Black Powder
GUN DIGEST

Edited By Jack Lewis

with

Dan Cotterman

Sam Fadala

Bob Furst

Dean A. Grennell

Turner Kirkland

Bob Learn   Bob Zwirz

Claud Hamilton

Eddie Parl

John Ross

Richard Smith

Hal Swiggett

Ralph T. Walker

DBI BOOKS, INC., NORTHFIELD, ILLINOIS
(Formerly Digest Books, Inc.)

Most black powder buffs today are using modern replicas for their shooting activities, rather than risk damage and wear and tear to their valuable originals. This, coupled with the fact that the "real thing" is quite expensive, is what got the replica black powder industry going nearly twenty years ago.

Our covers show two excellent examples of the state of the art. The long gun is Parker-Hale's faithful reproduction of the 1861 Enfield Musketoon. P-H uses the sealed pattern and original gauges in producing the gun for complete authenticity. This highly-accurate .58 caliber carbine has been approved for use by the North-South Skirmish Association.

There are a number of Dragoon replicas on the market, but only one is made by Colt. Shown is the massive Third Model Dragoon in .44 caliber with a weight of four pounds two ounces and an overall length of 14¾ inches. When Colt resumed production in 1974, serial numbers picked up at 20,901, where they stopped in 1860.

Charger Productions

Editorial Director
BOB SPRINGER

Technical Editor
DEAN A. GRENNELL

Research Editor
MARK THIFFAULT

Art Director
JOHN VITALE

Staff Artists
BILL MYERS
RICK RIVADENEYRA

Production Supervisor
WENDY L. WISEHART

Associate Publisher
SHELDON L. FACTOR

ISBN 0-695-80714-5   Library of Congress Catalog Card Number 72-86645

CONTENTS

INTRODUCTION

I'D LIKE TO think that Davy Crockett, Daniel Boone and Fess Parker all had something to do with the returned interest in the black powder shooting sports. There is no way, of course, of determining precisely what really has affected this interest, but I do know that, after I portrayed Davy Crockett in the Disney series, I began to receive a great number of letters from black powder buffs. Even then — well over a decade ago — there were more individuals interested in this form of recreation than one would have suspected.

Then, about the time that I started the Daniel Boone series, I found the mail from those interested in muzzleloaders reaching a new high. And I suppose that puts me in something of a chicken-and-the-egg situation, wondering whether the TV series helped spark interest in black powder shooting or whether it might have been the other way around.

Whatever the reasons, both Daniel Boone and, although not in true historic sequence, Davy Crockett did much to develop my own interest in target shooting and even hunting with muzzleloaders.

As a boy on my grandfather's ranch in Comanche County, Texas, I started with a BB gun, graduating in turn to a .22, then a .410 shotgun. In those Depression days, rabbit stew was a frequent part of the family diet.

But I didn't handle a black powder firearm until cast as Davy Crockett, when I had to learn to load and fire with enough authority not to arouse the black powder brotherhood. After that, I was asked to ride on the National Rifle Association float in the Rose Bowl Parade. From that, I began to learn just how much interest there really was in caplock and flintlock shooting.

My son, Eli, is almost 16 at this writing and I enjoy taking him into the mountain country to introduce him to the way in which his ancestors hunted and protected themselves.

In helping him to load and fire the replica muzzleloaders of today, I cannot help but feel he is gaining a slight taste of what it took to build this country...and perhaps I'm re-experiencing some of those feelings, too. I've never tried to analyze the feeling of comradeship during those periods when we're shooting together, but I know they're good. And I want to keep them that way!

Fess Parker

Fess Parker

Santa Barbara, California

HARNESSING THE POWDER DEMON CHAPTER 1

"From a puff of white smoke came a hell-based missile that would doubtlessly be steered by an unseen demon into the breast of some hapless knight. Armor, long the amulet of nobles in combat had ceased to be effective."

Fireworks May Be Spectacular, But Gunpowder Became A Force With Which To Reckon After It Started Hurling Projectiles!

WHILE THE CHINESE are rightfully credited with the invention of gunpowder as such, it was used in the Orient primarily for celebrations and novelty use, until Marco Polo and other early Europeans recognized some of its potential as a propellant.

Not that the Chinese did not use their version of black powder in warfare; they did, but again it was on a limited basis. The fire lance and whoosh bomb of the early Chinese were weapons of defense and were employed more for their value in terrifying an enemy than their abilities to inflict physical harm. First recorded use of gunpowder in the context outlined above was as a defense against barbarian raiders through the Han Dynasty.

Whatever parallel may have existed between Chinese and European feudal systems, there appears to have been no equality between the happy, content philosophy of the Orient and the grumbling discontent of the European vassal

who, with growing unwillingness, pledged loyalty to a band of overlords. This striking difference takes much from the logic of those who exalt the Chinese for using black powder primarily as fuel for fireworks in public celebrations.

The development of firearms cannot, however, be laid so conveniently upon a comparison of philosophies. An objective appraisal of centuries past shows alternate patterns of progress and stagnation. Of contradictory significance is the fact that the Thirteenth Century, whose crest lifted our Roger Bacon to pinnacles of achievement, gave way to virtual regressiveness that was to last for nearly two hundred years. However, it was during that period, represented by the Fourteenth and Fifteenth Centuries that, beginning with the cannon, the gun was subject to one of its most significant eras of advancement.

Somewhere between sanity and the outer reaches of chaos we will find proof, with all scientific authority, that acknowledge the first type of gun which could be carried, pointed and fired by one man: the matchlock.

The multitude of weapons throughout the Fourteenth and Fifteenth Centuries were found in the hands of armies not yet equipped to progress from the use of longbows and catapults, the hand cannon among them. The matchlock, though at first little more than a meager refinement of the hand cannon, represented an advancement in design and usefulness, but did not make itself known to any marked extent until about the middle of the Fifteenth Century.

The name, "matchlock" contradicts our image of a match by present definition. In its broader extremes, the word, "match" referred to a thick length of cotton string set on fire at one end. The string was held by a C-shaped device which was attached to the right side of the stock just aft of the rearmost extension of the barrel. The "C" could be tipped so as to bring the lighted end of the string in contact with a tiny priming charge which was cupped around the ignition hole or "touch" hole. Later the "C"

This soldier of the mid 1500s is most likely armed with an "une arquebuse du calibre de Monsieur le Prince," French for an arquebus of calibre of the prince as it was known then.

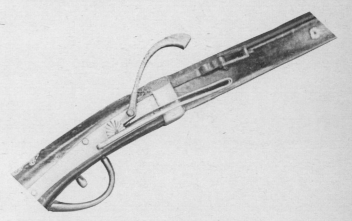

Nearly identical in design, these two Japanese matchlocks from the 1600s feature S-shaped serpentines. The match was held in place by a U-shaped ferrule and struck forward, not back towards the shooter as had C-shaped matchlocks.

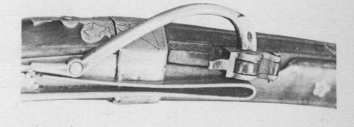

the first gun was a mortar in which black powder was being mixed with the first projectile being the pestle. We will, with greater satisfaction, surmise that the first gun was a tube which, in one crude manner or another, had been fashioned with the specific intent of containing a powder charge capable of firing a projectile. The method of ignition is determined by the necessity of setting fire to the charge behind the projectile. There is no point in speculating on the degree of success attained through these elementary experiments — guessing at the number of overloads, blow-ups or misfires — since any importance is overshadowed by the greater significance of realizing what it meant.

Whether by accidental discovery or invention, man had progressed, through trial and success, to a point where he was ready to shoot something of potentially greater accuracy than the arrow or quarrel. The longbow was on the threshold of being replaced as a weapon of war, though it was destined to endure in coexistence with the gun for many centuries. The catapult, the nightmare of countless medieval sieges, would yield during competition with the cannon.

Granting full credit to the use of field artillery and the indispensable role it played in the eventual death of feudalism, we move into the birth and development of smaller, more portable firearms. The natural transition from field cannon to hand cannon probably began taking place sometime during the latter part of the Fourteenth Century. Without getting stuck in a mire of definitions, we will

configuration was replaced by an "S" or serpentine string holder whose fulcrum point was located to have a heavier amount of the "S" on the down side. This intentional unbalance was doubtless in favor of helping to prevent unintentional discharge as a result of having the serpentine accidentally tip forward. This development may be regarded as a blackboard diagram for a kindergarten project. However, any system that kept kindling and gun together was better than grasping the gun with both hands while trying to touch off the charge by means of a burning straw held between clenched teeth!

To achieve a longer lasting, more uniform glow, the cotton string used for the matchlock was soaked in a saltpeter solution and allowed to dry before lighting. Whether this process lessened the tendency of the string to drop unwelcome sparks into the powder charge is not known.

The design of this soldier's hand cannon is advanced for its time. Note how the match is levered to the touchhole. Earlier models were designed so that the cannoneer touched the match to the touchhole with his free hand, which was then quickly withdrawn to save fingers from flash.

Probably nothing short of squeamish concern on the part of the shooter ever avoided such accidents. Add to spark dropping the uneasy tendency of those first free-swinging serpentines to tip forward when brushed by a twig or an excess of clothing and you will appreciate the need for some means of greater mechanical control!

It is appropriate to note some of the other drawbacks of the first serious attempt at solo shooting before we can fully enjoy the improvements that will come later. The wind, then as now, existed as a deterrent to accuracy and, in larger proportions, as an outright prohibition to shooting. The first stout puff would blow away that precious pinch of priming that surrounded the touch hole. If not lost in the wind or scattered by an ill-timed sneeze, a priming charge could be tipped away by the slightest cant of the gun. Finally, as if all this weren't enough to justify a factory call-back of everything in production, those early models were cursed for blowing a cascade of sparks into the shooter's face. The absence of shooting glasses in those medieval times should have been cause for protest, even among the most stout-hearted men.

By the beginning of the Sixteenth Century, gunmakers had brought forward a number of matchlock ignition mechanisms, each with some most welcome safety features. Quite possibly as an inheritance from the crossbow, the gun now had a trigger. It also had become heir to the power of spring tension, used to conspicuous advantage in gaining further control over the movement of the serpentine. In one form or another, both the trigger and the spring are in widespread use today. Still another component, the sear, which releases the strength of the spring when the trigger is squeezed, is well known to modern gunnery.

The expansion of thought and innovation also brought about a more satisfactory method of holding the priming powder. The touch hole was now drilled in the side of the breech where the primer could be contained in a small, covered pan which had a lid to shield it from wind and at least a minor amount of rain. Still another shield to the rear of the flash pan protected the shooter's face from sparks.

And, instead of being hand-held at arm's length or, for the bravest, against the chest, this newer matchlock had wood that looked like a real gun stock!

While the breech end of the earliest hand cannons had been simply welded shut, the latter part of the Fifteenth Century witnessed the blessing of a threaded breech plug. To the breech plug there was attached a flat piece of metal which extended from the rear of the barrel back over the stock. This metal extension, better called a tang, helped provide a more solid mating of barrel and stock when the tang was firmly secured to the stock by a large screw. To say that the coming of the tang meant an improvement in accuracy would be a modest understatement.

The matchlock, as it reached maturity, emerged as a monument to the determination and skill of the gunmaker's art. Craftsmen throughout Europe had worked to bring their best efforts to a firearm that represented the greatest advancements of their time. Not merely a tool of defense, the matchlock posed proudly with its precisely machined exterior, mirrored bore and glistening finish. Stocks, too, were selected from the most beautifully grained woods and extravagantly carved and inlaid with silver, ivory and gold. This was treatment man traditionally reserved for his most favored treasures. Had he at last accomplished perfection in a personal weapon? Could this basically simple firearm, with its serpentine, match and flashpan, be the best of design and craftsmanship?

As one might expect, the improvements brought into the design and making of guns were, in a sense, paralleled by a continuing improvement in the manufacture of black powder. In the century that followed Roger Bacon's declaration of a formula, there was a growing tendency to increase the amount of saltpeter in proportion to the amounts of sulphur and charcoal. Bacon was aware of the importance of purity of the three ingredients, but perhaps not as keenly as later experimenters. The purification of saltpeter, for example, was a subject that involved repeated processes of crystallization. As discussed in Chapter One, the dry method of powder making was replaced by

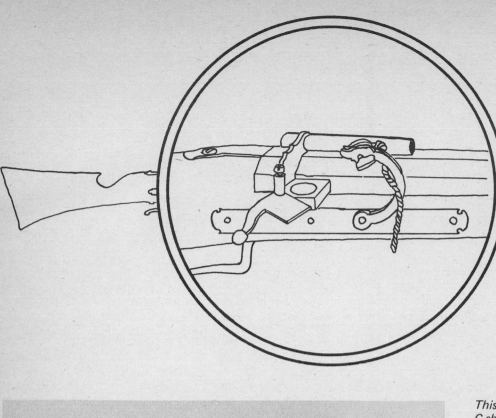

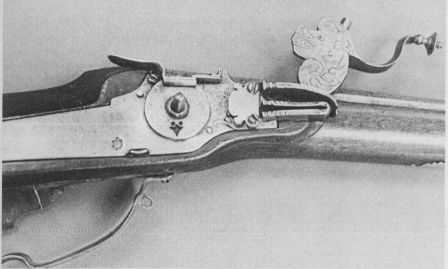

This drawing of an early C-shaped matchlock shows now dangerously the match ignited the primed flash pan, sending a shower of sparks back into the shooter's eyes.

This wheellock, although appearing rather crude in design, was expensive and hard to produce during the 1600s. This is the reason that matchlocks were used.

advanced techniques involving the use of damp cakes which were then sieved into granules which could be sorted according to size and combustion rate.

It can be observed that neither gun nor powder were actually ready for each other when they got together. Ideally, the propellant would have burned completely to shoot a projectile at maximum speed while leaving no residue in a gun that was capable of standing up to any pressures generated in the process. It didn't happen that way. Even the most casually interested firearms enthusiast is aware of the gobs of fouling that accumulate as a result of burning black powder and the complete destruction of guns because of overladen powder chambers is not unknown to historians.

The problems of improper loading had reached at least partial solution by the middle of the Sixteenth Century when musketeers are said to have benefitted from the use of prepared charges. A small, elongated paper or cloth sack would contain a measured powder charge — presumably classified for use in the firearm for which it was prepared — and, at one end, a ball. The "cartridge" was tied at each end to prevent spillage and a third length of string encircled the sack and was driven tight to keep ball and powder separated. This, truly, was the first belted cartridge.

Fouling of gun bores must have been known — if not so much a problem — even to the shooters of stones. However, the tighter bore-to-projectile seal made possible with the introduction of the metal ball, along with an increasing dissatisfaction with woefully inaccurate shooting, strengthened the need to minimize the effects of fouling. Adding emphasis to the need for a gun and powder combination that would remain reasonably clean through the ordeal of sustained shooting was the military significance of firepower: The more frequently a shooter was forced to stop loading and firing in order to clean a hopelessly fouled gun, the less effective he was in battle.

It is speculated that some unknown gunmaker, probably during the Fifteenth Century, hurried to his shop and tooled a number of equally spaced grooves into the bore of a gun. These grooves subsequently served their intended purpose by trapping some of the combustion residue of black powder. The grooves were straight along the length of the bore and so had little effect on the bullet's flight. Regardless, there was at last a means of overcoming fouling and this contributed a significant step in firearms development.

The next important development was the twisting of the grooves. In addition, someone reasoned that longer grooves of about the same width and depth would hold more fouling. Deepening or widening the grooves would either weaken the wall of the barrel or, in effect, change the caliber of the piece. The logical answer was to make the grooves longer by cutting them so that they would follow a spiraling path down the length of the bore.

Whether, with the introduction of fouling grooves, anyone expected the added benefit of improved projectile accuracy is not known. The helical fletching of arrows for the betterment of flight characteristics was known to the ancient Egyptians. Whether or not this knowledge was generally widespread, it is important to recognize that cutting straight grooves presented less machining difficulty than would have been encountered in attempts to spiral

At one time guns were only owned by the wealthy. This is reflected in the ornately finished butt stock at left and the gun held by its owner Turner Kirkland above.

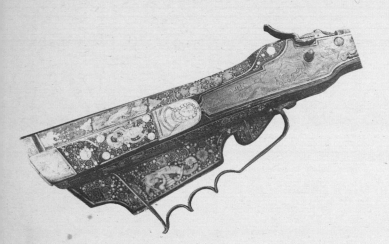

them. It is supposed that several decades elapsed between the cutting of straight and spiraled grooves in gun bores. Whether the interval was necessary to allow for the improvement of machining techniques and tooling or an expanded awareness of the nature of projectiles in motion is another matter for speculation.

As if to stand in defiance of the demonstrated superiority of the matchlock's range and penetrating power, longbow shooters were persistent in their allegiance. This weapon, whose prowess had been established by kings and noblemen throughout the centuries, could let fly a dozen arrows while the gunner prepared and discharged a single ball. In a social sense, archers were gentlemen while shooting was something within the capability of the commonest peasant. As a general rule, the rank and file serfs were too busy working to afford the time necessary to achieve proficiency with bow and arrow.

The sustenance of the longbow and its kin, the crossbow, as significant influences in battle were destined to yield to the gun, regardless of noble sentiment. The soldier could be trained to a satisfactory level of proficiency with a gun in a fraction of the time necessary to make a good archer. The importance of whether the trainee could intentionally hit anything was offset by the gun's equal value in frightening an adversary. Invader and defender

alike respected and feared the mere presence of a gun in battle. The dull "thunk" of the bowstring had been replaced by the roar and flame of an even more impressive weapon. From a puff of white smoke came a hell-based missile that would doubtlessly be steered by an unseen demon into the breast of some hapless knight. Armor, long the defense of nobles in combat, ceased to be effective.

Medieval physicians and surgeons were not unaware of the necessity for quick treatment of bullet wounds. The danger of infection were such as to nearly equal the effects of the ball itself. According to Boothroyd, one favorite recipe for treating gunshot wounds called for mixing equal parts of oil and wine and injecting them into a live dog which was then boiled. Finally, a poultice of the boiled dog meat was applied. None of the benefits of the foregoing treatment seem to have been recorded. We may, however, reflect upon the humane aspects of allowing the dog to get smashed before the moment of his execution.

The penetration of armor breastplates an acknowledged capability of the swift projectile, its tendency to err in flight was still in question. That is, prior to the boon and revelation of the spiraling grooves already discussed. This significant innovation, along with the fixing of some means of sighting to the weapon, settled the contest that had been raging between whether projectiles were guided by the gods or individual's accuracy. The rifle balls now flew with predictability and at last the shooter could call his shots. The gunner who previously had been proud to shoot a hole through a wine barrel at a hundred paces could now send a ball whistling into a tankard at the same distance.

Regardless of his improved accuracy with barrels that would spin the projectile, the smoothbore was to continue in favor. Man had begun to hunt with his solo gun and the small birdshot used in hunting could not be effective when

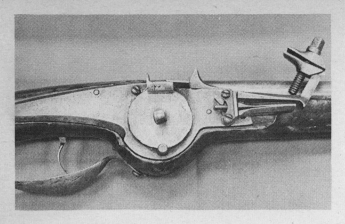

Not all wheellocks were elaborately finished with ivory and mother of pearl inlays, but were rather drab and only functional in their design. These were mainly military arms.

All types of devices were used, or at least thought about, that would give armed forces an advantage over one another. Here soldiers use an elevated platform to expose the enemy.

discharged through a bore with twisted grooves. Experiments show that the shallow rifling impressions in today's barrels will spin shot into a doughnut-shaped pattern. Imagine the spraying effect that must have resulted from shooting an ounce or two of tiny pellets through barrels with much deeper grooves.

Reviewing the saga of weaponry brings about a distinct awareness of type overlapping. Like shingles on a roof, each representation of the technology of its time continues for a while, coexisting with its replacement. After competitive tests it is either abandoned to the archives or sustained for sentimental reasons. The bow, for example, remains in use today, having endeared itself to many as an object of romantic background whose mastery demands the best abilities of the archer. To another extreme, catapult and cannon might represent two shingles that overlapped only briefly. Who could get sentimental over a catapult?

The development of the matchlock was still in a state of progress when, during the first quarter of the Fifteenth Century, the wheellock appeared. As the name suggests, this newer idea incorporated the use of a wheel with a rasp-like edge. The wheel was wound a little less than one turn by use of a small wrench, something like a rollerskate key. At this point, the wheel was held in readiness by a sear whose tip had been automatically indexed into a hole on the inside of the wheel.

The squeezing of the trigger animated a conglomerate of components into the following mystery of actions and reactions: Wheel, a small segment of which protrudes into flashpan, begins rapid rotation when pulled by a tiny chain which is held taut by the tension of a spring; cover over flashpan moves aside allowing fool's gold (iron pyrites) which is clamped in jaws of pivoting "doghead" to move into union with wheel; the resulting sparks set fire to the priming mix in the flashpan. Consequently, the powder charge was ignited and the shot was on its way.

Marvelously, the muddled mechanics of the wheellock took only a split second; trigger pull and shot were nearly simultaneous. Quickness of locking time was insignificant among the wheellock's advantages when compared to its readiness. The pyrite ignition meant that the arm no longer had to be carried about with the hazard of a glowing wick hanging uncomfortably close to the priming charge. The wheellock could be loaded and stored or carried afield where it would be ready to shoot as quickly as the need arose.

Possibly for the first time, the hunter was ready to carry the gun into forest and meadow in search of game, probably in the company of one or two humorously skeptical archers. In the case of the wheellock, the nimrod provided an embarrassing share of laughs as his fool's gold crumbled uselessly into the grass or, worse yet, he stood drenched in a shower of sparks. Or the blush of humiliation that must have come upon being left sprawling on the ground by a horse frightened into sudden acceleration by the boom of black powder. The bow and arrow lads were justly amused.

Distrust of the wheellock system was exemplified by shooters having an auxiliary serpentine and match built on their guns. Thus, if the complex parts in the wheellock's mechanism became inoperable as a result of the inevitable accumulation of powder residue, the old dependable "match" was available. The cost of the wheellock, to say nothing of the added expense of a second ignition system, rendered guns with double ignition the exclusive property of the wealthy. The best of both was not good enough. Something better had to come.

Progress in design suffered from the diversity of several attempts to improve on the old spinning wheel concept before it was abandoned. Such examples of the wheellock as may have endured were preserved for the value of precious metal inlays and artful carvings, rather than for their actual efficiency as working firearms. Perhaps by reason of simplicity, better ways to create the spark continued to elude discovery.

Flint had first been tried with the wheellock, but due to

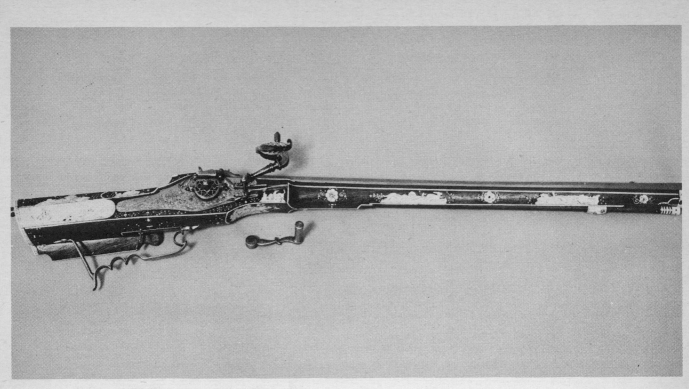

This modern reproduction of the wheellock design rifle is an example of the artistry used to make each gun one of a kind. Note the key in upper photo used to wind lock, which threw sparks toward shooter.

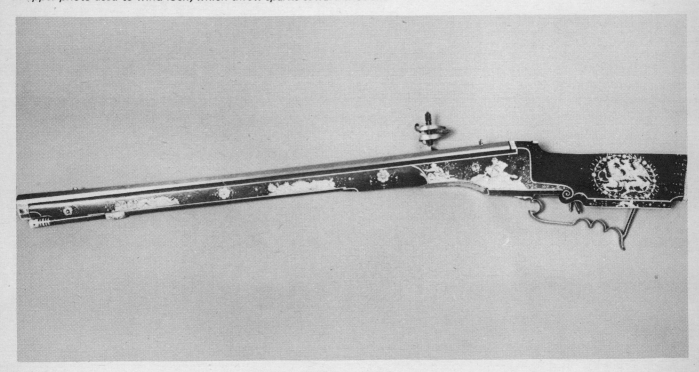

its hardness, it wore the peaks off the roughened surface of the wheel. Pyrites was softer and would ultimately see use in a system known as the pyrites lock. Grand-daddy of the flintlock, the pyrites lock seems to be a logical stepchild of the matchlock. Variations involved only the substitution of a "cock" for the earlier serpentine and a roughened plate, called the battery or frizzen, for the pyrites to strike. The brief appearance of the pyrites lock is mainly significant because once again, an attempt had been made to get rid of the match and its inconveniences. The difference this time was that it had been done without approaching the com-

plication of an alarm clock.

At about the same time, still in the middle of the Sixteenth Century, the snaphance or "snapharmce," made itself known. This one reached back and picked up one of the good ideas that had been put to work in the design of the wheellock, namely a covered flashpan as featured in yet another of its variations, the miquelet. Pyrites lock, snaphance and miquelet seem to have been different names for guns that, except for variations of mechanical detail, were essentially the same.

Admirers of matchlock, wheellock and the pyrites-snaphance-miquelet trio just described continued to tug in different directions (probably to the snickering of loyal bow and arrow enthusiasts) until the first part of the Seventeenth Century. Gunmakers of the era at last agreed to advance from the confusion of over two centuries with a uniform effort in the interests of standardization. The resulting harmony of thought and idea crystallized in the form of a better gun, the flintlock. It preserved the simplicity and low manufacturing cost of the matchlock, with a lock time that rivaled that of the wheellock. Coupled with its use of flint, more generally available and less given to crumbling than pyrites, the flintlock had retained such features of convenience and safety as the covered flashpan, unhesitatingly hailed as an outstanding advantage of the wheellock.

This early 1500 woodcut by Erhardt Schoen depicts the firemaster of a mercenary force. His task was to supply fire for matchcords and braziers, as well as cooking fires. At left an arquebusier loads his matchlock.

This 16th Century Arquebusier is armed with a spring driven matchlock. The cost of these weapons was so great that many countries had to continue arming their forces with the older matchlock until the discovery of flintlocks.

No agreement with respect to measurement of shot was to come until the middle of the Sixteenth Century. Throughout Europe medieval "wildcatters" sought to promote their own system of bullet measurement, knowing certainly that they would thereby achieve a sort of paper immortality. As measurement of lengths, widths, depths, et al., varied in different areas between inches and millimeters, the only hope rested in some system that correlated values of weight.

In England, royal proclamation officialized the pound in favor of commerce. Each pound contained a prescribed number of ounces, each of which was divisible into scruples, grains and so on. Scales with surprisingly high capabilities of accuracy aided in establishing the number of lead balls of a given size needed to constitute a total weight

of one pound. The number thus required, sixteen, for example, was assigned to every ball of that particular size. Henceforth, every gun taking such a ball could be referred to as a "sixteen bore." There were numerous bore sizes and an equally wide assortment of balls, some more popular than others. In modified form the bore system reamins with us today and is used in references to shotgun gauge.

The transition in usage from "bore" to "caliber" brings to light an interesting bit of word history. At first the word "caliver" (corrupted pronunciation can be blamed on medieval Englishmen) was used to name a particularly awkward eleven-bore with an overall length of about six feet. In weight, the caliver would challenge the heftiness of many of today's benchrest rifles. Regardless, the word has no roots in common with the origins of any gun: In mean-

From a 1566 book entitled The Hunt of Beasts, Birds and Fish, this woodcut engraving by Jan ver der Straet shows common people hunting ducks. This book was one of the earliest to depict firearms use for the taking of wild game, probably the first to show bird hunting.

ing, "caliber" is directly attributable to a contraction of the Latin "qua libra," a phrase that asks, "How much?"

Just how much shooters have loved the flintlock over the centuries can, to some extent, be appreciated with the knowledge that thousands of them are still in use today! Author Charles Edward Chapel, writing near the close of the 1930s, made clear reference to flintlock rifles still being used in this country, not necessarily as novelty arms but as practical tools of hunting and home defense. True though it may be that the bulk of flintlock arms in use today are in the hands of black powder hobbyists, no concession is made as to the practical usefulness of these guns. They have, by reason of sound design and practicality, managed to outlive numerous systems which were said to be superior.

The piercing of armor by the rifle ball established a significance for the shoulder weapon in military matters. In an attempt to re-establish a comfortable degree of invulnerability for knighthood, tailors of armor, for want of superior metallurgy, made thicker plates. The process continued to ridiculous extremes. Knightly knees wobbled and the mighty steeds of combat snorted under the growing burden of iron.

Even as the warring nobility collectively sweated and swooned beneath their useless shell, others found pleasure in the leisurely indulgence of hunting. On the Continent, large parties of bird hunters flaunted nature's abundance by amassing kills that numbered in the hundreds as the result of a single day's slaughter. In the name of sport, deer by the thousands were shot by hunters who knew neither the limit of law nor conscience. We must remember, however, that the term "deer" was used by many to describe just about any animal of the forest. Carnage in the name of target practice and gentlemanly pastime persistently foreshadowed the coming of more and more restrictive hunting laws.

Records do not generally show the popularity of large and extravagant hunting parties in Britain. The hunter existed somewhat more within the bounds of sportsmanship. While he may at times have been wasteful of game and given to indiscriminate plinking, he hunted as much out of necessity as for recreation. Had not the political and economical significance of the common peasant been altered by the gun? In addition to soldiering, his training and familiarity with firearms had taught him to hunt in order to augment his family food supply.

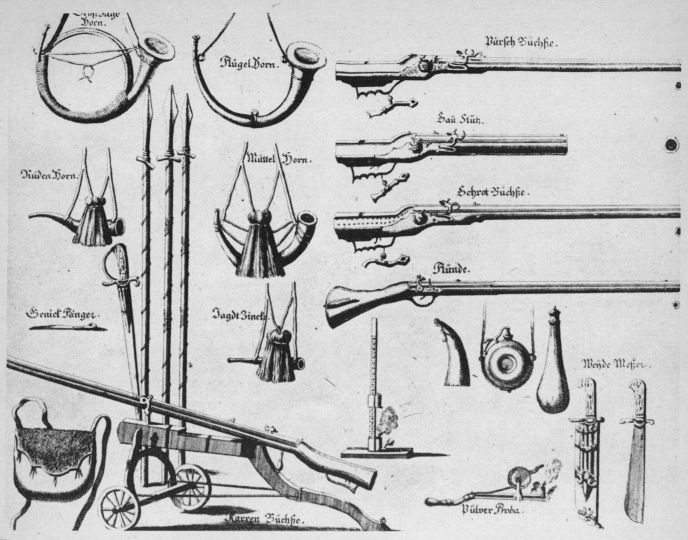

The wheellock duck gun mounted on the carriage, the three wheellocks and flintlock, five horns, two knives, game pouch, three powder flasks, and two powder testers are all 17th and early 18th Century hunting implements. Duck gun would fire several pounds of shot at waterfowl.

The classic Puritan of Seventeenth Century England who sought freedom and a new life in the world to the West considered his destiny somewhat less uncertain because of his confidence in the gun. Whether matchlock, wheellock or flintlock, it was his companion in defense as well as his assurance of food when game was available. The Algonquin hosts of the New World may in some measure have been responsible for an enhancement of appreciation of game animals as a natural resource. Although the colonist was far from conservation-minded, at least it seemed that the slaughter parties common to Continental Europe would not establish themselves in America...not until annihilation of the buffalo absorbed the attention and energy of his descendants in the decades ahead.

No view of early American pilgrims seems complete without at least token attention to the blunderbuss. If a carbine existed in relationship to the long Brown Bess flintlocks, it would have had to be the short, Dutch "thunder gun." Popularized in history and subject to an immortality of exaggeration and falsehood, it probably drew the greater part of attention because of its odd, funnel-shaped barrel. Its value seems to have been based on its handiness, credit the short overall length, and its capabilities for short-range shooting. The stubby barrel, incorporating no choke, suggests that the blunderbuss would have been well adapted to the rapid dispersement of birdshot.

It looked like a cartoon gun and in "blunderbuss" found a name that added to its clumsy appearance. The term is a translation of the Dutch, "donderbuchse."

For all its usefulness, the blunderbuss did not enjoy the popularity of its longer kin. The English shoulder gun of wide use by the middle of the Eighteenth Century was the Brown Bess. Bess, for Queen Elizabeth, who is said to have endorsed the making of the prototype and brown, in description of a color that was imparted to the metal through a process of oxidation.

Despite the known superiority of accuracy possible for bullets shot from twist-rifled barrels, the majority of guns used by early Colonials were smoothbores. "Musket" was the accepted name usually applied to these. German guns of the American Colonies were mostly of the rifled type, probably because both the grooving and spiraling had been a result of German thinking. Yet, while the rifled barrel held greater possibilities for accuracy, the smoothbore was the more versatile by reason of its ability to handle either rifle ball or birdshot.

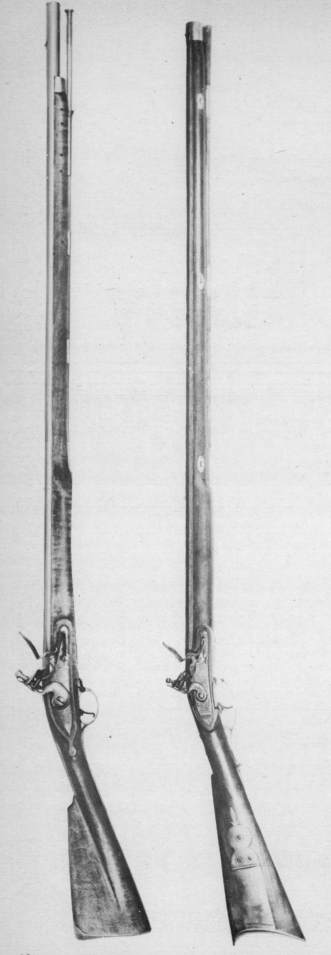

American makers of long guns in the years before the Revolution were dependent on the importation of locks from Europe. Guns were fashioned so as to conform to variations imposed by the origin of European supply. Locksmiths in England, Germany, France, the Netherlands and Austria sent flintlock systems for use on guns of the Colonies. Overall design, however, took a decidedly greater balance of influence from the pattern of English guns.

In 1775, in anticipation of the inevitable revolutionary conflict with England, a Committee of Safety was formed in each of the thirteen colonies. Each committee appointed selected gunmakers to manufacture as many weapons as they could and, within all possible limits, to standardize on design and caliber. It was, however, that a lack of accord which left any uniformity of bore size a matter of ragged perspective. Generally, the most popular caliber, about .75, was ruled by that of the most popular gun, the Brown Bess. Others of .70 to .80 are said to have been used.

The simplicity of flint raking across roughened metal was to continue to have its irresistible appeal to shooters far and wide until the middle of the Nineteenth Century. Even thereafter, the romance of the flint guns was to earn the admiration of shooters who had guns of greater sophistication and efficiency. It is possible for a good thing to survive something our reasoning tells us is better...especially if it challenges our primitive wiles.

The Reverend Alexander Forsyth, Scottish experimenter and wildfowl hunter, is credited with taking advantage of the explosive properties of fulminates, known to science before his time, for the ignition of powder charges. To make the most of his idea, Forsyth designed a special lock and, in 1807, got a patent for it. His idea involved a hammer which would strike a tiny quantity of fulminate and thus create the spark of ignition. The Reverend's inspiration and its consequent development represent strides of immense significance in the story of firearms and, indeed, ammunition itself. The usage of the pressure building properties of fulminates served as a foundation in the development of breech loading and metallic cartridges.

By 1836, the advantages of Forsyth's percussion cap and the Forsyth lock, in production for nearly a quarter-century by that time, were recognized by the military in Britain. The Brown Bess could, without prohibitive expense or difficulty, be converted from flintlock to the new system. It is said to have seen its first use in the hands of British troops in China in the year 1841. By the middle of the Nineteenth Century, American shooters also were in full appreciation of the percussion cap.

Subsequent evolution from muzzleloading to breechloading and, eventually, to self-contained ammunition seems to have taken nothing from the intrigue of the flintlock. For all their practicality and superior technology, the later innovations did not possess the primitive mystique generated by the sound of stone on metal.

Today, the flint and pyrites guns exist in distant harmony with the modern generation of firearms whose roots trace themselves to the authorship of Alexander Forsyth's invention. Each extreme in technology represents a branch of firearms history that is distinguished by reason of its deep-felt influence on virtually every aspect of our lives. For evil and for good, the discovery of the fire drug has meant much to us all in terms of our social lives, our economics and, in fact, our sciences. Those Taoist alchemists would be impressed.

Two early flintlocks used in this country were the Brown Bess (left) and various styles of long rifles such as the one shown on the right. The Brown Bess was the official arm used by British troops in Colonial times, long rifles were used by colonist to hunt game and during Revolution.

CHAPTER 2

A History Of Handguns

The Chronological Evolution Of The Handgun From Its 14th Century Beginning To The Introduction Of The Cartridge And Smokeless Powder.

JONATHAN SWIFT, THE IRISH-BORN satirist, philosophized at the turn of the Eighteenth Century that necessity is the mother of invention. Necessity did have much to do with the early development of firearms, especially handguns.

Although it isn't totally agreed upon by historians, the introduction of the smallarm appeared in the form of a crude hand cannon sometime during the third quarter of the Fourteenth Century. However, in the monastery of St. Leonardo in Lecetto, Germany, paintings clearly depict soldiers carrying and firing small handgun tubes around three feet in length. These early scenes had been painted by Paolo del Maestro Neri during the period from 1340 to 1343.

Hand cannon, such as this, first appeared sometime during the 14th Century. This particular hand cannon is much more refined than the majority, displaying the well advanced styling of the modern day pistol.

Even though these paintings supposedly are the same as the original artist had done them, some historians feel that the hand cannon may have been added by a later artist who tried to modernize the image projected by the scenes. If these paintings are original and untouched, they may well be the first to depict the use of handgunnes, as they later became known in Britain.

Military ledgers and log books of the last quarter of the Fourteenth Century and the first quarter of the Fifteenth Century make mention of the use of and procurement of touches, drivells, tampions and frypannes.

To load his gun or piece, the cannoneer first charged it by pouring a desired amount of powder down the muzzle. This usually was done with the use of an elongated hollow tube, the end of which was cut to form a scoop. The tampion — a wooden disk used to separate the powder from the ball and to form greater chamber pressures for harder hitting shots — then was seated over the powder.

The cannoneer seated the tampion firmly over the powder with the drivell — referred to today as a ramrod. Next, the ball was seated above the tampion. The balls used for these early black powder guns were made usually from lead or brass, but those made from bronze or even iron are not uncommon. If supplies were limited or required too great a length of time in acquiring, soldiers occasionally used balls that had been hewn from stone, just as the balls for cannon were made, except somewhat smaller in size. The bores of hand cannon rarely exceeded three-quarters of an inch in diameter, although many of the early wood-cut scenes and paintings show hand cannon with bores better than twice that size.

Occasionally the touchholes required that the cannoneer place a minute amount of powder into it to serve as a primer for the main charge in the chamber. More often than not though, the touchhole went straight through to the charged breech.

Hand cannoneers never were far from the frypanne, a pan or brazier of hot coals, usually heated until they glowed. These were for heating the touche — a short piece of wire, a burning stick or even a hot coal.

Taking a somewhat hasty aim in the general direction the projectile was intended to fly, the cannoneer would ignite the charge of powder by inserting the touche through the touchhole or by igniting the priming powder just above the touchhole. If the hand cannon didn't explode in his face, killing him and anyone foolish enough to be standing close at hand, the round was on its way, more or less in the direction of the target.

Being a cannoneer had its problems, not only in being a poor way of arming oneself but in that the deadly bow and arrow remained superior when it came to accuracy and speedy reloading. It wasn't until sometime around the end of the first quarter of the Fifteenth Century that cannoneers began thinking of ways to improve their abilities by devising ways of aiming their armament.

This had been done previously to some extent by merely sighting down the top of the barrel and lining up on the target, be it man or animal. This again proved a problem in itself.

To aim in on the target in such a manner required the cannoneer to use both hands in order to hold the gun steady. Who then would apply the touche to the touchhole to ignite the round? Had man been created with a third hand, all would have been well enough. As it was, however, the cannoneer was very ineffective unless a means of aiming or firing the cannon could be established.

As a remedy to this problem, some forces enlarged the size of the hand cannon and assigned two men to aim and fire each. While one man aimed and supported the gun — by now better than five or six feet in length and having a bore in the neighborhood of .80 or .90 caliber — the other would apply the touche upon command of the first or when he signaled that the gun was aimed in on the target. This worked to a certain degree, but it then jeopardized two men instead of one once the gun had been emptied into the ranks of the enemy.

As an even more practical remedy — in a way giving the cannoneer a third hand — someone at an unknown date in an unknown country built the first matchlock. Historians have pondered these two unanswered mysteries and, although not backed by any historical documents or significant happenings, Genoa, Italy, may have been the place and about 1440 the date.

In this original form of matchlock hand cannon, the lock was nothing more than an S-shaped lever to which a slow burning piece of cord or match was attached. When aiming the gun all the cannoneer had to do was grasp this lever with several of his fingers and lever the match into the touchhole as soon as he was lined up on his target. To keep the match from accidentally setting off the powder charge, the lower half was made longer and heavier purposely. The extra weight balanced the arm in a vertical position, keeping the match away from the touchhole, which was now the flashhole.

Up to this point, the hand cannon had been the early development for both the shoulder weapon and the handgun. With the introduction of the matchlock, the two forms began to develop in their own forms even farther.

The majority of the matchlocks were built as shoulder weapons, but a few were fashioned after the earlier hand cannon, but given a short one-handed handle to serve as a grip. These were fitted with shortened barrels — less than two feet in length. Crude in design, the match still had to be levered into the touchhole that was located atop of the breech, requiring use of both hands.

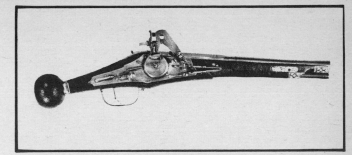

Wheelocks, such as this late 16th Century Austrian, revolutionized the pistol, allowing for the first time a gun to be loaded, primed and stored or carried, but ready to shoot.

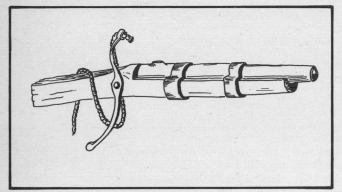

This sketching depicts the design similar to the first matchlock small arms. The serpentine holds the matchcord in the nose of a pivoted arm, is levered into touchhole.

It wasn't long before the matchlock won wide acceptance and replaced the touchhole hand cannons. It was evident, however, that the location of the touchhole was rather precarious. As a deterrent to the hazards that rain and wind had on the exposed touchhole, it was moved to the side of the breech, appearing in the form of a pan.

Along with the improvement of the flashhole — some having a plate that would slide or slip over the priming powder to prevent it from spilling or being blown out by the wind or even dampened by an unexpected shower — came improved matches. Early matches consisted of nothing more than twisted cords, which probably were hard to get burning, let alone keep burning for any length of time. It was found that, by soaking the cord in various solutions of saltpeter and allowing them to dry, the matches would burn better and for a longer period of time; these eventually became known as slow matches.

The true mechanical matchlock was developed sometime during the third quarter of the Fifteenth Century. Together the matchlock and the improved match remained the principle means of armament of the world's forces until the Seventeenth Century.

Although the development of the matchlock was instrumental in the evolution of the handgun, a pistol fitted with this type of lock saw little use in Europe. Several pistol-like arms were made at this time, but these, for the most part, were produced in Japan and India. With the exception of a few matchlock pistols made in Poland during the Eighteenth Century, European armsmakers considered a firearm of this sort to be of such uselessness as to not even warrant limited manufacture.

With the coming of the wheellock, handguns took a giant stride forward. As with the origin of the matchlock, hand cannon and black powder itself, the inventor of the wheellock is yet another mystery to arms buffs. Many believe that the first wheellock was the result of the work done by several men. One such man was Leonardo da Vinci, who designed an early form of the wheellock as early as 1508.

Along with the wheellock came the first practical pistols. This lock allowed a short, easily maneuvered gun to be carried and fired with a one-handed hold. The absence of the burning match also made it possible to hide or conceal the arm, or at least to have a gun that would readily fire without having to worry about adjusting the match.

The pyrite or flint of a wheellock pistol is held in the jaws of the dog head — the vise like section of the cock — and the wheel is spanned, or wound in place. The pyrite then is placed against the area of the wheel that is located nearest the flashpan. If the powder and ball have been loaded in the proper sequence, the rotation of the wheel should provide enough spark from the iron pyrite to ignite the primed pan as the trigger is released and the pistol should fire.

As mentioned, the date and place of the first wheellock is not clear, but it is certain that they were being used widely during the first quarter of the Sixteenth Century. The development of these locks met some opposition from a large number of people. Many were not familiar in how they worked and classified them as being dangerous. Emperor Maximilian I made it illegal to manufacture the dangerous wheellock in 1517. His actions were followed closely by similar authorities, all contending that such guns made the job of thieves and robbers easier by affording them a gun that could be hidden and concealed.

Europe was war-ridden during the first half of the Sixteenth Century, giving the wheellock ample opportunity to prove its value as a military arm. Attacking or defending forces would line up in ranks, many of them armed with nothing more than pistols, and fire in volleys. While the front rank would be firing, the others would be busy reloading their pistols; the ranks continuously going forward and falling back to reload.

Wheellocks were expensive to produce and perhaps this is why many of the major armed forces continued to use matchlock rifles until the Seventeenth Century. With the exception of some military pistols that were made more functional than fancy, pistols were the property of wealthy gun enthusiasts. These were usually decorated with numerous inlays of ivory, bone, horn or mother of pearl. The metal on these guns usually was ornately engraved and

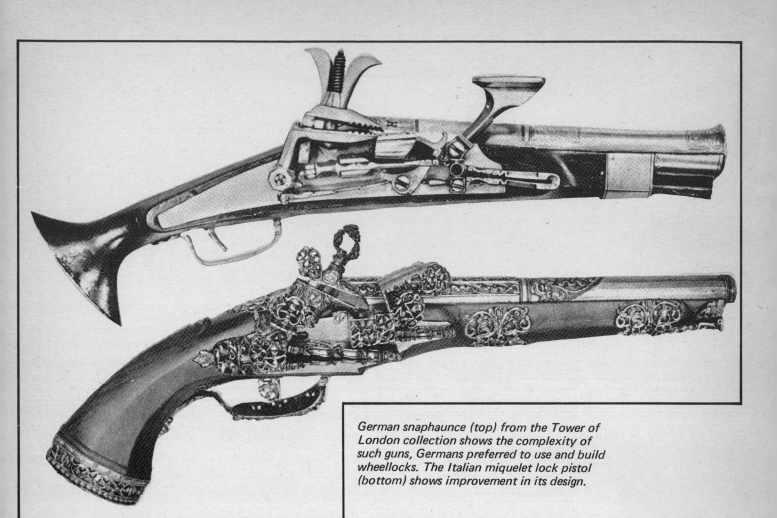

German snaphaunce (top) from the Tower of London collection shows the complexity of such guns, Germans preferred to use and build wheellocks. The Italian miquelet lock pistol (bottom) shows improvement in its design.

sported gold and silver inlays. The lock, barrel, trigger guards and mounts were also blued, richly browned or even enameled.

Gunsmiths all across Europe tried feverishly to produce work superior to their counter-parts in yet another country. The result of this competition is evident in many of the exquisite guns of the period that are now in many private collections and on display in museums. The word pistol itself is of reputed origin, possibly the result of such international pride in craftsmanship.

Italy, in which many paintings show the early use of handguns, has some claim to being origin of the wheellock pistol, the name supposedly derived from the city of Pistoia. Czechoslovakia also lays some claim to origin of the word, the word coming from a short Bohemian handgun known as a pist'ala or pipe.

Use of flint and steel to ignite a primed flash pan was established through the use of wheellocks, but the expense of producing them made it impossible for common working people to afford such guns. Breaking away from the complex design of the wheellock, the Dutch snaphaunce did much to do away with the smoldering match of the matchlock and the expense of the wheellock.

This lock was an early forerunner to the flintlock, as also was the miquelet. All three types of locks used the flint against steel to produce spark principle. To fire, the cock or hammer was drawn back and held under the tension of a spring by some type of sear. As the trigger was pulled, the sear released the hammer and the tension of the spring

drove it forward, causing sparks as the piece of flint held in the jaws of the cock struck against the steel arm located above the flash pan.

These sparks are actually minute particles of molten steel being scraped away from the hardened frizzen or pan cover. By dropping into the primed flash pan, they ignited the priming powder and the gun would discharge.

The first snaphaunce locks appeared during the late Sixteenth Century and were made in and around the European countries of Germany, England, and France, although there is evidence of such locks from as far south as Italy. The sear protruded through the side of the lock plate on the earliest of these locks. This would engage a notch on the cock itself, either on the rear of the cock or a slot that had been milled or cut into the inner face.

To prevent the powder from spilling from the pans on these early handguns as they were being carried in whatever way the owner saw fit — belt, makeshift holster, lanyard, et al. — the flash pans were fitted with a cover that mechanically slid out of the way as the pistol was cocked. Few, if any, of these pistols featured a half-cock position.

Miquelet locks were an improved version of the flint and steel or snapping lock. Two different styles of this lock were common to the mid-1500s: the Spanish miquelet and the Italian miquelet. Although there is considerable debate over just where this type of lock first appeared, it is believed that the Spanish were the first to utilize it on pistols. If Spain had been the first country to use the miquelet lock at all, it may be the first time credit can be given the

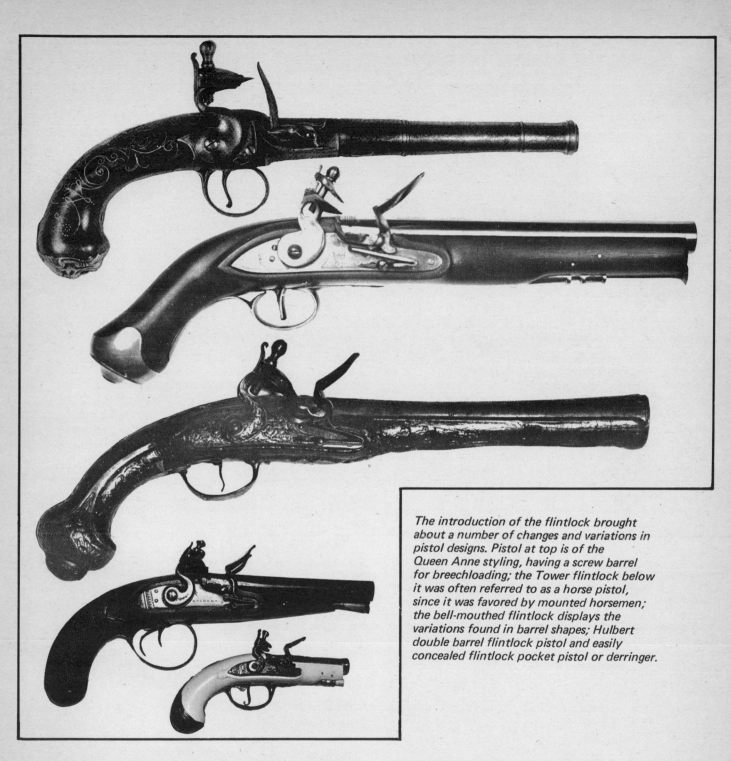

The introduction of the flintlock brought about a number of changes and variations in pistol designs. Pistol at top is of the Queen Anne styling, having a screw barrel for breechloading; the Tower flintlock below it was often referred to as a horse pistol, since it was favored by mounted horsemen; the bell-mouthed flintlock displays the variations found in barrel shapes; Hulbert double barrel flintlock pistol and easily concealed flintlock pocket pistol or derringer.

inventor. Supposedly the lock was invented by Isidro Soler, a Madrid gunmaker.

There were several differences between snaphaunce pistols and miquelet pistols that made the latter superior. First of all, the miquelet was the first to utilize the pan cover as the actual frizzen. On pistols with snaphaunce locks the cover and striking arm — frizzen — were two separate parts. Combined into one L-shaped part, the combination frizzen and pan cover made the lock simpler by doing away with internal parts that were needed to move the pan cover as the lock was cocked.

Another desired feature on this newer lock was the addition of a half-cock or safe position of the hammer. This was made possible by the addition of a second sear. This sear — on both Spanish and Italian versions — worked horizontally through the lock plate. On the Spanish miquelet, both sears passed through the lock plate. The half-cock sear appeared as a stud and the full-cock sear as a flat blade. On the Italian version, half-cock was achieved by one arm of the sear engaging the toe of the cock; full-cock was achieved by the second sear to the rear of the cock engaging the heel.

The use of the Spanish miquelet lock for pistols never really caught on throughout the rest of Europe, but handguns made in that country continued to be so produced until the end of the flint and steel period. Even more backward were the oriental countries, still relying on the match principle until introduction of the percussion lock in the 1860s after Perry's opening of the Eastern Empire; they never really went through the flint transition period, but

Collecting fine old original pistols has become both hobby and profession for such men as Bob Elz (right). Here he examines one of a cased pair of fine Manton flintlock. Looking on is collector Gary Saunders.

Many originals are fitted with now declared unsafe damascus steel barrels.

past it instead.

Not an original lock in true design, yet another type of pistol lock was produced in England during the Sixteenth Century. This was the English dog lock. Combining features found on both the miquelet and the earlier snaphaunce, pistols fitted with this particular lock were for the most part produced during the period of about 1640 to 1650. This rather crude lock featured a horizontal sear to the rear of the cock much like had the snaphaunce lock, but was fitted with the L-shaped pan cover and frizzen found on miquelet pistol locks.

Although the exact date or year in which the French lock — the first true flintlock as we know it — was introduced first isn't exactly clear, the invention of the first flintlock can, with reasonable certainty, be accredited to Marin le Bourgeois. It is believed that the first appearance of this type of lock, especially for pistol use, was either during the last few years of the Sixteenth Century or the first decade of the Seventeenth Century.

Surprisingly enough, the gunmakers during the Sixteenth and Seventeenth Centuries were ingenious and some were even several centuries ahead of themselves. Examples of this would be the various experimental breechloading and revolving repeater pistols of that time, some of which were quite practical and well advanced. Pre-dating Samuel Colt's famed introduction of the revolver are quite a few practical revolving handguns. Repeaters and breechloaders were too complicated for the period, however, and perhaps this is why they weren't refined until later dates.

The flintlock remained the most commonly used pistol until the first percussion locks had been perfected during the early 1800s. With the exception of a few small, privately run gun shops, the American armsmaking industry didn't start taking shape until the turn of the Nineteenth Century. American revolutionary forces had been armed mostly with guns that had been stockpiled as they could be obtained and were nearly all manufactured in European plants.

One of the biggest problems encountered in the manufacture of early pistols was the lack of standardization. By 1763, however, the French had remedied this problem to

some degree and began producing the first standard military flintlock pistol. Some fourteen years later the plants in St. Etienne and Charleville began producing the Model 1777 new cavalry pistol. In 1799 the newly formed government of the United States contracted these plants for five hundred of these pistol at $6.50 each.

This contract had been obtained by Simeon North of Berlin, Connecticut, along with his brother-in-law, Elisha Cheney. Eventually two thousand of these pistols were manufactured in France for shipment to the United States. The only difference between the U.S. North and Cheney, as they were known, and the French pistol was that the former had an extra inch added to the length of its barrel. Also the French pistol was fitted with a belt hook; none of the North and Cheney pistols sported this attachment. Of importance is the fact that this was the first pistol to be manufactured for the newly formed American government.

Necessity again played a vital role in the introduction of the first percussion type lock. Reverend Alexander John Forsyth, a sportsman and amateur chemist from Belhelvie of Aberdeenshire, Scotland, unhappy with the way his flintlock's primed pan would scare wildfowl before the main charge had been ignited, set about to discover a new type of lock that would offer instantaneous ignition.

After several years of experimenting and even total rejection by the military, Forsyth took out a patent on his new lock and, with the assistance of one James Purdey — later to become renowned in the firearms field — set up business at No. 10 Piccadilly, London, in 1808. Their first successful lock was the of scent bottle type. This type of lock was used on some of the Joseph Manton pistols made after the introduction of the Forsyth lock.

A number of different handguns with locks similar to the principle of the Forsyth lock cropped up during the years between 1810 and 1820, most of which had little appeal to handgun fanciers or were of such uselessness they were dropped from further testing.

Several handguns were fitted with locks that were primed with a formed priming charge that appeared in the form of a round ball. This was placed in a shallow receptacle that formed a sort of flash pan. A solid nose striker would ignite the globule of powder and discharge the main body of powder inside the breech. The biggest downfall of handguns featuring such a lock was that the priming charge was easily knocked from its position and was susceptible to moisture.

A few other handguns were manufactured about this time that used a tubular percussion cap-like ignition system. The tube lock was primed with a copper tube five-eighths of an inch in length and approximately a sixteenth of an inch in diameter. This tube was open on both ends and filled with percussion powder. To prime the lock, the tube was inserted into the flashhole until about an eighth of an inch protruded; this rested on an anvil-like piece of metal that acted as a sort of flash pan. The impact of the blunt nosed hammer or striker ignited the powder inside the tube, which in turn ignited the loaded charge. In addition to occasionally throwing sparks back into the face of the shooter, this lock proved undesireable in that it had a tendency to crimp the tube to a point that it would lodge in the flashhole.

A percussion cap is nothing more than a small copper cup about an eighth inch in depth and diameter. Open on one end, a minute amount of fulminate of mercury is placed on the inner surface of the closed end. This is placed over a short hollow nipple, the inner passage leading to the powder charge in the breech. As the blunt nosed hammer falls on the cup when the trigger is pulled, it explodes the fulminate of mercury and sends most of the flash or sparks down the hollow cavity of the nipple to ignite the main charge of powder.

With the percussion cap, shooting was immune to weather, misfires and hangfires, providing the caps had been manufactured with good quality. The change in pistol locks — and rifle locks — from flint to percussion was the swiftest ever to take place. By 1830, the percussion caps had all but replaced flintlocks. The shooters of the latter were greeted on the field with the same amusement as today's black powder shooter.

During this period James Purdey left Forsyth to open a business of his own, today a world famous name in firearms. Some of Purdey's first guns were beautifully designed

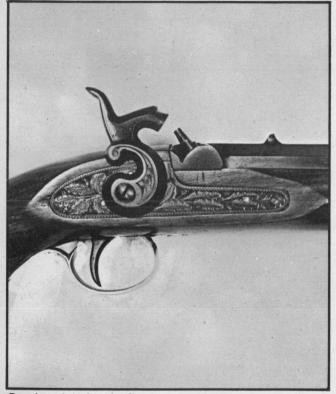

Developed during the first quarter of the 19th Century, the percussion caplock was the first really dependable ignition system.

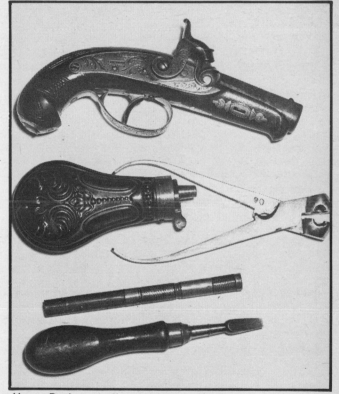

Henry Deringer built pocket pistol similar to the one used in the assassination of President Lincoln, such pistols since then have continued to be classified as derringers.

All of these, however, were early forms of the percussion cap lock; all working on the principle of igniting the priming powder by striking it between two hardened surfaces — the blunt nose of the hammer and whatever the globule of powder or tube rested on.

The first true percussion cap appeared sometime between 1814 and 1820, possibly invented by an American or an Englishman. There is some controversy over the originator of this principle. But by the mid-1820s pistols featuring a true caplock appeared in both countries. The percussion cap operated on a simple principle and, with its reasonably reliable firing capability, won the acceptance of shooters world-wide.

percussion combination duelling and target pistols. These first guns were all handmade and, since they were intended for the defense of one's honor or for just plain plinking, they were made without provisions for attaching the ramrod. This usually was kept in the pistol case along with all the other loading accessories.

The simple design of the percussion lock made it possible to produce pistols that would fit easily in pockets, boots or wherever the owner desired to conceal his miniature firepower. These small percussion pistols were known as pocket pistols, later to become known as the derringer.

Henry Deringer was an American gunsmith who started business in Easton, Pennsylvania. He later moved to

Although still predated by numerous early revolving handgun designs, the Collier flintlock revolver was probably one of the first actual practical designs. Type of ignition robbed it of becoming popular.

Philadelphia, where he began to produce guns. His first rifles and pistols began appearing around 1806 and all were fitted with the principal lock of that time, the flintlock. Many of these guns were produced under contract for the U.S. Army.

The notoriety, rather than fame, of the Deringer pistol — a short and easily concealed percussion handgun — stemmed from the number of homicides comitted with them. Among these was the assassination of President Lincoln by John Wilkes Booth. The public identification of the murder weapon resulted in the international use of the word, derringer, to describe the type of pistol, the second 'r' added to differentiate the Deringer-made pistol from the general type.

The single-shot percussion pistol continued to be the standard military handgun until perfection of the revolver. As mentioned earlier, there had been numerous experimental versions — many quite practical — of revolving type handguns since the Sixteenth Century, but it wasn't until the Nineteenth Century that actual refinement of this type of handgun took place. One reason for this late development of the revolver can be accredited to the fact that there had been a lack of machinery for the manufacturing of firearms until this time.

For the most part, these early revolvers employed a crude or unorthodox mechanism to rotate the cylinder or relied upon the shooter to manually turn the cylinder and line up the chamber and barrel by hand. Perhaps the earliest practical automatic cylinder rotation appeared on a revolving handgun built by John Dafte of London in about 1680. The method used to rotate the cylinder is nearly the same as that used later by Colt and may possibly be the source of the idea for his first single action cap and ball revolver. Actually, the same principle is used on Colt single action Army revolvers still being produced. The Dafte revolver, however, used a snaphaunce type lock.

One of the first revolvers to appear in the United States was the Collier. This five-shot flintlock — the accredited invention of Captain Artemus Wheller of Concord, Massachusetts — appeared around 1820. The handgun had one strike against it; it featured a flintlock instead of the percussion cap that was increasing in popularity. Later percussion models were introduced, but they never became

popular and were discontinued.

Although Samuel Colt can hardly be given claim for the invention of the handgun, he probably did more in the development of such guns than any other individual. The first revolvers produced by Colt were several different versions of the folding trigger Paterson model, so named since they were manufactured in Paterson, New Jersey. Colt ran a business that was constantly on the verge of going bankrupt, until he landed a government contract for one thousand revolvers in 1847.

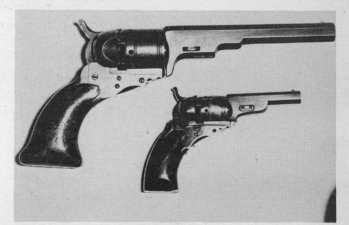

Colt Paterson was the first of the famous Colt made percussion revolvers to be produced. Top revolver was known as the Texas Model, bottom pocket pistol known as a Baby Paterson.

Mass-produced for Colt by Eli Whitney, Jr., in his Whitneyville, Connecticut, plant, these pistols were issued to the U.S. Mounted Rifles for use in the Mexican War. To aid in the speedy production of the Colt Whitney Walker Model, production also was moved to several different shops in Hartford.

With business now booming, Colt began to refine the revolver even further. By the time of the outbreak of the Civil War, Colt had refined his wares to the point of near absolute perfection. Revolvers had become the accepted handgun and Colt soon found himself contending with

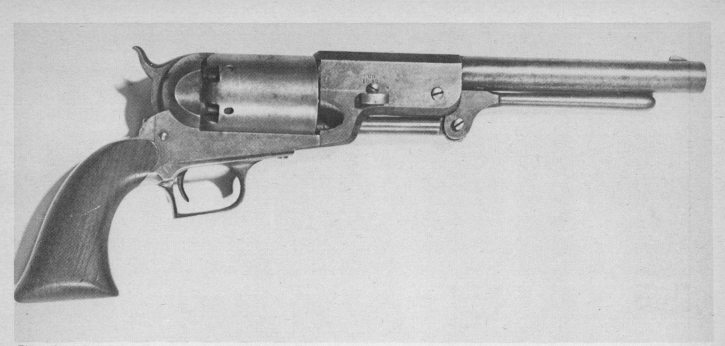

First of the Colt Dragoon pistols was the Whitneyville-Walker of 1847. This percussion revolver gave U.S. troops the added firepower needed to help win the Mexican War.

numerous counterfeiters, making nearly exact reproductions of his originals. A number of European revolvers were spawned at that time also. Among these were many Colt look-alikes that were manufactured under the authority of Colt.

The Civil War brought about the manufacturing of even more copies of Colt's revolvers, especially the Navy and Army model revolvers. Most of these domestic imitations were made in Texas for use by Confederate troops and, since most employed a considerable amount of handwork, they usually varied some from one to the other.

In America, the firm of E. Remington and Sons of Ilion, New York, was Colt's chief competitor. In 1857, Remington started production of the firm's first percussion cap and ball revolver. This gun had been designed and patented by Fordyce Beals, also the designer of the famous walking beam model. Patented in 1854 and manufactured by Eli Whitney, Jr., the Whitney Beals featured a solid frame that encircled the cylinder completely, something that Colt revolvers lacked.

The Remington Beals First Model of 1857 differed from the Whitney Beals in that it featured a conventional means of rotating the cylinder. On the Whitney Beals the cylinder had been rotated by first forward movement of the trigger, the rotation ending as the trigger was returned to the original position. The gun then was fired by pulling the trigger in the regular manner, by squeezing it to the rear.

Several early models of the Remington revolver saw use before the production of the Beals Army revolver from 1860 to 1862. Users generally favored the solid frame and the more robust feel of this revolver over that of the Colt. So it was only a matter of satisfying its public that Remington introduced a near identical version of this gun in the smaller .36 caliber instead of .44. Improved models of the Beals Army and Navy revolvers appeared in 1861 and were referred to simply as the 1861 Army and 1861 Navy, being .44 and .36 caliber respectively. These guns remained basically the same until the introduction of the Remington Army Model cartridge revolver in 1875.

Undoubtedly the revolver was produced in larger

numbers in the United States than anywhere else in the world. The Civil War demanded a step-up in their production so great that U.S. and Confederate manufacturers couldn't meet the demand of their armies. To solve this problem, both sides turned to foreign manufacturers, both occasionally buying arms from the same source.

In addition to the revolvers made throughout Europe for the American forces, many fine sporting cap and ball

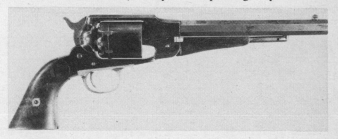

The New Model 1858 Army was designed for Remington by Fordyce Beals, who seemed to favor the solid frame. The design proved so successful that the 1861 Navy Remington (below) remained practically unchanged.

Combustible cartridges were commercially made and sold during the 1860s. They made loading cap and ball revolvers less tedious.

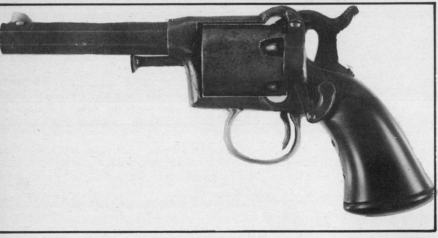

This Remington Beals First Model pocket revolver is an example of the various types of designs introduced during the percussion revolver era.

Many Colt replicas appeared during the Civil War, top revolver is a Metropolitan made Navy replica, middle pistol is authentic Colt. Bottom revolver is an early Belgian pin fire revolver.

revolvers were also produced. Much to the surprise of many Americans who believed that today's modern design of handgunnery originated in the United States as a result of Yankee ingenuity, such developments as the first solid frame revolver and double action revolver were invented and saw their first commercial use in Britain.

Perhaps the earliest form of a double action revolver to see commercial production was Robert Adams' self-cocking revolver. Actually, this British five-shot featured a trigger action instead of a true double action, not allowing the hammer to be cocked manually. Through its internal design, lifting and camming action — the hammer was drawn back mechanically — and released as the trigger was pulled. There was no means of cocking the revolver manually and there was no half-cock position, but instead a hammer catch that would allow the hammer to be drawn back and locked in place for ease in loading and rotating of the cylinder.

The first true double action revolver was the Beaumont-Adams revolver of 1855. The appearance of this pistol and that of Adams' pistol of 1851 patent is nearly the same. The loss of accuracy with a gun that required a tug of the trigger to fire it apparently became noticeable to both shooters and its inventor. To remedy this, a small spring-loaded pawl and an extra notch on the breast of the hammer were added. This allowed the 1855 Beaumont-Adams to be manually cocked and fired, at the same time offering the shooter double action firing for point blank shooting when accuracy wasn't critical.

Paper cartridges for cap and ball revolvers appeared in many makeshift forms, usually contrived by the individual shooter for the sake of convenience. These usually were nothing more than the bullet — a round ball in most cases — and the powder rolled together in a piece of paper. The problem with this was the necessity of removing powder and ball from the wrapping before loading them into the chamber. What was really needed was a loaded unit — ball, powder and paper — that could be seated hastily in the chamber and fired.

The Remington Army Model of 1875, although having a reliable extraction system, didn't become as popular as Colt single actions due to excessive fouling and its often difficulty of operation.

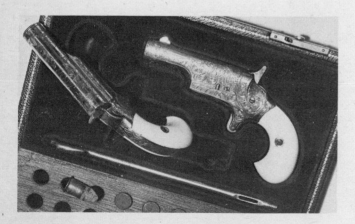

The Colt No. 1 derringer was chambered for the .41 short rimfire cartridge. These small guns were a favorite of gamblers and others of similar professions from the days of riverboat fame.

A number of experimental cartridges resulted from this need. In addition to a cartridge that would have to be completely combustible, the round would have to be durable enough to withstand reasonable handling and, to some degree, impervious to moisture. Among the first early

attempts that proved successful was a cartridge wrapped in a paper hull made of gunpowder and collodion; although burning completely and reasonably waterproof, it proved too fragile.

The most successful of these attempts was the skin cartridge of Captain John Montague. As described in his patent of September 1856, "a skin or membrane (prepared from the gut of animals, pigs or birds or reptiles) is used instead of paper for cartridges, which are made without a seam. A covering of net-work or thread may be used to strengthen the cartridge."

Following the paper cartridge era, or overlapping and running concurrently with it, were experiments in developing the breechloading arm and ammunition, some of which featured either internal or external ignition. The first satisfactory self-primed metallic breechloading cartridge was the pin-fire cartridge. This type of cartridge is known to have been around as early as 1841, but development of its potential didn't really occur until the late 1850s.

In its original form, the pinfire case was similar to the paper shotgun hull, having a brass base and paper walls. Later pinfire cartridges appeared in an all-brass form. Both types had a small hole through the case wall near the head of the brass. A percussion cap was pressed into this small hole, followed by a small pin.

The cap was retained in position by the pin and the walls of the chamber. The pin protruded through an opening of the loaded chamber and the round was fired by the force of the hammer striking the pin, which, in turn, exploded the priming cap. Many European cartridge companies manufactured pinfire pistol cartridges up until the mid-1930s.

The first self-priming cartridges resembled a percussion cap that had been increased in size. The idea of the cartridge — a brainstrom of Louis Nicolas Auguste Flobert — was derived probably from the percussion cap, since it used the same principle. These cartridges were intended for indoor target practice, so didn't feature any range or great amount of velocity. The copper case wasn't much larger than the standard percussion cap and the bullet was propelled by the fulminate, also used as the primer. These cartridges didn't support the rim that is so prevalent on today's .22 rimfire, but the rear area of the case was swelled to prevent the case from being driven all the way into the chamber as the hammer struck the rear of the chambered round.

Further development of the rimfire cartridge was done by the American plant of Smith and Wesson. Developed by Douglas Wesson during the years of 1856 to 1858, the No. 1 Pistol Cartridge or .22 short was an advanced form of the Flobert cartridge. There was a difference in bullet design, however, and the brass case also contained three and four grains of black powder in addition to the fulminate priming. This cartridge and the pistols chambered for it won such wide acceptance that by 1871 more than 100,000 of these cartridges were being produced each day.

Many of the existing cap and ball revolvers were modified to accept rimfire cartridges as those in suitable calibers were produced. A number of new make handguns also were produced to handle the rimfire cartridges, including numerous derringers. One such pistol was Colt's No. I Derringer chambered for the .41 short.

The development of the metalic rimfire cartridge and the later introduction of the primer-ignited center-fire cartridges put an end to the muzzleloader and cap and ball revolver era.

By the turn of the Twentieth Century the handgun had evolved as we know it today; smokeless powders and automatic handguns the chief advancements in the last quarter of the Nineteenth Century.

CHAPTER 3
THE WALKER
by
COLT

Lost For Many Years, Captain Samuel Walker's Colt Is Found Among A Southern California Collection!

THE ORIGINAL "WALKER" COLT — the Colt's Army Revolver, .44 Caliber, Model 1847 — which was the personal property of its designer, Captain S. H. Walker, is in the collection of Shelly Horton of Santa Ana, California.

At the time of manufacture in late 1846, two of the revolutionary handguns with numbers 1009 and 1010 were specifically marked as personal arms to be sent to the soldier and gun designer, who at that time was involved in the Mexican War.

The gun in Horton's collection bears the stamped serial number "1010," and has been certified as one of the handguns made especially for presentation to the captain by Samuel Colt; the other still is in the family of Captain Walker in Baltimore.

This particular Walker was "lost" for many years. It had disappeared and no trace of it was found until it came into the possession of the present owner in about 1940. According to Horton, his late father an avid collector purchased the black powder revolver from a stranger, ascertaining only that it was a "Walker" Colt, but not checking the number until several days later. By that time, the seller had disappeared, leaving no means of tracing the hands through which it had passed since its manufacture.

In all, there were only 1100 of the Walker Colts manufactured. A special lot of 1000 was turned out for the United States Mounted Rifles, a new cavalry unit to which Captain Walker had been assigned. The other log of 100 was turned out as presentation pieces for such persons as Walker and other notables.

Of the original lot of 1000 of the .44 caliber handguns, today there are approximately 85 known to exist, most of

them in the hands of collectors and museums. Of the additional 100, the location and existence of 15 has been verified to date.

The order manufactured exclusively for the Mounted Rifles was divided into lots of 200 handguns each, with each revolver in each lot having the letter designation of the military company stamped on it with the numbers from "1" through "200" following. Companies of the U.S. Mounted Rifles were designated as running from "A" through "E." The additionally produced 100 handguns, of course, bore no letter and were numbered consecutively from 1001 through 1100.

Walker, a professional soldier and lawman, first had served in the army as a corporal in the Florida Indian Wars of 1837. Later, as a Texas Ranger, he had become familiar with the deadliness of Colt's Paterson revolver. He had made several visits to Colt, suggesting improvements in a handgun which he had in mind specifically for the mounted soldier. Finally, prior to his assignment to duty in the expeditionary forces in Mexico, he worked out the model for the "Walker" Colt and was instrumental in having it ordered by the War Department.

The model designed by the soldier was patterned to a large degree after the .36 caliber revolver produced earlier by Colt, but had numerous refinements. In addition to being more compact, it was much better suited to the needs of a fast-charging cavalryman.

At Walker's suggestion, a loading lever was fashioned as a part of the handgun, working on a hinge; a precaution against the lever being lost during battle or at a time when

29

The big Walker Colt disassembles for easy cleaning. Enclosed trigger and loading lever were big improvements over earlier Paterson.

Both Shelly Horton (right) and his brother, Roy are avid collectors. Even after more than a hundred years of hard use, machine marks are still evident on the Colt Walker below.

the horseman or soldier might need it most.

Colt, of course, had secured his first patent on a revolver in 1836 at the age of only 21 and is said to have drawn plans for his first practical model while serving as a plain seaman on a voyage to India. He later formed the Colt Patent Arms Manufacturing Co. at Paterson, New Jersey, with his father and 25 stockholders, turning out his earliest models.

At the time Walker had convinced himself of the need for the new .44 caliber model for his U.S. Mounted Rifles, Colt had suffered some financial reverses and it was necessary to have the handguns made at the musket factory of Eli Whitney, Jr., son of the inventor of the cotton gin.

Since a model of the earlier .47 caliber handgun was not available from which to draw plans for the new pistol, Colt copied it entirely from memory, incorporating the new innovations supplied by Captain Walker. At the time, Whitney was intensely worried about getting his money for turning the new model in its limited order in spite of the government contract which Colt had received. The "Walker" Colt, as it is popularly known rather than by its official designation, was purchased by the Army for $28 each.

(The original price is of interest when compared to the amount which a Walker Colt is considered to be worth in this day and age.)

Under the terms of the government contract, the first 1000 .44 caliber Colts were completed on July 6, 1846, and arrangements made to ship them to the supply unit of the Mounted Rifles. The weapons did not catch up with the cavalry unit until it already was involved in the Battle of Vera Cruz; the heat of battle was not considered the ideal time for uncrating the revolvers.

As a result, although there is considerable dissension both pro and con, it is doubtful whether Captain Walker ever actually received the two Colts — Nos. 1009 and 1010 — which had been sent for his personal use. He was slain in the battle, when a Mexican civilian killed him with a wooden spear.

Under the terms of the Army contract, the Walker Colt was to be .44 caliber (using 32 conical and 48 round balls to the pound); the barrel, nine inches in length, was marked with the words: ADDRESS SAMUEL COLT NEW YORK CITY.

The handgun boasted a cylinder measuring two and seven-sixteenths inches in length with six chambers, as well

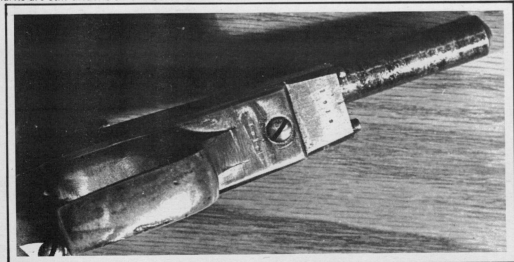

as oval locking slots and one locking pin at the rear. On the 1000 revolvers turned out for the Mounted Rifles, there was the design of Indians and soldiers engaged in a battle scene engraved in the metal. The barrels and cylinders all were fashioned of Sheffield cast steel.

The all-important loading lever was designed without an end catch. Instead, it was held in place by a slender "T"-shaped spring, which entered a slot in the lever near the plunger joint.

On the Walker Colt, the trigger and bolt screws did not pass completely through the frame; in later models — improvements upon this pistol such as the Dragoon — the screws penetrated completely through the frame.

Walker's improved model boasted a "V"-shaped mainspring, while the frame was curved in at the rear, where the grips were designed to enter. The grip-strap was of iron, the trigger guard of heavy brass, while the rear housing was angled at the junction of grip and frame.

The grips themselves, sometimes referred to as "Slim Jims," were in one piece and fashioned of black walnut holding a particularly deadly grace.

The wedge, holding the revolver firmly together, entered from the right side of the barrel. When well oiled, it could be driven out with the haft of a light knife or even with pressure from the fingers, making the handgun easy to dismantle.

The cylinder, barrel and gripstrap of each pistol had a blued steel finish, while the loading lever and hammer were case hardened. Weight of the handgun was standardized at four pounds, nine ounces.

Clumsy though it may appear by today's standards, the Walker Colt constituted a major improvement in firearms, as did Colt's first revolver. The improvements designed by Walker — including the loading lever — were included in the Dragoon model, which also was .44 caliber and was manufactured for the Army from 1848 to 1860.

Horton's Walker Colt No. 1010 is in excellent shape considering the fact that it is well over a century old; it still fires and Horton's father, the late Roy S. Horton, a retired optometrists, conducted target practice with the handgun on numerous occasions.

The lost years of its history before it came into the possession of the present owner probably will never be recounted, but it is not unlikely that the revolver saw service along the frontier, helping to win the West in the days after Captain Walker was slain.

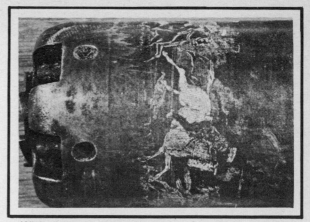

With chalk rubbed into the lines of the cylinder engraving, the scene sketched by Captain Samuel Walker is clearly seen on Walker's revolver.

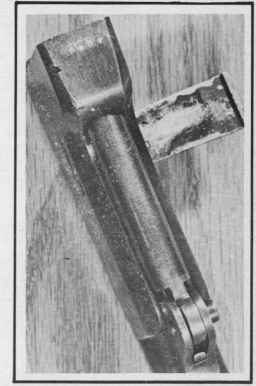

The barrel and loading lever assembly are fastened to the frame — holding cylinder in place — by a metal wedge. Below, the serial number 1010 is stamped several times.

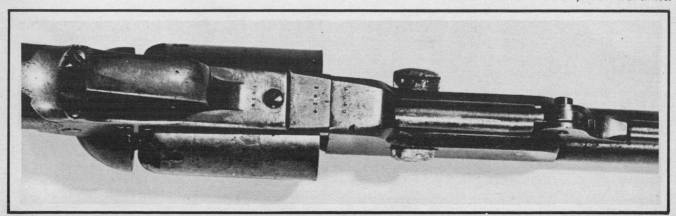

CHAPTER 4

THE ORIGINAL REPLICAS

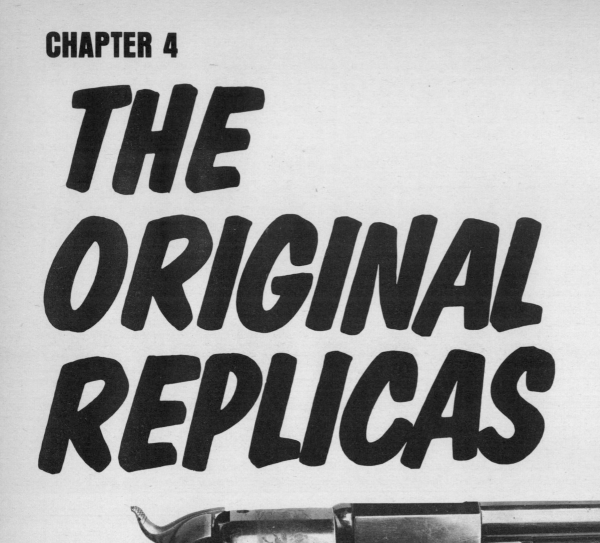

COUNTERFEIT

Sam Colt Called Them By
A Less Refined Term: Counterfeits —
And Devised Ways To Tell The Real Thing!

REPLICAS ARE NOTHING new. Even as early as the 1840s Samuel Colt himself was hard pressed to discourage the illegitimate production of his cap and ball revolvers. The idea of a repeating handgun was beginning to win wide acceptance and more than one get rich quick armsmaker tried his hand at copying any of the several designs produced by Colt during the period of 1836 to 1872.

An unusual and distinctive feature of the original Colt revolvers produced during this period were the scenes that encompassed their cylinders. The large and heavy .44 caliber Walker and Dragoon revolvers made during 1847 and 1848 were engraved with a panoramic view of mounted troops battling a horde of Indians. Pocket revolvers had a stagecoach holdup scene with one of the passengers blazing away at the fleeing bandits — presumably using one of Colt's pistols — stamped on its five-shot cylinder. Engraved upon the cylinder of Colt's famous Navy revolver was the scene of warships of the era engaged in battle.

Often looked upon as an ornate addition to the handgun's design, these engravings are really more. Although the fact is only vaguely understood among many collectors, Colt included these engravings as a means of telling his original pistols from fakes, or as we have come to call them today, reproductions.

The numismatist — a collector or individual that studies coins, tokens, medals and other similar objects — often numbers among his cherished possessions an illustrated sheet showing a vignetted illustration of numerals and other banknote details known as a counterfeit detector. Most of these originally were issued to bank tellers to enable them to readily identify or to check the authenticity of monies or banknotes from other such firms.

For this reason, Colt marked the cylinders on his handguns with scenes that could be readily identified. He then issued his own form of counterfeit detector. The only one that was ever issued, however, appears to have been printed in 1849. In addition to the scenes printed on the counterfeit detector there was a peculiar design of the Dragoon type revolver also printed in assembled and disassembled form. It is believed that this was an experimental model that was produced in that same year.

Samuel Colt had the uncanny knack of always choosing the right man for the right job. Perhaps this is why he chose W. L. Ormsby to engrave the three scenes previously mentioned.

Ormsby, a banknote engraver by profession, occasionally put his artistic talents to work on other projects, among which were the patterns for the Colt cylinders. Although the scenes on the Walker and Navy were his renditions of sketches forwarded to him for copying, the engraving on the cylinder of the pocket pistol was entirely of his own design.

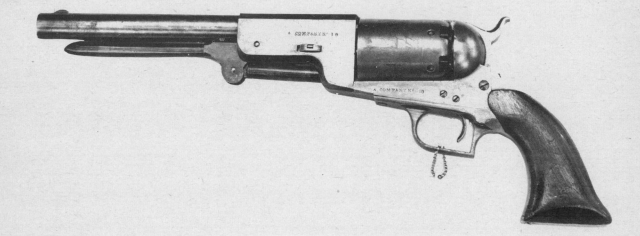

Of these three Colt Dragoon type revolvers and the Walker below, only two are actual Colts. The Dragoon at top on opposite page is authentic Colt, as is the Walker, other two are replicas.

The story has it that Ormsby was travelling aboard the ill-fated stage on his way West when the holdup occurred. It is believed that he was armed with one of Colt's older model Patersons with a folding trigger. Since the first of the new pocket pistol models were first produced in 1848 — the same year in which Ormsby allegedly thwarted the holdup with his Colt revolver — it is not impossible that he might have been armed with one of these.

The first of this Colt design to be produced were engraved with a portion of the fight scene which appears upon the cylinders of the Dragoon and Walker models. It was also during this time that Colt revolvers came under their heaviest attack by counterfeiters.

The scene which appears on the Walker and Dragoon pistols was done from a sketch by Captain Samuel Walker of the U.S. Mounted Rifles, also a former member of the Texas Rangers. Armed with Colt Paterson revolvers, Walker and about fifteen members of the Texas Rangers attacked a large force of Comanche braves that had them outnumbered by better than five to one. Putting them to flight, they managed to kill or wound nearly half of the raiding renegades.

Due to the fire power of their six-shooters, the Rangers managed to escape the battle with only minor wounds. Although Captain John Coffee Hays was in charge of the command at the time of the battle, it was Walker — impressed with the extra fire power of the sixgun — who later encouraged the supplying of pistols of this type to mounted troops.

Colt had an abundance of competitors during the 1848-1850 period. He travelled all over Europe selling production rights to numerous minor gunmakers to make and market his patterns. Under Colt's Austrian PATENT 1849, for example, Joseph Ganahl of Innsbruck was licensed to make Dragoon revolvers. The same type of agreement was made with some of the Liege, Belgium gunmakers also.

Most of these production rights were made under the stipulation that the manufacturers would not export these weapons back to the United States or to England, where Colt also had his London plant. To help with the production of guns in Liege, he even shipped sets of unfinished parts. Once the parts had been finished, the Belgium gunmakers would stamp the parts with the markings COLT BREVETE, which meant that they had paid Colt ten Belgian francs royalty.

As agreed, most of these guns were marketed only in the European countries, but the American market seemed more appealing to some. So, eventually many of the guns started filtering back into the United States.

The cylinders on the European made revolvers — with the exception of some Belgium-produced guns — lacked the engraving of the Colt produced revolvers. To avoid being undersold by a product of his own design, Colt began printing his counterfeit detector. This way a dealer or purchaser could at least assure himself of buying an original instead of a foreign made copy.

Drawn up by Ormsby — who had originally sculptured the engravings — the counterfeit sheet was marked with the firm's name and address, ordering instructions, the warning **BEWARE OF COUNTERFEITS & PATENT INFRINGEMENTS**, and Sam Colt's signature. With the exception of a very few Belgium made imports, the fashion for engraving American pistols did not spread abroad.

Prized by collectors today, the Walker Colt had Indian fight scene engraved on its cylinder, big gun weighed nearly five pounds loaded.

Even among the arms manufacturers here in the United States the practice of cylinder engraving did not spread, except for maybe an occasional presentation gun. The only exception to this rule would probably be the Whitney arms, but even so, there were few mass produced revolvers that bore engraving to match the intricate Indian fight, Naval battle and holdup scenes used by Colt.

As Benjamin Franklin once said, there is much difference in imitating a good man and counterfeiting him!

It is also interesting to note that, although engraved on the cylinder, there was no known comparison or counterfeit sheet printed for the Paterson. Perhaps at that time Colt hadn't thought of the possibility to use the engraving as a means of detecting originals from fakes that were made outside of his Paterson, New Jersey, plant without his permission.

Why Walker was chosen to lead the U.S. Mounted Rifles during the Mexican War is still a mystery; there were many other better qualified military men at the time, including Hays and Ben McCulloch. It is said that his brother, Jonathan, had many political ties in Washington and was instrumental in getting him the command

Walker, however, made several design recommendations to Colt and was influential in the remodeling of the handgun. Produced by Eli Whitney, Jr., in his Whitneyville, Connecticut, factory, the new model was designated the Whitneyville-Walker Dragoon pistol. The gun later became the official sidearm of the U.S. Mounted Rifles and the cylinder of the large revolver — weighing approximately four pounds — was engraved with the Indian fight scene sketched by Walker during his earlier Texas Ranger service.

In the sketch, Walker depicted himself in command of the charge, although it was Hays who actually was commanding the troops. Since Hays was riding a white mule during the battle, it is believed that it is he that Walker sketched riding just to his rear, partially hidden by his dark mount.

The Navy pistol scene bore stampings that depicted the Texas Navy and Mexican Navy battling it out in the shallows of the Gulf. This scene also commemorates one of the early exploits of the Colt Paterson and, incidentally, is the same batch of revolvers later used by the Texas Rangers during the Indian fight.

The cylinder of this Colt Pocket Model also includes the gun's serial number. Engraved metal is evidence that this was presentation gun; note the words COLTS PATENT on gun.

On May 16, 1843, the Texas armada — quite the worse for wear and drastically undermanned — met with Mexico's well armed and heavily manned warships near the port of Campeche.

The Mexican ships were well built shallow draught steam vessels and were well suited for use in shallow flats of the Gulf. The Texas ships, on the other hand, were nothing more than some old sloops and schooners that had been hastily prepared for use as armed warships.

Under the command of Commodore Edward W. Moore, the Texans sent shot after shot crashing into the heavily manned Mexican ships. Hardly a shot was fired that did not hit its mark, taking some of the attackers with it. Mexican shells did a considerable amount of damage to the Texas ships, but since they were undermanned, many of the rounds failed to hit anybody.

During a later visit to New York in 1850, Moore — excited in telling of the battle — sketched out the battle scene for Colt to use on the cylinder engraving on his then new model Navy revolver. This gun was to replace the earlier pistol as the official issue gun for Naval forces.

To manufacture the engraved cylinders, the scenes were first cut into a plate of iron. Through a hardening process the iron plate was then turned into a somewhat soft grade of steel, from which yet another impression was made onto another soft piece of iron. This second piece of iron was in the form of a roller. After the sculptor had made any last minute changes or touchups that he cared to, the roller was hardened into steel.

The cylinder blank — already bored and milled out for the placement of nipples and cylinder locks — was then placed in a device resembling a lathe. The engraving roller was then brought against the cylinder blank under a considerable amount of pressure. In doing so, the raised etchings of the scene were incised into the much softer metal of the cylinder.

On the early engraved scenes were included the markings COLT'S PATENT. The cylinder engraving on the Whitneyville-Walker and the Whitneyville-Hartford Dragoons were additionally marked MODEL U.S.M.R., later on the First Model Hartford Dragoons appeared the stamping U.S. DRAGOONS. The pocket pistol and Navy revolver cylinders were also marked with the gun's serial number.

Although worn through years of hard use, the Naval battle scene on this Colt Navy is clearly legible; revolver was .36 cal.

CHAPTER 5

FIREPOWER ALONG THE MASON-DIXON

It Took An Assortment Of Rifles And Muskets To Fight The Civil War. The North Found Quantity An Asset Over Quality When It Came To Markmanship!

WAR ALMOST ALWAYS NECESSITATES an extreme step-up in the production of suitable arms for the armies involved. The great Civil War between the North and the South was no exception.

Although the Northern states were much better prepared to meet the increasing demands of the wartime forces, they too were hard-pressed to maintain an adequate supply of such guns flowing from their arms plants. The South, however, was far worse off. They were hardly prepared to meet the demands of war when the first shots rang out over Fort Sumter.

For the most part, the majority of the arms used by the South's ill-equipped forces at the outbreak of war were guns that had been captured from such raids as that at Harpers Ferry. Despite the beliefs that such raids did much to arm the South's soldiers, the take from those raids was relatively small, when compared to the great number of rifles, handguns and artillery pieces that it would take in later attempts to defend their homelands from the invading Northern forces.

The lack of standardization of armament on both sides resulted in a motley assortment of firepower. Hardly a single unit was uniformly armed. The South's raids had

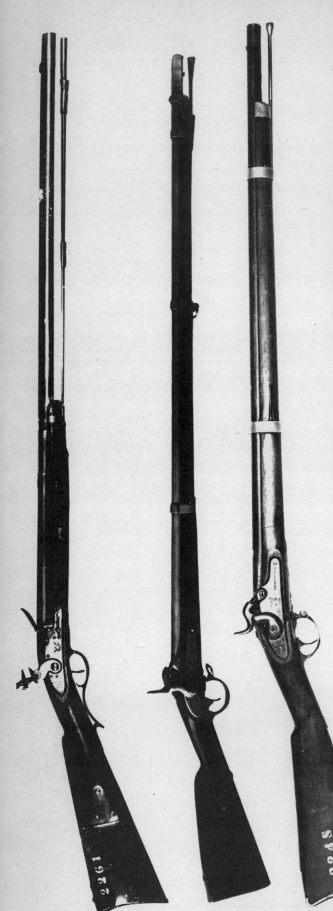

Early in the war, Confederate
soldiers carried such guns as
the 1814 Harpers Ferry flintlock
at far left and the 1842 Model
Mississippi rifle (middle).
Rifled musket at right was made
in a Fayetteville, North
Carolina, armory. Pictured above
is a Confederate cartridge box
and .577 caliber Minie bullets.

mostly resulted in obsolete military guns, many of which
were flintlocks that had to be converted to a percussion
ignition system before they were of any value. The lack of
these large captures in early battles, however, would probably have resulted in an early collapse of the Southern
armies.

The rifles and muskets used by the Confederate forces
fell into eight different categories. During the early days of
the war, Southern armory-made rifle and 1855-61 musket
models became standard issue. Another favorite was the .54
caliber M1842 Mississippi rifle. In 1858, the .54 caliber
bores on some of these guns were bored out to take the .58
caliber Minie. These were also fitted with adjustable sights
and issued to U.S. Army troops as an infantry rifle.

The third type of rifled musket used by the Southern
forces was the imported British Enfield and the South made
copies of this particular gun. This was a fifty-four-inch
rifled musket of .577 caliber. Adequately named the short
Enfield, a shortened version of this gun was commonly used
by mounted infantry units. Not an actual carbine in the
true sense, the short Enfield was nearly as accurate as the
full length musket while being somewhat manueverable like
a carbine, only more effective.

Muskets were almost always accompanied by some sort of blade. Note the difference between the Enfield bayonet above and Dahlgren design below.

The U.S. Springfield percussion rifled musket model of 1855 was the standard armament of the Federal troops. This one is fitted for Maynard tape-priming system.

Although scattered Southern records don't reveal the exact number of these guns used by Confederate forces, it is believed that some 700,000 Enfields were obtained through purchases, captures and the constant supply of blockade runners.

The fourth type of Confederate shoulder armament was the Austrian or Texas Tyler rifle. This gun appears to be a cross between the Austrian Lorenz rifle and the French Minie. This same type of cross is prevalent in the Tallassee carbine produced at the Tallassee Armory in Alabama. In lock and fittings this rifled musket resembles the Enfield, but the stock lines followed more along the lines of the U.S. musket; in 1864, this firearm was adopted as the standard pattern for the Confederate cavalry.

The fifth type of long gun to appear in the South was the breechloading cavalry carbine. A number of novel breechloaders were produced in the South's armories, but the most interesting was a slightly modified version of the Sharps that was produced in Richmond, Virginia. Among numerous other breechloaders, the Tarpley and Perry stand out as fairly good breechloading designs.

The sixth group of rifles to arm Confederate soldiers were those made abroad for the Southern forces. The Calisher & Terry was one such rifle that saw some use during the Civil War. In Great Britain, where the gun was manufactured, United Kingdom services passed over this gun in favor of the arms produced by Westley Richards.

Other imported guns were far less popular, such as the different Belgian guns. A good number of those muskets were so unreliable that they were properly labeled worthless by the troops who were so armed. Many a Southern soldier quickly rid himself of the arm the first chance he got, usually to replace it with one of the North's finer rifles — which was commonly picked up from the battlefield.

Such battlefield salvage can be considered as the seventh category of Confederate armament. Many of the Enfields

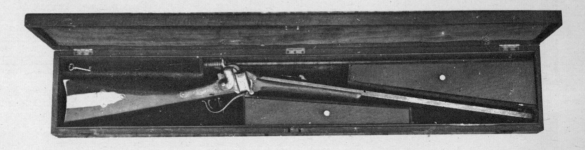

Springfield musket (top) was produced in a contracted armory, markings include 1861 date and stamping "Trenton." Colt revolving rifle (middle) was early repeater. Regular issue, custom cased Sharps (below) were reliable armament.

and Springfields of the Northern forces were almost always the first to be picked from the battlefields. Many of these may have needed repair work done but the South's armories were capable of doing this; it was far easier to repair a gun than to produce one from scratch.

The final category of the South's rifles and muskets were the flint and percussion guns that had been stored in the U.S. arsenals. Many of these guns were of patterns dating from as far back as the late 1700s and were originally to be used to arm the state militias; in 1808 an act by Congress established a system of arming able-bodied men in the event of state emergencies. A considerable number of these guns were originally fitted with flintlocks, but had been converted to accept the percussion system.

Springfield muskets were the standard firearms used by the Northern Union forces. Eli Whitney, along with numerous other armorers, produced some 670,000 of these rifled muskets for the Union armies. In addition to these,

the Springfield Armory produced another 793,434 of the guns that bears its name from the period of 1861 to the end of 1865.

A big .58 caliber infantry gun, the Springfield rifled musket was quite accurate. A few old sources claim that ten-shot groups having a twenty-seven-inch diameter could be made at five hundred yards and that the 550-grain Minie fired from one of these rifled muskets would easily penetrate four inches of pine at a thousand yards.

Coupled with the devastational powers of the Minie bullet, the muzzleloading Springfields, Enfields and numerous other imported and domestically produced rifled muskets were unquestionably the most employed firearms of the war. Actually, when speaking or referring to the guns of the Civil War, the topic is more on guns that were produced before the war began.

By 1860, Colt had developed his revolver about as far as

they could before the introduction of rimfire cartridges. Remington had done the same with their solid-framed Beals' designed cap and ball revolvers and the general design of the rifled musket had remained the same since about the end of the first quarter of the century; the only changes being improved ignition systems. Of course, there were other revolvers and rifled muskets produced and used in addition to the ones we have already discussed here, but few are of general interest.

What about the guns that actually were developed during the Civil War? Actually, only a few new designs came about at that time, as most of the changes were just improvements over existing patterns. To win a war, however, one of the opposing armies must have a definite edge or advantage over the other. Additional firepower on the battlefield

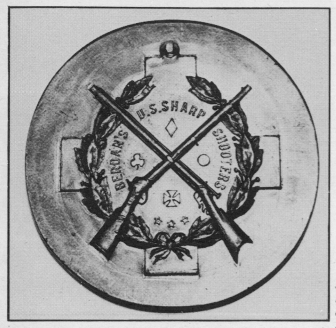

could be credited as an added advantage and it is a good bet that such was the idea during the development of the first really successful repeating rifle and carbine designs.

The Civil War was the first modern war: Mathew Brady recorded the actual bloodshed through the lens of his camera; important messages could be sent in a matter of minutes instead of days through the telegraph, and the greatest development in armed warfare since the Minie came into being — the repeating rifle. Although Colt's revolving percussion carbine and several other percussion repeaters had been around since the early 1850s, it wasn't until March 6, 1860 that U.S. Patent 27,393 was granted to Christopher M. Spencer for the first really successful repeating cartridge rifle.

A seven-shot repeater, the Spencer was slow to win acceptance by the Army Ordnance Department. Spencer had managed to impress Commander John A. Dahlgren, inventor of the famous Dahlgren naval cannon, and Chief of Navy Ordnance Andrew A. Harwood during a demonstration at the Washington Navy Yard in June, 1861.

During the two-day test fire, he had demonstrated the effectiveness of the gun by successively firing 250 rounds each day without stopping to clean the rifle. During this initial introduction of his rifle to the war department officials Spencer even surprised himself by surpassing his own estimated rate of fire of fifteen shots per minute by increasing the number of shots to twenty one rounds per minute. Harwood was so impressed that he immediately put in an order for seven hundred Spencers to be used by the Navy.

The Army Ordnance Department apparently wasn't as enthused about the repeating Spencer as were the Navy officials. Most of this hesitation to accept the new rifle has been credited to the then Chief of Army Ordnance,

Sharpshooter's badge (left) worn by Berdan's marksmen displays a long range sniper rifle and the reliable Sharps. Lieutenant George A. Custer (below left) and General Plesanton shortly before Custer's promotion to general.

Spencer's seven-shot repeater was slow to be accepted by Ordnance Department officials but soon became a favorite of the troops.

Union cavalry commander, Major General Phillip H. Sheridan in photo taken by Matthew Brady. Cavalry troops found the Spencer to be an ideal choice of firepower.

Brigadier General James W. Ripley. Often described as "old Army," he apparently still favored the muzzleloaders over Spencer's new repeating concept.

The majority of the Spencer rifles and carbines used by Federal troops were of .50 caliber and were chambered for the .56-56 Spencer rimfire cartridge, having a big 350-grain bullet propelled by 42 to 45 grains of black powder. The magazine on these rifles and carbines was located inside the butt stock and was virtually protected from possible damage should the arm be dropped.

Although Spencer had made a government contract to deliver 10,000 of the guns on December 26, 1861, delivery of the arms didn't start until better than a year later. It is believed that this delay was caused by the design change of

the extractor. The first of these repeaters were fitted with an extractor that closely resembled the edge of a saw blade. As the action was worked the teeth on the extractor would latch onto the rim of the cartridge and pull it from the chamber. This was later changed to a superior side position extractor.

Spencer's seven-shot repeaters saw their first real action during the extremely bloody battle of Antietam. Until then, the Southern sharpshooters, many of whom had been firing their armament since their rural boyhood days, had brought heavy losses to the Northern forces. Perhaps this is one of the reasons for adopting the superior cartridge breechloaders and repeating Spencers and Henrys.

In an indecisive battle, both North and South suffered

heavy losses at Antietam, but the repeating Spencers had given the inexperienced Federal troops the added firepower they needed to turn Lee's first attempt to invade the North. The battle had proved one thing however: The repeater was to see further use during the war.

Some sources claim that as many as 200,000 Spencer rifles and carbines are thought to have been used during the war. Procurement records, however, clearly show that only 94,196 Spencer carbines and 12,471 rifles were purchased officially by the Ordnance Department during the period of January 1, 1861, to the end of the fiscal year, June 30, 1866; this is not counting the seven hundred rifles purchased by the Navy.

In addition to these purchases, better than 58,000,000 of the Spencer cartridges were purchased, many of which were used in the Ballard and Joslyn carbines of the same .56-56 Spencer caliber.

The Spencer became so popular among troops that when units were denied issue of such arms they occasionally took it upon themselves to personally purchase the guns. One such case was the order of 4000 Spencers by Colonel John T. Wilder to equip the men of his brigade. Actually, he had no authority to make the order and the Ordnance Department promptly refused to purchase the guns for him. Wilder asked his men if they would mind purchasing the guns with their own money and the brigade voted in favor of his suggestion.

Armed with the seven-shooters, Wilder's brigade soon won the title of The Lightning Brigade as they turned the Confederate troops from Hoover's Gap in the Cumberland Mountains. With the Confederate troops unable to reinforce those already at Chickamauga, Union soldiers won the battle in a smashing victory several weeks later.

The most widely used repeating rifle of the Civil War, the Spencer wasn't the only one to be employed. In the opinion of many modern Civil War buffs the fifteen-shot Henrys were the best rifles available during the war. Although about 10,000 of these repeating lever actions were eventually purchased by individual soldiers, not one was officially purchased for issue to Federal troops.

An extremely accurate close range arm, the Henry was fitted with a twenty-four-inch barrel that was first bored to .42-inch and then rifled to .43-inch. The .44 Henry Flat, the rimfire cartridge for which these guns were chambered, lacked something in the power department. Propelled by 26 to 28 grains of black powder, the 200-grain bullet was pushed from the muzzle at a velocity of around 1100 feet per second, developing a muzzle energy of just under 600 foot/pounds. Even with this power shortage it nonetheless became a popular sporting cartridge. These early Henrys were the first milestones for the later Winchesters, which were greatly improved through the use of such center-fire cartridges as the .44-40.

Combined with the fact that the Spencer was slow to be fully adopted for use by Union cavalry units, the limited use of the Henry may have added to the length of the war. Many historians and arms buffs believe that if the Spencer had been adopted earlier and produced in large enough numbers, along with full utilization of the Henry's firepower, the war could have been shortened by as much as a year, maybe two.

Burnside, Joslyn, Merril, Gallagher, Maynard, Remington, Smith, Starr, Ball, Gibbs, Hall, Ballard, Linder, Palmer, Warner and Cosmopolitan are a few more names that were known among arms producers of the Civil War.

For the most part these were carbines and, although many gave good service, they never quite matched the firepower of the big bore muzzleloaders or repeaters such as the Spencer.

Union cavalry soldier in full uniform, including sabre and Spencer repeating rifle. While mounted, rifle was carried in this manner, attached by lanyard.

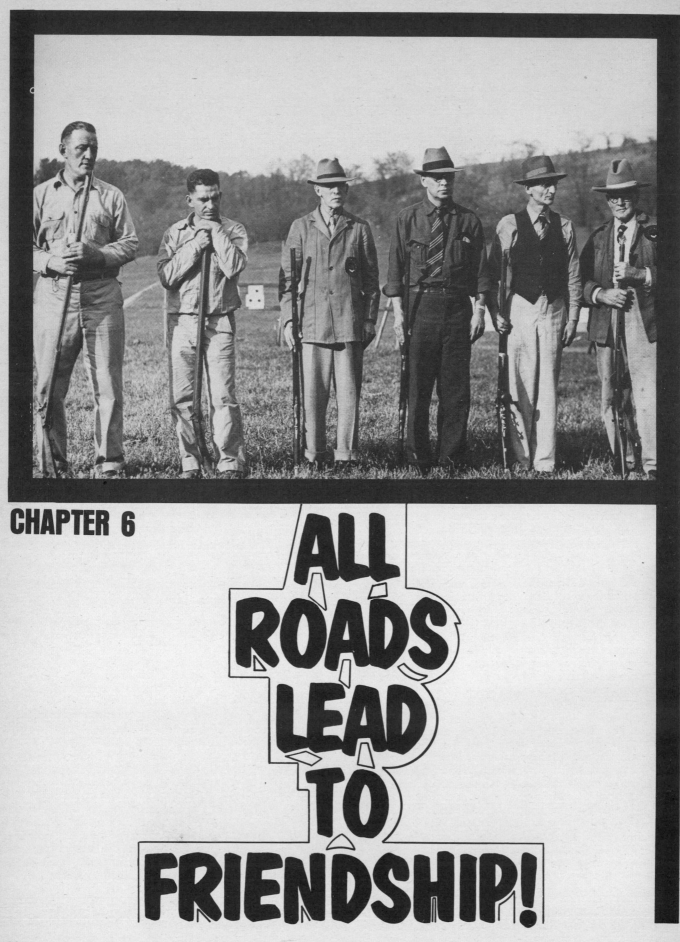

CHAPTER 6

ALL ROADS LEAD TO FRIENDSHIP!

Every Sport Has Its Big Yearly Event And, After A Quarter-Century Now, This Indiana Annual Meet Is It For Muzzleloaders!

IN THE GENTLY ROLLING, wooded hills and farm lands of southern Indiana lies the village of Friendship, population 120. Here, fifty miles west of Cincinnati, is a piece of Hoosierland from the pages of James Whitcomb Riley, where you can see and take part in competition in historical America. Here, too, you can see and take part in competition in not just plain target shooting, but marksmanship with muzzleloading guns firing only black powder. There are matches for pistols, rifles and shotguns.

Each Fall, a six-day shoot is held to determine the muzzleloading champion of the United States. This Fall shoot always ends on Labor Day. In addition to "this big one," a two-day Spring shoot is held as well as a two-day turkey shoot in November.

The National Muzzle Loading Rifle Association conducts these matches on its own ninety-two-acre range located on the eastern border of the town of Friendship, north of Laughrey Creek.

On August 24, 1781, a band of Indians attacked the command of Colonel Lochry, which was on its way to join Clark's forces at Vincennes. The colonel and thirty-six of his men were killed and the survivors made British prisoners. This action took place on the north bank of the stream that somehow became Laughrey Creek.

The NMLRA Labor Day Shoot is, to the black powder fan, what the World Series is to a baseball fan, what Camp Perry is to the breechloading clique — pure magic. You rarely hear the shoot called by its correct name; rather it is referred to as, "the shoot at Friendship," or just plain "Friendship." So, if you should hear a couple of characters mumbling something about "friendship," with a queer look in their eyes, they aren't talking about undying loyalty to each other, they're discussing ways and means of getting to the Big Shoot back in Indiana.

Just how old the sport of marksmanship is, no one knows. Civilization started to emerge from the mists of time when man and vegetation appeared in the forms we recognize today; we are told this was at the end of the Pleistocene Epoch, about one million years ago. It is not improbable that some Stone Age kids became the world's first marksmen by throwing stones at some whitening skull. The adults were too busy fishing and hunting to play games.

We read of a Roman Emperor during the Second Century A.D. who must have been the greatest marksman of them all. Once he killed a hundred raging lions in the great arena with exactly one hundred arrows.

By 1375 the crossbow began to supplant the long bow and shortly after 1400 A.D., the sound of firearms was heard at the shooting festivals.

At Augsburg, Germany, home of many of the best artist-armorers of the Dark Ages, handguns and muskets were used in the 1429 matches. The 1508 match was attended by 544 bowmen and 919 gunners. This great turnout so protracted the meet that thereafter efforts were made to limit the number of invitations to four hundred.

Today, all the best traditions of the ancient shooting festivals are still carried on at Friendship. The NMLRA, with its 7,500 members, 150 affiliated clubs and the wonderful ninety-two-acre shooting facility didn't just spring into being; it did have a double start, though, because two separate groups started about the same time and, when they joined forces in 1935, the NMLRA was formed.

Early in 1931, E. M. "Red" Farris and Oscar Seth of Portsmouth, Ohio, decided to hold a shooting match with oldtime muzzleloading guns. The event was held February 22, 1931, with great success, as sixty-seven shooters attended.

The atmosphere at Friendship is a relaxed one during the yearly shoot. Umbrellas are used to ward off the scorching sun.

The next year, another shoot was held at Portsmouth. In 1933, an organization was formed with Seth as president and Farris as "ramrod." The hat was passed and there was ten dollars in the treasury. Radio WLW of Cincinnati featured a popular story teller known as Boss Johnson. Boss had an especial friend among his host of followers, W. F. "Pop" Neighbert, storekeeper and police chief of Friendship, Indiana. These two cronies decided to hold a black powder shoot.

Boss "talked it up" on WLW and the response was all they hoped for. He asked his boss, Powell Crosley Jr., owner of WLW, to put up a prize. It was a silver loving cup about the size of an umbrella stand and was hotly contested for; today nearly forty years later it is still being battled over and is the most important single trophy of all, next to the National Championship Cup.

Some of the other awards for that first Friendship shoot were: A pair of rubber boots donated by S. H. Sickerman, a hunting coat donated by Neighbert, a suede jacket offered by the Friendship State Bank, a half barrel of flour by the Friendship Milling Company and several more of which I have no record.

Today, the first three places in every event are awarded medals: gold, silver and bronze. In many cases, the winner receives a handsome trophy in addition to his gold medal. There are fourteen different championship aggregates consisting of two or more of the seventy events and in a

Wearing authentic costume and beard, this shooter appears as if he just stepped out of the pages of a history book. Not all shooters are quite this authentic in dress.

Slug gun shooters and spectators both enjoy an informal practice session before the heat of the actual competition is on.

46

Firing their heavy barreled black powder rifles, competitors shoot for top honors in the Alvin York Match. Shooter above is Bill Furst.

Floyd Resor of Union City, Indiana, is a regular at Friendship. He is known for his extremely accurate black powder guns.

number of cases, a single event may be part of several different aggregates.

In 1935, the two groups joined to form the NMLRA with Boss Johnson as president. The 1937 shoot was held at Rising Sun, Indiana, next year the matches were moved to the Sugar Bowl, amid the larch and maple trees, one time camping ground of the Shawnees near Dillsboro, Indiana. The Dillsboro Health Resort became the association's headquarters for the next two years. This establishment is the nearest complete hotel accommodation to Friendship; Del Ross, Margaret Turner and the rest of the staff always do everything to make the visiting shooter happy.

Since 1938, all matches have been held on the association's own range, a piece of land bought from the late Walter Cline, author, a founder and long time M-L enthusiast. The present range is named the Walter Cline Range. The association's monthly magazine, Muzzle-Blasts, was started in September, 1939, and goes out monthly to each member.

No organization grows without the leadership of industrious men of ability. Only a few can be mentioned in a short story like this. In addition to those mentioned above: Walter Grote, Bull Ramsey, Clarence McNeer, James Lemon and about a dozen others should be listed as founders. B. LeRoy Compton, M. G. Van Way and James Lemon are some of the businessmen who helped the lusty infant reach its present status. Today the headquarters address is: P.O. Box 67, Friendship, Indiana 47021.

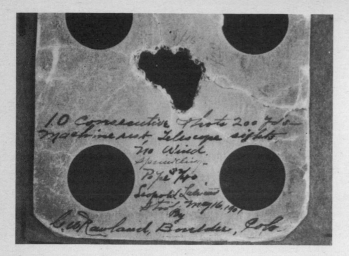

Somewhat of a record at the annual
muzzleloading meet is this ten shot, two
hundred yard group made by C.W. Rawland.

The purpose of the association remains the same as the day it was founded: To promote shooting, collecting and building muzzleloading guns and equipment, along with the joy of research into the history of these items.

Each year, when the order to commence firing is given, some are made bold, some irresolute, some strengthened and some paralyzed by buck fever. Some consider the loss of an event the way most people would regard the loss of an eye. Others are as keenly downcast, but hide behind a stoic front. To be a winner, you have to be a competitor;

With the competition still not underway, the parking lot at the Walter Cline Range fills rather quickly with arriving shooters.

this spirit of competition seems to be what brings us back each year, for maybe "the next time," our efforts to excel will pay off. The rifle events — both round ball and slug, offhand and bench — make up the bulk of the program on the 175-position rifle range.

Over the years, complete and detailed rules and procedures have been developed and are published in the NMLRA Rule Book. All round ball rifle events are five-shot matches, the slug-gun and pistol events are ten-shot affairs and the number of birds for the shotgun matches varies. Each string of five shots must be fired in forty-five minutes, then the range is closed for fifteen minutes while the crews change targets. Firing starts at 8 a.m. and continues straight through until 5 p.m. All scores are posted hourly on the seventy different event sheets. Each shooter selects the events he wants to enter and he may fire these events in any order he chooses. Because of this, the winner of every event is in doubt until the final relay on Labor Day morning.

Most competitors enter the four events, the aggregate of which makes up the National Championship. These events are: the Mike Fink Match, twenty-five yards offhand, any iron sights; the Powell Crosley Match, fifty yards, benchrest, open iron sights; the Alvin York Match, fifty yards, benchrest, any iron sight and the Walter Cline Match, one hundred yards, benchrest, any iron sight.

Your gun will qualify, if you can lug it up to the firing line, it shoots black powder, is loaded from the muzzle and can be fitted with the specific sight equipment and fires the proper bullet for the match — either a round ball or a slug. Several events do have a weight limitation on the gun, but its vintage is of no importance. Loading benches are provided to the rear of the firing line, but a sturdy folding shooting bench and chair are a must.

Because each man and woman is firing the events of his choice in the sequence of his choosing, the outcome never "hangs on the next shot." This does not make for keen spectator interest; after the novelty of the flash, boom and smoke has been observed, a muzzleloading match is about as exciting to the casual observer as watching grass grow.

To a competitor, it is a different story. If he has turned in a good score the first day, he finds himself checking the score sheet for that event several times a day to learn whether anybody has beaten him yet. If his score holds up, the suspense grows.

The pistol range and of course the trap field hold more

spectator value. To add more color for everybody's enjoyment, shooters and their families are urged to wear authentic costumes of earlier days, especially for the Sunday morning parade to church. The Lutheran Church of the nearby hamlet of Farmers Retreat conducts services Sunday morning. All shooting is stopped for an hour while the Jim Bridgers, Wyatt Earps and Colonial girls parade to church and for a moment barbers, salesmen, lawyers, doctors, engineers, laymen and ministers lose their identity and become characters of the past. Those not attending church use the time to renew cherished friendships or repair a piece of equipment. The ladies of the church also operate the dining room in the club house, as well as the lunch stand outside throughout the shoot. Three meals a day are served and the menus range from hot-dogs to a full chicken dinner, including all the trimmings — even blueberry pie. A feature of the noon meal is the special fast service table for shooters only.

each state. The registration area is on the main floor near the west door. Scoring is done on the second floor, secure from helping hands. South of the clubhouse the camping area is laid out in "streets" with 110-volt juice available for the individual lots. Modern rest rooms and bath houses are permanent installations. The shooter's camping equipment ranges from a sleeping bag under the sky to the most luxurious self-contained house trailers. A strict five-mile per hour speed limit is enforced throughout.

Commercial Row lies to the west and here permanent wooden booths flank a wide street area to accommodate our modern gold and silversmiths. If the demand for space overflows the booths, space for tents is made available. All kinds of equipment and supplies are for sale. Remington still makes percussion caps, Hodgdon has black powder and the ancient art of flint knapping flourishes in Brandon, England. In recent years, several new sources of flints have been developed in our South.

This photo, taken in 1953, shows the interest already prevalent at that time. These shooters were busy practicing for match four days before.

A few years ago a new event was added: the Seneca Running Offhand. Here the contestant — preferably in buckskins — must fire five shots from five widely separated stations on surprise targets. Each man must be fully equipped to load between stations and, since a time element is involved, each must move at a fast trot and after the last shot race back to the starting point. The shadows of Colonel Lochry and his men must certainly watch in approval; for the Seneca course is laid in the bed of Laughery Creek.

Any person shooting a five-shot possible in competition automatically joins the exclusive 50 Club and receives a gold lapel button, is a guest at the 50 Club dinner and may enter the 50 Club Match.

The two-story clubhouse is equipped with kitchens, dining room and a main hall capable of seating five hundred people. The great memorial fireplace contains a stone from

The number of shooters registering each year varies from 500 to 600. They come, some with families, from virtually every state and territory. On the holiday weekend the crowd exceeds 2,000.

So, we come to the real purpose of the whole enterprise: The shooting events, the best individual shooter, etc. In my opinion, the greatest individual accomplishment was the 100 — 9x record score fired by John Baldinger in the two hundred-yard Billinghurst match, not only because of this record, but because John was seventy-eight years old at the time. What a wonderful example of the joy a target shooting competitor can experience long after more strenuous sports have to be given up.

For a fine outdoor hobby for the entire family, try muzzleloading target shooting and, if you do I hope you never have a misfire.

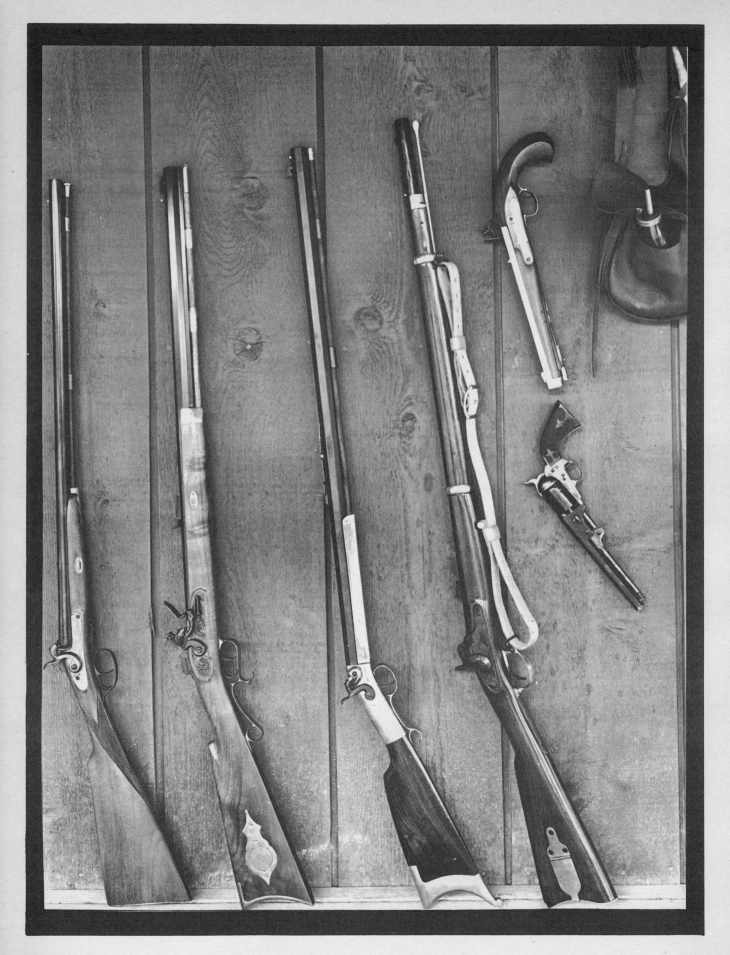

REBIRTH OF AN ERA

Nostalgia, Low Cost And Anti-Gun Laws Have Much To Do With The Rebirth Of The Black Powder Sport!

THE SCARCITY OF fine old original black powder arms in safe shootable condition can be accredited for the introduction of the numerous replicas and reproduction guns that are being offered today. Few, if any, serious collectors would even entertain the thought of putting such fine old originals through the rigors of everyday shooting. Once these guns are lost to irreparable damage, they are lost for good.

The idea of producing a modern reproduction or replica of these early arms took hold in the second half of the 1950s and, through the efforts of such men as Val Forgett of the Navy Arms Company and Turner Kirkland of Dixie Gun Works and others, there now are a good number of replica models to choose from. For the most part, the majority of these guns are almost exact reproductions of the originals they copy. There are changes on some, however, that actually make these guns far superior to their predecessors. Most of these changes are internal, making the guns more dependable without changing the overall appearance.

It's hard, if not impossible, to credit any one individual with the introduction of replicas. It's a known fact that Sam Colt, himself, was hard pressed to discourage the illegal manufacture of Colt copies and there are a number of guns still around that were assembled from surplus original parts, many known to have been produced well before the rebirth of black powder shooting in the last several decades.

In 1955, Turner Kirkland began marketing his Dixie

Ruger recently entered the black powder field with this percussion version of their famous Blackhawk single-action, dubbed the Old Army.

squirrel rifle. Made in Liege, Belgium, this rifle was the first modern-made black powder muzzleloading arm to be introduced in the United States. As could only be expected, this .45 caliber rifle was accepted quickly by the contemporary black powder crowd.

The shortage of vintage Kentucky and Pennsylvania long rifles, coupled with the fact that the vast majority of these guns were handmade, and the growing rarity of such guns caused the prices to skyrocket out of the average shooter's reach. The Dixie rifle, however, had two extremely pleasing features. In addition to being reasonably priced, the gun actually was superior to most of the originals in that it utilized much stronger modern steels in its construction.

Dixie Gun Works' rifle opened a new field and it wasn't long before other replicas and reproduction guns began to hit the market. In 1958, Val Forgett formed the Navy Arms Company; his first gun was a near exact replica of the 1851 Colt Navy. This was the first of the cap and ball revolver replicas to come into this country.

The story behind producing this first pistol is somewhat interesting in itself. It seems that Forgett experienced some trouble from the Italian customs people in trying to get an original Colt Navy to Brescia gunmaker Vittorio Gregorelli. Customs officials wouldn't allow the pistol to be shipped to the gunmaker, who hadn't received a license to produce firearms. This problem was easily solved, however, by calling on a friend, who was in the service and stationed in Italy at the time, to deliver the gun to the armsmaker.

Of the first sixteen of these guns produced — ten copies of the original Colt Navy and six of the Confederate Griswold & Gunnison brass framed .36 caliber Army revolver — Forgett quickly noticed nearly a dozen changes in their design. These were all prototypes and he soon had them straightened out.

The Italian hand craftsman had changed the bead front

sight to a dovetailed blade and among the other changes that robbed the guns of an original appearance were the enlarged screw heads of the guard screws and the extra width of the brass guard plate. The inner curve and beveled angle on the back of the guard plate was deliberately changed slightly to distinguish the copy from the original. This also results in yet another slight change in the shape of the grips.

Replicas and reproduction guns have come a long way since the introduction of the aforementioned two. Today's black powder enthusiast finds a large number of such guns available at most any sporting goods store and through a multitude of arms distributor catalogs.

Why all this fuss over shooting dirty, smelly and ballistically inferior black powder guns?

Of all the logical reasons, from nostalgia to the growing legal complications involved in possessing and discharging firearms of modern design, especially handguns, perhaps the single best reason is that black powder guns are fun. How many times have you been firing at a range with your conventional armament to suddenly notice a giant puff of smoke belch forth some ways down the firing line? It sure catches your interest and, before the day is over, it's a good bet that you'll mosey on over and see what said shooter is firing. Black powder guns are interesting!

Beginning muzzleloader and cap and ball revolver shooters would be wise to stay away from the cheapies on the market. Even though these guns are fully proof-tested before being imported into this country and are declared safe for shooting, their sloppy manufacture make them undependable and the trouble they present detracts greatly from the pleasure of shooting them.

As with modern cartridge-type guns, black powder guns are classified into one of three main categories: rifles, shotguns and handguns. Each of these categories can be broken down even further — single-shot, multiple-shot, double barrel, single barrel, etc. — but for this brief introduction of replicas and reproduction guns we will leave them in the three main categories. Subsequent sections will go into detail on the background and development of many of these guns. This is a look at some of the better black powder pieces available on today's market.

CENTENNIAL ARMS has been in the black powder arms business since the early 1960s, following closely the developments made by Val Forgett. Among the numerous pieces now offered by them, two stand out as about as close a reproduction as can be obtained — their New Model Colt Army replica and 1863 Zouave Remington reproduction.

Both of these guns are imported from Italy and both are strong, well built shooters. The Army replica is .44 caliber and has an eight-inch rifled barrel. A big .58 caliber, the reproduction of the Zouave is a perfect choice for North/South Skirmishes or big game hunting.

COLT: Getting back into the black powder scene this early developer of the cap and ball revolver has again begun reproduction of the 1851 Navy. This is a top quality cap and ball revolver that is not a replica, but a reproduction of the same gun. Colt had to work out a few bugs when production was first started on these revolvers, but they are now stronger shooters than the originals.

CONNECTICUT VALLEY ARMS is a relative newcomer to the field of black powder manufacture, with most of their products being made to their specifications by a Spanish factory that works only for CVA. As well as finished armament, ready for shooting straight out of the protective carton, the Connecticut firm also turns out do-it-yourself kits for all of the firearms they offer in finished condition. The kits come with easily followed instructions and have been pre-checked for safety in firing, we're told, if the directions are followed to the letter.

DIXIE GUN WORKS: A pioneer in the replica business, Turner Kirkland has built this firm into one of the largest black powder gun distributors in the country. Among the numerous replicas now offered are the Dixie Deluxe Pennsylvania rifle and the Dixie First Model Brown Bess. The Dixie Pennsylvania rifle isn't an exact replica of any given make, but is a copy of the general type, roman nose shaping of the butt stock, beautifully inlaid brass patchbox, cherry-stained hardwood stock. The Dixie Brown Bess is a big .75 caliber long land smoothbore musket and is about as close a reproduction of the original available today.

EARLY & MODERN FIREARMS — known throughout the trade simply as EMF — was one of the earliest firms to recognize the future of black powder shooting. Through mass mail order marking, EMF also has been able to bring good quality firearms to the public at a price most shooters can afford.

With a broad variety from which to choose, one of the firm's top sellers is a full-scale replica of the Walker Colt. EMF currently is entering the field of modern imported cartridge handguns as well.

LYMAN, a firm well known for its sighting equipment and reloading presses, now offers two cap and ball revolvers. The Lyman New Model Army is a six-shot, 44 caliber revolver and the Lyman New Model Navy is its smaller .36 caliber version. Both guns are made in Europe under Lyman's supervision and the result is two fine black powder revolvers that are dependable. Both the Army and Navy follow the solid frame Remington pattern, a design favored by shooters interested in installing adjustable target sights.

NAVY ARMS, known for its spearheading the development of replica cap and ball revolvers, offers a complete line of single-shot percussion and flintlock pistols. The Navy Arms Kentucky pistol is a copy of the type of pistol used during the late 1700s and early 1800s. Having a .440 bore diameter, this is a reliable shooter backed by an experienced distributor of black powder guns; it is available in flintlock or percussion.

For the serious competitor, Navy Arms also offers special target percussion revolvers. These .44 and .36 caliber revolvers are of the solid frame design and have full-length top ribs with ramp front sights and fully adjustable rear target sights.

NUMRICH ARMS: For some time now this developer of the Hopkins & Allen underhammer rifles has offered a complete line of wares for the hunter and serious competitor. The H&A Deluxe Buggy rifle is a light, short rifle that makes an excellent hunting piece in brushy country. This rifle is in .36 or .45 caliber. Available in the same calibers,

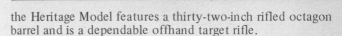

Lyman — long known for its sighting and reloading equipment — is another new entry. This is the .36 caliber New Model Navy revolver. The firm also produces a .44 caliber New Model Army and numerous other black powder shooting aids and accessories.

the Heritage Model features a thirty-two-inch rifled octagon barrel and is a dependable offhand target rifle.

RICHLAND ARMS, new to the field of muzzleloading arms, is a longtime distributor of fine imported breech-loading shotguns but now offers a 12-gauge muzzleloading shotgun. This gun sports twenty-eight-inch barrels that are cylinder bore. It is a rugged lightweight shotgun and should make an excellent upland bird hunting gun. The walnut stock is set off by the engraved lock plates — purposely left in the white — and the beautifully plum-colored browned barrels.

RUGER now is producing a black powder .44 caliber version of its famed single action Blackhawk. Featuring a completely modern internal mechanism, this is one of the most dependable cap and ball sixguns. The revolver, dubbed the Ruger Old Army, features a fixed blade front sight and fully adjustable rear target sights. In appearance, the Old Army is similar to the firm's line of cartridge revolvers, the frame being modified to accept the loading lever, substituting a capping groove in place of the loading gate.

There are numerous other top quality replicas and reproduction guns available. As mentioned, there still are cheap black powder guns on the market even though the trend is toward quality. Never settle for anything less than top quality. It pays in the long run, even if it costs more initially!

THOMPSON/CENTER, of Rochester, New Hampshire, is producing an American-made modern version of the Hawken rifle. This rifle was the prized possession of the westward adventurer and today is one of the most sought after collector pieces. Thompson/Center's modern reproduction differs slightly from the original, utilizing modern coil springs in place of the original flat type springs in the lock work. The rifle, however, maintains the husky and robust feeling of the original.

THE CONFEDERACY'S LAST ARSENAL!

Tumer Kirkland's Tennessee Arms Stronghold Is Enough To Stagger The Civil War Buff's Imagination!

NEED A NEW hammer for your well-used 1819 Halls rifle? What about an original main spring for that mint condition Charleville musket hanging over the fireplace — which could have been in the boat with Washington as he crossed the Delaware? Or perhaps your needs are more in the line of an original lock for a rare Green carbine.

An old gun fancier could spend a lot of time searching for any of these parts. Charleville muskets are hard to come by and it's doubtful that a collector owning one would be willing to part with his main spring anyhow. Equally rare are Green carbines — with less than a thousand produced in 1856 and 1857 — so chances are that, if you could locate a hammer for the 1819 Halls rifle, it would be quite the worse for wear. As a matter of fact, replacement parts for just about any antique firearm is near impossible to locate, unless you happen to know where to look!

One such place is Dixie Gun Works of Union City,

Rebirth Of An Era: Part B

Tennessee. Here, Turner Kirkland — founder and president of the firm — has stockpiled an unknown quantity of old original parts for these guns and many others. Today, Dixie Gun Works is perhaps the largest retail black powder catalog order store and antique gun parts supplier in the country. How it grew to reach this status is a story in itself.

"The first gun that my father bought me — being quite young at the time, I paid for the gun, but father bought it — was an old Colt 1849 Model .31 caliber pocket pistol that

Remington pistols, not to mention near mint condition Civil War rifles and muskets could be had for as little as fifty cents each, with mint condition guns bringing as high as two or three dollars. Collecting these guns had not yet reached the level of interest we know today and there were plenty of guns to be had; nearly every home had at least one or two just collecting dust.

"Of course, he said he was buying them for me," recalls

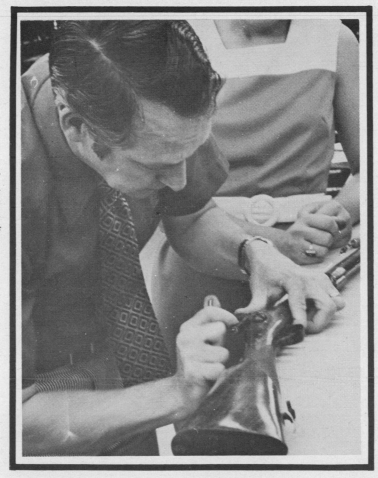

Dixie Gun Works' vice president Ernest Tidwell replaces faulty nipple on one of firm's muzzleloaders.

was pretty well used up. But the gun only cost seventy-five cents, so I couldn't complain much about that. I liked the gun so well that I would carry it to bed with me each night," states Kirkland. "I loved that gun better than just about anything else."

He had no idea at the time, but that worn out old Colt probably was part of the foundation on which Dixie Gun Works was formed. It was 1932 and the country was suffering from the effects of the depression. Small businesses folded under the stress of just day to day living; in short, it was hardly a time to be spending money on guns.

Kirkland's father, however, ran a small men's clothing store that just managed to survive the times. Although his sales were small, he always managed to scrape together enough money to buy an occasional rifle or pistol.

Money was scarce and hard to come by and, when anyone did manage to earn a few dollars, it almost always went for food to feed the family; rarely was it spent on guns. Consequently, fine original Kentucky rifles, Colt and

Turner Kirkland, "but really I think he was just buying them to hang on the walls in his store so they would help bring in a little more traffic and consequently make people spend a little more money.

"I didn't really know the difference between gunpowders then and didn't even know that black powder was available, but I would take firecrackers and stuff them in the end of the old Colt's barrel and light them, holding the gun out while it shot. A couple of years later, about 1934, I took out the silver powder by cutting open and unrolling the firecrackers. I loaded this into one of the chambers of an old Remington revolver.

"Well, the gun blew up! The solid strap on the frame that ran across the top of the cylinder just disappeared into thin air when the powder ignited. The chamber of the cylinder blew outward and, of course, ruined the gun. I can't remember what I ever did with that particular gun, but I guess I traded it off to someone way back. Anyway, I had learned my lesson about using smokeless powder in a black powder gun!"

Kirkland would travel with his father to visit relatives in Memphis every chance he got or at least that's the excuse he used to go along on the trips. Almost as soon as they would roll into Memphis, Turner would just disappear, but could always be found at York Arms, looking at their great display of guns and ammunition. "I was in my seventh Heaven visiting York Arms," recalls Kirkland today with a faint smile.

At that time York Arms was selling black powder for around sixty-five cents a pound, percussion caps ran around fifteen cents for a tin of a hundred. Today, Dixie gets nearly three dollars for that same pound of powder and a tin of percussion caps runs a dollar.

Five years after buying his first gun — the old Colt 1849 pocket pistol — Kirkland had managed to build his collection to more than a hundred guns of various makes. For the next few years, college took up most of Kirkland's time and gun collecting underwent a temporary set back.

When World War II broke out, he joined the Army and for the first time began meeting other gun collectors. Looking back, he remembers that "during the war I began to run into other collectors and started going into gun stores, among which was Bannerman's in New York City. I would spend hours walking around in Bannerman's just looking around.

"I couldn't afford to buy anything, but my mouth watered when I saw all the bargains they had. Back then you could buy a Sharps rifle for around $3.50 and good Spencer rifles were only $3. Mint condition .58 caliber Civil War muskets with bright and shiny bores could be had for less than five dollars apiece.

"Bannerman's even had new cast model cannon barrels for sale. Because I saw these at Bannerman's and liked them so well, is the reason I sell them today."

After the war — even more interested in gun collecting than he had been before — Kirkland began trading off the hundred-gun collection he had acquired before WWII. This was not to get rid of his guns, but instead to upgrade each piece in this collection.

There were few serious collectors in western Tennessee, so he did most of his trading and selling with collectors in other states through the mail. This was when he first discovered that there was a good demand for selling and buying through the mail.

Business continued to grow and in the May, 1948 issue of Muzzle Blast Magazine, Kirkland ran his first commercial ad. It was short and to the point: He had ten muzzleloaders — giving a very brief discription of each — he wanted to sell and he was looking for prospective buyers. In a very short time, all ten of the muzzleloaders were sold and Dixie Gun Works became a consistent advertiser in several of the shooting magazines.

In 1950, Turner Kirkland took a job selling jewelry and found himself doing a lot of travelling throughout his home state of Tennessee and neighboring Arkansas. Most of his work was done during the day and he had a lot of free time on his hands at the end of each day. To pass this time, he began to look up local gun collectors in each of the towns he travelled. Carrying quite a stock of merchandise with him, he did a lot of swapping and buying out of the trunk of his car.

His magazine advertisements began to receive a lot of attention from gun dealers all over the country and Europe. As a result, he made important contacts in England, Belgium, Spain and Italy.

During his jewelry selling travels he discovered there was a definite need for replacement locks, triggers, tenons, barrels and various other parts. He began importing these from manufacturers all over Europe and his business prospered even more.

He then purchased a small metal working lathe from

More than a dozen different kits are available from the Union City, Tennessee, firm. There are an even dozen displayed here but there are several not shown.

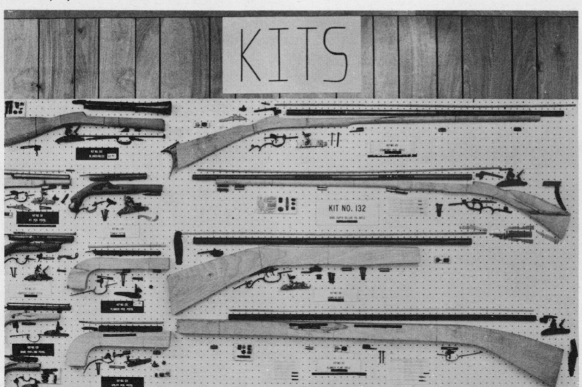

Two of the numerous visitors to Dixie Gun Works are almost lost among the forest of gun barrels as they browse through the old guns on sale there.

Part of the Dixie collection that isn't for sale. Many of these guns were a part of Turner Kirkland's early gun collection.

Sears-Roebuck and began milling bullet moulds out of commercially made cast iron hair straighteners. The demand for these moulds was so great that he could make as much as a hundred dollars a week making and marketing them in his spare time.

By 1954, mail order for his imported parts and bullet moulds, not to mention the occasional batch of guns he advertised for sale or trade, reached the point of forcing him to quit his selling job. He moved the business into a revamped coal house and this was Dixie Gun Works' first home.

Six months later Dixie Gun Works offered its first catalog, a twelve-pager selling for twenty-five cents. Business really boomed and in less than a year, the operation outgrew its coal house facilities and had to be moved into a larger building.

In 1955, Dixie Gun Works introduced the first reproduction rifle ever to be marketed in this country. Built in Belgium to Kirkland's strict specifications, the Dixie Squirrel Rifle was an exact copy of the type of rifle that is referred to so fondly as the Kentucky rifle. The gun featured the rounded symetrical lines of the original Kentucky types and the quality of the Belgium-made rifle soon won wide acclaim among the growing black powder crowd.

Dixie Gun Works continued to grow until it once again outgrew its existing facilities, doubling in size in five years.

In 1961, the firm moved into yet a larger building, where it was based until 1968, when it had again increased

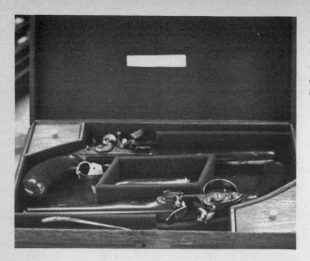

Among the many replicas for sale are actually quite a few antique arms, such as this cased pair of duelling type pistols.

It's always hard on muzzleloaders to dry snap them. Visitors that must snap a gun are given the chance, but with a flare pistol.

to the point of having to be moved into a still larger structure. Today, Dixie Gun Works occupies a spacious 31,000 square-foot building on the outskirts of Union City.

Turner Kirkland today is as fascinated with firearms as he was when he bought that first 1849 Colt. He now spends a good part of his time travelling throughout the country and Europe trying to locate forgotten stockpiles of antique gun parts, old leather goods and other relics, including medieval armament, antique reloading equipment — and even scalplocks.

Dixie Gun Works has done much to promote the sport of shooting black powder guns, as evidenced by their participation in the National Spring Shoot of the National Muzzle Loading Rifle Association at Friendship, Indiana, each year. The firm has been represented at every match since 1951, with Kirkland attending most of the matches himself.

The initial success of Dixie's Squirrel Rifle reproduction led to an ever-growing market of reproduction black powder guns. Today the firm imports close to forty different makes of replicas, as well as being a distributor for many of the other replicas being made or imported by

Prospective buyer gets the feel of a reproduction gun.

numerous other firms.

If you are the type of gun fancier who likes to thumb through gun magazines, you've probably come across a short seven-word ad that reads, "Visit Dixie Gun Works for Antique Arms." Turner Kirkland encourages anyone that might be travelling through that section of the South to stop in and visit.

A visit to Dixie Gun Works is like walking through an antique firearms museum and, better yet, many of the old guns are actually for sale. There are countless old military muskets and rifles filling the spacious gun racks, several showcases jammed full of hundreds of mint and near-mint condition Colt and Remington cap and ball revolvers. Adorning one complete wall of the building is Kirkland's personal collection of fine old original Kentucky rifles and rare and unique military arms. Some of these have been in his collection since before World War II and a few now have collector values of over $2,000.

The current Dixie Gun Works catalog is a far cry from the twelve-page 1954 catalog that sold for a quarter. To get all of their wares into a single publication, the present day catalog consists of some 362 pages, selling for two dollars.

Having become known as an authority on antique firearms, especially on Philadelphia derringers and Kentucky rifles, Kirkland receives as many as a hundred inquiries each day concerning old guns that someone is interested in buying, selling or repairing. Their questions range from "what is the gun's value?" and "can it be repaired?" to "would you like to buy it or know of anyone that might?"

Kirkland is always interested in buying old guns, but to answer questions such as the first two, he has included in his latest catalog more than fifty pages of helpful information on how to clean, care, repair, test and determine the date of manufacture for many of the more common black powder guns. Also listed are several pages on Civil War proofmarks that help give the reader some personal information on guns made during this era.

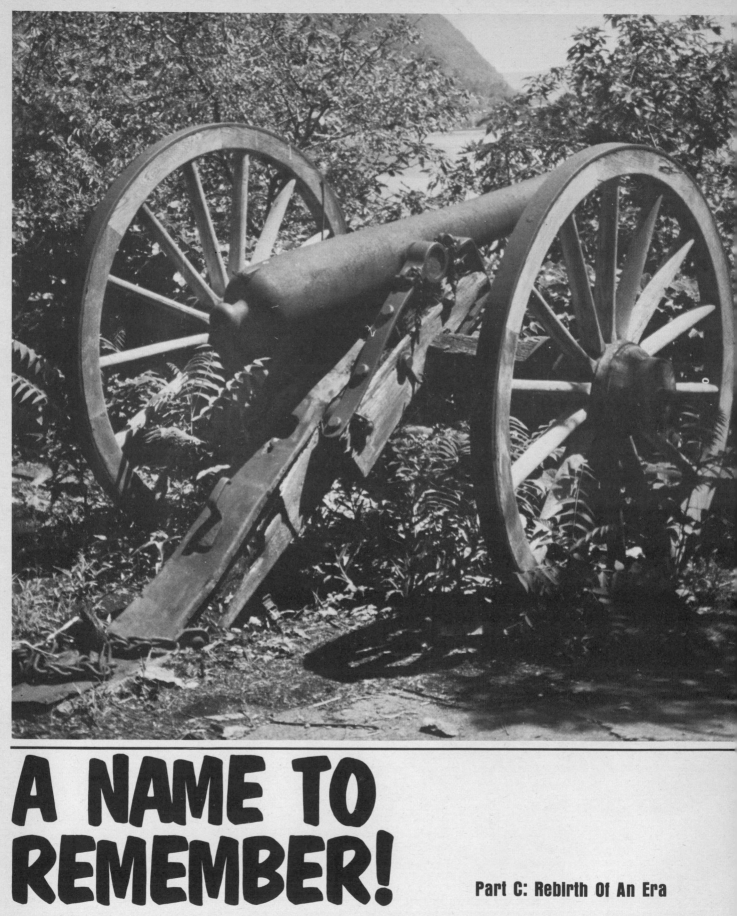

A NAME TO REMEMBER!

Part C: Rebirth Of An Era

Today's Burgeoning Business In Black Powder Replicas Is A Phenomenon Of Fairly Recent Growth And This Is The Saga Of A Man And His Company Who Helped Pioneer It!

Nearing nine inches in length, this fourteen pounder James projectile is just one of the many types Forgett encountered on Bannerman's.

"THE WHOLE ISLAND had been cleaned off in keeping with my contract and that was probably one of the oddest documents in history," Val Forgett, a quiet, soft-spoken gent, recalls. "It was necessary to take off everything of an explosive nature before the insurance company would even allow anyone else on Bannerman's Island."

The boat was about to pull away from the pier that jutted out from this castle on the Hudson River, but Forgett noted that, at the end of this dock, there stood like flanking sentinals two naval war shells from the Spanish-American war. They were some fourteen inches in diameter and at least nine feet in length.

"With a Stillson wrench in my hand, I shinnied up one of the shells like I would a palm tree. I unscrewed the plug and discovered that the shell was still loaded!

"It had been sitting out there in summer suns, hot and ready to go, since 1898 or thereabouts. And as I looked into that supply of powder, I suddenly had the feeling I might be the first man on the moon. And that was before anyone learned to spell astronaut."

Undaunted, the man from Teaneck — then his home — climbed the adjoining shell, removed the plug from it and, just before he and his boat sailed away into the sunset of the Hudson River, he tipped the two shells off the pier — and into fourteen feet or so of soft mud!

This experience has much to do with Forgett's initial success in the field of antique arms sales. As the story goes, the insurance agents covering what was known officially as the Bannerman Island Arsenal, a 5½-acre piece of land loaded with obsolete but nonetheless dangerous explosives, had sought to have the Army, the Air Force and even the Marines send demolitions experts to defuse what could have created the greatest stir in Greater New York since the last passing of Halley's Comet. By everyone's admission, the island — loaded with decomposed Civil War and Spanish-American War explosives — was a bomb that was simply waiting for the right opportunity to do its thing.

At the time Forgett was contacted and contracted to clean up the island arsenal, his own business, Service Armament, was in being and doing well, dealing largely in antique and war surplus armament, most of it out of the muzzleloading era.

Forgett long had been a student of the armament of the Civil War and the decades following and, in addition, had a thing about cannon. He had, at one point, as many as sixty Civil War artillery pieces on his farm. His idea of a quiet Sunday's entertainment was to load one up and hold target practice at several hundred yards. He since has cut the collection to some eight prime pieces.

While Service Armament already was a thriving business even Forgett admits that the old arms he purchased from the Bannerman arsenal did much to make the business even better known. After all, Bannerman's had been a leader in the surplus business after the Spanish-American War and, at one point, had advertised in several New York City newspapers that they had just received three whole trainloads of

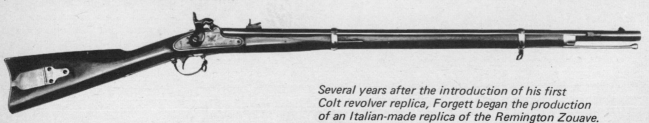

Authentically reproduced, the Navy Arms copy of Baby Dragoon has nicely engraved cylinder.

war surplus goods, much of it captured from Spain.

The near legends regarding the so-called Bannerman castle are countless, but most have a basis in truth. For example, the Bannerman firm admitted the manner in which the huge structure came into being in the first place. It seems that a soldier of fortune approached the firm with the idea of purchasing arms to begin a Latin-American revolution. The Bannerman's, of course, refused such an arrangement and the adventurer went elsewhere to find the needed goods.

He eventually was arrested, along with his supply of contraband armament. All of the smallarms had been dismantled and hidden in bags of cement.

When the Federal Government ordered the arms — and the cement — sold at auction, it was the Bannerman's who purchased them. The armament was put up for sale and the cement was hauled to the island to be used in building the vast structure that sprawls across the 5½ acres.

A front view of Bannerman's Island Arsenal. Despite everlasting appearance of the building, poor concrete caused the castle to crumble.

The erstwhile gunrunner may have had the final laugh, however. The cement was of low quality as might be expected. The structure was hardly finished before it began to show crumbling fissures and wide cracks in the concrete.

The breakwater flanking the castle had been created by driving the barrels from artillery pieces into the mud until they formed a continuous series of pilings. The cannon from the flagship of Admiral Farragut, the naval hero, was emplaced on the top level of the castle to guard the entrance.

In these surroundings, one would expect to find a hoard of collector trophies that should be worth thousands upon thousands of dollars — and a few of these were found, Forgett admits. But for the most part, the valuable collector items long since had been sold through the Bannerman operation. What remained was largely rubble. In one courtyard, there were thousands of pith helmets strewn about, literally all that remained of the once proud British regiments that had fought in North Africa and India in the last century.

Countless Gatling guns had been smashed by vandals, the brass fixtures hauled to the mainland and sold as scrap. A number of the watchmen hired over a period of years also seem to have made up for the low pay by going into the scrap iron business on their own. And almost everywhere were unexploded shells, some of them nearly a century old, when Forgett and his own small crew of explosive experts landed on the island to make it safe.

According to Forgett, the State of New York wanted, at that time, to purchase the island for recreational purposes, but the sale was being held up by the fact that those insurance companies would have nothing to do with it until the island was literally defused.

With only forty days in which to accomplish this monumental chore, Forgett had to draw upon his own experience, designing special tools for dismantling some of the shells.

As they were disarmed, some shells were turned into scrap and hauled away to a smelting plant in Pennsylvania, while some of those in better shape were made into safe

Several years after the introduction of his first Colt revolver replica, Forgett began the production of an Italian-made replica of the Remington Zouave.

collector items. In fact, Forgett put together a collection of every shell known to have been used by either side during the Civil War, disarmed the lot, then donated them to the Smithsonian Institute.

This explosive adventure took place early in 1958 and more than a decade later, when the Bannerman Arsenal finally did catch fire — again the victim of vandals, it is reported — it was not the holocaust that it once could have been.

But that experience convinced Val Forgett more than ever before that he was on the right track. Here again he had noted that the supply of collector type black powder armament was becoming scarce. The prime pieces all were in collections and the price was beginning to rise.

For the man who — like Forgett — reveled in the idea of loosing a cloud of smoke from the muzzle of a cap and ball handgun, it had the makings of a mighty expensive hobby. In fact, at the prices that original black powder guns were bringing, it was not wise to shoot them. It just wasn't the economic thing to do.

In 1956, several businessmen met in Alexandria, Virginia, to discuss the feasibility of having replica revolvers made abroad. After some debate and considerable study of the venture, it was determined there might possibly be a market for this type of gun. No one was certain, it was a hit or miss proposition, but the deal was on. A replica Colt

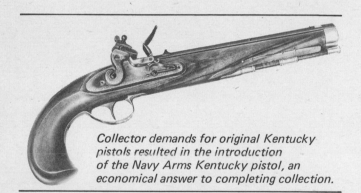

Collector demands for original Kentucky pistols resulted in the introduction of the Navy Arms Kentucky pistol, an economical answer to completing collection.

Navy would be made in Italy for importation into the United States.

Actually this informal business meeting was the beginning of the Navy Arms Company. One of those men bold enough to take the gamble of producing a replica cap and ball revolver was Forgett, now president of the aforementioned firm as well as Service Armament.

There was more to getting an authentic looking replica built in Italy than just a handshake with a couple of business associates, as Forgett soon found out.

The first and immediate problem was to get an original Colt Navy to the Brescia gunmaker, Vittorio Gregorelli. Italian customs officials refused to let the gun be shipped to the subcontractor for the Beretta factory. It seems that Gregorelli did not make complete guns; only parts for the M-1 Garand for Beretta; not making complete guns, he didn't have a firearms manufacturing license. The Colt Navy was returned.

The problem was remedied by delivering the Colt in person to Gregorelli and the latter soon had the prototype run of sixteen guns under way; ten were copies of the 1851 Colt Navy and six had brass frames and round barrels, like that found on the Confederate .36 caliber Griswold & Gunnison Army revolver.

When these guns finally reached Forgett's office, it didn't take him long to notice nearly a dozen design changes. The majority of these changes were of minor significance and were easily cured.

Most detectable was the change of the original front sight bead to the more conventional dovetailed blade. Another change was the size of the guard screw heads. These were much larger than should be. Also, the guard plate had been widened to surround the larger screw heads.

These changes were transformed back to the original pattern and the first production run got underway. The inner curve of the replica was purposely changed slightly as the Italian craftsmen had done so on the prototypes. This was to ensure an accurate means of determining an original from the replica.

The black powder revolver, marked NAVY ARMS CO. along the barrel top, began to hit the U.S. market in 1958. Built from quality materials and assembled by hand, the replica was accepted immediately by modern black powder shooters and collectors needing such a copy to fill a gap in their collection.

With the success of the Colt Navy replica, Forgett considered producing a replica black powder rifle. His choice was the Remington Zouave — often referred to as the most colorful of all Civil War guns. The rifle was also a success and the Navy Arms Company was now a well established business.

Since the introduction of the Colt replica in 1958, Forgett has built Navy Arms into what is possibly the largest black powder gun supplier in the country. Since then he has introduced a number of near exact replicas of many famous guns, the originals of many which are all but impossible to find for sale or otherwise.

A favorite of North/South Skirmish shooters, the Navy Arms' reproduction of the 1863 Zouave is so exacting that the firm claims that parts from it will interchange with those on the original. The big .58 caliber rifled musket is fitted with a thirty-three-inch rifled barrel and is fitted with a folding rear sight that adjusts in elevation for ranges from one to three hundred yards.

Another authentically reproduced gun is the firm's Harpers Ferry musket. In .58 caliber, this rifled musket sports a thirty-five-inch rifled barrel, but instead of being blued, it features a browned finish, as did the originals. This gun is of the half-stock design and has a flintlock; the walnut stock on the Navy Arms' gun is fitted with a large hinged patchbox as were original Harpers Ferry muskets.

For percussion revolver fans — especially Colts — Val Forgett is importing numerous different revolver replicas. A copy of the Colt 2nd Model Dragoon in .44 caliber is about as exact a copy of that revolver as can be found. The frame and loading lever of this revolver are beautifully color case-hardened and are set off by the deep bluing of the barrel and cylinder and the polished brass frame and back strap. The cylinder of this gun is engraved with the same Indian fight scene found on the original.

Competitive cap and ball marksmen usually favor the solid frame Remington design over that of the Colt. Reasoning is simple; the Colt's open frame doesn't allow the installation of adjustable sights, whereas the Remington's solid top strap is ideal for such sights.

Navy Arms has redesigned the Remington Army Model revolver by fitting these replicas with a set of micro adjustable target rear sights. Often considered the magnum of Civil War revolvers due to its ability to withstand greater pressures, the Navy Arms' target version of this gun is no exception. The quality of the material used in the construction of the solid frame allows the use of heavy maximum charges. Late outdoor writer and pioneer of handgun hunting Al Georg killed a near record black bear with a prototype of this particular gun.

OUT OF A CONNECTICUT VALLEY

CVA's mountain rifle is available as either a finished gun or in kit form as an easy challenge to the buff.

THROUGHOUT THE HISTORY of the American arms-making industry, New England always has been the heart of this very important part of our economy. Such revered names as Eli Whitney, Simeon & North, N. Starr, Sharps, Colt, Winchester, as well as such important factories as the Springfield Armory and many others have been situated in Gun Valley. In fact, from the years 1850 to 1940 an average of better than sixty percent of all firearms products, capital and firearms workers were situated in the small area of New England.

If New England was the heart of arms-making in the United States following our Revolution, the Connecticut River Valley was the heart of New England gunmaking. It would seem only right that one of the major companies in the business of reproducing our early flintlock and percussion firearms would be located in this historically important region. Even more fitting, this company sits virtually on the banks of the river from which it has taken its name. That company, of course, is Connecticut Valley Arms, Incorporated, located in Haddam, one of the most picturesque points along the entire Connecticut River Valley.

The name, Connecticut Valley Arms, was arrived at after a great deal of thought. The president, David L. Silk, who originated the company, elaborates: "In starting up a muzzleloading company, I felt the history involved in the sport of muzzleloading was equally important to the shooter as the gun itself. I wanted a name that not only sounded historic, but was tied to the history of the firearms and kits we sell. Connecticut Valley Arms seemed to sound right, and unquestionably belonged in the history of arms development."

Connecticut Valley Arms — or CVA, as it is referred to by most muzzleloaders — has grown to a position of prominence in the muzzleloading field in just five years.

In 1971, when Silk founded the company after twenty years in the export gun business, he really didn't know what he was getting into. He describes it this way: "I could see a real nice business in supplying the avid history buff or amateur gunsmith with reproductions and our now well-

CVA Is A Relative Newcomer, But Its Black Powder Arms Are Finding Favor

known do-it-yourself muzzleloading kits. But at that time, we were just starting and had a number of growing pains to survive.

"I remember our first shipment coming in and being quite a bit different from what we expected. The one bright spot was that the do-it-yourself kits all managed to go together quite easily and soon became one of our most popular items."

Silk related also that he feels the kit idea has become popular, because it involves three important aspects: shooting enjoyment, do-it-yourself craft appeal and historical

Part D: Rebirth Of An Era

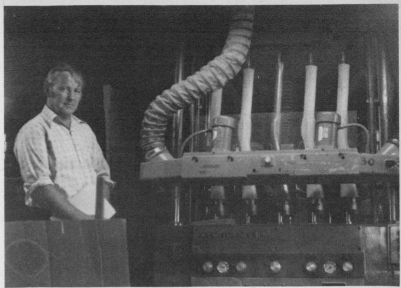

Dave Silk, CVA president, pauses beside a piece of sophisticated machinery on which stocks for black powder arms are turned. (Below) Stacked stocks comprise only a small part of wood factory's production in an effort to supply nation's muzzleloaders.

Craftsman fits the tang to one of the Connecticut firm's Kentucky rifles. As is evident, a great deal of hand work goes into turning out each of the muzzleloaders.

interest. There is something about taking a bunch of parts and putting together your own antique-style weapon, then displaying and firing it.

As time went on, CVA learned some lessons to achieve success. It wasn't all a bed of roses, however, as Silk describes: "As we began our development of the line, we worked to increase the quality of the parts and fit in our guns and kits. This proved extremely valuable and showed measurable results. After a while, however, it became evident that, no matter how well we made the product, we were not helping our customers unless we provided them with complete instructional material. Since this revelation, we have made a consistent effort to provide the most complete and easily understood instructions available. Most people who want to build one of our kits are not professional gunmakers but are knowledgeable and interested hobbyists, who may even look at a kit as a way to learn gunmaking. We try to help them with our instructions, as well as with a well-made kit."

CVA's product line, by and large, is manufactured overseas and is imported in a similar fashion to that used by most other muzzleloading companies. There are some exceptions that Silk feels sets CVA apart: "Until recently, virtually all of our products were manufactured in Spain and brought in exclusively by us. We enjoy a unique relationship with our manufacturer in Spain. He produces exclusively for us and gives us complete freedom in product design. As the years have gone by, we have developed a strong friendship with the company and a great deal of interplay back and forth between here and Spain. Our people have been there and their people have been here numerous times. A real benefit to us and our customers is that they know the CVA product is exclusively ours and that we and our manufacturer will stand behind it."

CVA kits and guns are being used in almost every part of the country by amateur gun builders and competitors. This involvement goes back to the company's beginnings, as Silk describes: "The muzzleloading sport has been good to us and we go out of our way to support the sport. We have actively supported the National Muzzle Loading Rifle Association and feel that any muzzleloader should do likewise by joining, but I remember when we first got involved and went out to one of the NMLRA's national competitions to display our product.

"We were overwhelmed by the quality and authenticity of the muzzleloaders competitors were using. Here we could see, in one place, all of the custom-made, high-priced, authentic firearms, as well as talk with people who made and used them, provided they would talk to us. On our first few visits, that wasn't easy.

"We felt like outsiders with these experts; but after a brief period of time, they were more than happy to provide us with valuable constructive criticism and suggestions."

The current CVA line includes nearly seventy kits, guns and accessories at this time, and that number may increase in the future. Twelve kits, available in either flintlock or percussion, allow the budding apprentice gunmaker and hobbyist to choose from a variety of styles and degrees of difficulty. He can build anything from a small pocket Philadelphia Derringer up to a big .50 caliber mountain rifle, which is just the ticket for most American big game.

In addition there is a three-fourths-inch bore cannon kit that is a current favorite. For the less daring, CVA offers the same models in ready-built form. While sacrificing a certain amount of personal, do-it-yourself satisfaction, the individual may get out and enjoy the sport of muzzleloading a great deal quicker by picking up one of these ready-made front-stuffers.

Most muzzleloaders seem prone to carry around what appears to be a truckload of accessories. CVA can provide the shooter with all the accessories commonly used, from powder horns and flasks to measures and cappers plus the necessary shooting expendables like lubricant, patches, balls and caps. For the fellow in a rush — the guy who may have bought the ready-made gun — CVA has a special Shooter's Kit that puts all the necessary supplies in one package. This saves a lot of time and energy in sorting out what one really needs.

The length and breadth of CVA's line is impressive and should be of interest to most any muzzleloader or do-it-yourself fan. The line is broken down between kits, finished guns and accessories. Any finished gun offered is available in kit form.

The kits provide the do-it-yourselfer with all the parts needed to make a fully shootable muzzleloader. All the parts in every CVA kit are in a finished or near-finished state, allowing the kit builder to do only final fitting and finishing of wood and metal. He can, of course, embellish the kits with his own niceties by carving, recontouring or even engraving.

The biggest difference between a do-it-yourself kit and a box of parts is the instructional material provided. As Silk indicated earlier, this is an area upon which CVA has concentrated. The instructions provide a thorough step-by-step explanation of the construction process as well as providing hints on finishing. Most CVA kits can be built easily and successfully by the first-timer using CVA's instructions, although CVA does recommend starting with one of the smaller, more manageable pistol kits before commencing construction on a rifle.

The hottest item in CVA's line at the moment is their new mountain rifle kit. This new rifle is an excellent copy of the Hawken Brothers now-famous mountain rifle. This new front-stuffer has a large number of features that make it an authentic reproduction. The most striking of which are all-steel furniture; no brass, two barrel wedges rather than one and a pewter-type nose cap.

On the finished gun all metal parts, with the exception of the German silver wedge plates, nose cap, and German

At right is the Napoleon III cannon, when it has been completed by a home craftsman. It is authentic in every detail. (Below) The cannon started as a kit, with the individual parts carefully packaged against any damage.

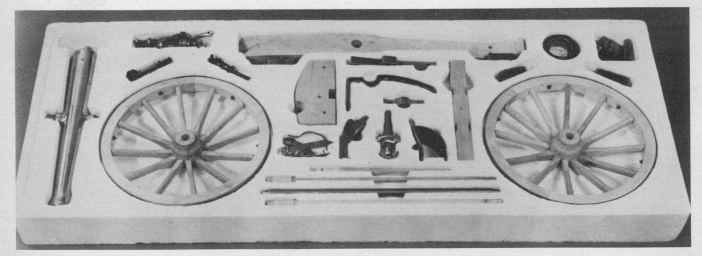

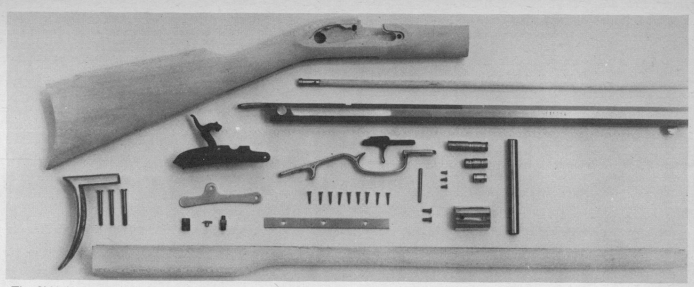

The CVA Kentucky rifle, fresh out of the box in its percussion configuration, looks complicated, but isn't. (Below) Flintlock version is available also in either kit form or as finished firearm, but the difference in price is quite substantial.

CVA's Philadelphia Derringer has found great favor among muzzleloading buffs. Short barrel, small grip and lack of a rear sight make it poor for accuracy, maker admits.

silver patchbox, are browned to provide an additional degree of authenticity.

This half-stock gun is choice for most people considering muzzleloading hunting as it is available in both .45 and .50 caliber. Incidentally, this will be the first gun CVA has ever produced in the United States and features an American maple stock. This should delight most muzzleloaders, as that particular wood seems to be the most popular among the front-stuffing clan.

The other rifle in the CVA line is their popular Kentucky. This long rifle is designed to get people started in the muzzleloading sport with minimal expense. To that end, it is designed with a two-piece rather than a one-piece stock, which reduces the cost of the stock by two-thirds. Available in .45 caliber, it carries a lot of brass and one of CVA's locks with a rifled barrel.

CVA has a number of pistols and pistol kits available; one of the most popular is their Tower pistol. This isn't a reproduction of a real honest-to-gosh Tower. It's more of a shooter's version with the lines and looks of the Tower pistol in a little bit more manageable size. A .45 caliber bore lets one fire the gun more economically with some of the more readily available components. The finished gun is available only in percussion, but the kit is available in both flintlock and percussion.

The CVA Kentucky pistol, a companion piece for their Kentucky rifle, is .45 caliber and uses the same lock as the rifle, with a full stock running out to a brass nose cap. It is available also in percussion version only for the finished gun. The kit builder can make either flintlock or percussion.

Also available are small belt-style pistols which are called the CVA Colonial pistol and a Derringer. The latter is popular even though it is not much of a hunting or target arm. Something about it just intrigues people.

CVA's scale model of the Napoleon III cannon is one of the most complex reproductions ever manufactured. This little dreadnought has a three-fourths-inch bore and fires a .690-inch round ball. Over two hundred individual pieces go into each finished gun and kit; however, the kit builder has a lot of these pieces assembled for him prior to his commencing construction.

A few features of this cannon never fail to draw comment. The most immediately obvious is the beautifully flared, steel-rimmed wheels on each side of the carriage. These wheels are made up and fitted with individual spokes just like the originals to add to the authentic look of the piece, with steel ammunition boxes on each side of the axle. They are hinged and latched and function fully. To complete the authentic look, a variety of bucket hooks, ramrod holders and other small appointments make a showpiece that can be dragged out to the back lot for the Fourth of July, New Years, births, deaths and other momentous occasions that require the pomp and dignity that only a cannon salute can punctuate.

EMF: BLACK POWDER'S SUPERMARKET

Twenty-Seven Years And A Massive Inventory Have Made This Firm Just That!

BEING SATISFIED with what you get has become, sadly, the normal mode in the last few years. The haughty stares and icy "If you don't take it, someone else will" attitude has replaced the genuine desire of suppliers to meet consumer desires in a wide range of products.

The same applies, in some cases, to gunmakers or distributors. Sure, some of the larger makers have reintroduced specific models. But it took a goodly number of years before those firms recognized that buyers weren't content to settle for other offerings. The gun-buying public knew exactly what it wanted and was vocal enough to finally get it, according to Mark Thiffault, who made a thorough study of the firm for this volume.

Black powder gunners long have been victims of this syndrome. Because their numbers are relatively small in comparison to the size of the gun-owning populace, importers or makers could pretty much dictate what was

Boyd Davis, EMF president, holds the replica of Walker Colt in his left hand, modern Super Dakota .44 magnum in his left, affording an idea of comparative sizes.

guns and consequently tooled-up and began producing them. Their judgment was correct and the guns sold extremely well.

"We purchased Great Western lock, stock and the proverbial barrel in 1958, then relocated the entire operation to North Hollywood," continues Davis, seated behind his desk in EMF's Burbank, California, headquarters building, across from the NBC studios. "We continued manufacturing and selling retail and supplying the trade with the single-actions.

"We recognized that the American public was interested in this historical weapon — in our two retail stores we had some original single-action revolvers as well as original black powder revolvers and muzzleloaders, and it was around this showcase the browsing public always seemed to gather. They were intrigued with these guns because they formed a part of our history. We knew that they would purchase a piece of America's past if it was well-made and affordable."

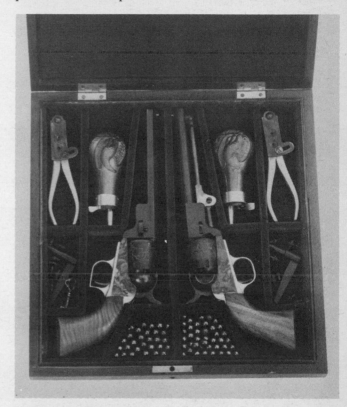

Double cased set of .31 baby dragoons comes complete with two pistols, two flasks, two moulds, deluxe case.

going to be available to whom and when, like it or not.

This hasn't been the case with Early and Modern Firearms Company, Incorporated. They've gone overboard in the other direction, much to the delight of the discriminating black powder gunner who knows exactly what he wants and won't settle for less.

EMF, as it's better-known in the shooting field, can supply a reproduction of just about any black powder gun in any configuration that's been manufactured. Take the 1851 Navy percussion revolver as one example. EMF can supply it in .36 caliber, brass frame, engraved cylinder, round barrel; .36, caliber casehardened frame, engraved cylinder, octagonal barrel; .36 caliber, casehardened frame, octagonal barrel with silver trim; .36 caliber, brass frame, fully engraved, octagonal barrel; .36 caliber, Mason-Dixon Commemorative with nickel frame, octagonal barrel; .44 caliber, brass frame, round barrel with plain cylinder; .44 caliber, brass frame, fully engraved, octagonal barrel; ad infinitum.

And this doesn't even consider the various barrel lengths available, or the cased sets with accessories, or the consecutive serial numbers for cased sets with two revolvers! In short, if it's ever been produced, EMF can supply you with an authentic reproduction of that black powder gun.

EMF began in 1950 as a retail gun store operating across from the world-famed Farmer's Market in Los Angeles. Business was sufficient that, a couple of years later, another branch of Early and Modern Firearms began trading in North Hollywood. The two stores were conventional in their offerings for the most part, but imported war surplus hardware was added and EMF began supplying dealers throughout the country.

The firm was incorporated as EMF in 1956 and the group of far-sighted partners providing financial and physical support to the growing firm closely watched the manufacturing operation of the Great Western Arms Company in south-central Los Angeles.

"Prior to World War II, Colt had discontinued the manufacture of their single-action revolvers," relates EMF president, Boyd A. Davis. "The Great Western Arms Company thought there still was a market for these two

Joe Karas of EMF's shipping crew checks available stock in preparation for making shipment of black powder guns.

Enfield cavalry carbine has 22-inch smoothbore barrel, swivel ramrod, teak stock, brass butt plate, trigger guard.

Ironically, it was the latter factor which led to the shutdown of Great Western in the mid-1960s. "The other gunmakers in the United States realized they'd misjudged the buying taste of the American populace and began importing from Germany and other European countries similar models to those we were selling," Boyd Davis notes. "We couldn't compete with their foreign imports on a cost basis and finally shut down the plant. The single-actions and derringers made by Great Western are becoming something of a collector's item now, since less than 100,000 units were produced and sold."

But all was not lost in the closure of Great Western: EMF had realized there indeed was a steadily growing market for black powder guns and that Europe was the most economical place to produce them.

Davis and his four-man board of directors began studying what course their corporation should take as the Sixties were crashing to a close. They ceased the sale of war surplus items back in 1968 and decided to test the black powder gun importation business on a firsthand basis. The signing into law of the Gun Control Act of 1968 spurred their decision, since mail-ordering cartridge guns was outlawed, while black powder remained legal. Then, too, original guns that once were plentiful and cheap had begun disappearing into private collections. The sources for originals were drying up as demand for them was mushrooming.

"I had spent a goodly amount of time in Europe, specifically Italy, checking production techniques and laying the groundwork for our eventual participation in the importation of black powder gun reproductions," Boyd Davis states. "By this time, the foreign gunmakers already had been conned a few times by Americans who promised huge orders and failed to place them. They naturally were cautious.

"But when we decided to push ahead, I went over with lots of money and ordered conservatively," continues the salt-and-pepper-haired Davis. "I promised only those things I knew I could deliver. In this manner, EMF has built up, in the last eight years, an excellent working relationship with the Italian companies currently making reproductions for us. They know we're as good as our word."

And that's a facet of the EMF operation that applies to prospective customers, as well: If they say they've got it, you'll get it. None of this foisting off an alternative gun that's not exactly what you wanted or saw advertised.

The first order for reproduction guns wasn't necessarily large by EMF's standards today and was for a half-dozen of the most popular models of black powder guns around.

"You know, the 1851 Navy revolver that everyone seems to buy, the 1860 Army revolver, the Zouave rifle and other steady sellers," comments Davis. "We gradually began to expand our product lines to other styles of the guns, started bringing in black powder accessories and even

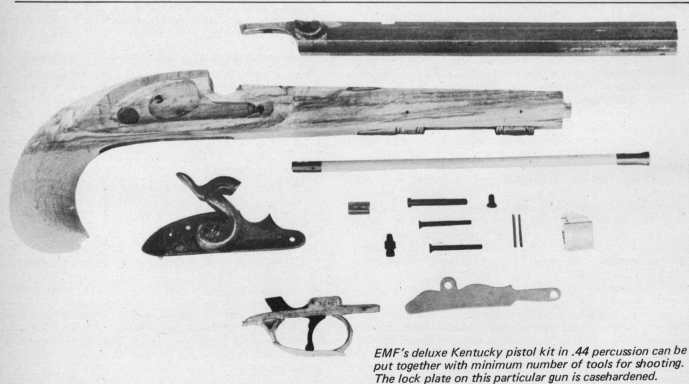

EMF's deluxe Kentucky pistol kit in .44 percussion can be put together with minimum number of tools for shooting. The lock plate on this particular gun is casehardened.

Above: Double-barrel muzzleloading shotgun is 12 gauge, with 32-inch barrels, cylinder bored for shot or solid balls. (Left) Replica 2nd Model Dragoon is .44 caliber; frame, hammer, lever are casehardened. The cylinder is engraved; 7½-inch barrel.

imported rifle kits for the do-it-yourselfer."

Authenticity is what EMF promises and partly is the reason for their wide product line. "There are, as our catalog shows, many variations available on each and every black powder gun," Davis adds. "Each reproduction we offer has been made at some point in America's frontier history, though some of the differences between models of the same gun may be cosmetic only. But they were made with those modifications, which is why we're forced to stock such a wide variety of the same gun. And I can truthfully say that if we don't have it, it's simply not available."

EMF's reproductions, Davis hastens to add, actually are better than the originals. "The steels used in these guns today are much superior to those available to early American gunmakers," he explains. "Production techniques have advanced, also, so the finished product is much better cosmetically and structurally."

Some American gun buyers still seem bothered by the bugaboo regarding foreign-made products and their alleged inferiority, especially regarding metals. There may have been justification for this harangue in the early days, but Davis feels it's not so today — a statement justified by the weighty fact that most American gun manufacturers are importing either components or some of their finished products from foreign makers who build them to rigid American specifications.

"In the early days, there was only one Italian gun manufacturer of any consequence," adds EMF's president sincerely. "He has since acquired three or four major competitors who are vying for a slice of the lucrative American market. As a consequence, production has improved, as has the finished product. There is no longer reason to criticize Italian-made guns."

EMF has ridden the crest of the wave of interest in black powder guns. It has expanded into five busy sections under its corporate roof: inventory, retail and dealer sales, telephone sales, advertising and a direct-mail department that contributes so much in mail charges each month that it's a wonder the U.S. Postal Service stays in the red!

The key to the operation, along with management, is EMF's inventory department. This group scrupulously records each item, from front-loader to nipple wrench, received and distributed so Boyd Davis knows the exact time to reorder. But even with such tight controls, EMF

sometimes is hit with bemoaned shortages.

"The Italian political situation, striking dockworkers, fluctuation in the respective values of the lira and dollar all can have influences over our supply," says Boyd Davis. "We try as far as is humanly possible to stay on top of the situation and only rarely, through no fault of our own, are caught short. But we don't like it, nonetheless, for it means an unhappy dealer or customer who may not patronize us again. Thankfully, it doesn't happen often."

Throughout the EMF enterprise runs the continual demand for personal contact with wholesale or retail buyers. Each letter received is answered by a staff member, though more often than not by Boyd Davis, himself. This personal approach has been instrumental in EMF's twenty-seven years of continued business where others have failed, he feels. And Davis looks forward to the continued growth of EMF and black powder-related activities.

"This isn't just a gut feeling. I can see it," Davis says.

"Just a couple of weeks back I drove off into the San Bernardino Mountains where a reenactment of the Civil War was to be staged," he continues. "There weren't many spectators, but there were perhaps one hundred participants in both the Union and Confederate armies.

"Cannon were blasting, men charging and falling, and women attired in Civil War-era garb attending to the wounded — it was incredible!" he exclaims. "After the battle was over, young children just old enough to understand what the scene represented were gathered around, listening and watching wide-eyed with wonderment and fascination. These are the kids who will one day be buying black powder guns, and their generation after them, ad infinitum.

"The reason for this is because of the continuing interest in America's heritage," Davis says softly. "These black powder guns are part of our past and people today want to hold a bit of it, want to own a piece of our past. It's not a fad — we sold no more black powder guns in the Bicentennial year than in any other — but a deep feeling for those things that shaped our future. Nothing has been more instrumental in this regard than the black powder gun."

So, while Boyd Davis might not be sitting in his chair to see it, or this writer to record it, EMF will continue to quench this historical thirst of the American people. There's just no question about it.

PRACTICAL BLACK POWDER GUNS

Here's An Approach To Muzzleloading Fun Minus Fuss

From left: First two bullets are 600-grain .58 caliber Minies, made in a Lyman 570 mould. Text explains reason for difference in weight designations. Bullet on right is prelubed with Hodgdon's Mini-Lube; other isn't lubed.

CHAPTER 8

FSSST! POOF! CLICK. All part of the fun in black powder shooting? At first, maybe, but when the aura wears off, the modern shooter — product of the Space Age that he is — often becomes totally dismayed with hangfires, misfires and no fires. He gets bored. He may decide that all that pampering, wading in black soot up to the elbows, plus clicking instead of shooting at that big deer, are not worth the aesthetic pleasure of watching that burst of blue smoke accompanied by the shower of colorful sparks. The black powder guns are quietly laid to rest in a dusty corner of the closet seldom to be used again.

In spite of an atavistic urge to regain some of the charm of yesteryear, the modern shooter is a person of his time, a man on a schedule. He enjoys the soothing effect of shooting the old-style guns, the handloading, the slow shooting, the historic satisfaction. But a lot of initially enthusiastic shooters do lay the replicas away all too soon. And that is too bad, especially when something can be done to cure a lot of the black powder blues. The purists won't agree. The more casual black powder shooters, however, would do well to turn to more practical measures that will bring those guns back out of the closet, or send these fellows to the gun store for other models that can be lived with.

The idea is to have a lot of fun, and success, with the guns without having to lose chances at game, without all those annoying misfires and without having to scrub quite so long and hard after a day's shooting. Through smart initial buying, and/or modification of existing arms, plus some loading techniques and ignition cures, black powder can be a practical marriage of shooter and gun with a long association.

Which guns to buy? Since the objective is practicality, by all means the pirate pistols and tiny six shooter, plus the ornate flintlocks should be sought after, and used, but with the clear understanding that they are not the everyday — not even the every week — black powder gun. The oddball shotgun gauge is fine, too, for the occasional firing and a lot of wall decoration. And the funny calibers — the .42s and .37s — make excellent conversation pieces.

The idea is to purchase calibers and arms that can be fitted out neatly and speedily with accouterments and ammunition. In a handgun, for example, caliber .44 is a wise choice. The ball often is available precast and ready for use. Or there are many styles of moulds for do-it-yourself ammo. And there are at least two good bullets available in moulds; one a 200-grain that Lee offers. Real power, easy loading, modern enough to be useful in our day, historic enough to be pleasing to the sense for yesterday, a handgun of this caliber is a large enough bore not to require frequent between-shot scrubbings, too.

We found that Sam Fadala, who holds forth up in the hills around Sugar City, Idaho, pretty well goes along with these thoughts, so we asked him to offer some ideas on how to keep the fun in black powder shooting without all of the tribulations that seem to go with it.

"My first black powder shotgun was a 24-gauge fun gun, but soon the honeymoon was over and I found this partner had faults. She required hand-cutting of wads and special diets of powder and shot, and I soon tired of cutting everything from cardboard to toilet paper to stuff down her throat and relegated the piece to a corner of the basement," Fadala admits.

"A rifle has to be percussion for me. The flintlocks are beautiful and fascinating; especially the time lag between the pan smoke and actual detonation. The purist may have the patience to take down the flint often and prime it up, but most shooters do not. The percussion, still a primitive form indeed, offers a more practical way to go for most of us."

In the handgun, Fadala's personal choice is the Army .44 in the Remington model replica, which is distributed by many companies today. To his eye, this is the most appealing of the sixguns; the long and graceful lines are practical, too. The top strap frame is tough and stout loads hold well in her. She points well.

"I like the ingenious safety factor of the built-in notches between the cocking notches. By rotating the cylinder to these spots and lowering the hammer into them, the gun is locked up in a safe position. Ignition is good and that is a big plus.

"There are many good percussion rifles and the choice is up to the buyer. My personal choices were the Hopkins & Allen Underhammer for my use, and the Harrington & Richardson Huntsman for my beginning son's use. In big .58 my H&A is a practical hunting rifle. I don't care to wear shooting glasses in the field and the underhammer design, an American innovation, means that any sparks and soot will blow downward. Also, rain and snow is kept out of the works. The arm is sound and strongly made. I have shot big loads of black in her for several years without trouble.

"My son's H&R is a practical arm for the beginner. In caliber .58 it is powerful, and boasts the closed action (not legal in some states for hunting, however). This closed action means the sparks stay out of the eye and the elements stay out of the powder. Cleaning is a cinch. The entire breech plug is knocked out easily with the cleaning rod and the bore is open for end-to-end scrubbing. Neat. The design, too, is familiar to all of us and takes no getting used to."

Modification of existing guns is a good way to gain even more practicality. If the .44 Army is selected, the sights probably will be less than desired and may have to be modified, even changed, in order to shoot right on the money. Target sights are available, though they give the gun a look of a mixture between the old and the new that may not be pleasing to everyone. Misfire being no big problem,

Removable breech plug from Harrington & Richardson's Huntsman has been fitted with Fusil V ignition system. Note recess for large pistol primer with the flash hole showing. Cap to go over primer is at right of the plug.

The Navy Arms Magnum black powder shotgun in model 12-gauge size takes one piece wads, handles heavy charges.

this piece comes from its maker just about ready to please the shooter.

Black powder shotgunning never really has caught on in the United States to any appreciable extent, as evidenced by a glance through the latest listings of black powder guns; one will find dozens of pistols and rifles, only a tiny handful of shotguns. The early black powder shotguns were often off-gauge pains in the posterior, such as the 24 gauge already mentioned.

"My own black powder shotgun is a 12 gauge, right on the money. No modification was necessary on this baby. Navy Arms sells her under the name Magnum and she is able to handle old 10-gauge loads of about 1½ ounces of shot and a dram equivalent sufficient to match modern loads of the baby 12 magnum. Ignition was no problem. If it were, the gun would soon wear a couple of Fusil V igniters under those big rabbit ear hammers," Fadala reports.

"The two .58s did take a good bit of important modification. The underhammer took on a reducing program in the form of six inches of barrel lopped off. I wish Numrich would offer the rifle with that barrel length for hunters. The long unwieldy thirty-two-inch original needs that extra six inches like Durante could have used a six-inch extension on his nose. The front sight was changed from a rather thick outfit to a standard bead, but the back sight was left alone."

After removing the six inches of barrel, two little wings of metal were soldered to the tang because, with heavy loads, the buttstock had a tendency to loosen up. The metal wings fit into slots cut into the wooden buttstock and will not allow the tang to turn at all. The old percussion nipple was exchanged for a Fusil V unit. This is a small screw-in item that accepts regular primers, large pistol in this case. Foul play? Fadala doesn't think so: "I never found much sportsmanship in having a rifle go off as it pleased. Positive ignition is safer and much more practical. The underhammer has never had a misfire since the Fusil was screwed into place."

His son's .58 misfired often at first. That was cured with the Fusil, too, but not quite as simply as merely screwing one in. The unit would not fit, because it rested too high, and the action couldn't close. A gunsmith recessed it for a few bucks and now ignition is one hundred percent sure.

Loading for the black powder guns is a trade all its own, truly the first form of handloading. And the best thing a shooter can do is feed his arms what they require, which means carefully working up with easy loads; no different, really, from modern loading of smokeless arms. But there is more argument concerning black powder loads than we care to recount. Fadala once did a short piece for a small Arizona magazine on black powder loads and one reader wrote in saying he surely was going to kill himself. An American group hunting in Africa had up to 600-grain bullets backed up by 175 grains of powder, making Fadala's loads seem undernourished.

"The range of loads is great, but one thing is for sure — no one should try to make a high-velocity rifle out of a black powder arm. They were not intended to be such. Power in these arms means driving projectiles of great mass at modest speeds and I have no qualms about a man shooting the biggest elk in the woods with a 600-grain Minie taking off at only 1200 foot-seconds. That bullet is liable to chop a tree down on the other side of the elk after going through his shoulder blades. At the same time, the extreme of loading way down is foolish and the practice castrates what otherwise would be macho loads."

Old-timers used to shoot over clean, fresh snow, starting easy and loading more and more powder until unburned flecks showed up black against the white. Fadala tried this

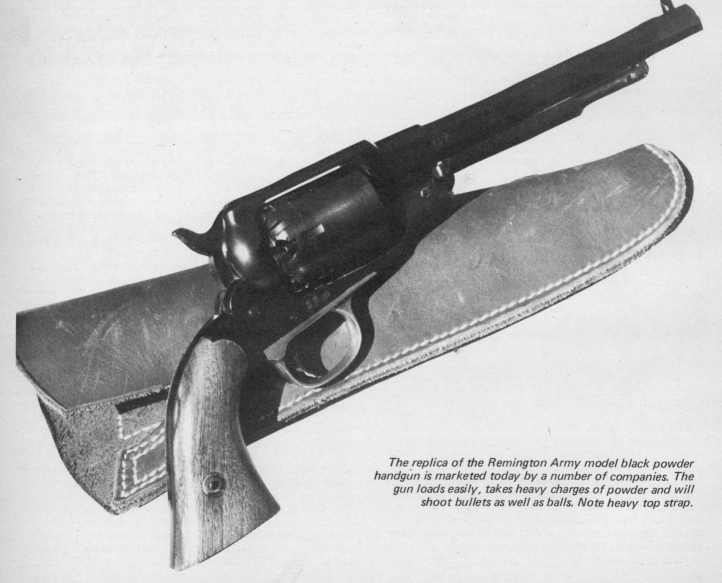

The replica of the Remington Army model black powder handgun is marketed today by a number of companies. The gun loads easily, takes heavy charges of powder and will shoot bullets as well as balls. Note heavy top strap.

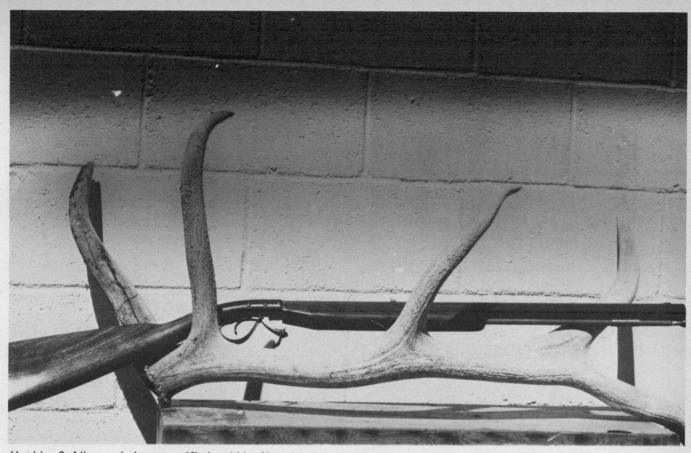

Hopkins & Allen underhammer rifle is sold by Numrich Arms. It is strong, reliable and fitted with the Fusil system. Six inches of the barrel have been cut off original 32-inch length. This specimen was manufactured in .58 caliber.

on butcher paper and it seemed to work well, because he had an Oehler Skyscreen chronograph right next to him, taking accurate readings. When a buildup of soot did begin, velocity seemed to peak off. Also, the ear does help here, because a crack will take the place of the throaty boom when the rifle reaches 1100 foot-seconds, which breaks the sound barrier. However, for hunting big stuff, he prefers to go above the 1100 mark and feels it is entirely possible, with safety.

Loading the big rifles is careful work. There is no case to show primer pocket expansion, no primers to crater, none of the indications we are used to. The powder-burning test in a good rifle, however, should be safe enough. Using someone else's top loads, even in similar rifles, is taboo, just as it is in modern loading practice. Load your own, carefully.

"I'm certainly not recommending loads to anyone, but my big .58 shoots a 460-grain bullet at a chronographed 1600+ with 150 grains of FFg and a 600-grain at 1300+ with 125 grains of the same powder. Minies are the thing for big power, though ball seems more accurate in my rifles. The Minie has the mass, and in black powder rifle shooting, mass counts for much."

Sometimes the moulds are misleading, however, and a 570 Lyman Minie, for example, actually weighs 600 grains. This is because Lyman apparently checks their moulds with an alloy that is lighter than pure lead. When pure lead is used, which it must be for the skirt of the Minie to flare out and fill the bore for the gas seal, the bullet weighs more than indicated on the mould.

One of the most important aspects of making black powder guns practical is prelubing and preloading. Prelube is simple and merely constitutes wrapping a Minie up in plastic food wrap with a coat of lube around it. The lube will fill the grooves of the Minie, as well as coat the bullet well. When ready to fire, the bullet is slipped out of its plastic dressing and popped down the bore, already lubed. We have had good luck with Hodgdon's Mini-Lube in this respect, as it seems to coat the projectile well.

Preloading is a good way to prevent spilled shot and powder, as well as a lot of cussing in the field when more than one shot is to be fired in haste.

"In only a handful of seconds, I once got off two hits on a javelina boar with a .58 rifle, using preloaded ammo. For a rifle, I glue two plastic medicine vials together; one for the prelubed bullet, the other for the powder charge. This unit is carried in an ammo pouch or possibles bag. The top is popped off the powder, then the granules are poured down the barrel followed by another top popping and the bullet follows. Cap and fire."

Preloads for the shotgun are even more important, and here is where that standard gauge really comes in handy. Fadala puts all preweighed powder charges in plastic tubes, then into ammo pouches on his belt. Into his possibles bag goes standard 12-gauge one-piece plastic wads. A shot charge rests in another pouch in plastic bottles, over-the-shot wads also in the possibles bag. Down the bore goes the powder charge, then the wad, then the shot, over-shot wad, then cap and fire. The pistol is about the same, really, using preweighed powder charges and lubed bullets.

Techniques for working up your own premeasured loads and a means of carrying them depend upon the quality and

Fusil V ignition has been set in place in underhammer model. Fadala found that improved the gun's performance.

size of the gun, but a safe way to go is to demand from the manufacturer that he give you a starter load. Sometimes this will be low, but it is a start. Black powder is not to be toyed with. A little common sense applied will pay off.

For the shotgun, again, the manufacturer should suggest beginning loads. Fadala's 12 gauge came with instructions that it will handle up to 10 gauge, by old black powder standards. Looking this up, we find that to be 1½ ounces of shot and five drams equivalent, which is a powerful load. Turning to drams broken down to grains, we learn four drams — as high as the chart happens to go — is worth 109 grains. If one dram equals 27.5 grains, then adding that to

the 109 we come up with a stout 136.5 grains. That's too much for us; we don't hunt jet airplanes. Fadala, incidentally, settled on 110 grains of powder and 1½ ounces of shot for geese. Patterns are good. The load is, to our experience, as deadly as a modern 12.

With all this talk about updating the black powder loads, making things easier, ignition more positive, why not simply stick to modern loads and forget the old-style guns? The answer is simple: Fun, enjoyment.

Cleaning has become easier, too, by using the modern black powder solvents, and by firing a new kind of propellant — a replica black powder, not really the old soot and ashes stuff at all. The new stuff is decidedly cleaner to burn, and more shots can be fired before swabbing is necessary. That is another plus of the new powder. It acts much like the old black and loads in the same weights, though it seems to take up about twenty percent less space than the old soot. This means the limited chamber dimensions on the heavy black powder handguns can get more powder behind the bullet when such is appropriate. The new stuff is still hygroscopic — in other words, it still attracts moisture and the old swabbing with hot water is necessary. But it comes off easier, especially if a modern lube has been used along with the Pyrodex, as well as solvents. (Pyrodex is explored at length in a later chapter.)

"I have heard the argument that updating muzzleloaders will put them on par with the modern arms. One state game department won't open special black powder seasons, because its people believe the old gun styles have no disadvantage," says Fadala.

Even with modern care and feeding, the muzzleloader is a single-shot, hard-to-reload, short-range proposition. We've heard all the stories about the old-timers knocking a feather off the Indian chief's hat at six hundred yards — and even believe some of them. These boys lived with their guns. We don't. Few modern black powder shooters can handle their smokepoles anything like they shoot their scoped-up smokeless magnums.

"I am not asking anyone to closet his old flintlock or pirate pistol. They are fun, but a steady diet of these can cause disuse altogether in the black powder area and that is too bad. Sometimes I go all the way back, use my beautiful powder horn with the scrolls and decoration, soot things up right proper, and go home and bathe myself and my guns.

"But for week-to-week shooting I will take the black powder practicals. Admittedly, mine is a middle-of-the-road attitude, not a purist form.

"I want all that fun without all that fuss."

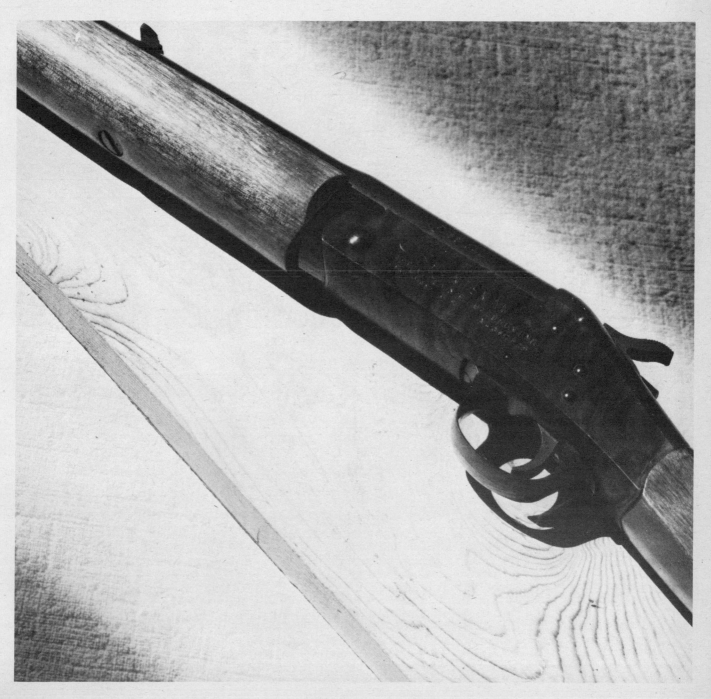

LOADING AND SHOOTING BLACK POWDER GUNS

A Complete Step-By-Step Guide To Loading And Shooting Cap And Ball Revolvers, Single-Shot Pistols, Muskets, Rifles And Muzzleloading Shotguns!

CHAPTER 9

As authentic looking as any hundred year old handmade original, the powder horn above is commercially produced.

DROP A CHARGE of black powder down the barrel or into the chamber mouth, seat a round lead ball or conical minie over this powder, prime the flash pan or place a percussion cap on the nipple and you're ready to indulge in some black powder shooting!

Sounds like a simple operation, doesn't it? Really it is quite simple, provided the proper components have been used in the loading process. Even so, how these components are loaded can make a big difference on just how well the rifle or handgun will group its shots on paper or bring down game.

So, in keeping with our policy that, if you want expert advice, you go to an expert, we approached Turner Kirkland, the ramrod of Dixie Gun Works up in the Tennessee hills. What follows comes from the experience of the field, the range and T. Kirkland's own personal experiences.

A question most commonly asked by the beginning black powder shooter is, "How much powder is actually too much?" A good rule to follow when working on starting loads is to begin by matching the caliber of the ball with the same number of grains of powder.

For example, a good starting load for a .36 caliber rifle would be in the neighborhood of 35 grains of FFFg. Although this rule will apply to most of the replicas on the market today — as well as their originals — there will be an occasional case where it will not hold true.

A good example of this would be the Colt 1862 Police pistol. Try as you like, about all the powder you can get into the small revolver's chambers is in the neighborhood of 20 grains. Although the police pistol resembles the New Model 1861 Navy in appearance, it is more like the 1849 pocket pistol in actual size. Even with as little as 20 grains of powder, it sometimes is difficult to seat the lead ball far enough below the one-half fluted and rebated cylinder's chamber mouth to allow it to rotate freely enough to fire.

Black powder is available in several different grades, based upon the fineness of the granulation. Powder with a single Fg designation is quite coarse and is used mostly in many of the old black powder center-fire cartridges and muskets with bores as big as the .70 caliber Brown Bess. This overly bored shoulder arm fires a patched .680-inch ball powered by 70 to 80 grains of Fg powder. Powder of this granulation will pass through a screen opening of .0689, but not through a .0582 screen opening.

Used extensively for the loading of muzzleloading shotguns, FFg powder is somewhat finer than Fg. This powder also is a good choice for loading big bore rifles and Tower-type pistols having a bore diameter of .540 to .690; having a faster burning rate, it is still popular among old arms buffs that handload .44 Colt, .44 Webley and .45 Colt center-fire black powder cartridges.

Perhaps the most commonly used, FFFg powder is used in loading practically all of the cap and ball revolvers, small-bore single-shot pistols and rifles ranging from .36 up to and including some of the .54 calibers. This powder has a much faster burning rate than the two grades previously mentioned and is a better choice when loading short-barreled guns.

Black powder guns are practically immune to being overloaded, although heavy charges many times are the most inaccurate. When loaded with too much powder — which has an extremely slow burning rate when compared to smokeless powders — a black powder rifle or handgun will merely expel the excess charge out the muzzle as it is fired.

If you ever have watched a cannon being fired you've probably noticed all the fire and sparks that shoot from the muzzle. This is the excess powder still burning as it leaves the barrel. This is also the reason why most black powder rifles have long barrels; to utilize all of the propelling force caused by the burning powder by allowing it to be ignited fully while still in the barrel.

The following chart from Dixie Gun Works clearly shows how the velocity is increased as the barrel length is increased:

Solid framed Remington design revolvers are broken down by dropping loading lever, pulling cylinder pin forward and rotating cylinder out of the frame.

VELOCITY TABLE*
CAL. .40 DIXIE CAPLOCK RIFLE
Barrel Charge Wts. in Grains Of DuPont FFFg Blk. Powder

Length	38	47	56	65	75	84	94	104	114
40"	1551	1770	1884	1987	2059	2178	2260	2356	2437
38"	1567	1747	1879	1992	2099	2216	2306	2347	2359
36"	1543	1735	1836	1994	2079	2189	2194	2301	2274
34"	1493	1610	1828	1966	2063	2186	2272	2246	
32"	1527	1654	1819	1913	2017	2098	2199	2233	
30"	1460	1642	1796	1932	1984	2052	2088	2064	
28"	1492	1623	1742	1903	1973	2095	2089		
26"	1445	1596	1734	1838	1902	1944	1952		
24"	1449	1593	1710	1784	1894	2019	2092		
22"	1468	1553	1668	1733	1844	1879	1937		
20"	1420	1509	1631	1703	1818	1863	1976		

* Velocity averages, expressed in feet per second, are for 5-shot strings. Firing with increasingly heavy charges was discontinued when recoil and muzzle blast became objectionable.

Extremely fine in granule size, FFFFg powder seldom is used, except for priming the flash pans of flintlocks. On occasion it is used for loading small pocket pistols and smallbored derringers of a .31 caliber or less. This is the fastest burning grade of black powder and, although many shooters claim that FFFFg burns much too fast and creates pressures that are too excessive for most black powder guns, there are those who argue the point that it is safe and that it gives a hunting rifle a little more punch. This is something of a personal debate, but certainly FFFFg should not be used in guns that are in poor condition. Usually these guns shouldn't be shot with any grade of powder!

In loading each type of muzzleloading firearm, each varies a little from the others, but basically they are loaded all the same — from the front to the rear!

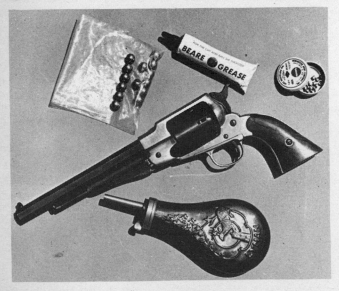

CAP AND BALL REVOLVERS

Samuel Colt, Eli Remington and a few other early armsmakers probably would turn in their proverbial graves should they witness the large numbers of reproductions — many of which actually are built better than the originals — that are being made to exact specifications of some of their early designs.

The cap and ball revolver is being produced in larger numbers today than at any other time in history. Nostalgia probably has accounted for the largest number of the modern day sales, but a few shooters have made tack drivers out of some of the better made replicas.

Navy Arms, Replica Arms, Dixie Gun Works, Centennial Arms, to name a few, all import modern-made replicas. Although basically the same as the originals in design, these are produced from materials superior to those used a century or better ago. These guns are fully proof tested before leaving the factories in Belgium, Spain and Italy for export to the United States, today the largest black powder shooting country in the world.

A black powder revolver is simple in design and operation, but there are a few steps which make loading, shooting and caring for them a little simpler and a lot more enjoyable.

Presuming you have just purchased your black powder cap and ball revolver, there is an important task one must take care of immediately before trudging off to the range with the expectation of punching a few holes into a paper target or two. As packed in the factory, most replica revolvers are doused thoroughly with a number of different types of lubricants. If not cleaned from the chambers of the cylinder, the first attempts to load them can end in one gooey mess.

Colt replica revolvers can be broken down easily for cleaning by removing a small wedge located just forward of the cylinder. The wedge is tapped back through its slot from the right side of the revolver.

Placing the hammer on half-cock, rotate the cylinder until the end of the loading lever will make contact with the metal between two of the chambers when levered down. This works as a lever and removes the barrel and loading lever unit from the frame and cylinder pin.

This initial cleaning doesn't have to be an out and out complete scrubbing of each and every part, especially if you plan to go right out and do some shooting with the gun as soon as you finish cleaning it; that's what you'll have to do

Colt replica is broken down by first removing wedge located in front of the cylinder. Such replicas as the Lyman below are actually safer than originals.

again when you're through firing it.

A quick examination of the insides of the chambers will probably reveal that they are well coated with lube. To clean this out rather quickly, simply dip a cotton swab into a cleaning solvent such as Hoppe's No. 9 or Birchwood-Casey bore solvent.

Swab out the insides of the chambers with the solvent, making sure that you clean all six — or in the case of five-shot cylinders, all five. Surprisingly enough, its easy to lose count!

Next, place the cylinder — chamber mouths down — onto a folded piece of cloth or paper towel to drain. You might have to swab the chambers first with a dry cotton swab, if you splashed on the solvent rather heavily. The paper or cloth will absorb the excess as it drains out.

While the chambers are draining, it might be a good idea to make a few passes through the barrel to remove any lube that might be packed into the rifling. Using a wire brush of the right caliber, make several passes through the barrel. Hold it up to the light and visually check to see if it is clean; if not, push the brush through a few more times, this time using a little solvent on it. Run a clean patch or two through it and it should be clean enough for firing.

By this time, the chambers should have drained any excess solvent. If there still is solvent visible, either let it drain a while longer or swab it out. Reassemble the gun in reverse of the way it was broken down.

The Remington-type revolver has a solid frame that completely encircles the cylinder. To remove the cylinder from this type of gun is simpler than with the Colt type.

The loading lever is brought down as if a round is being loaded into the chamber. With the lever in this position, grasp the T-shaped wedge that rests tightly against the flat bottom area of the octagon barrel and pull it toward the muzzle. By placing the hammer on half-cock and returning the loading lever to its upward position, the cylinder should rotate out of the frame.

The cylinder then is cleaned the same as the cylinder from the Colt-type replica. The barrel on the Remington-type revolver, however, does not separate from the frame and must be cleaned from the muzzle. Cleaning techniques and the care of cap and ball revolvers are covered in greater detail in another section.

Before loading the revolver, place a percussion cap on each nipple and snap it. By doing so, the explosion of the percussion cap will remove any dirt or grease that may be blocking the ignition from reaching the chamber. Unless the cylinder was scrubbed thoroughly, it might be a good idea to place a second cap on each of the nipples and snap it again, burning any oil that is remaining inside the chamber.

Percussion caps are available in a wide range of sizes and it sometimes is a problem to find the size that fits best. Trying to match one manufacturer's size designation to another's is like trying to break a secret code of some sort.

For instance, the Eley No. F4-21 is nearly identical to the No. 11 Winchester cap, both having a .175-inch inside diameter. Unless the manufacturer designates in the literature that comes with a new cap and ball revolver the size and make of cap to use, about the only way to get the proper size is by the old trial and error method, actually fitting the caps to the nipple.

Most of the modern made nipples measure .163-inch across the top and taper to about .168-inch in diameter at the point where they thread into the cylinder. If it is impossible to find the exact cap size, it is wise to buy the size on the larger side. The larger cap can be pinched slightly with the fingers, giving it a tight fit on the nipple.

After the caps have been placed on the nipples and snapped, place the revolver's hammer on half-cock to allow the cylinder to rotate freely. Using a powder flask or some other means of dropping a measured charge of powder into the chambers, charge each chamber with powder. The amount of powder to use will vary with the caliber and model of gun. It is, however, impossible to overload a cap and ball revolver with black powder. There isn't enough room to allow for an over-charge of powder and still have room to seat the ball.

The soft lead ball used to load cap and ball revolvers is always oversize and is swaged with a tight fit. To load a .44 caliber Colt Dragoon, for example, a .453-inch ball is used. A good powder charge for this hefty handgun — the gun weighing in the neighborhood of four pounds — is 40 grains of FFFg behind the 145-grain lead ball.

As the oversize .453 ball is seated in the .440 chamber, a thin ring of lead is peeled off the sides of the ball to form at the chamber mouths. This is a good indication that the ball is being swaged tightly. It's important that the ball fit snugly in the chamber; if it doesn't, the ball would have a tendency to work its way forward as the gun is being fired.

This, in itself, would prove no great problem during the first shot or two, but there is a chance that the ball could work its way far enough forward that it would protrude from the chamber mouth and catch onto the frame as the cylinder rotated. The ball catching onto the frame wouldn't allow the cylinder to turn.

CHART OF BALL SIZES TO USE IN REPRODUCTION GUNS		
Revolver	Chamber Size	Ball Size
1860 Army, .44 cal. Centennial	.446	.450
1860 Army, 44 cal., Replica	.446	.450
Reb, .36 caliber	.375	.376
Model 60 Army, .44 caliber	.447	.451
Wells Fargo, .31 caliber	.315	.320
Patterson, .36 caliber	.378	.380
Yank, .36 caliber	.375	.376
Sheriff's Model, .36 caliber	.375	.376
1861 Navy Colt, .36 caliber	.375	.380
Baby Dragoon, .31 caliber	.316	.321
Leech & Rigdon .36 caliber	.375	.376
Walker, .44 caliber	.440	.441
Dragoon, .44 caliber	.440	.441
Remington Revolving Carbine, .44 caliber	.450	.454
Remington Army, .44 caliber	.450	.454
Remington Navy, .36 caliber	.375	.376

Once the ball has been seated in each of the chambers, a grease-type lube should be placed over each chamber mouth. This prevents the possibility of a chain fire — having more than just the intended chamber firing. This is not a recommended way of grouping the shots on the target and is dangerous to the shooter, most of the time resulting in a ruined gun.

Numerous types of lubricants can be used to prevent a multiple discharge; Crisco shortening is one of the most widely used. Hodgdon now offers a commercially made lube which is called Spit Ball. It comes in a hip

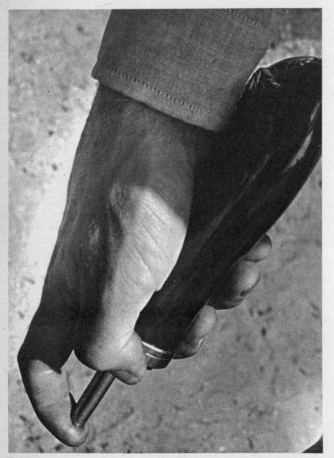

The charger on this flask measures out one exact charge for a .36 caliber cap and ball revolver such as this Colt Navy. Thumb opens and closes charger opening.

pocket-size plastic bottle that has a flip open or shut nozzle that allows you to get the lube down into the chamber mouth and completely cover the seated ball. In addition to

preventing a chain fire, this lube is also supposed to improve accuracy. Lubes of this type help prevent powder fouling from buidling up in the bore. There are several such commerical products now available.

As a rule, the hotter the powder load used, the less consistent accuracy you'll get from a black powder revolver. It is best to experiment with the gun until the right load is segregated. Usually this load is just enough powder to get the lead ball from the muzzle to the target with the least amount of drop in its trajectory. Hot powder charges have a tendency to spew the balls erratically and seldom puts them anywhere near the same point of aim for each shot.

The following chart is of recommended loads for certain models and calibers. These loads may seem on the mild side to you, but these are the loads we feel will give consistent accuracy.

Revolver	Ball Diameter	Apprx. Wt. in Grains	Charge in Powder Grains	
.31 Colt Pocket Pistol	.321 (0 Buck- shot)	45	FFFg	15
.31 Remington New Model Pocket Revolver	.321 (0 Buck- shot)	45	FFFg	15
.31 Remington Rider Double Action Revolver	.321 (0 Buck- shot)	45	FFFg	15-18
Other .31 caliber American revolvers	.321-.310	40-45	FFFg	8-18
.36 Colt Navy	.376-.380	80	FFFg	22
.36 Remington New Model Belt Pistol	.376-.380	80	FFFg	20-22
.36 Savage Model 1861	.376-.380	80	FFFg	20-26
.36 Modern Manufacture Reproductions	.380	80	FFFg	18-22
.36 Colt Police Pistol	.380	80	FFFg	12-15
.44 Colt Dragoon	.451-.453	140	FFFg	40
.44 Remington New Model Army	.451-.453	140	FFFg	26-30
.44 Rogers and Spencer	.451-.453	140	FFFg	30-35
.44 Modern Manufacture Reproductions	.451	140	FFFg	28-30

With hammer at half-cock the cylinder on the Navy Colt replica can be easily rotated to charge each chamber with FFFg powder from charger on the flask.

Although cap and ball revolvers normally are loaded without any kind of wad or patch, there are those who choose to place a treated felt wad between the ball and powder charge. These wads are made by treating a piece of thin felt — like that used in the making of your favorite Stetson — in a melted liquid consisting of beeswax and beef tallow. The felt material then is laid out to dry.

Wads are cut to the exact chamber size with a wad cutting device, which is simply a punch with a recessed head and sharpened edges. This is placed on the material and

Slightly oversized soft lead ball is placed sprue down or up over the charged chamber. Cylinder is then rotated until ball is directly below loading lever. Below, the ball is firmly seated over the powder by fulcrum action of loading lever.

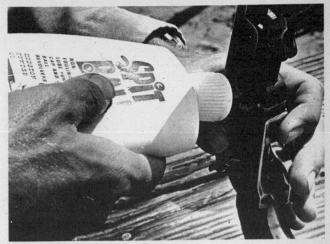

The final step to loading a percussion revolver is to place a lube of some sort over loaded round. This seals the round and prevents a possible chain fire.

heartily rapped with a hammer; cutting a circular wad from the felt the exact size of the chamber diameter.

When loading with felt wads, the powder charge is dropped in the same manner as before. Instead of seating the ball directly over the powder charge, however, the felt wad then is inserted, the ball seated over this wad. Lubricant at the chamber mouth no longer is needed, as the wad completely seals off the powder charge from any possible exposure to the flash as another chamber is being fired.

Wads are a little less messy and easier to load than smearing grease at the chamber mouth, but they do little to help prevent powder foulings in the bore and make sustained firing of the revolver more difficult.

If you've ever watched a shooter at the local rifle and pistol range make several trips back and forth to his car before he is ready to do any shooting, you probably realize that shooting a cap and ball revolver requires more than just the gun and a few bullets. There are numerous accessories that aid in shooting these black powder sixguns.

There is probably nothing more frustrating than trying to fit a percussion cap onto a nipple with the fingers. Half the attempts resulting in a cap lost in the grass or among the piles of .22 brass that are a part of almost every range.

If a capping device is used, however, it then becomes a simple operation; simply slip the cap on the nipple and pull the capper away, moving to the next nipple until all the chambers have been capped. Most of the large black powder gun suppliers carry a capper of this sort. Dixie Gun Works even handles the circular spring-loaded capper for the Paterson Colt.

If Crisco is your favorite lube at the chamber mouth, for both economic and acquisition reasons, a good way to dispense it into the chambers is by filling a cake decorator with the shortening, then squirting it over the loaded chamber. This not only speeds the process, but helps keep the Crisco in the chamber and not all over the hands and, eventually, the gun.

MUZZLELOADING SINGLE-SHOT PISTOLS

Single-shot muzzleloading pistols have come to be known as pirate pistols, duelling pistols and even a few are referred to as horse pistols. Although they vary greatly from one to the other — from the extremely short barreled derringers of riverboat fame to the duellers used in the early 1800s — they are all loaded in just about the same manner, with the only variance being the size of the ball and the amount of powder used.

Certainly you wouldn't load a short, three-inch barreled derringer of .44 caliber with the same amount of powder as

This well photographed explosion of a primed flash pan should be enough to convince anyone why it causes flinching.

you would a Kentucky pistol of the same caliber having a nine-inch or longer barrel. With chamber and barrel being the same — one-piece barrel and breech — more powder can be loaded into this type of handgun than with the revolving cylinder type. With the cap and ball revolver, the ball must be seated below the chamber mouth to allow the cylinder to rotate. If the ball is left protruding partially from the chamber, more likely than not, it will catch on the frame as the cylinder rotates.

Being a single-shooter, the muzzleloading pistol has no moving or rotating chamber that must be aligned with the barrel before it can be fired. Consequently, the ball does not have to be seated to any significant degree.

A shooter should be ever cautious when loading this type of gun. It is easy to overload these guns accidentally, usually a double charge dropped from the powder flask. Occasionally a shooter can't remember whether he's already charged the gun with powder. This is especially true when busily engaged in conversation. So, it is wise to pay attention to what you're doing.

If the gun is well made and manufactured from strong modern materials, it should be able to withstand the double charge. The problem would be the effect on the shooter. As an example, the .58 caliber Springfield pistol of approximate 1855 manufacture usually is loaded with 40 grains of FFg or FFFg powder behind a 265-grain .570-inch ball. A double charge of 80 grains is 20 grains more than the recommended load for the .58 caliber Zouave rifle. In probability, the excess powder would only be expelled from the muzzle, the gun's short barrel not allowing the slow-burning powder complete ignition.

Unlike the cap and ball revolver, the single-shot pistol always is loaded with a ball actually smaller than its bore diameter. This is patched with a thin piece of cotton or linen to fit the ball tightly against the rifling, if the pistol happens to be rifled.

Many original flintlock and caplock pistols, as well as some of today's reproductions, are fitted with smoothbore barrels. These guns were intended originally for use at rather close range and longer range and pinpoint accuracy wasn't one of their better virtues. The exception to this rule

might be some of the early military wheellock designs, with barrels as long as eighteen inches, and a few of the duellers.

Today, numerous smoothbore muzzleloading pistols are being imported from all over Europe. These can be loaded just as their rifled relatives or without the patching material, if the gun is going to be fired as soon as it is loaded. The patching keeps the ball from rolling back out the muzzle, if the pistol is going to be carried with its muzzle toward the ground. In addition to loading with the lead ball projectile, this type of gun can be loaded with birdshot much the same as muzzleloading shotguns are loaded.

The following chart gives recommended loads for several of the various types of derringers, duellers and horse pistols.

Pistol	Ball Diameter	Powder	Charge Weight in Grains
.28 caliber derringers made under various brand names	.260	FFFg	10
.31 caliber derringers made under various firm names	.300	FFFg	10
.36 caliber Dixie target pistol	.355	FFFg	22
.36 caliber Hopkins & Allen Boot Pistol	.340	FFFg	18-22
.41 caliber Dixie brass frame derringer	.395	FFFg	10
.40 caliber Dixie Flint Pistol	.395	FFFg	25
.44 caliber Replica Arms Kentucky percussion pistol	.410	FFFg	25
.45 caliber Hopkins & Allen Boot Pistol	.435	FFFg	25-28
.45 caliber Dixie Flint and Percussion Pistol	.445	FFFg	25
.54 caliber U.S. Pistol Models 1819-1842	.535	FFFg	30-35
.56 caliber Navy Arms 1806 Harper's Ferry Pistol	.555	FFFg	35
.58 caliber Navy Arms Harper's Ferry Dragoon	.575	FFg or FFFg	35-40
.58 caliber U.S. Springfield Pistol Model 1855	.570	FFg	40
.67 caliber Tower Flint Pistol	.650	FFg	40

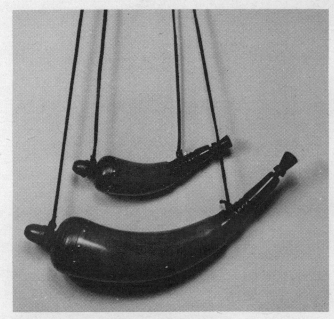

Flintlock pistol fanciers usually have two powder horns. The larger horn carries the powder for the main charge, the smaller horn holds the powder for charging the pistol's flash pan.

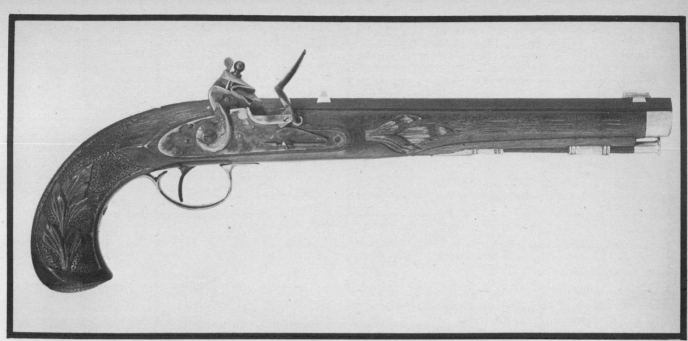

Some of today's black powder guns are copies of the general type, such as the Replica Arms Kentucky pistol above. Others are exact replicas, like the Navy Arms 1855 Harpers Ferry below.

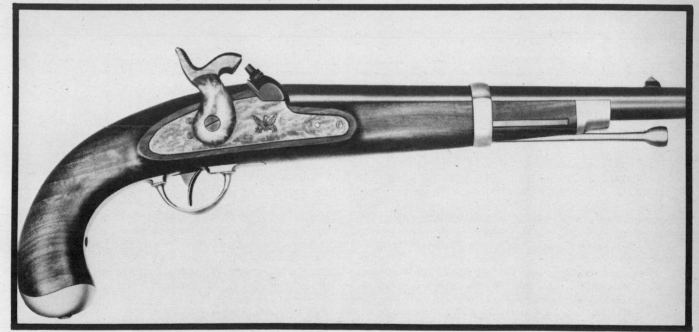

Two more of today's replicas to show the wide variety available are the Hawes derringer and the Tower flintlock pictured at left. All imported guns are fully proof tested and quite safe.

If continuous shooting is planned for the better part of an afternoon, it is best to use patching material that has been dampened with sperm oil, Hodgdon's Spit-Patch lubricant or something similar. The lube will keep powder fouling soft and allow more shots between cleaning, which is necessary when accuracy is the goal.

The U.S. flintlock musket Model 1835 was the last such gun to be adopted by the Army; old guns should be thoroughly checked out before they are fired.

There are now several .58 caliber replicas of this original 1841 Mississippi rifled musket on the market; original was .54 cal.

THE MUZZLELOADING MUSKET AND RIFLE

WEBSTER'S DICTIONARY DEFINES nostalgia as a wistful or excessively sentimental, sometimes abnormal, yearning for return to or of some past period or irrecoverable condition. Certainly the yearning to shoulder a long barreled black powder rifle and to wander almost aimlessly through the timbers, fields and over hill after hill can hardly be defined as being abnormal. It may be the result of some nostalgic feelings, but whatever the reasons, this is an enjoyable pursuit that can be made even more pleasant through proper loading of the rifle or musket being carried.

Although basically the same in design and functioning, there is a world of difference between the heavy-barreled Kentucky, Hawken and Pennsylvania rifles and their distant relative, the thin-barreled rifled or smoothbore musket. How the two types of guns are loaded also are similar in many respects, but there is a difference here too. Although not a complete loading guide for shoulder weapons, this section should help you find the right load for the type of rifle or musket you shoot.

As already mentioned, the main difference between the muzzleloading rifle and musket is the thickness of the barrel walls. Rifles almost always have rather thick and heavy rifled barrels, while the musket — which may either be rifled or left smoothbore — is fitted with a barrel that more resembles the barrel of a shotgun than the rifle. For this reason, the musket should not be loaded with a patched ball. Instead, it is loaded with a conical minie bullet.

There are still quite a few shootable original .58 caliber Civil War muskets to be had. The prices of these will make the average black powder shooter's wallet suddenly lose weight and result in the silent treatment from his wife.

During the 1930s and 1940s, these guns could be ordered from Bannerman's in New York for the lordly sum of three to five dollars apiece. Today, this same gun, in good condition, will bring upwards of $200 and, even if in poor condition, in the neighborhood of a century note. By the time the latter has been restored to shootable condition, it is probably worth more than the musket in good condition that originally cost twice as much.

The .58 caliber muskets of the mid-1800s receive more attention from black powder enthusiasts than probably any other make or design. To cope with the shortage of fine old originals — that really shouldn't be shot anyway — a number of firms are importing from European manufacturers a variety of reproductions that are quite safe and fun to shoot.

One of the most copied and currently reproduced versions of this type of early military shoulder arms is the .58 caliber Remington Zouave. Navy Arms' copy of the 1863 Zouave is about as fine a reproduction of this type that you're bound to find and, selling for just under a hundred dollars, it is within the price range afforded nearly any shooter's budget.

There are numerous other reproductions for less money, but their quality seldom matches that of the Navy Arms Zouave. Before being imported into this country, however,

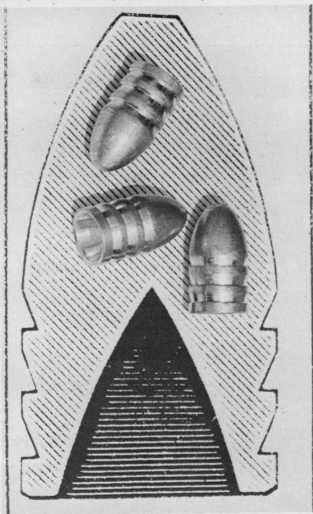

The Navy Arms firm imports from Italy a well built replica of the Zouave rifled musket. This was the general type of gun used during the Civil War and best results are obtained when firing Minie bullets such as those below; hollow base expands into rifling.

complete scrubdown of the musket, but should be thorough enough to remove excess oil and lube from the barrel and breech. Usually a swab dipped in the soapy solution and run the length of the barrel several times should do the trick. It is also a good idea to place the hammer at half-cock and make sure that some of the cleaning solution is forced out through the nipple or vent hole on the downward stroke of the rod and cleaning jag.

The wet, soapy patches should be followed by several clean, dry patches to absorb any water left in the bore. A few patches slightly saturated with a bore solvent, such as Hoppe's No. 9 or Bucheimer's black powder solvent, should be run through the barrel, allowing some to trickle through the vent. The solvent will help prevent rust, the worst enemy a muzzleloader can have. To remove any excess solvent, shove another dry patch down the bore. Now you're ready to do some shooting!

Even after thorough cleaning it is a good practice to snap a few caps on a percussion rifle before loading it.

all of these guns are proof-tested with a charge of powder that exceeds any that should be used during day-to-day shooting.

As with nearly all guns that come straight from the factory, these guns usually are well lubricated and will have to be cleaned before they are loaded and fired. If there happens to be quite a bit of lube down the breech, the result can be a gooey mess, if the powder charge is dropped in before cleaning.

Hot soapy water is as good as anything else with which to scrub the bore. This initial cleaning doesn't have to be a

If this first outing is to be done at a local rifle range, remember to keep the muzzle pointed downrange. Place a percussion cap on the nipple, if the gun happens to be a caplock, and snap it. This should remove any grease that might be obstructing the nipple vent; if the explosion of the percussion cap reaches the breech, a small amount of smoke will be emitted from the muzzle.

It is a good idea to carry a nipple prick — a piece of wire small enough in diameter to be inserted through the flash hole of the nipple — to punch through any obstructions in the nipple. Unless percussion caps are hard to come by in your area, it also is a wise practice to snap two, maybe three,

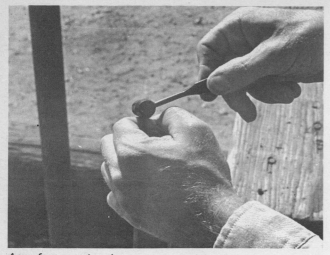

A perfect powder charge can be weighed out each time with the Lee powder dippers, great for range shooting, not while hunting.

Adjustable powder measures such as this are available from a number of black powder suppliers; never charge directly from flask.

more caps before loading.

When dropping the powder charge down the muzzle, always hold the muzzle out and away from your body, keeping your hand away from it at the same time. Never charge a muzzleloader directly from the powder flask! This is only asking for trouble in the event that there is an accidental discharge — having a flask full of powder explode in your hand can prove quite discouraging.

If the musket being loaded is of the flintlock type, it is best simply to make sure that the flash hole is clear by punching it with the nipple prick, which, in this case, becomes a vent prick. It is, however, a common practice to prime the pan and dry fire the gun to check whether the flint and frizzen are sparking enough to ignite the FFFFg powder used to prime the flash pan.

In either case, loading a caplock musket of the Zouave type or a flintlock musket of the Brown Bess type, always keep the muzzle at a safe distance.

The .58 caliber musket can be loaded with either FFg or FFFg powder. While many black powder shooters swear by FFg powder, others faithfully stand by FFFg. So, it is best to experiment to see which powder best suits your wants and needs. It is actually safe to use either powder since black powder will not create pressures enough to create a problem in this caliber.

The .575 diameter minie used in the .58 caliber Zouaves weighs in at just around 500 grains, enough lead to drop just about anything that wanders the North American continent provided the shot is well placed. A good starting load for this caliber would be 65 grains of FFg or 60 grains of FFFg. This load is good for a muzzle velocity just around the 1000 feet per second mark and enough foot-pound energy to knock game as big as moose off its feet for good one-shot kills.

There are a number of ways to measure the correct amount of powder to drop for each charge. Occasionally you will probably run across a musket shooter that uses the "looks like enough to me" system, guessing at the charge weights. This is hardly recommended since rounds so loaded are usually very inconsistent.

If shooting is confined to just target shooting at rifle ranges, the No. 230 dipper from the Lee powder measure kit is the answer for consistent charge weights. A level dipper full of powder will measure out a consistent 60 grains of FFFg every time.

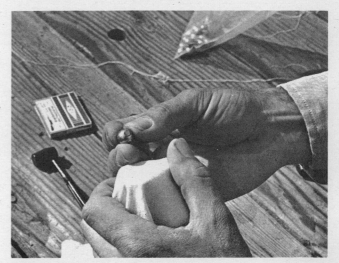

When not using pre-cut patches, drape proper thickness material over muzzle. Sprue on ball should either be seated straight up or straight down. It can be partially pushed into muzzle with thumb.

If small plastic containers are available, these make excellent powder containers. Using a powder scale of reputable manufacture, an exact powder charge can be poured into each of the containers before heading for the range or out to fill the freezer with a winter's meat supply.

With the muzzle held out at an arm's distance, drop the pre-measured powder charge down the muzzle, making sure that the finger tips are clear of the barrel opening.

The conical minie is then started into the barrel with the finger tips. Always take care to make sure that it is started into the muzzle as straight as possible. Next, pull the ramrod from its position beneath the barrel and firmly seat the bullet over the powder charge. Never slam the bullet down the bore; instead, take care and try not to batter the soft lead.

If hunting in the field, replace the ramrod in its original position below the barrel; if at the range, it can be laid on the bench. Place the hammer at half-cock and place a percussion cap on the nipple, pressing it down firmly with the thumb to make sure that it is firmly seated. Bring the hammer to full cock and aim in. The gun is ready to fire, providing the components have been loaded properly.

Of course, the .58 caliber Zouave wasn't the only military musket, but it was one of the best known during the Civil War. In addition to the muskets used during that period, there are a number of carbines and rifles ranging from .54 to .75 caliber that are loaded in this same manner; many of these so-called rifles are really muskets that were designated rifles because of their rifled bores.

Above: After the ball has been pressed into the muzzle, the excess patching material is cut off with a knife. (Below) The patched ball then is started into barrel. The instrument being used is termed a short starter.

The means and equipment for patching the round ball are almost as old as black powder, but less complicated.

MUSKET/RIFLE	BALL DIAMETER	POWDER	CHARGE GRAINS
.54 caliber U.S. Mississippi Rifle	.535 or minie	FFFg	75
.54 caliber U.S. Rifle, Models 1804-1814-1817	.535 or minie	FFFg	75
.577 English Enfield Rifle	.570 to .575	FFg	60
.58 caliber Civil War Muskets (Confederate)	.570 to .575 or minie	FFg	60
.58 caliber U.S. Civil War Rifle, Models 1855-1861-1863	.570 to 575 or minie	FFg	60
.58 caliber Navy Arms Model 1863 Remington Zouave	.575 or Lyman No. 575213, 575494, or 575602 minie	FFg or FFFg	60-65
.69 Whitneyville Plymouth Navy Rifle	.680	FFg	70
.69 caliber U.S. Muskets Models 1808-1842	.680	FFg	80
.69 caliber U.S. Muskets Models 1821-1840-1842, re-rifled from smoothbores	.680	FFg	70
.70 caliber Navy Arms Brown Bess	.680	Fg or FFg	70-75
.75 caliber Dixie Gun Works Brown Bess	.740	Fg or FFg	70-80

After the ball has been seated four to five inches into the barrel, ramrod is used to seat it over powder charge.

There are actually no set rules to loading and firing muskets. True, patched balls can be fired in them, but seldom do they perform as well as the minie bullets. The musket just doesn't allow enough powder to be loaded to get the utmost accuracy from their large bores with round ball projectiles. The one exception to this would be the Brown Bess musket.

Dixie Gun Works now offers a reproduction of this once favorite arm of the early East Coast settlers — provided they could get one from an unsuspecting British soldier. This particular gun is fitted with a forty-two-inch smoothbore barrel and is loaded with a patched 610-grain .740-inch ball in front of 70 to 80 grains of FFg.

The accompanying charts are by no means a complete list of loads for the different guns listed, but instead give some good starting loads for the given guns and calibers. There were numerous foreign-made muskets that were made especially for the Civil War and imported to the United States, some being sold to both Union and Confederate forces. As a rule, these are basically built to the specifications of the Springfield rifled muskets and should be loaded as such. Calibers may vary, so it would be wise to learn the exact caliber before attempting to shoot any of them.

The loading and shooting of heavy barreled muzzleloading rifles is basically the same as with the thinner barreled musket. For better accuracy, however, the long barreled Kentucky and Pennsylvania rifles, as well as the short barrel Plains and Hawken type rifles, always are loaded with a patched undersize ball.

The Minie bullet at left is superior to the round ball when it comes to speedy reloading. Patched ball, however, usually proves to be the most accurate of the two.

RIFLE	BALL DIAMETER	POWDER	CHARGE-GRAINS
.36 caliber Hopkins & Allen Offhand Rifle	.340	FFFg	35-45
.38 caliber Replica Arms Plainsman Rifle	.360	FFFg	40-45
.44 caliber Navy Arms Kentucky Rifle	.434	FFFg	45-60
.45 caliber Dixie Gun Works Standard Percussion or Flint Rifle	.445	FFFg	65
.45 caliber Thompson-Center Hawken	.440	FFFg	50-65
.45 caliber Hopkins & Allen Target Rifle	.435	FFFg	55-70
.50 caliber Thompson-Center Hawken	.490 or No. 445599 Lyman minie	FFg	50-70
.58 caliber Hopkins & Allen Deer Stalker	.570 or No. 575213 Lyman minie	FFg	60-70

Reproduction muzzleloading double barrel shotgun is copy of type of gun used a hundred years ago.

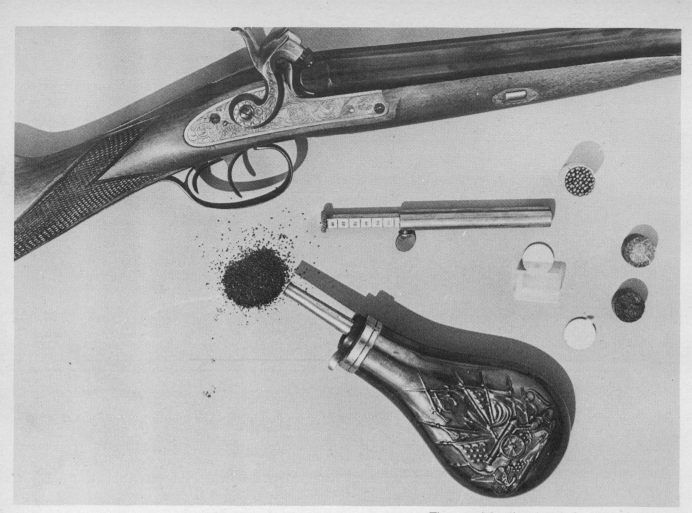

The muzzleloading double from Richland Arms, some shot, powder, wads and percussion caps are the ingredients for a day of shotgunning.

MUZZLELOADING SHOTGUNS

> To ram the Powder well, but not the Ball (shot);
>   One Third the well-turned Shot superior must
> Arise, and overcome the nitrous Dust,
>   Which, dry'd and season'd in the Oven's Heat,
> Has stood in close-mouthed Jarr the dampless Night.
>   Now search for Tow, and some old saddle pierce:
> No Wadding lies so close or drives so fierce.
>   And here be mindful constantly to Arm
> With Choice of Flints, a Turn-Screw and a Worm;
>   The accidental Chances of the Field
> Will for such Implements Occasion yield.

Written in 1727, this segment of a poem entitled *Pteryplegia: Or, The Art of Shooting Flying* by A. B. Markland goes into some detail concerning the components needed to load an early fowling piece, the early name for the muzzleloading shotgun. The poet even goes so far as to warn of some of the hazards and the need of a turn screw and worm to remove the loaded components from the breech should they fail to fire.

With "One Third the well-turned Shot superior must Arise," Markland was trying to get across the point that as much as one and one-half as much shot is used as powder. When referring to the search for tow or saddle pierce, he

Same flask used to charge the percussion revolver will double as shotgun powder container, Lee dipper measures the charge.

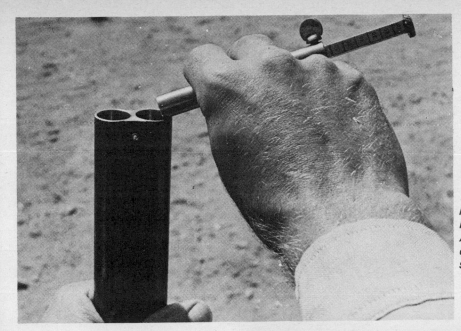

Measured powder charge is loaded into muzzle (left). Above, the wads used to comprise load and what they should look like loaded.

Felt wad of right thickness is first inserted over powder (right). Plastic shot protector such as that available from Federal is then inserted.

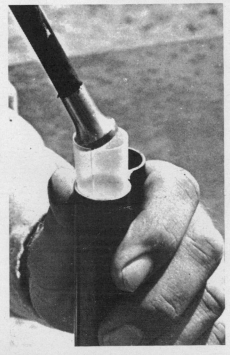

was referring to the most commonly used materials for wadding between the powder and shot.

Black powder apparently was not the propellant that we know today. For one thing, powder mills were usually just small businesses employing little, if any, quality control over their product. Atmospheric moisture must have been something of a problem then also, since Markland writes of placing the powder in a "close-mouthed Jarr the dampless Night" to dry in the warmth of the oven's heat. Hopefully, the powder was kept well away from the flame!

Just as these early fowling pieces were loaded in 1727, the currently made muzzleloading shotguns also are loaded, except that you don't have to place your powder in a jar to dry overnight or rip apart old saddles to get the tow padding to use as wadding. The components, though, are basically the same; powder, wadding, shot and a wad over this to keep the shot from rolling out the muzzle.

Missing, however, from many of the modern black powder shotguns are the forty-inch or longer barrels that were used on the early fowling pieces. This, perhaps, is where the idea of an extra long barrel giving a shotgun added range originated. This is true with shotguns that are loaded with black powder, since the long barrel gives the powder more distance to be completely burned or ignited.

With breechloading shotguns using smokeless powder shells, this isn't the case. The powder, in most cases, is completely ignited by the time it has traveled less than half of the gun's twenty-six or twenty-eight-inch barrel. With these guns, the longer barrel only tends to improve the gun's pattern at maximum ranges, not make it shoot farther.

As a starter, if the gun happens to be a new black powder reproduction, clean the bore to remove the excess lubricant that usually is all but poured down the bore at the factory. Muzzleloading shotguns can be cleaned in the same manner as the rifled or smoothbore musket.

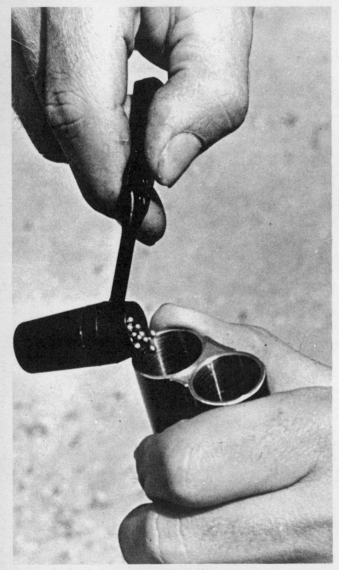

Proper load of shot is poured into the muzzle of the shotgun. Muzzle should be held away from body for each loading step.

If the gun happens to be a caplock, snap a few caps to clear the nipple and burn any moisture away that might be in the breech. In the event that the gun you are shooting is

Wildfowler (left) is imported by Century Arms. The accompanying double-barrel muzzleloader now is imported by the Dixie Gun Works.

fitted with a flintlock, prime the pan with just enough FFFFg to insure that the flint is sparking enough to ignite the powder; clean the flash hole leading from the pan to the breech.

A muzzleloading shotgun is loaded in almost the exact manner as a shotgun shell; it might not be a bad idea to cut open a shell and examine how it is loaded.

A measured charge of powder is first dropped into the breech through the muzzle. The amount of powder used will vary according to the intended target. If claybirding is the afternoon's activities, a good medium velocity load is best. Again this will vary, according to the gauge of the shotgun.

The powder is followed by a thick felt or cardboard wad. This should measure around 3/32 to one-eighth inch in thickness. If the gun's bore is close to being the exact diameter of one of the standard 12, 16, 20 or 28-gauge breechloading shotguns, there is a wide variety of components in the line of wads that can be used in the black powder gun also. This includes plastic shot cups that will greatly improve the gun's pattern.

Powder having FFFg granule size tends to throw the shot in erratic, inconsistent patterns that vary too much to be dependable. Most muzzleloading shotgun manufacturers and shooters who have done countless experiments with the guns agree that the best granulation to use in shotguns of 12, 16, 20 and 28-gauge is FFg. Shotguns of 10 gauge or larger should be loaded with Fg powder.

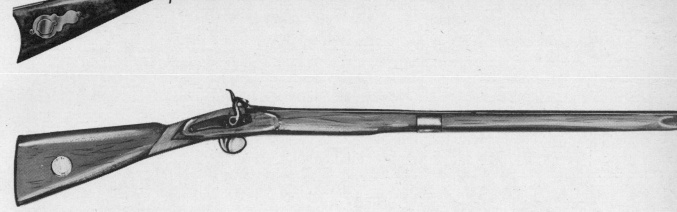

The shotgun at top is a lightweight 12 gauge from Numrich Arms, below is a full-stock 28 gauge from Century Arms.

At one time it was common practice to use the smooth-bore muzzleloading shotgun to hunt big game, especially the large bore 4, 8 and 10 gauges, which were used on dangerous game in Africa. The smaller gauges were used extensively for taking whitetailed deer and black bear in this country and Canada. Of course, these weren't loaded with regular lead shot, but with a large round lead ball that is referred to as a "pumpkin ball."

These are loaded just as the regular shot load, except that the ball is used instead of the shot. The accompanying chart from the Dixie Gun Works gives recommended loads for firing round lead balls from muzzleloading shotguns.

Although the loads on this charge hold true for loading today's modern muzzleloader, it was originally compiled in February, 1896 by the Gunmakers Company and the Guardians of the Birmingham Proof House under the authority of the Gun Barrel Proof Act of 1868. All charges were based on FFg powder for those gauges of 12 or smaller and on Fg powder for the larger bores.

It does prove that muzzleloading scattergun loads have changed little in the past century!

GAUGE	POWDER GRAINS	DRAMS	BALL GRAINS
4	273	10	1531
5	213	7-15/32	1217
6	179	6-17/32	1025
7	154	5-5/8	889
8	135	4-15/16	793
9	122	4-15/32	725
10	109	4	656
11	96	3-1/2	574
12-13	89	3-1/4	547
16-18	75	2-3/4	437
19-21	68	2-1/2	383
22-30	55	2	328

With the wad seated over the powder, drop in the shot. Lead shot comes in a variety of sizes and — again depending on the target — there is a proper size shot. For the medium velocity trap or target load, No. 7½ and No. 8 shot work the best. The small size of the shot allows more pellets to be loaded in a given 1-1/8 or 1-1/4-ounce shot charge, making the pattern more dense.

To keep the shot from rolling out the end of the barrel, another thin felt or cardboard wad should be seated in front of the shot. Tissue paper that has been blotted with a commercial lube such as Dixie Gun Work's Bear Grease or Hodgdon's Spit-Patch makes an excellent over-the-shot wad. The lube helps hold the wad in place and allows more shots between barrel cleanings.

The following chart gives light, medium and heavy loads in drams. To figure how many grains each load is made up of, simply multiply it by 27.34 grains; a one dram equivalent. It is recommended that you start by loading the light load first, then if it doesn't seem to be up to your desires, go to the medium, then to the heavy, if even more is needed.

All loads are based on the use of FFg powder. If FFFg powder is used on the smaller 28 gauge, 32 gauge and .410, reduce the load slightly.

GAUGE	DRAMS POWDER	SHOT CHARGE (OZ.)	
4	10	3	Medium
8	5-1/2	2-1/4	Medium
10	5	1-3/4	Heavy
10	4-1/2	1-1/2	Medium
10	4	1-1/2	Light
12	4-1/8	1-3/8	Heavy
12	3-3/4	1-1/4	Medium
12	3-1/4	1-1/8	Light
16	3-1/8	1-1/8	Heavy
16	3	1	Medium
16	2-1/2	1	Light
20	2-3/4	1	Heavy
20	2-1/2	7/8	Medium
20	2-1/2	3/4	Light
28	2-1/4	7/8	Heavy
28	2	5/8	Medium
28	1-3/4	5/8	Light
32	1-3/4	5/8	Heavy
32	1-1/2	9/16	Medium
32	1-1/2	1/2	Light
.410	1-1/2	5/8	Heavy
.410	1-1/2	1/2	Medium
.410	1-1/4	1/2	Light

CARE, CLEANING & BLACK POWDER

If Cleanliness Is Next To Godliness, Muzzleloaders Should Create Believers!

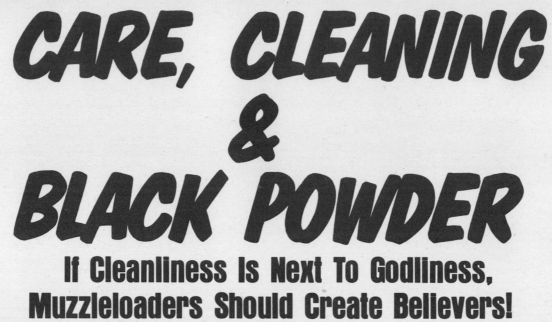

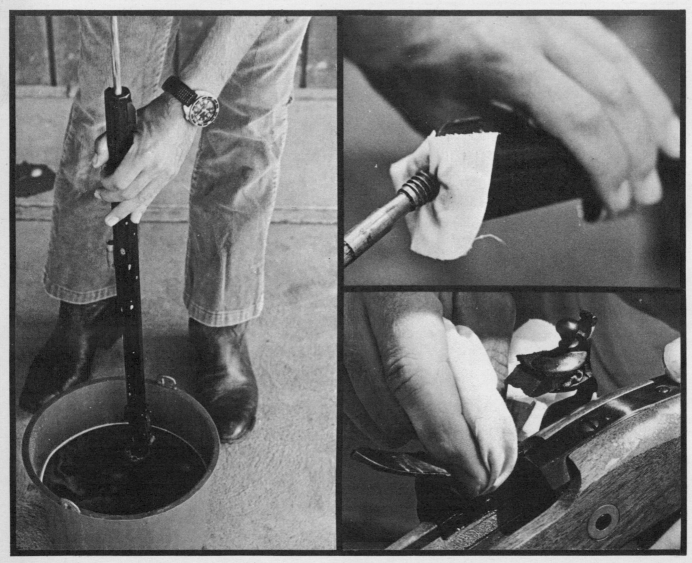

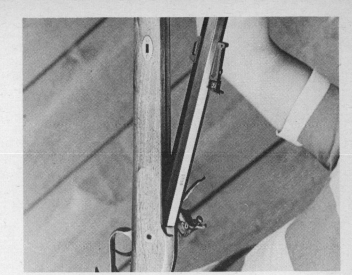

With wedge out, barrel can be lifted free of the stock to disengage the hooked tang at rear of breech

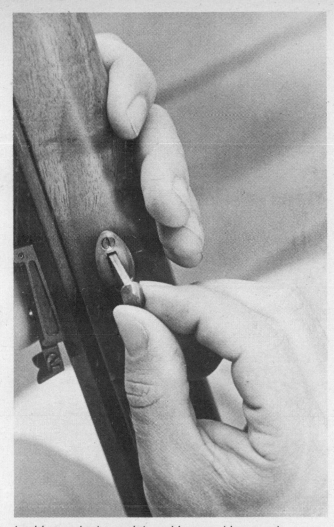

Locking wedge beneath barrel is tapped loose and withdrawn as preliminary in disassembling certain designs, so as to protect woodwork during cleaning.

HERE AND THERE in this book we have touched upon the subject of cleaning and caring for the different forms of black powder rifles, revolvers and shotguns. However, little has been written to give an in-depth description of the cleaning procedures that will keep your favorite charcoal burner in top condition for years to come.

As a starter, let's take a look at black powder, itself. As you know, black powder is extremely corrosive and the reasons behind this are simple.

Corrosion of metal is actually an oxidation process, the hydrogen molecules of the metal's surface combining with the oxygen. This dehydrogenation commonly appears in the form of hydrated ferric oxide, or in plain English, good ol' red rust. When left unchecked for any length of time, this surface rusting action penetrates deeper and deeper into the metal.

Black powder presently being manufactured consists of approximately 11.85 percent sulphur, 13.51 percent carbon and 74.64 percent saltpeter, the latter being the propellant's corrosive ingredient. More properly designated potassium nitrate, saltpeter provides the oxygen needed to enable the confined powder to burn, or better yet, ignite and burn fast enough to cause propelling pressures.

Chemically, potassium nitrate — KNO_3 — is made up of three atoms of oxygen for each atom of potassium and nitrogen. Roger Bacon and earlier chemists seeking the discovery of an explosive mixture found potassium nitrate in the form of cyrstalline salt that had resulted from nitrification of the chemicals in arable soil.

Loaded and fired in a muzzleloading gun, black powder leaves a considerable amount of residue inside the barrel and chamber area. Although the majority of the potassium nitrate is consumed during the burning of the powder charge, there is always an extremely small amount left clinging to the barrel walls. Remembering that potassium nitrate is actually a salt and that salt attracts moisture, visualize the condition of a muzzleloader's bore, if left uncleaned for several weeks, months, or even a year.

Too often a fine reproduction as well as beautiful old original guns are subjected to such treatment from thoughtless owners too lazy to take a few minutes to clean such guns after a day of shooting. It makes little difference if the gun was fired once or a hundred times; the result will be the same, unless time is taken to clean the gun before putting it away, possibly a totally ruined bore.

It's not unusual to get carried away during a shooting session and realize suddenly that you've overstayed your visit. Upon your arrival back at the homestead, you find yourself in a spot: To please the little lady and rush into the shower for that dinner date or to thoroughly clean that pet benchrester.

With the rapidly growing number of new moisture displacing lubricants and special black powder solvents available today, luckily incidents like this can be avoided.

Bucheimer's black powder solvent and Black-Solve are only two of the rapidly growing lines of special black powder solvents that now are available. When presented with the decision of either taking valuable time to clean the bore on a black powder gun or wait until a more convenient time, it now is a quick chore to spray a corrosion-preventing coat of the new solvents into the dirty bore. With the solvent preventing the oxidation process from taking place, cleaning can now be put off for as much as a week. One thing is certain, however, and that is the necessity of cleaning out the gummy residue before the next firing session.

A number of cleaning solvents, including the previously mentioned two, make some of the cleaning easier and less

When design permits, breech end of the barrel can be dunked into the bucket of hot, soapy water and rod pumps the solution in and out through the nipple.

The black powder solvent also serves as rust-preventing compound and can be used on cleaning patches for use in wiping down exterior of the gun as well as in the bore.

Cleaning jags usually are furnished with the gun, can be turned onto end of ramrod to pull patch up, down.

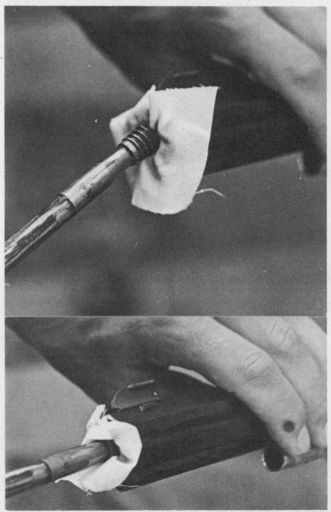

messy, but when used in confined areas, they occasionally leave a strong odor and give off some eye-stinging fumes. For this reason, the majority of today's black powder shooters not having an open, well aired place to clean their guns prefer to use a simple solution of hot soapy water.

When mixing this solution, the hotter the water the better it will clean. The soap — although some shooters prefer one particular brand over the other — can be of the general dish washing variety found at any super market. If lots of suds are your thing, squirt into an empty plastic pail a fairly generous amount of detergent, then fill with the desired amount of hot water.

Of all the muzzleloading rifles I have shot, the easiest to clean is the Thompson/Center Hawken. The hooked breech system on this particular gun allows the barrel to be completely removed within the matter of a few seconds. A wedge through the forearm on this rifle's half-stock also travels through a rectangular slotted loop located on the bottom flat of the octagon barrel. By tapping this wedge to the right, it disengages the loop and frees the barrel from the stock.

The breech plug on the Thompson/Center rifle is in the form of an upward swept hook. This hook fits into a recess located on the barrel tang; with the forward portion of the barrel free from the stock it can be removed by lifting it from the rest of the rifle and allowing the hook to disengage from this recess.

Completely removed from the stock and lock work, the barrel now can be submerged into the soapy water solution. A cleaning method I find quite effective is to place the vent hole end of the barrel into the bucket of water, place a cleaning patch on the ramrod cleaning jag and start pumping. As the ramrod and patch are drawn toward the muzzle, it causes a vacuum which, in turn, causes a fresh supply of hot soapy water to be drawn in through the submerged vent hole. After a few pumps, I find it easy to draw the solution the entire length of the barrel, for a fresh barrel full of cleaning solution with each pump. This system of cleaning hooked breech guns is very effective and results in about as clean a barrel as can be obtained.

Unfortunately, not all rifles and muskets have the hooked breech and cleaning is a little more difficult. Even without a barrel that is removed easily like the Hawken's, there still are easy ways to clean the majority of the muzzleloading rifles and shotguns without having to remove the barrel at all.

If you have lots of time and plenty of cleaning patches, the solvents will do an excellent job of removing powder fouling from not overly dirty bores. For really dirty and built up bores, however, the hot soapy water solution is hard to beat.

A simple but effective way of cleaning the barrels on percussion caplock rifles is to slip a piece of neoprene surgical tubing over the nipple, then drop the other end into a bucket of the soapy water solution. By pumping the ramrod in the same manner as mentioned earlier, the solution will be drawn through the tubing and into the barrel.

Of course, the tubing should form a tight fit to prevent possible leakage of the soap and water onto the stock. Although a small amount of the soapy solution that I commonly use has yet to have any effect on the stock's finish — for the short period of time it is on the wood — there is a possibility that a few of the detergents available could ruin that beautiful high-gloss shine, so be careful not to slosh any out of the muzzle.

Now and then the pumping of the dry bore won't cause enough vacuum to draw the soapy water through the tubing. If you've ever had to use a water pump, you should be familiar with the term priming the pump, which is what you'll have to do to get the water flowing from the bucket and into the barrel. To prime the barrel, for the sake of terming this step, pour a small amount of the water into the muzzle before inserting the cleaning rod and patch, which could also be dipped into the solution first. It is a good practice to place a piece of absorbent cloth around the muzzle to prevent water from running back down onto the stock.

Scrubbing with soap and water should be followed by a thorough rinsing with clean, hot water. This removes the soap film and the surface of the metal dries quickly. As soon as the barrel is dry it should receive a thin coat of moisture displacing oil, such as WD-40 or G96 Gun Treatment. As an extra precaution against rust in the bore, I

G-96's black powder solvent can be sprayed down the bore of black powder firearm as means of temporary protection or after a full course of proper cleaning.

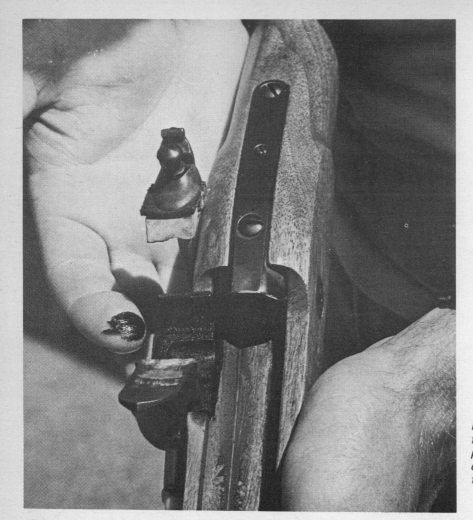

Flintlocks can build up heavy fouling deposits in the priming pan, requiring thorough cleaning and maintenance in this area for protection.

usually follow the drying with a patch soaked in Hoppe's No. 9 solvent run the entire length of the barrel several times. This is followed by several dry patches, then yet another patch sprayed with one of the super lubricant/rust-preventers, such as WD-40.

With the exception of a few late 1700 and early 1800 duellers, few single-shot pistols employed the hook breech. For the most part, these pistols having a caplock can be cleaned in the same basic manner as rifles and shotguns with conventional breech plug. As with the rifles produced by Thompson/Center, however, the firm also uses the hooked breech on their Patriot pistol. The short nine-inch-barrel on this pistol can be totally submerged in a bucket of water, making for easy cleaning.

Unless the barrels can be removed from flintlock rifles, shotguns and pistols, the cleaning of these is a little more time consuming. One of the best methods is to place the bucket of soapy solution near the muzzle, dip the patched cleaning jag into it, then make several complete up and down strokes through the barrel. The patch then is dipped into soapy water again and the process repeated; it may be necessary to change patches after several repetitions to make certain that the bore is getting cleaned thoroughly.

When using a water solution to clean flintlock guns, care should be taken to make sure that some of this water doesn't slosh out of the flash pan's vent hole and onto the stock. It is possible that even the slightest amount of moisture seeping between the metal and wood could result in the bottom of the barrel or the inside of the lock work rusting unnoticed.

Undoubtedly some shooters prefer one particular oil or grease over another, but for the most part, today's scientifically developed gun oils and lubes are just about equally suited for any cleaning and preserving needs. Once a favorite of the black powder shooting crowd of quite a few years ago, sperm oil still is available from several muzzleloading accessory distributors and gunsmithing houses. Brownell's of Montezuma, Iowa, is just one source from which sperm oil is readily available. When using this natural preservative rendered flesh-up from the sperm whale, it is a good practice to place the oil in the refrigerator overnight to allow the fats to harden; the pure oil then can be poured off and this is what should be used.

Kept clean and free of moisture, metal parts on a muzzleloading rifle, musket, pistol or shotgun will last indefinitely. Wood, on the other hand, will deteriorate rather quickly -- at least much faster than the metal — if not well cared for. Oil seepage from the barrel and lock work is one problem that causes discolored and damaged stocks. I never apply more oil than is necessary to coat the metal surfaces in question. Excess oil won't be absorbed by the metal and can only take one other course, running into crevices that usually lead to one area or another of the wooden stock.

Even stocks need an occasional cleaning; the powder fouling that commonly occurs around the nipple or flash pan vent must be wiped off continually or eventually it will ruin the finish in that area of the stock and could possibly soak into the wood and discolor it. Using a dry lather, a mild soap and very little water, the stock can be easily cleaned with the aid of a soft cloth and a soft bristled brush for hard to reach angles and checkering. Wiped clean, a little paste wax and gentle buffing will result in a beautiful luster.

Of all the black powder guns, cap and ball revolvers win the title of being the easiest to clean and care for. Almost all of the replicas and reproduction revolvers presently being sold are generally of two designs, either following the pattern of the open frame Colt or the solid frame Remington. Both of these guns are easily broken down to allow thorough cleaning of each and every part.

To dismantle the Colt, a wedge located just forward of the cylinder is tapped to the left, the hammer is placed at half-cock and the cylinder is rotated until the loading lever comes in contact with the metal separating two of the chambers. By applying pressure on the lever the barrel assembly will disengage the remainder of the percussion revolver. With this removed, the cylinder freely slips off of the cylinder pin or arbor; for general cleaning, this is as far as you should have to break the gun down.

The solid-framed Remington-designed revolvers are almost equally as easy to dismantle. Dropping the loading lever down to where it lies at about a forty-five-degree angle from the barrel, the cylinder pin can be pulled forward. The loading lever is then placed back to its original position and by placing the hammer at half-cock the cylinder should rotate out of the encircling frame.

Of the two types of revolvers, I still find the Colt-patterned guns the easiest to clean. The majority of this cleaning is done to the barrel and cylinder; the frame and grips usually can be wiped clean with a soft cloth and a little oil applied to the metal should be adequate. The barrel and cylinder, however, require a much more thorough cleaning to remove the powder residue left from firing.

The feature that I like best about the Colt-type revolver is the barrel being separate from the frame. This allows the barrel to be scrubbed from the chamber end. Again hot soapy water is about as good as anything for cleaning out residue left from an afternoon's shooting session, but occasionally a really dirty barrel may require a little more. Recently Armite Laboratories of Los Angeles, California, introduced an amazing new bore cleaning agent known as Gun-Soap. My first impression of the product upon opening the glass jar-type container was that it reminded me of lime jelly, if there is such a thing.

The barrel on a Navy Arms' Colt Navy replica that I picked up for little or nothing looked as if it hadn't been cleaned, since it was purchased by its neglectful owner several years earlier. It was almost impossible to make out the rifling because of the built-up powder foulings.

Dismantling the .36 caliber revolver I soaked the cylinder and barrel in a hot soapy water solution for twenty or thirty minutes. Using a wire brush and the Gun-Soap,

G-96's black powder solvent is sprayed in liberal dose over the pan and frizzen of gun as cleaning premininary.

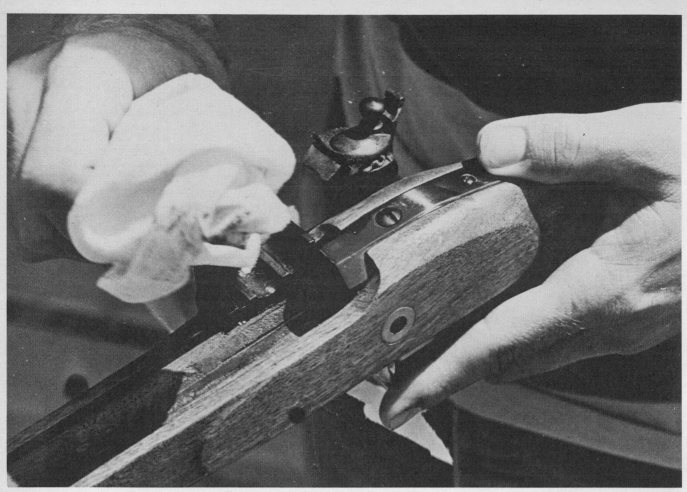

Cleaning rags, as well as old toothbrushes, can be used
in removing solvent-loosened fouling residue in pan.

With cleaning completed, breech hook is re-inserted
under the tang and wedge is replaced to reassemble gun.

along with a little elbow grease, the bore soon was returned to nearly new condition. Although I haven't tried the new cleaning solvent on the barrels of any of my muzzleloading rifles, I personally believe that it would do wonders for a rifle that has become heavily fouled.

The nipples of a percussion revolver usually are one of the little areas that consume a large amount of time when being cleaned. A fast and simple remedy for this is to use an old toothbrush to scrub out residue accumulated in the numerous machined grooves surrounding the nipples.

Again, all cleaning with a detergent and water solution should be followed by a good rinsing in hot and clear water. As an extra precaution to preventing rust, I often find it a good idea to place the washed revolver parts in a warmed oven — 250 degrees or so — to assure that all of the water is completely dried. With Colt-type revolvers this usually consists of just the barrel assembly and the cylinder. On Remington reproductions, however, it is advisable to first remove the wooden grips before placing the rest of the gun into the hot oven; removing the grips before the entire cleaning job is even more advisable.

Reasoning behind the removal of the Remington design revolver's grips before cleaning is to allow the barrel to be scrubbed with water without damaging the finish on the wood. Unlike the Colt replicas, the barrels on these pistols do not separate from the frame. Instead, they must be scrubbed from the muzzle end and, if completely submerged, the internal parts will have to be lubricated after each cleaning. With the removal of the grips, however, the majority of the internal parts can be reached with a pen oiler by the simple removal of the trigger guard.

Never reassemble any gun that has been cleaned in water until each and every part has been oiled or, as is the case with the cylinder pins on a cap and ball revolver, greased.

It's not uncommon to run into an occasional shooter who is experiencing all sorts of trouble in cocking a cap and ball revolver. Part of the time this can be attributed to the lack of enough clearance between the chamber mouth and the breech of the barrel or the lack of lubrication — grease — on the arbor or cylinder pin. There are all sorts of fancy special purpose greases that will work nicely, but one that I find to be just as suitable and much cheaper is regular automotive grease.

Muzzleloaders have a way of mellowing with age, especially if they are well taken care of and cleaned regularly. Remember, it's nearly impossible to over-clean a black powder gun, but one that isn't cleaned properly is just as bad off as one that isn't cleaned at all.

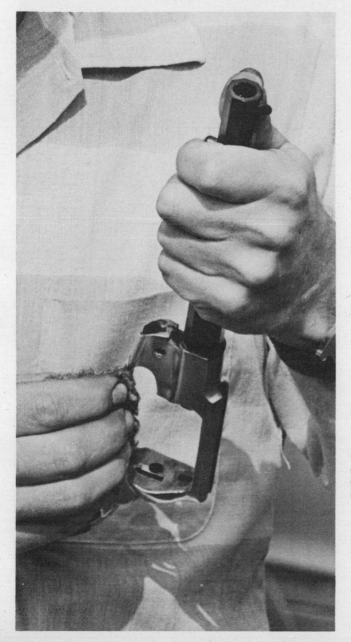

Since guns of the Remington pattern are not readily capable of separating barrel and frame, care must be taken, as discussed here, to prevent damage to the lockwork from water or fouling.

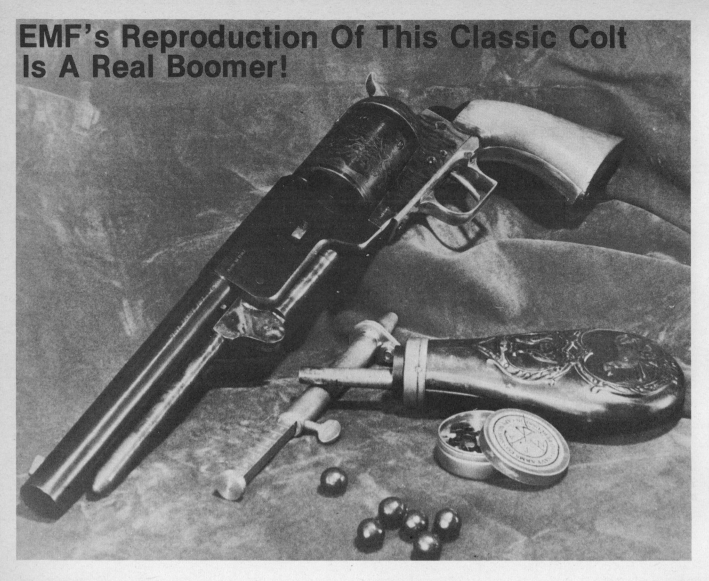

CHAPTER 11

WRINGING OUT THE WALKER

CAPTAIN SAMUEL H. WALKER of the Texas Rangers was a massive man, as mentioned in an earlier chapter. Consequently, he fit well into the territory where he did a big job with a rugged organization.

Samuel Colt was a genius in the field of firearms. His ingenuity was obvious in both the inventive and manufacturing fields.

When Sam Walker teamed with Sam Colt to design and build a handgun for military use, the outcome could not have been anything less than what it was; the Colt Walker Dragoon.

This hybrid would stand out from other handguns for its huge engineering. The ponderous Walker obviously thought big when he told Colt what the military needed and Colt was the man to deliver.

A gent named Eddie Paul is one of those who was smitten by an advertisement from Early & Modern Firearms proclaiming their version of the Colt Walker to be the "largest of the Colt percussion pistols."

"Up until then, I had considered my modest collection of firearms complete in that, at least, it partially covered the whole spectrum. They range from a miniscule Derringer on the lower end of the scale up to my .44 magnum Ruger Blackhawk.

"It didn't bother me, knowing there were smaller guns than the particular Derringer I possessed, but when I

The replica of the Colt Walker, with its four-pound, nine-ounce weight, 15½-inch overall length, even tends to dwarf the .44 magnum Ruger blackhawk. Unlike other Colt models of the era, Walker had no catch on rammer lever.

thought there might be a gun out there larger than my .44 magnum, I couldn't rest until I had one of these replica Walkers."

After phoning in his order, Paul then became even more anxious and drove from his Los Angeles home to nearby Glendale, where EMF is headquartered.

"I exchanged my hard-earned cash for a large, rectangular box," he recalls. "The shipping weight was marked at seven pounds, so it had to be the Walker, reputedly the largest handgun ever manufactured."

On hefting the Walker, Paul rapidly came to the conclusion that it never was meant for fast draw. "On the other hand, I can't imagine anyone challenging a man who had one," he states, referring to history.

Aside from a few Italian proof marks and a serial number above 8000 (the original Walker never reached 1001), it is a good copy. The metal to metal was the same quality as that of his Ruger .44 magnum Blackhawk, Paul insists.

The grips finish off the 15½ inches of a purely functional, no-nonsense design (except for the engraving on the cylinder) and are in keeping with the original Walkers. When you hold the Walker you know why the Comanches are not around now. The dragoon was built for men and no others need apply.

Possibly the most unusual feature of the Colt Walker, aside from its Paul Bunyan size and its four-pound nine-ounce weight, is the left-handed arrangement of the barrel wedge. This was contrary to the arrangement of the wedge on the preceding and succeeding models made by Colt. Southpaw Sam Walker made this gun an extension of his own personality and, ironically enough, never took delivery of one. He was killed in combat before the gun was in production.

"Although this particular gun sounded better than most replicas when checked out unloaded and would satisfy most people, I always take the two hours or so that is required to tune any new gun I acquire," Paul advises.

A single-action revolver is checked by slowly drawing back the hammer while holding the gun up near the ear. You not only can feel but hear any roughness in the mechanism as the hammer, bolt, cylinder and trigger go through their cycle. After a tune-up this should be a smooth, quiet operation.

Although a gunsmith quite often needs an array of files and abrasive stones, a Dremel tool and emery cloth will clean up the parts in most replicas. Paul found them exceptionally smooth, which eliminated much of the basic filing.

He polished the face of the hammer where one finds the trigger notches, the trigger nose, bolt cam face and the limb of the bolt with rubbing compound, then reassembled the gun. On rechecking, he found the action as smooth as that of any single-action revolver in his collection, he reports.

The next thing was to truck it out to the firing range for testing. A good stout horse will do in lieu of a truck. Needless to say, everyone wanted to examine the dragoon, but they gave Paul a wide berth when he prepared to fire it.

"I loaded the Walker with 40.0 grains of FFFg, followed by a 128-grain .44 ball and topped off with a liberal amount of Hodgdon's Spit Ball to prevent the possibility of a chain fire. Six number 11 Navy Arms caps were installed and the gun was ready to speak its peace.

"The Walker sometimes was used with a detachable rifle stock and, after raising the heavy weight onto the target, I began to wish I had one. But until I did, I would have to use both hands to hold up the Walker. At that time, I realized how light my .44 magnum Blackhawk was by comparison.

"The hammer was drawn back slowly and I noticed the small crowd taking one step backwards with each progressive click of the hammer until it was at full cock. I took a deep breath, lined up the hammer notch with the target and lowered the front brass sight into the center of the target. I slowly squeezed the trigger. A flash of fire, a sound of thunder and a cloud of smoke preceded the longest length of silence this firing range had ever known, as everyone tried to figure out what caused the explosion," Paul relates.

Paul next was bombarded with a barrage of questions pertaining to his new Walker. With all the commotion, he forgot to look at the target. He later found it was in the 8 ring at one o'clock.

"If you purchase a Walker, you will save a lot of money on powder, despite the fact that the Walker uses twice the load of a normal .44. You shoot it once and answer twenty questions, shoot again and answer another twenty questions, ad infinitum.

"Because of this strange side effect, it is beneficial that you become an expert on the history of the Walker, so you can amaze your new-found friends with trivial information.

"There are many old stories about the devastating effects of being on the receiving end of the Walker and, although I can't attest to their validity, I know that, from being in the operator position for six rounds, the receiving end has to be a lousy location.

"After fighting off the crowds, I managed to complete the testing and, with a little practice, could get 3½-inch groups at twenty-five yards for as long as the powder held out," says Paul.

Although following the same general principles of design, the replica of the Walker Colt appears mammoth when it is compared in size with a modern reproduction of Samuel Colt's New Model Navy revolver, made during the same era. According to claims of Early and Modern Firearms, the replica comes close to being today's most powerful handgun.

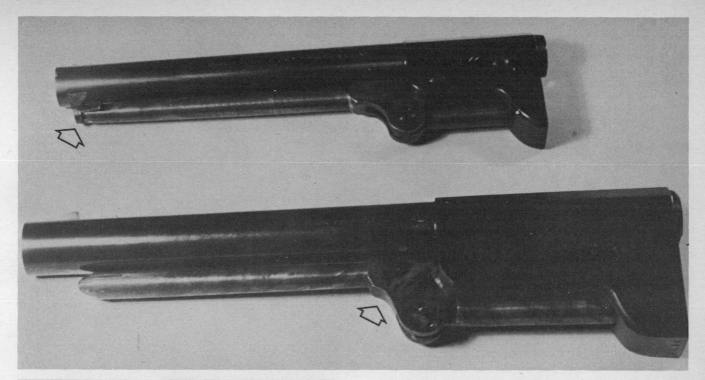

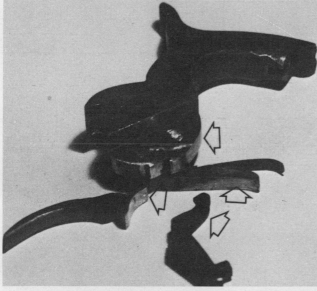

The nine-inch barrel of the Walker replica (at bottom) shows the loading lever catch near the pivot point, while catch on Navy model is at end of the loading lever.

Arrows indicate areas that were polished with rubbing compound. Included are the face of the hammer, trigger nose, bolt cam face and limb of the bolt. Little work was required, we found, and polishing smoothed up action.

The next step was a trip to the Angeles National Forest for some magnum loads. The results of which were, to say the least, unexpected.

The Walker was loaded to maximum capacity of 50.0 grains of FFFg, with balls of 127.5 grains. Upon touching off the first round on the .44, it was evident the Walker would be quite capable of stopping any Comanche.

In fact, after shooting test rounds into a water-logged telephone directory, Paul found the Walker would penetrate deeper than a .45 auto with a 173-grain, round-nose lead slug.

"I also found that, with the ball-to-powder ratio I was using I could expect a velocity of over 1800 fps and a muzzle energy in the neighborhood of 1100 foot-pounds. This is compared to my .44 magnum loads of 1570 on velocity and with an energy of 1313."

We should point out our feeling that, while Eddie Paul might expect 1800 fps of muzzle velocity with his 127.5-grain round lead ball and 50.0 grains of FFFg powder, there is grave doubt that an accurate chronograph would confirm such performance.

Lyman's Black Powder Handbook lists 960 fps as the velocity for a .451-inch round ball weighing 138 grains, when driven by 37.0 grains of FFFg from an eight-inch barrel. It seems doubtful that Paul's load could exceed 1100 fps, as nearly as we are able to extrapolate from the Lyman data.

In any event, the laws of physics being as they are, 127.5 grains at 1800 fps comes out at 917.5 foot-pounds of energy rather than the 100 figure he mentions. The same projectile, fired at 1100 fps, would carry 324.6 foot-pounds, as we interpret it.

As of this date, Eddie Paul has sent some thirty pounds of lead through the nine-inch barrel of the Walker with no problem other than a strange limp acquired from carrying the Walker on his right hip. He has been assured by Ed Spinney of EMF that this problem can be easily rectified by purchasing another Walker and carrying it on his left hip.

"Now if I can only convince my wife that the next Walker is for medicinal purposes, I've got it made!"

RETURN OF THE HAWKEN

Thompson/Center's Modern Reproduction Of The Hawken Half-Stock Rifle Is One Of The Finest Muzzleloaders Available Today!

CHAPTER 12

THE PROFESSIONAL HUNTER and mountain man of the early 1800s usually carried among his prized possessions a short and heavy barreled half-stock muzzle-loading rifle. For the most part, these were nearly always well built and were so made that they would withstand a considerable amount of hard use, be it on the trapline, following the buffalo herds, putting camp meat on the meat pole or fighting Indians, the latter being a peril often en-countered while in pursuit of the first three.

One such rifle favored and highly prized by these hardy individuals was produced by Jacob Hawken and later by his brother, Samuel, at their St. Louis, Missouri, plant. Jacob was the first to go into the gunmaking business and perhaps the earliest remaining record of his exploits in the manu-facture of firearms is his listing in the 1821 St. Louis directory. It seems that all records of the Hawken factory

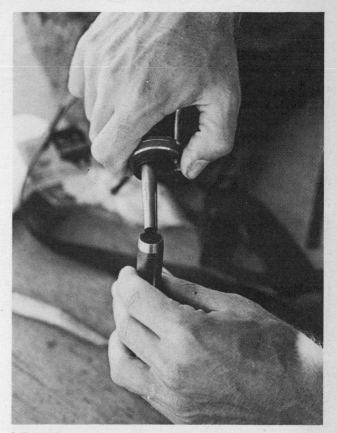

Not an exact copy of the original, the Thompson/Center Hawken does feature the styling and feel of the famous Hawken gun.

Adjustable powder measure makes weighing exact charges simple. Below, the patched ball after the excess patching is trimmed.

were destroyed upon Jacob's death during the cholera epidemic of May, 1849; the loss of all such record is perhaps the reason that a cloud of mystery and uncertainty hangs over the authenticity of many early Hawken type rifles of reputed manufacture. Genuine Hawken-built rifles are among today's most sought collector pieces and their value is so great that few, if any, are taken to the field for actual hunting or continuous firing.

Originally built as an extremely rugged hunter's rifle to withstand the hardest of use, the Hawken rifles featured heavy octagon barrels and were commonly of large caliber for use on game as large as buffalo or elk. The stocks almost always were cut and shaped to be strictly functional without any fancy frills; for the most part these were of half-stock design, although there were a few full stock Hawkens produced. Since these guns were handmade there were slight differences from one rifle to another; placement of sights, shape of the iron butt plate, stock lines, et al.

Ten years after his brother's death, Samuel Hawken moved the gunmaking operation to Denver, Colorado. With the assistance of his son in carrying on the family tradition, he continued to produce the Hawken rifles in Denver until 1861, returning to St. Louis and reopening the shop there once more. A year later, he sold the shop to former employee John P. Gremer, who continued to turn out rifles under the Hawken name for some years.

Through the popularity of such rifles, the name Hawken is occasionally used to describe the general type of buffalo, plains or mountain man rifle built on the lines of the Hawken-built originals.

With collectors placing high value on original Hawkens, such rifles are nearly always only seen at gun shows. For the hunter wishing to own this type of durable hunting black powder rifle, however, a reproduction of the Hawken now is being produced at the Rochester, New Hampshire, plant of Thompson/Center Arms Company.

Available in .45 and .50 caliber, the Thompson/Center Hawken does feature some design changes, a number of which make the reproduction gun even more reliable that were the originals. The rifle does, however, retain the husky feel and eye-pleasing lines of the original; the firm admits that their Hawken isn't an exact replica, but is a well built and dependable gun of the general type.

Unlike the iron furniture found on the original Hawken-built rifles, the Thompson/Center rifles sport polished brass

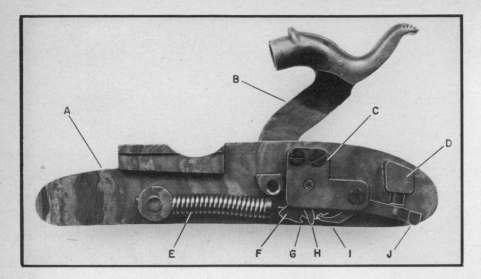

Hawken lock: (A) lock plate; (B) hammer; (C) bridle; (D) sear spring; (E) coil main-spring; (F) tumbler; (G) half-cock notch; (H) detent; (I) sear nose engaging full-cock notch; (J) sear. Below middle, ball is started down barrel with wooden short starter. Bottom, flash pan of flintlock is primed.

ramrod thimbles, butt plates, patch boxes, and nose caps on the short half-stock walnut stock; few originals were fitted with patch boxes. The trigger guard on guns produced before 1972 were made from beautifully color case-hardened iron. Since then, however, the firm has been installing polished brass trigger guards on the new Hawken rifle.

The double-set triggers on the new rifle are designed so that the rifle can serve a dual purpose, as both a fine hunting rifle and a reliably accurate target rifle. The clever design makes it possible to fire the Hawken by completely bypassing the rear set trigger, should a snap shot present itself while hunting. On the other hand, the front trigger can be set so that it will release at the slightest amount of pressure by first pulling the rear trigger. This hair trigger makes the Thompson/Center gun a fairly accurate off-hand or light benchrest target rifle.

A feature that should be equally pleasing to the black powder shooter who can't stand the messy chore of cleaning his favorite smokepole after an afternoon of shooting it is the easy removal of the Hawken's barrel from the rest of the rifle. This is accomplished through the patented or hooked breech system; the rear of the breech plug forms a hook that fits into a recess of the tang and the front of the barrel is held in place by a wedge that travels through two plates in the stock and a loop located on the bottom flat of the octagon barrel.

To remove the barrel, the ramrod is first removed from the thimbles and placed aside. The hammer is then placed at half-cock, or in the safety position. The barrel wedge is carefully tapped from the slot through which it holds the barrel in place. With this done, all that remains to do is grasp the barrel near the muzzle and lift upward until the hooked breech frees itself from the recess in the tang. This makes cleaning easier and prevents accidental staining of the stock with strong solvents.

With the barrel removed, the breech end of the Hawken's barrel can be placed into a pail of hot soapy water. The ramrod — with the cleaning jag attached — and a cleaning patch are inserted into the muzzle. Each time the ramrod is drawn toward the muzzle the air-tight fit of the patch will cause a vacuum and the soapy solution will be sucked into the barrel through the vent hole. This pumping action will keep a constant fresh supply of hot water coming into and leaving the bore of the barrel and results in as clean a barrel as possible. As soon as all powder foulings are removed the barrel is removed from the water and swabbed with dry patches until it has cooled; this is followed by running a patch lightly coated with lubricant

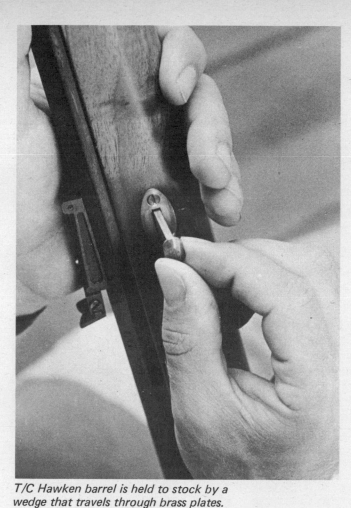

T/C Hawken barrel is held to stock by a
wedge that travels through brass plates.

The hooked breech results in easy takedown.

the entire length of the barrel.

Of all the design changes on the new Hawken, perhaps
the most interesting are those that have been made in the
lock itself. On both the flintlock and percussion lock
models, the flat springs usually found in these mechanisms
have been replaced with coil springs. A flat spring may be
more original, but the coil springs are less likely to break,
especially the heavy duty type used in the new Hawken. To
utilize the coil spring, however, several other internal designs had to be changed; such changes may make the lock
different from the original on the inside, but the outside
appearance remains basically the same as that of locks
found on rifles manufactured better than a hundred years
ago.

Both the .45 and .50 caliber Hawkens are fitted with a
twenty-eight-inch button rifled barrel. This high quality
octagon barrel features a one turn in forty-eight inches
twist rifling. To the beginning black powder enthusiasts this
may seem rather slow, and it is. Black powder rifles have to
be rifled with long land patterns to make them accurate
since they have relatively slow muzzle velocities.

When care is taken to load the Hawken properly, it is
about as accurate a black powder rifle as can be found.
Fitted with a high-bladed front sight and an open rear sight
that is fully adjustable for windage and elevation, the gun is
an ideal hunting rifle. Although not standard equipment on
the rifle, Thompson/Center also manufactures an accurate
vernier tang rear sight. This aperture type "peep sight" is
easily attached to the barrel tang which is already drilled to
accept the sight.

Packed with each rifle that leaves the factory is an in-

formative booklet containing information that the beginning black powder shooter would be wise to know before venturing afield with the new Hawken. Within its sixteen pages, the booklet explains how to care for the rifle, gives some background on its original manufacture and most important, it gives good starting loads for the beginner.

Thompson/Center recommends the following loads:

POWDER CHARGE	CALIBER/BALL DIAMETER	MUZZLE VELOCITY	MUZZLE ENERGY
50 grains FFFg	.45 caliber/.440 ball	1605 fps	732 ft. lbs.
50 grains FFg	.50 caliber/.490 ball	1357 fps	761 ft. lbs.
60 grains FFFg	.45 caliber/.440 ball	1720 fps	841 ft. lbs.
60 grains FFg	.50 caliber/.490 ball	1434 fps	850 ft. lbs.
70 grains FFFg	.45 caliber/.440 ball	1825 fps	947 ft. lbs.
70 grains FFg	.50 caliber/.490 ball	1643 fps	1115 ft. lbs.
80 grains FFFg	.45 caliber/.440 ball	1929 fps	1054 ft. lbs.
80 grains FFg	.50 caliber/.490 ball	1838 fps	1396 ft. lbs.
90 grains FFFg	.45 caliber/.440 ball	2003 fps	1140 ft. lbs.
90 grains FFg	.50 caliber/.490 ball	1950 fps	1570 ft. lbs.
100 grains FFFg	.45 caliber/.440 ball	2081 fps	1231 ft. lbs.
100 grains FFg	.50 caliber/.490 ball	2052 fps	1739 ft. lbs.
110 grains FFFg	.45 caliber/.440 ball	2158 fps	1324 ft. lbs.
110 grains FFg	.50 caliber/.490 ball	2135 fps	1883 ft. lbs.

Black powder buff Ray Taylor gives Jock Mahoney some personal tips on muzzleloading practices during the range session with T/C's Hawken.

Although the loads having the greatest amount of powder displayed more punch — on both ends — we found that most of the milder loads were the most accurate. Tests were made with both a .45 caliber percussion lock and a .50 caliber flintlock Hawken, in both guns patched round balls were used for the most part; some tests were made with Minie bullets moulded in a Lyman No. 445599 mould.

Working with the .45 caliber percussion Hawken first, 50 grains of FFFg printed five of the patched 128-grain .440 round balls into something resembling a group eight inches below the point of aim when fired from a hundred yards; 60 grains brought the shots up to the point of aim but did little to improve the group tightness.

An increase of another ten grains proved too much as far as accuracy was concerned; dropping to 65 grains of FFFg the Hawken consistently printed its shots into the four-inch bullseye. One charge of 100 grains was all we needed to decide that it was more than necessary, sending burning

powder several feet from the end of the muzzle; the short twenty-eight-inch barrel didn't allow enough room for this much powder to be ignited completely and we doubt if those flames chasing the ball to the target are that beneficial once it leaves the barrel.

This rifle had been fitted with one of Thompson/Center's Puma pistol scopes before test firing. This scope is easily fitted to the rifle and requires no additional drilling on the octagon barrel. To install, the rear sight of the Hawken is removed by unscrewing the two small screws in its base. The base of the scope is then attached to the barrel by the same screws and holes, both matching perfectly. The scope tube is then attached to the base mount by two hex screws that align with two notches in the flat rail that travels the bottom length of the 1½X scope.

Using the standard open sights that come on the Hawken, there was little difference in the results obtained

Jock Mahoney's offhand shot with the half-stocked T/C Hawken replica results in cloud of black smoke as the first ball is sent toward the target in the range test.

Mahoney points with obvious pride to the X-ring hole left by his first shot with Thompson/Center Hawken.

with .50 caliber flintlock. We did notice, however, that the pre-ignition of the primed flash pan was enough to occasionally cause the shooter to flinch slightly and ruin his groupings. Working with a variety of powder charge weights, we finally established 70 grains of FFg as the best all-around load; 65 grains of FFFg worked nearly as well but the groups weren't as tight. One thing was evident: These .50 caliber balls carried a lot of punch, making the rifle an ideal choice for primitive weapon big game hunts.

Thompson/Center recommends that the patching be lightly coated with lubricant such as Vaseline, Crisco or one of the commercially produced black powder rifle lubes. Hodgdon's Spit Patch was used extensively during the test firing and worked very well. We did find it necessary to wipe the bore partially clean of powder fouling after every six to ten shots, varying according to the amount of powder used; the more powder used, the more the bore would build up.

The nipple of the .45 caliber percussion rifle uses standard No. 11 caps; although the sizes of caps have a tendency to vary from one source to another — like trying to fit a pair of number seven shoes on a number eight pair of feet — both No. 11 caps produced by Remington and those offered by Navy Arms fit the nipple with just the right amount of snugness. The flash pan on the flintlock is best primed with FFFFg black powder, but FFFg will work almost equally as well.

Selling at $175 for the percussion and $190 for the flintlock, the price seems quite reasonable when you consider that Thompson/Center backs these guns with a lifetime warranty. For $20 more the guns come complete with an accessory kit that includes everything to get the purchaser to the range and the bullet to the target — except for the black powder, cap and balls, that is!

THE GREAT KENTUCKY COME BACK

Navy Arm's Reproduction Of The Kentucky Pistol Is A Boon To Both The Serious Collector And Shooter!

CHAPTER 13

OFTEN SOUGHT by today's dedicated antique arms collectors, the Kentucky pistol was the first truly domestic handgun of the United States.

Prior to the Revolutionary War, American gunmakers were practically nil. Almost all arms still were being produced in Europe, where gunmakers had been in the business for several hundred years. It was during the years leading into the Revolution, that U.S. armsmakers began to produce their long rifles, most of which are erroneously labeled as Kentucky rifles. It was through this mislabeling, though, that the Kentucky pistol may also have received its unwarranted title. Actually, the majority of both pistols and long rifles were handcrafted by gunsmiths in other gunmaking states, such as Pennsylvania, New York and a few other East Coast colonies.

In form, the Kentucky pistol was commonly far less fancy than those produced in Europe; ferrules on the forestock were often left off, ramrod thimbles were simpler in design, and the barrels — sometimes made of brass — were commonly much heavier than, say, a British dueller. The pistol did, however, fulfill the need for an accompanying sidearm for the American long rifle.

Now considered an important piece of Americana, collectors have placed so much emphasis on Kentucky pistols that it is about impossible to find them at any price — reasonable or otherwise. As mentioned, these pistols were produced before the introduction of mass production, being completely assembled from parts made entirely by the same method.

To make available a pistol of this type for those collectors and shooters that can't afford an original — or can afford but are wise enough not to subject them to the rigors of everyday firing — several of today's black powder gun distributors are offering modern-made replicas of the general pattern.

One such replica that stands out in both quality and authenticity is the Kentucky pistol available from the Navy Arms Company. This particular pistol is the result of years of studying the Kentucky pistol designs and the evaluation of numerous prototypes by Navy Arms' president Val Forgett.

Like the first American-made pistol of nearly two hundred years ago, this Italian replica is assembled by skilled hand craftsmen. The parts, however, are produced in larger quantities through modern mass production. Actually these parts are probably much more uniform than the handcrafted ones built during the late 1700s, each built to a standard pattern. Original handmade gun parts almost always varied from one piece to another, even when built by the same gunsmith.

Truthfully, a pistol of this type has little practical use in the field. The fixed sights are hardly target quality, the cumbersome shape of the gun makes it impractical to carry for any length of time and its single-shot concept practically rules it out as a choice for a hunting arm. They are, however, an economical answer to filling the gap left in many collections that are in need of such a gun.

The Navy Arms Kentucky pistol is available in either percussion or flintlock. Both guns are fitted with an oil-finished walnut stock as well as a 10¼-inch rifled brass barrel. The lock plates, hammers and flash pan on the flintlock models are beautifully color case-hardened. The lock screws that run through the stock are held in place by an inlaid press side-plate on the left side, screwing into the lock plate itself on the right.

The solid walnut stock is set off by polished brass thimbles, trigger guard and forend schnabel. The ramrod appears to be made of hickory, stained with walnut tones so it matches the stock. The metal tip on this is also made of polished brass.

Of all the Italian proof marks on the .44 caliber brass barrel, two are easily identified. One appears as two bayonet-equipped rifles in the crossed position, back-grounded by a hammer. This is encircled by an outline resembling a medieval shield and topped by a single star over something resembling a toothed gear. This is the house proof mark of the Gardone Val Trompia Proof House. The other proof mark is yet another gear background star over the upper case letters PN. In 1950, this mark was adopted to distinguish black powder arms that rated a definitive proof of 8,800 psi.

The lock bolt plate on the replica is similar to the lock design used on the pistols produced by Joseph Long in his Snyder County, Pennsylvania, gunsmithery around 1800. The stock, on the other hand, is quite different from Long's pistols. Instead of the rounded butt commonly found on early Kentucky pistols, the Navy Arms model features a definite edge in place of the rounded contour.

The barrel is well inletted into the stock, as is the lock and brass trigger guard. The two brass ramrod thimbles are attached firmly to the stock by several pins through the wood and matching holes in the ferrules.

Although the sights are fixed and, as mentioned, are a far cry from target sights, the gun shoots with fair accuracy. The best results were obtained when firing a patched .430 ball in front of twenty-six grains of FFFg powder. When a ball closer to the actual .440 diameter bore was used, the patching wouldn't allow the lead ball to pass into the muzzle at the projectile's widest point.

Several shots were made with just the ball and without the patching. As can be expected, the results were less than desirable. No two shots flew in the same direction; one shot would hit high and to the left, the next low and to the right, etc. The smaller the ball — of less diameter than that of the bore — the more erratic the placement of the shots.

Possibly the gases escaping around the open space left by the smaller projectile can be credited with the extreme deviation of the points of impact. This theory is partially backed by the betterment of the results as soon as cotton patching of .011-inch thickness was used.

With the aforementioned 26-grain loads and the patched .430 balls, the placement of the shots were a little more consistent. By consistent, it is meant that they at least hit the cardboard holding the target — and occasionally even hitting the latter — from a range of twenty-five yards. If the groups were to be measured, it is a safe estimation to say that ten shots were placed into an area of around two feet in diameter, hardly a match winner!

Surprisingly enough, quite a few shooters become so accustomed to firing a pistol of this type that they become quite proficient with it. Usually, this is after many test firing sessions to find just the right load for that particular gun and, more often than not, after some tinkering around with the sights; with usually around an eight to ten-inch barrel, it only stands to reason that such guns should be somewhat accurate.

Originally these guns were built as a sidearm to accompany the early domestic long rifles, so what could be more challenging than to carry a replica of this particular design as a back-up gun when hunting with a black powder rifle? This should have a certain amount of appeal if the target of the hunt is to be such ill-tempered game as the wild boar.

Lock plate of the Navy Arms Kentucky pistol is color case-hardened and adds greatly to the overall appearance of reproduction gun.

Of all the proof marks on the 10¼-inch rifled brass barrel, shooter would be wise to follow warning to use only black powder in pistol.

The dovetailed brass front sight blade is similar to those installed on original pistols of more than a hundred years ago. Schnabel and ramrod fittings are also made of brass.

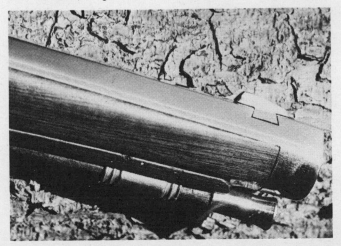

As a safety precaution, shooter at left first measures out correct powder charge with the aid of powder measure.

With Kentucky pistol braced against knee, patched ball is seated.

Although the barrel of the Navy Arms Kentucky pistol is longer than that found on the majority of the black powder pistols, it still isn't long enough to allow large charges of powder to be fully utilized. Simply, this means that large amounts of powder will only result in much of this powder to be still burning as the ball leaves the barrel. This does little to improve accuracy or increase the projectile's penetrating capability.

It was found that any charge of more than 33 grains of FFFg was only a waste of powder when fired from the 10¼ inch brass barrel. This load, however, proved to be one of the most inaccurate, but displayed the most penetrating power — a good point to keep in mind if the gun is to be used as a back-up gun on a primitive hunt. With this load the soft lead ball easily penetrated the thickness of a two by six pine board, good enough to put the finishing touch to a wounded wild boar, bear, cougar or other game that could be listed as being dangerous, especially if wounded.

The Kentucky pistol leaves a lot to be desired when it comes to target shooting or hunting, but they are an interesting part of American history and still are a lot of fun to shoot.

Pistol of the Kentucky type are awkward to load, best method is to place butt against the ground and keep muzzle away from face (right). The flash pan is primed (below) and the pistol is ready to fire.

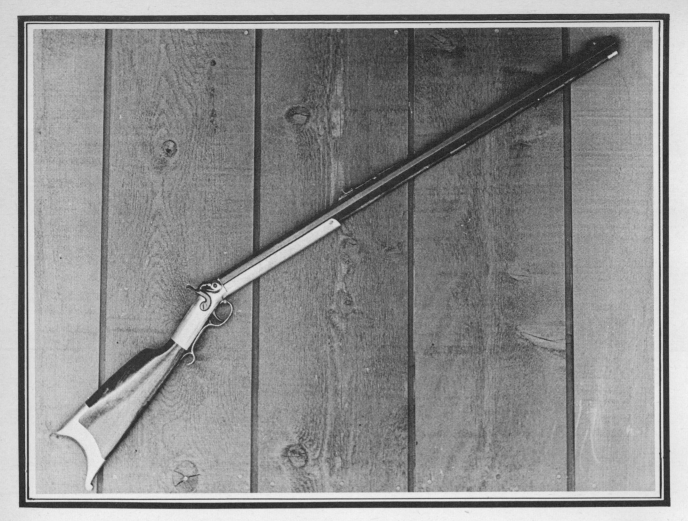

MOWREY'S ETHAN ALLEN RIFLE

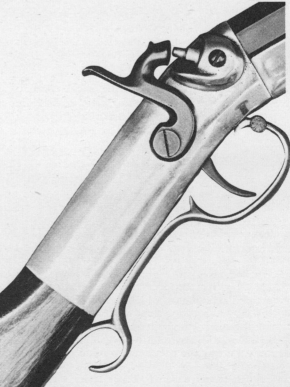

As discussed here, the action is notable for its sleek lines and simplicity. Round object at the front of the trigger guard is a nail which supports it on wall.

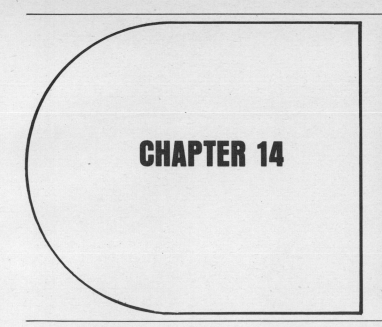

CHAPTER 14

Once A Favorite Of Early Frontiersmen, The Allen & Thurber Rifle Is Once Again Being Built For Today's Discriminating Black Powder Enthusiast!

Below: a simple blade foresight is attached near the muzzle by means of a dovetailed base mount.

OF ALL THE MUZZLELOADING RIFLES produced by the Nineteenth Century gunmakers, the excellent long rifles produced by Ethan Allen at his Grafton, Massachusetts, gunmaking facilities are probably the least understood — and undoubtedly the least written about.

Little known, except by those dedicated to studying the history of the firearm in the United States and the serious antique arm collector, is the fact that Allen actually was the first maker of pepperbox pistols in this country. In 1834, he was granted the first U.S. patent for handguns of this design. His was a revolving pepperbox, no doubt a refinement of similar guns being built in Europe at the time.

For a number of years after he began production of his pepperboxes, he was the only mass producer of such handguns; his competition was mainly from numerous small gunsmithing firms, most of which either soon folded or sold out to larger operations.

In his book, "Roughing It," Mark Twain's writings concerning the Allen pepperbox pistol made the gun famous, if not notorious. The small multi-shot handgun delivered tremendous firepower considering its size and was easy to conceal, a perfect choice of armament for some shady characters. The majority of today's so-called up-to-date and comprehensive publications on firearms, however, fail to make any mention of the rifles made by Allen. Even when the authors and editors of such books cast some light on this mystery to the black powder shooter, they usually do so briefly.

As mentioned, Ethan Allen began producing his pepperbox pistols in his plant at Grafton, Massachusetts, after receiving his patent of 1834. Several years later, in 1837, he formed a partnership with his brother-in-law, Charles T. Thurber, and the firm's name was changed to Allen & Thurber. Under this name — at the Grafton, Massachusetts,

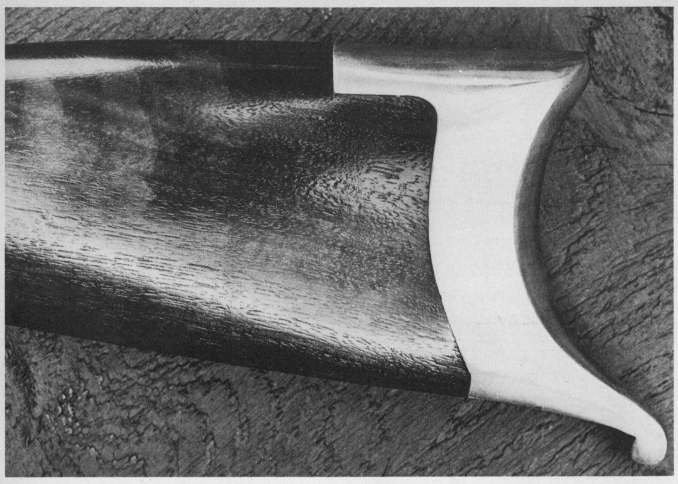

The highly polished brass butt plate is fitted meticulously to the walnut of the stock, which has had ten hand-rubbed coats of oil finish applied.

location — they continued to make pepperbox pistols, some single-shot pistols and an accurate, well built rifle.

Apparently, family ties weren't all that strong between Allen and Thurber, for in 1856 Allen dissolved the partnership with his by-marriage relative, only to form yet another partnership with another brother-in-law, Thomas P. Wheelock.

Under the firm name of Allen & Wheelock — located in Worchester, Massachusetts, having moved from Norwich, Connecticut, yet another previous move made while still in partnership with Thurber — they continued to produce their line of wares on through the Civil War.

In 1865, the name was changed once more, this time to E. Allen & Company and was so named until Ethan Allen's death in 1871. Allen's two sons-in-law, Sullivan Forehand and Henry Wadsworth, took control of the company and ran it under the name of Forehand & Wadsworth; in 1890 this was changed to the Forehand Arms Company.

Although at one time or another the Allen firm, run by him or by later members of his family, produced numerous styles and designs of both percussion and cartridge revolvers, rifles, pistols and even shotguns, it is the rifles produced under the name of Allen & Thurber that are probably of the most importance to today's black powder enthusiast.

Allen & Thurber rifles aren't as well known as their pepperboxes, but those shooters and collectors that are familiar with them consider them of top quality. Of simple design and solid construction, many a westward traveller and frontiersman chose to shoulder one in place of such well known rifles as the famous guns produced by Jacob Hawken in his St. Louis shop.

The W. L. Mowrey Gun Works of Olney, Texas, now is producing an exact replica of the Allen & Thurber rifle for those shooters wanting what the makers consider the ultimate in a black powder hunting muzzleloader. As on the original Allen & Thurber, simplicity of design is one of the rifle's strongest selling points.

Unique in design, the lock features only two actual moving parts, the trigger and tumbler. The lack of numerous moving parts on this simple lock almost guarantees the shooter years of trouble-free shooting. The internal lock work is housed inside a hollow, high density brass casing. This brass action housing also serves as the wrist of the stock, breech plug and nipple seat; even the cleanout screw threads into this.

In addition to the trigger and tumbler, the lock is made up of two springs and a single pin. The shaft of the tumbler passes through the right side of the brass casing and attaches to the hammer on the outside. Anyway you look at it, it's about as simple as you can get!

The thirty-one-inch barrel features eight-groove rifling; the lands and grooves of about equal width. Although only

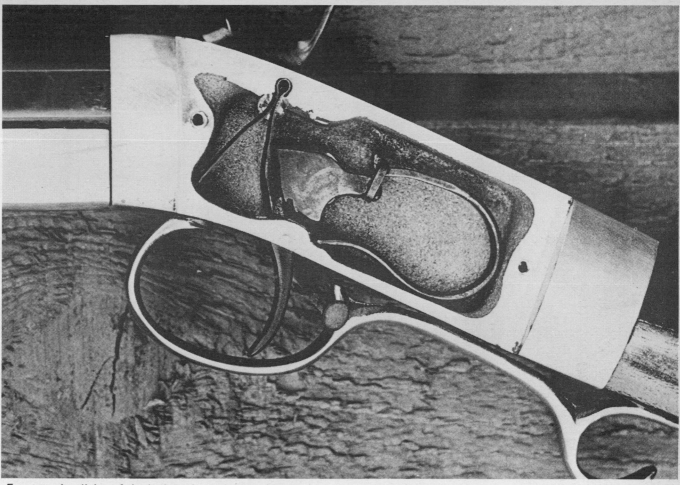

*Extreme simplicity of the lockwork can be seen here.
Trigger and tumbler are the only moving parts.*

.010-inch in depth, shallow rifling of this type has actually proven superior to rifling with much deeper grooves. As black powder burns, it tends to leave a considerable amount of residue within the barrel. Deep grooves only result in a bigger build up of this residue and actually make loading subsequent shots only more difficult.

By utilizing eight-groove rifling in the Mowrey replica of the Allen & Thurber, the shallow .010-inch lands and grooves hold the patched ball just as securely as six or four-groove rifling having a deeper cut. Not only does this make it possible to load more shots between barrel cleanings, but it also resists stripping under heavy charges.

Conventionally, the barrels on muzzleloading rifles have a twist somewhere in the neighborhood of one turn in forty-eight inches. The Mowrey, however, has a somewhat slower rate of twist in its barrel, at one turn in sixty inches. Combined with the thirty-one-inch length of the barrel, this slow twist allows the usage of heavy charges without noticable loss in accuracy. Again, the slow twist resists stripping of the bore when heavy charges are being used; this is especially an added advantage when target shooting or hunting on a windy day.

Each gun produced at the Olney, Texas, plant can be considered sort of a semi-custom job, with many of the processes in its manufacture being either done partially or completely by hand. One example of this is the beautiful walnut stock. Each stock is custom fitted to the rifle, a process that can only be accomplished through hand labor.

In addition, each stock receives ten coats of hand-rubbed oil finish to give the walnut the high luster it deserves. As on the Allen & Thurber replica, only the butt-stock is of walnut, the forend is made from the same Inco brass used in the action housing. The result is a good looking and well balanced rifle well suited for either bench or off-hand shooting.

Available in .45, .50 and .54 calibers, this long barreled black powder rifle is capable of developing muzzle velocities around 2200 to 2400 fps, which should interest hunters who choose to go afield each fall after their buck with a muzzleloading rifle. When loaded with 115 grains of FFFg powder, the patched .490 ball of the .50 caliber leaves the barrel at around 2250 fps and has enough energy at fifty to a hundred yards to drop even the biggest buck in his tracks.

When firing the .50 caliber Mowrey Allen & Thurber rifle, however, I achieved the best results with powder charges ranging from 70 to 85 grains. Even a charge of this mildness pushes the patched 175-grain ball out of the muzzle at around 2000 fps and still has enough punch to bring down game as big as deer and black bear, and although not exactly an ideal small game rifle, it is still a good choice for some of the larger varmints in the coyote

Serial number of the rifle is stamped on brass butt plate along its lower edge.

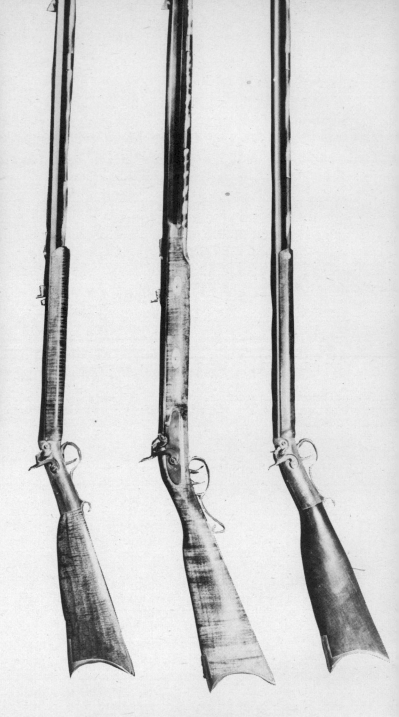

From left: the Mowrey Hawk has wood forend and Hawken -type butt plate, as does same firm's Hawken model; at right is Mowrey 12-ga shotgun.

and bobcat class.

During the testing of the .50 caliber rifle, I packed it along with an array of other guns on one of my coyote calling sessions. After pulling a sixty-yard, one-shot kill on a coyote called in with the aid of a Circe jackrabbit distress call, I had nothing but praise for the gun.

Several weeks before the hunt I began taking the rifle with me to the range during my visits there several times each week. Working with the gun on numerous occasions, I consistently achieved the best accuracy with a load of 75 grains of FFFg and the patched .490 ball.

Mowrey claims that anywhere from a 100 to a 125 grains of FFg powder is the ideal load for this gun. When I tried this granulation of black powder, however, I found that it delivered its best groups when reduced to anywhere from 80 to 90 grains. But the results were no better than what I had previously gotten with the finer FFFg powder, which I have plenty of on hand for my smaller caliber black powder rifles.

The combination of 75 grains of FFFg and the .490 ball weighing in the neighborhood of 170 to 180 grains was more than ample to drop the coyote I called in. Truthfully, I don't think he would have noticed the difference had I been shooting twenty or thirty more grains of powder. He

*Above: Rear sight is adjustable for elevation by means of notched blade.
Lower: Thimbles for rod are well made.*

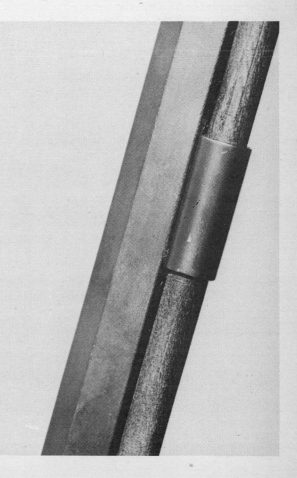

was dead by the time I covered the sixty yards separating us.

The Mowrey replica of the Allen & Thurber rifle is an extremely well balanced gun, well suited for carrying in the field and for off-hand shooting. It was a pleasure to shoot and bearable to carry!

Presently selling for $149.50, the Allen & Thurber is probably one of the best muzzleloading buys on today's market. For twenty bucks more, a presentation model of the gun featuring a hand-rubbed northern maple stock and furniture made of bronwite — having an appearance similar to nickel silver — is available.

Other fine muzzleloading guns from Mowrey include a wooden forend model dubbed the Allen & Thurber Special. With the exception of the wooden fore-stock, this is basically the same rifle as the Allen & Thurber replica. Also of similar design but having a Hawken-type butt plate is the Mowrey Hawk; Mowrey's 12-gauge shotgun also features the enclosed lock and Hawken style butt plate.

Of completely different styling than all of the other Mowrey guns, the firm's Hawken half-stock replica is an exacting reproduction of the gun once favored by the hardy mountainman. This is built only upon special order and to the individual shooter's or collector's specifications. The gun features a select hand-rubbed maple stock, polished Inco brass furniture, percussion lock and double set triggers. Interesting to note is that each and every part used to construct the Hawken half-stock is completely hand shaped and fitted.

Mowrey has a lot to offer the discriminating black powder shooter, most of it at a reasonable price and built to last the owner a lifetime.

CHAPTER 15

HANDY & ACCURATE

Actually, H&A Stands For Hopkins & Allen, Original Builders Of This Design Which, Again, Is Winning Popularity!

The Heritage model Hopkins & Allen replica in .45 cal.
has proved itself in the field as a deer gun for the
so-called primitive arms season in numerous states.

THE UNDERHAMMER RIFLE first appeared in New England during the 1830s. Unlike the side action locks of the earlier Kentucky and Pennsylvania long rifles, the understriker action on these percussion hunting and target rifles was completely of American design, perhaps making these rifles more distinctly American than any other domestically produced arm up until that time.

Simplicity of the lock made the underhammer a favorite among hunters, while instantaneous ignition proved a boon to the serious target competitor. The sad fact is, though, few underhammer rifles ever were produced. Firearms development was going through a rapid change in design and the birth of breechloaders was just around the corner.

Although target competitors hung onto the underhammer design for several decades after the introduction of breechloading rifles, hunters all but abandoned their use. Besides being usually superior in design and more accurate, the breechloader was far easier to care for and less tedious to load. The underhammer muzzleloader wasn't singled out as an inferior pattern to be discriminated against, for metallic cartridges were slowly putting an end to most muzzleloading guns.

Today it's not unusual to encounter an occasional muzzleloading benchrest shooter meticulously loading and firing a rifle of underhammer design. Many of these are century-old originals that probably couldn't be bought from said shooter for any price, and if one could be purchased, probably for more than the average shooter is willing to fork over. Not all such guns are hundred-year-old originals, but the price for such guns is still astounding, since they are almost always custom built to the individual shooter.

For the budget-wise shooter wanting a top-quality underhammer rifle at a reasonable price, Numrich Arms of West Hurley, New York, markets a complete line of Hopkins & Allen underhammer rifles. Completely American-made, the Hopkins & Allen line includes a model to whet the appetites of most all muzzleloading aficionados, whether serious target shooter, hunter or plain plinker.

At the top of the Hopkins & Allen underhammer line is the Heritage model. As on all the rifles comprising this line, the action is extremely simple. The only two moving parts on the lock are the trigger and the hammer; the trigger guard doubles as the mainspring. The underhammer is fitted to the solid metal receiver by a fairly large bolt, as is the trigger. The result of this simple design is a solid lock that is designed to give the rifle's owner years of trouble-free shooting.

A unique feature of the Heritage — as well as on the rest of the Hopkins & Allen rifles — is the rifle's easy takedown. A single tapered pin holds the barrel and fore-stock to the receiver. For easy storage during transportation, all of the Hopkins & Allen underhammer rifles can be broken down into the two pieces.

Available in .36 and .45 caliber, the thirty-two-inch barrel of the Heritage is precision rifled from a 15/16-inch octagon blank. The name of the model appears on the octagon flat immediately to the right of the barrel's flat/matted top. Although the rifle comes equipped with a receiver peep sight, there also is a square notch rear sight. The front sight is a hooded post and, when used with the

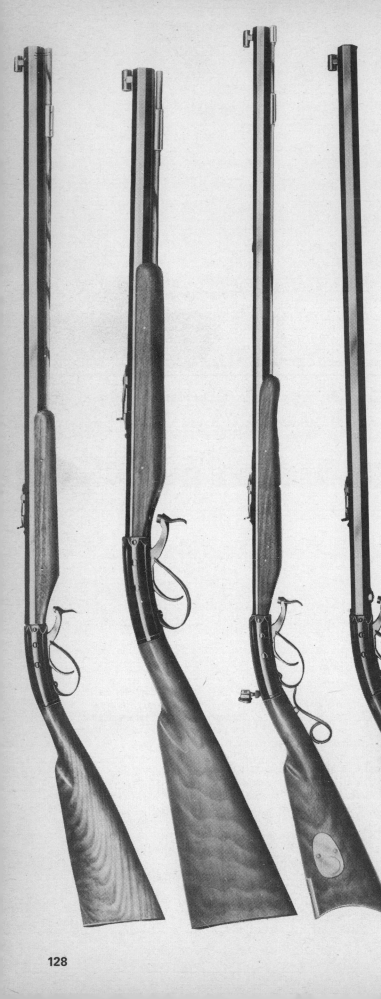

aperture rear peep sight, the rifle makes an excellent offhand target or hunting rifle.

Simple is the word best used to describe the brass furniture on the stock. In keeping with the rifle's simple utility design, Numrich Arms has avoided getting fancy with the rifle's functional patchbox, butt plate, trigger guard and single ramrod thimble. The oval-shaped patchbox on the butt stock can hardly be described as precision inletted, but on the other hand, it is a far cry from being crude and sloppy.

Working with one of the Heritage models in .45 caliber, my best groups were attained with a load of 72 grains of FFFg powder behind a patched .435 ball. First attempts to load with patching having a thickness of .016 proved unsuccessful. Combined with the diameter of the ball, the heavy material made it difficult to start and seat the patched ball. The recovery of one of the patches showed that the fit was too tight; the material was slitted where it had ridden on the rifling. Switching to .010 thick cotton patching, the fit of the ball in the barrel was perfect.

Groups of five to six inches at a hundred yards weren't uncommon. although most were around eight inches in diameter. When the powder charge was increased to 85 grains of FFFg, groups began to open up to twelve or more inches. Any attempts to go farther were dropped.

Slower burning FFg resulted in a considerably larger cloud of smoke at the muzzle and did little to improve accuracy. Using powder of this granulation in the Heritage did prove one thing, however, involving the difference in the pressures obtained between it and finer FFFg. Without measuring, I still believe that most of the groups obtained with FFg printed themselves on the paper a good three to four inches lower than those using FFFg.

Out of sixty or seventy shots fired with the Hopkins & Allen Heritage, I never experienced one misfire or hangfire. The direct path of the ignition flame into the charged chamber undoubtedly can be the reason; a hotter flame to ignite the main powder charge.

With the ability to group well within six inches from one hundred yards, the Heritage and the less fancy Offhand Deluxe model are both muzzleloaders well suited for packing in the field in hope of bagging that big racked buck or hard earned black bear. Basically, the Offhand Deluxe is the

Some of the rifles comprising the Hopkins & Allen line are, from left, the Deerstalker, the Deluxe Buggy, the Heritage and the all new .45 Target rifle.

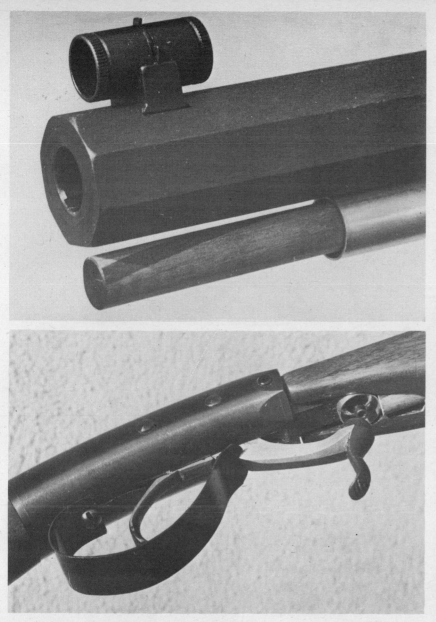

Left: Hooded front sight is standard on each Hopkins & Allen muzzleloader. (Lower left) The underhammer ignition system is positive. (Below) Original underhammer rifles such as antique used by this shooter are expensive.

same rifle as the Heritage, only it lacks the brass trigger guard extension, patchbox, butt plate and the aperture rear peep sight.

Perfect for carrying in brush country where extremely close snap shots usually are the order of the day is the Hopkins & Allen Deluxe Buggy rifle. This twenty-inch barreled muzzleloading carbine is actually just a shortened version of the Offhand model that was designed specifically for the Seneca Match competitor. Since its introduction, however, the short and light rifle has become very popular among black powder hunters that do their buck busting in close-range brush country. Like the Heritage and Offhand models, the Buggy rifle is available in .36 and .45 caliber.

Few if any hunters would attempt to use a .36 caliber muzzleloader for deer, most favoring the larger .45 caliber. Deer hunters demanding an even larger bore should find the Deer Stalker the ideal rifle. A bigger .58 caliber version of the Offhand, this rifle should give the hunter more knockdown power than should ever be needed. When fired from the thirty-two-inch rifled octagon barrel, .575 diameter

Minies should be extremely accurate.

With the growing interest in black powder competition, Numrich has introduced a special target/benchrest version of the Hopkins & Allen underhammer, the .45 Target. This rifle is produced without a forearm or ramrod ferrules, the lack of these combined with the heavier 1-1/8-inch rifled octagon barrel make the .45 Target an ideal benchrest rifle. Before the introduction of this mass-produced benchrest muzzleloader a shooter wanting an understriker competition gun could expect to pay well within the $300 margin for such a rifle.

In addition to the Hopkins & Allen line of underhammer rifles, Numrich Arms also offers two more top quality rifles. The Minuteman is a beautiful reproduction of the long rifle of early America that has become known as the Kentucky rifle. The other rifle is the firm's two-shot swivel breech rifle, perfect for the hunter wanting two spontaneous shots. Yet another gun available is the Hopkins & Allen Boot pistol, a six-inch barreled pistol of the underhammer styling.

CHAPTER 16
STAINLESS REPUTATION FOR THE OLD ARMY

Bill Ruger Designed A Black Powder Gun — Then Made It Rustproof!

WHEN YOU CHECK OUT Ruger's black powder cap and ball revolver, don't expect to find a replica model of any specific, historically famous gun. Neither will you find that the Ruger team has borrowed extensively from internal designs prevalent during the first dawnings of percussion pieces. Instead, you will note that the mechanism of Ruger's "Old Army" has much in common with their "Super Blackhawk" model.

But Bill Ruger didn't stop there. Four years later, he produced his Old Army model in stainless steel! This percussion revolver is an original Ruger design. It retains traditional handling and firing characteristics, while incorporating numerous improvements which mark the first significant advance in percussion revolver construction in more than a century. Needless to say, this new Ruger is intended solely for use with black powder. Never, under any circumstances should it be loaded with any other type of powder, no matter how light the load.

Like all other Ruger products, the two Old Army models are manufactured entirely in this company's Southport, Connecticut, and Newport, New Hampshire, plants. It is, as they say, one hundred percent Yankee-Doodle, with quality ordnance steels and music wire coil springs used throughout. Stainless steel nipples are standard and grip panels are turned from American walnut.

The caliber .44 percussion. Ruger's handgun has been designed to use a .457-inch diameter round ball or conical bullet of pure lead. The use of jacketed or alloy bullets is not recommended as accuracy is generally not as satisfactory as with the pure lead bullets. The bore of this

percussion piece is .443, with a groove of .451-inch. The barrel measures 7½ inches and features six grooves with a right twist of one in sixteen inches. The sights are the same as those on Ruger Blackhawks and Supers — a target rear, adjustable for elevation and windage, plus a ramp front with a one-eighth-inch wide blade, matted to eliminate glare. Weight is forty-six ounces, just three ounces lighter than that of their .44 magnum/.44 Special.

So that readers could get an idea concerning both guns, we assigned Bob Zwirz — on the East Coast near the Ruger facilities — to take a look at the first offering with its blued finish, while Dean Grennell — on the West Coast — was assigned to wring out the stainless steel version.

"When it came time for field testing sessions with two of these percussion revolvers, I was allowed to choose at random from the current Ruger production run. Both of these cap-and-ballers boasted serial numbers under 100. As for their finish, both showed the results of careful polishing and were richly blued/anodized. If it weren't for the variation in frame contour, the loading lever and plunger unit, the different appearance of the threaded nipples at the rear portion of the cylinder, the Old Army could almost pass for a Super Blackhawk," Zwirz reports.

"When Bill Ruger learned that his newest offerings were scheduled for test sessions, he voiced a desire to be on the scene and offered us the use of a large tract of land that he maintains in a rural sector of Connecticut. Before the day was over Steve Vogel, a Ruger executive, and his young son, Kurt, volunteered their services. Almost immediately so did Sandy Gleacher, obviously one of the world's youngest, ablest groomers of horses.

"Heather Williams also was recruited by way of a Ruger invitation, to join the festivities.

"Bill Ruger shares the opinion of this editor in feeling that shooting is not solely an adult sport. With proper supervision, it is both enjoyable and challenging to the younger set. Young Kurt, as an example, has become an exceptionally competent shooter in two short years, thanks in large degree to the patient efforts of his sports-minded dad. Naturally, it was Kurt that we chose to ready the two new percussion revolvers; without being told, he cleared the nipples by placing a Remington No. 11 cap on each nipple after ascertaining that the chambers still were unloaded."

The reason behind this, as most all know, is to guarantee that the nipple passages are rendered both clear and dry. This basic procedure completed, he then was ready to get down to the business of actually loading the revolver for firing.

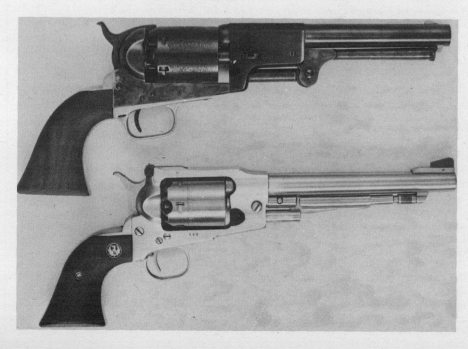

Bill Ruger's original version of his Old Army handgun resembled Super Blackhawk with the exception of the cylinder, which was equipped with stainless nipples.

Stainless steel Old Army has sleek lines when compared with big bulk of Colt's current Dragoon model.

Black powder expended for the day, Steve Vogel pops the cork on bottle of champagne to celebrate success of the Connecticut firing session.

Heather Williams, representing the distaff shooters, uses a two-handed hold for firing original version of Ruger's Old Army from sandbag rest. Note closed eyes, elevated barrel resulting from recoil as first round is fired.

As Bill Ruger and Zwirz pointed out to the less experienced, though it is completely safe to use as much black powder as the chamber will hold, leaving room for the bullet, such maximum loading is rarely the most accurate loading. End results of Ruger staff tests, along with our own, show that a good starting accuracy load, using a pure lead .457-inch diameter ball, is 20.0 grains of FFFg, plus sufficient filler (we used corn meal) to seat the ball approximately one-sixteenth inch below the chamber mouth.

For those who do not wish to bother with the extra step of using filler, then Ruger recommends 45.0 grains of FFFg. This gives excellent accuracy, though target sessions would seem to point out that the most consistent accuracy was attained while utilizing the filler over 20.0 grains.

Do not try 20.0 grains, unless you use filler. There will be no contact with the ball, for one thing, and there is good chance that you will have occurrrences where the detonating cap will fail to ignite the angled amount of powder lying in the chambers.

After clearing the nipples, you are ready to charge the chambers; now, place the hammer in the half-cock (loading) position so the cylinder is free to rotate in a clockwise direction. If you bring the hammer back too far, or if the hammer is put into the loading position by easing it forward from full cock, the cylinder will not be free to rotate.

Next, with one hand, hold the revolver by the grip with the barrel pointing upwards, but away from your own or anyone else's face or body. Using a powder dipper or other single charge measure, pour the correct amount of powder into one chamber. I personally use a custom, calibrated powder measure that prevents any mistakes. If you are to use the 20-grain load, don't forget to fill the balance of the chamber with the filler, leaving room enough to seat the bullet properly.

Now place the bullet in the mouth of the charged chamber and rotate the cylinder, until that chamber is aligned with the rammer. To execute the next step correctly, grasp the rammer lever and, with a firm, even stroke, seat the bullet on the powder or powder and filler. For maximum accuracy, the charge should be lightly compressed by the bullet.

Be certain that you have seated the bullet deeply enough so it does not interfere with the barrel and so the cylinder is able to rotate freely. When you look at a correctly seated ball, it will have the appearance of a wadcutter bullet and be almost one-sixteenth inch recessed. Repeat this procedure until all chambers are loaded with powder and ball.

And now you are ready for the simple chore of applying one of the commercially available bullet greases — we used Beare-Grease, produced by the Caution Tool Company, Incorporated, located in Southport, Connecticut — or one of the automotive water pump greases that also can handle the job. Whatever you choose, apply a liberal coating of the grease to each chamber mouth to cover the bullet fully and seal the chamber. The reason for this step is all-important; mainly so that the chance of a multi-chamber discharge is reduced.

And now for the capping procedure. Be sure you use only pistol caps, and that they be of good quality and the correct size (in this case No. 11). Whether you use an in-line cap feeder or one of other design, or prefer to position each by hand, the caps should be completely — and without pressure — seated on the nipples. Caps should only be tight enough that they do not fall off when the barrel is elevated. Never force a cap into place. Such extra pressure could cause it to detonate and that chain of events could put the gray into your hair.

The revolver is now ready to fire. If you do not intend to fire immediately, the hammer nose should be eased into one of the safety recesses which are provided on the rear of the Ruger's cylinder, between the nipples. This little operation must, in itself, be performed cautiously; should the hammer fall onto a nipple — you receive one demerit and a loud bang. Further, be certain the hammer is fully down in the safety recess and not just resting on the edge. The half-cock notch is provided for ease of loading only and should never be used as this revolver's safety.

With all of this data clearly explained to the troops assembled at Bill Ruger's shooting area, things progressed rather smoothly. Most of the offhand and benchrest shooting was run off from the twenty-five-yard mark. Groups, even when fired by Kurt and the two lasses, proved most satisfactory. Steve Vogel also managed to punch several dozen holes in targets, showing a not unsuspected professional hand.

There were only two slight difficulties encountered with the Old Army. First, it takes a fair amount of leverage to seat the bullet correctly in any gun of this type. This, at first, gave Kurt and Sandy a hard time; however, once the younger set got the knack of it, the problem pretty well worked itself out. Second, it does take some thought and practice for the uninitiated to disassemble the cylinder, cylinder pin and loading unit with any ease and no great loss of time.

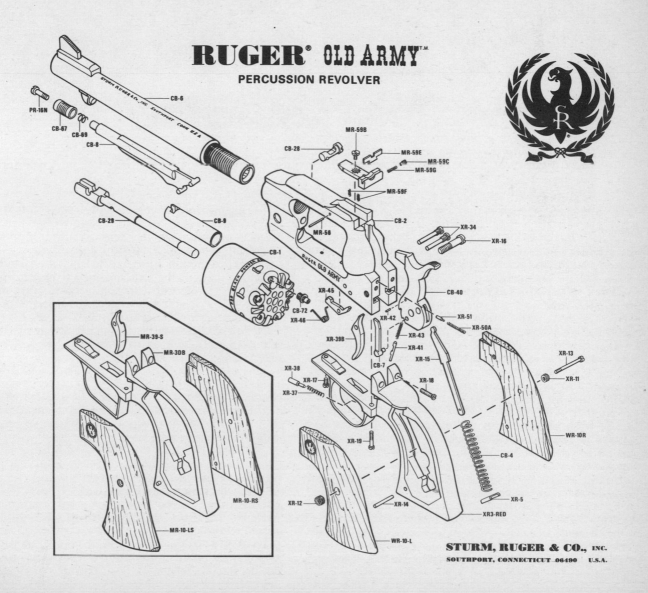

RUGER® OLD ARMY™
PERCUSSION REVOLVER

STURM, RUGER & CO., INC.
SOUTHPORT, CONNECTICUT 06490 U.S.A.

Finding right hold on lever in order to seat bullet properly was problem for the younger set, as evinced by Kurt Vogel. Steve Vogel, Sandy Gleacher observe.

What it takes, stated as simply as possible, is this: (Note: never attempt to remove a capped or loaded cylinder.) Place the hammer in the half-cock notch, being certain that the cylinder rotates freely. On the right side of the Ruger frame, just forward of the cylinder, you will see a large slotted pin. With a suitable tool turn this pin counter-clockwise until it stops at about 160 degrees. Now, unlatch the rammer lever and pull the rammer base pin assembly forward, toward the muzzle until it comes free of the revolver. The cylinder may now be removed.

Sight adjustment on the Old Army is there for the same reason as on any other fine shooting piece. On the Ruger, each click of the sight adjustment screws, either windage or elevation, will move the point of impact of the bullet three-quarters inch at a range of twenty-five yards. The height of the front sight has been preset to take best advantage of the elevation adjustment in the rear sight, considering the various ranges at which the gun is most likely to be used. Also to be considered is the simple fact that different load-ings will also call for readjustment of sights.

Sturm, Ruger & Company first introduced their percussion revolver in the summer of 1971.

It remained for Ruger to add one final touch of refine-ment to the Old Army and this turned up in 1975: a switch to stainless steel in place of the black-oxided steel used in the original.

The gun we received had been fired and not cleaned deliberately, Grennell recalls.

Since guns designed for use with black powder are pain-fully vulnerable to the highly corrosive residues left in copious quantity by the burning of that traditional propellant, the use of stainless steel makes irresistably good sense. This is not to infer that cleaning after shooting has become a thing of the past, because the residue continues to build up during extended firing sessions. That was pain-fully apparent when the stainless steel test sample — bearing the serial number 440 — was unpacked.

It required no more than a modest amount of time and effort, together with some Hodgdon's Spit-Bath cleaning solvent and a nipple wrench from Uncle Mike's of Oregon, to get the Old Army back in sanitary condition. Putting the cylinder and nipples into a stainless kettle and boiling them on top of a kitchen stove in soapy water removed the last of the impurities, revealing that the corrosion-proof chrome alloy suffered not the slightest trace of blemish as a result of this rather cavalier treatment.

As Grennell — who drew the cleanup detail — put it, "At least Zwirz was stuck for the postage on all that powder gunk, on top of what it cost to send the gun!"

Grennell proceeded to set up a rendezvous with Ray and Jackie Taylor, co-proprietors of The Flintlock, located in Anaheim, California. The establishment is a sporting goods store devoted primarily to muzzleloading guns and gadgetry. The Taylors are enthusiastic and knowledgeable aficionados of the archaic art of shooting with black powder firearms.

Zwirz, wearing Don Hume custom holster rig, displays targets shot on snowy day in New England. Six-shot groups measured 1-3/8 inches, fired from benchrest at 25 yards.

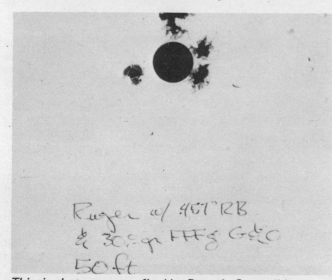

Ruger w/ 457 RB
& 30.0 gr FFFg G&O
50 ft

This six-shot group was fired by Dean A. Grennell in initial tests of the stainless steel Ruger Old Army.

The Taylors turned up at the range with a neat little accessory that proved so handy as to be all but indispensible: a loading stand designed for use with percussion revolvers. It eliminates the need for having a third and perhaps a fourth hand. Grennell, watching Ray Taylor make deft work of charging up the Ruger stainless, reflected that it would pose quite a challenge to reload one while pounding hell-for-leather across the prairie aboard a lathered cavalry mount, meanwhile trying to keep from getting skewered by a cloud of arrows launched by unfriendly redskins.

Grennell had cast up a quantity of conical bullets in a pair of Lee moulds, in both solid and hollow-point versions and had run some of these through his Saeco lube sizer, sizing them down to .4515-inch in the process. As it turned out, this proved to be a minor liability, since the unsized bullets grouped considerably better. The Lee mould is designed to produce an as-cast bullet whose base is a nice fit in the front of the Ruger chambers, with the front band being enough larger to provide the desirable tight fit.

Taylor predicted that the Ruger Old Army would give better groups with round lead balls and produced a sack of them, in .457-inch diameter, which he proceeded to load on top of 30.0 grains of Gearhart & Owens' grade FFFg powder and greased over-powder wads from Replica Products, Vienna, West Virginia. The improvement was noteworthy. When fired off the bench, with the butt of the gun supported by a cardboard box, this particular load put all six holes into a center-to-center spread of 1.525 inches at fifty feet, with the group neatly centered around the point of aim. Any of the six shots would have been capable of demolishing a ground squirrel at that distance, and Grennell noted with mild chagrin that several of his flossy, modern breechloaders would do no better, if as well.

Commenting that mild loads often showed further improvement in accuracy, Taylor refilled the Ruger, this time with 20.0 grains of FFFg in each chamber, topped with one 9mm case of cornmeal plus one of the grease wads and a .457-inch round ball. He warned that he thought he'd gotten one light charge of powder into a chamber in loading for that round and this proved correct. It came under the hammer for the second shot and resulted in a diffident report, with the ball striking about six inches lower on the paper. Four of the balls went into one ragged hole, spanning but .695-inch, but the final shot sailed high and right, nearly two inches from its nearest neighbor.

Taylor explained the purpose of the cornmeal filler, which keeps the ball up at the front of the chamber, preventing it from picking up too much velocity before the soft lead encounters the lands and grooves of the rifled barrel, thus preventing stripping and skidmarks. Jackie noted that blowing a promising group on the last shot is all too common.

"How do you explain it?" Grennell inquired, expecting that it might be due to a shift in center of gravity as the first five leaden globes had departed.

"Purely a matter of over-confidence," she replied with a quiet smile.

Like it's blued predecessor, weight of the stainless Ruger Old Army is forty-six ounces and its 7½-inch, six-groove barrel has a right-hand twist of one turn in sixteen inches. Sights of the stainless version are blued for improved, visual clarity. Bore diameter is .443, with .451-inch groove diameter. Music-wire coil springs are used throughout. Stocks are American walnut, with Ruger medallions. Cylinder is roll-engraved "For Black Powder Only."

CHAPTER 17

CENTENNIAL'S ZOUAVE

This Remake Of An Epic Arm Has Scored High On The Black Powder Hit Parade!

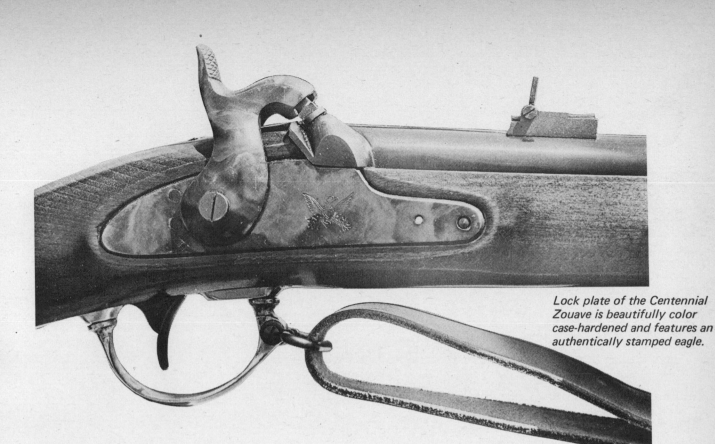

Lock plate of the Centennial Zouave is beautifully color case-hardened and features an authentically stamped eagle.

"THESE RIFLES ARE TO BE .58 inch caliber, and to have a three leaf rear sight, and cupped ramrod, with sword bayonet stud similar to those of the Harpers Ferry rifle, Model of 1855, in other respects of the pattern of rifles without bayonets heretofore made by you for this department."

Accepted by Eli Remington on August 6, 1861, this order for 10,000 of the described rifles from Chief of Ordnance General James Ripley marked the introduction of the famed Remington Zouave. Although only 10,001 Zouaves ever were produced, with an even less number of these seeing actual field use during the Civil War, the .58 caliber rifled musket still is considered to be one of the best and most colorful guns produced during that era.

Little is documented on the actual issue of the prized Remingtons and a large number of these guns in new condition are known to have been shipped to a number of Liege, Belgium, gunsmithing shops post war; many of these guns unfortunately were rebored to smoothbores to be used with shot and then were sent to Africa or South America. Combined with the scarcity of the Zouave due to its limited production, this rendering them into junk guns is enough to make any North/South Skirmish shooter cringe.

Though most U.S. Zouave regiments were armed with many different makes of foreign guns and even some transformed Springfields, the title also was used to describe the colorful Remington rifle, even though few Zouave regiments were lucky enough to be so armed. Exceptionally accurate, the dependable Remington was much like the graceful and elegant French Chasseurs de Vincennes rifle in appearance, having eye-pleasing styling and plenty of bright brass trimming.

The term, Zouave, is also of French origin and is used to denote a French Algerian military unit that became widely known for its colorful dress. Even more distinctive, however, was the Algerian unit's quick spirited drills. Later this title was used to acknowledge a light and highly mobile regiment.

Today, as was the case more than a hundred years ago, the individual fortunate enough to own one of the Remington Zouave rifled muskets is not apt to part with it. When such a gun is in mint or near-mint condition, it also is unlikely that said owner will pack it out to the local shooting range and put it through the hardships of firing the much desired collector's piece.

Centennial Arms of Lincolnwood, Illinois, is one of several muzzleloading arms distributors now offering reproductions of the famous Zouave rifled musket. The Centennial Zouave is so authentic that the original inspector marks are included on the stock.

Dubbed the Model 1863 Zouave Remington, the Italian-made replica is an exceptionally good looking and well built arm. The deeply blued thirty-three-inch barrel features three-land and three-groove rifling of the conventional right-hand twist. A close examination of the reproduction proved this three-land rifling to be about the only really distinguishing difference between it and the original Remington, which had five-groove rifling.

Just as Ripley had ordered on the Remington in 1861, Centennial Arms had the Antonio Zoli & Co. — the name of the Italian gunmaker as it appears on the Zouave's .58 caliber barrel — include the Harpers Ferry type bayonet mount. It is authenticity such as this that makes this modern day Zouave one of the most favored by North/South Skirmish shooters.

The nearly full-length walnut stock — ending approximately five inches from the muzzle — has a glossy oil finish and is accentuated by the polished brass butt plate, patch

There are numerous different types of lead projectiles available for the .58 caliber muzzleloader. Author used the two at left.

To prevent a build-up of powder fouling, author filled hollow base of Minie bullets with lube. Minie bullet, (bottom) is carefully started into muzzle; note cupped ramrod tip.

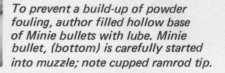

box, trigger guard, removable barrel bands and schnabel. These barrel bands are slipped into recessed grooves on the stock and are held in place by a spring that protrudes from the right side of the stock. To remove the barrel the tang screw must first be loosened, then all that remains to do is depress the band springs and slip the bands off; the barrel then should just lift out of the stock for easy cleaning.

The all-metal ramrod slips into a slot running the full length of the fore-stock. Keeping with the design of the original Zouave, the tip of the ramrod is cupped to prevent possible damage to Minie type bullets when being seated.

Other reproduced features that make the Centennial rifled musket authentically detailed is the color case-hardened lock plate, sling swivels and original type sights. The front sling swivel attaches to the front barrel band with the rear swivel located on the front curve of the brass trigger guard.

The three-leaf rear sight, graduated in increments of one, two and three hundred yards, intrigued me, as I studied it before making a visit to the local rifle range. A simple arrangement, the rear sight consists of three leaves that fold down and out of the way to allow the use of either a higher or shorter V-notch. The three hundred-yard notch is nearly a half-inch higher than the notch used for ranges of a hundred yards or less. This higher rear sight makes it necessary to elevate the muzzle in order to draw a bead on the

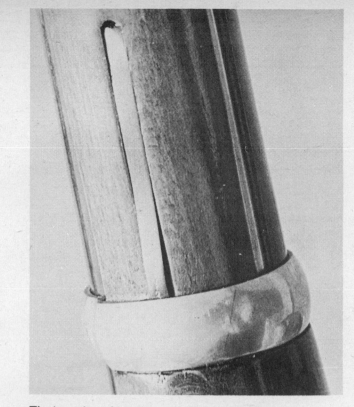

The brass barrel bands on the Zouave musket are slipped on/off, held in place by spring. Photos (below right) show the bayonet stud and rear sight.

target which in turn results in a rainbow trajectory from the muzzle to said target.

Curious to just how accurate the Zouave replica would be at the longer ranges, I concentrated the majority of my shooting with it at ranges of a hundred yards or more. Both .575 Minie bullets and patched .575 and .562 round balls were used with various loads of FFg and FFFg powder.

Firing a load of 65 grains of FFFg behind the Lyman No. 575602 Minie, I was really surprised when I put three consecutive shots right over the top of a hundred yard target. By dropping back to 50 grains of the same powder, the next three printed on the paper but in no way could they be considered a group; better than twelve inches separating any two hits.

Switching to FFg, a charge of 60 grains kept the shots on the paper and brought the "group" back to around ten inches. An attempt to load the round .575 ball soon had me digging through my box of loading accessories in search of thinner patching material. The .011-inch thick cotton pillow ticking I usually find ideal was much too thick since the ball was nearly the same diameter of the .58 caliber bore. When a small amount of .006-inch thick linen cloth was finally found it too gave an extremely tight fit, but it worked after a considerable amount of effort on my part.

With the .575 ball weighing in the neighborhood of 275 grains, I reduced the load to 50 grains of FFg as a starter. The thinner barrel walls of a musket won't withstand the pressures of heavier rifle charges, so it is a good practice to use some caution when firing patched round balls; these almost always, or should, weigh more than the Minie, resulting in increased barrel pressures.

With no adjustment for windage, there was little I could do as the first shot printed itself on the target just outside the last ring at approximately ten o'clock. After the last

group with the Minies, I was in store for a second surprise when I found that my next four rounds all hit within six inches of that first shot.

Patched with the heavier pillow ticking, the .562 balls gave equally pleasing results. Working with both patched ball loads I finally settled for a load of 55 grains of FFg as the most accurate for the .575 ball and 65 grains of FFg for the .562 round ball. During the hundred yard firing with the previously described loads, the barrel on the Centennial Zouave was wiped clean after every five shots. To see just how many shots could be fired with the patched balls without cleaning, I fired the next twenty shots without running the cleaning rod down the barrel.

Starting with the .575 ball — the patching receiving an application of Hodgdon's Spit Patch lubricant — the bore build up was so great after seven shots that the ball would no longer seat, with shots five, six and seven doing so after considerable wrestling with the ramrod. At the end of the twenty-shot test, however, the smaller .562 ball still could be seated without too much difficulty.

After cleaning the barrel with Bucheimer's black powder solvent and one big pile of patches, I fired the Zouave at two and three hundred-yard targets. Using the Lyman Minie — the preferred round of the Civil War — I found it quite difficult to keep any hits at all on the longer three hundred-yard target. Out of ten shots fired at this target, only two printed on the paper.

Things were a little different on the two hundred-yard target, with nine of the ten shots fired hitting the two foot square piece of paper. After that demonstation, and my shoulder feeling the afternoon's firing session, I have a little more respect for this piece of Civil War armament.

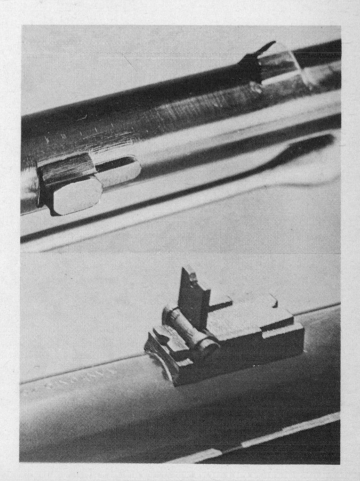

THE UNPREDICTABLE TASTES of the gun-buying public must have grayed many a hair and planted many an ulcer among the management of the venerable arms plant near the Connecticut River in Hartford over the century-plus of its activities.

Many a good model of Colt revolver has been discontinued from production, perhaps with regret, perhaps with a sigh of relief and, in later years, market conditions have necessitated setting the dies and jigs back up on the production line to churn forth additional units.

That's how it went for the legendary Peacemaker, Model of 1873: Sales had sagged to levels which made it econom-ically impractical, so production terminated. The fickle public became ever more enamored with the charm of the cowboy's traditional hogleg, prices soared to incredible heights. Other manufacturers commenced turning out replicas to satisfy the ever-growing demands and, with handwriting clearly legible on the wall, Colt resumed pro-duction: no great tragedy, considering the influx of green-backs generated by the western six-shooter in its second reincarnation.

So time inched forward, as it has a way of doing and that less-than-predictable group, the gun-buying public, not content to fire and admire their latter-day single action

CHAPTER 18

SON OF A GUN....

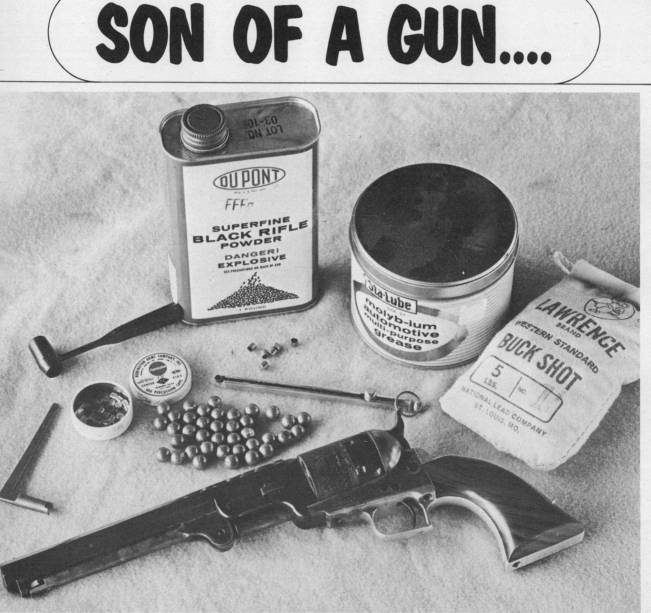

...Or How Does Today's 1851 Navy Colt Model Compare With The Original Of More Than A Century Back?

As the cylinder is pulled from the closely fitted arbor, the spiral-cut grease groves can be seen in latter.

six-shooters, began trending toward the old muzzleloading arms which had preceded the M1873. All of this may have disturbed the well earned rest of those earnest innovators such as Rollin White who had labored long and diligently to improve the breed by developing the principle of cartridge-loaded firearms.

Once again, the more adventurous competitors of the Colt works came forward, happily catering to this new penchant on the part of the g.b.p. and, once again, the Colt management noted substantial and growing sales which were having no effect upon Sam'l. Colt's check-stubs. It is easy — though surely not accurate — to envision some

board member at Colt's as he accepted the inevitable, staring moodily out the window at the bulbuous gilt dome which has been the plant's hallmark for generations. You picture him dropping a half-finished cigar into a mirror-polished brass cuspidor, smoothing luxuriant mutton-chop whiskers and gritting, "All right! Send someone into the back room to dig out the tooling on the Navy Colt!"

That's not the way it was, but it sounds plausible in a firm that has been surviving corporate shakeups since long before the great-grandparents of most people now living were wrestling with McGuffy's spelling books.

As with many of the more successful Colt Models, the Navy Colt of 1851 went through numerous modifications in its first career of production, many of them of a minor

Left: Small notch in nose of the hammer serves as the rear sight when hammer is cocked. Below: With locking wedge loosened and moved to the left, rammer is positioned between two of the chambers and the loading lever is used to force the barrel forward as first step in disassembly.

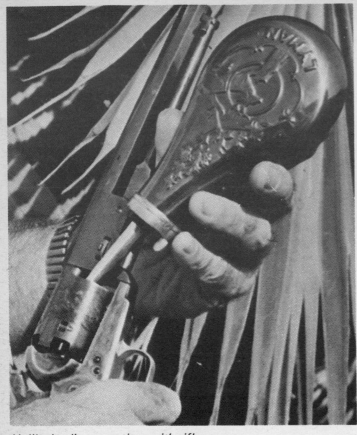

Unlike loading operations with rifles and other shoulder arms, it's common practice to pour charge direct from the powder flask into chamber mouth.

As discussed, the small plastic, dipper-type powder measures supplied for use with the Lee Loader kits can be used to dispense powder into front of each chamber, although the dipper is not quite as convenient as flask.

nature. Knowledgeable scholars of Coltly lore, such as James E. Serven, seem to agree that the Navy Colt was the most popular of all the muzzleloaders the firm turned out. It was the favored equalizer of the fairly late Wild Bill Hickok and a brace of them may have been tucked beneath his waistband on that fateful Dakota evening when he crumpled over his last poker hand: aces and eights, full.

The second-generation Navy Colt tips the scale at a hair over two pounds, nine ounces, carries the traditional 7½-inch octagonal barrel and its unfluted cylinder is embellished with a scene of naval combat, commemorating a successful encounter the Texas Navy had with some Mexican vessels. The words, "Colt's Patent," followed by the serial number appear on one line, and the line beneath says, "Engraved by W. L. Ormsby, New York." A third line, engraved around the forward perimeter of the cylinder, reads, "Engaged 16 May 1843." If memory serves, that was a Tuesday.

Barrel and cylinder are richly blued, with handsome case-hardening colors on the loading lever, rammer, frame and hammer. The trigger guard and backstrap — joined by a single screw at the lower front corner of the grip — are of a non-ferrous metal, presumably brass, heavily silver-plated. The stock of the Navy Colt is a single piece of wood — nut-brown on the sample gun, with attractive figuring in a deeper brown, so dark as to be nearly black, running diagonally — held by the trigger guard and backstrap encircling it in a closely fitted groove.

The trigger is blued, slender and graceful and set slightly to the left of center, as viewed from above and rearward in normal firing position. With the arm of the trigger scale

positioned midway up the trigger, pull on the test arm measured approximately seventy-six ounces — 4¾ pounds — although it feels lighter when firing..

The Navy Colt field-strips for cleaning into three assemblies: barrel, cylinder and receiver. The wedge at the lower rear of the barrel is tapped lightly with a non-marring tool such as a wooden mallet to loosen it, after which it is moved on to the left. It is not necessary to loosen the screw above the wedge on the left side and this should not be done. The screw serves to prevent loss of the wedge after being moved to the limit of its leftward travel. Some dingaling, into whose clutches the sample had fallen, was unaware of this and had split one side of the screw off in a vain attempt to loosen it.

Once the wedge is moved clear, the proper way to continue disassembly is to rotate the cylinder so as to place the rammer between two chambers and actuate the loading lever to force the barrel and receiver apart. The improper way is to grab the barrel with one hand and the receiver with the other, attempting to pull them apart. As they are fitted quite snugly, they will separate with considerable force applied and it is highly probable that the cylinder will fly loose and fall to the ground: a situation with little to recommend it.

The first type of Navy Colt had a novel design feature in that the cylinder pin or arbor had an open notch on its upper surface to accept the barrel wedge. In the second type, this was changed to a rectangular slot passing horizontally through the cylinder pin. The 1971 version follows the second type as to configuration in this regard.

Accuracy requires that the cylinder be a close fit on the

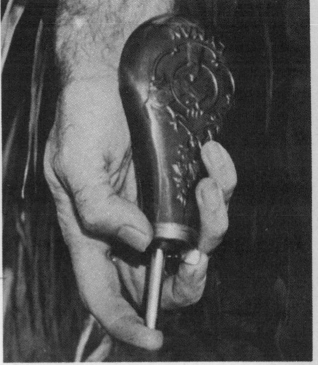

Engraving on the current Colt crop is the same as that on the originals, including patent dates, et al. (Right) When using a powder flask such as this one by Lyman, a finger tip is held over the nozzle, the flask then is inverted, and the gate lever is pressed and released. This allows the measuring tube to fill with powder, which, in turn, can be poured into cylinder chamber.

cylinder pin and a spiral grease groove is cut around the pin for about 1-1/8 inches. Here is where the passion for authenticity shows clearly. It would be quicker and easier to cut this spiral groove on a lathe, but the sample appears to have been cut free-hand, with irregular groove spacing being clearly evident.

The front sight is a brass bead, with tapering sides and a rounded tip. A notch in the nose of the hammer serves as the rear sight. Neither are adjustable, though the side-play of the hammer, under pressure, is well under 1/64-inch, making its sight steadier than many an arm of modern design that has been tested.

The top of the barrel bears the familiar legend: ADDRESS SAML COLT NEW-YORK CITY; no period after Saml, no apostrophe, though the L is of smaller size and has a line beneath it. This is but one of at least five different markings found in this location on Nineteenth Century Navy Colts and, as with countless other details, is almost painfully authentic.

The serial number appears in at least five places: lower surface of barrel lug, cylinder, lower front of frame and on both the trigger guard and backstrap.

The trigger guard is square-backed, in the manner of the second type. The third type used a small guard, rounded front and back and made of brass. Later, the guard was made bigger, still rounded and iron was used in some units instead of brass.

Rifling of the 1971 version consists of seven grooves, fairly deep and of approximately the same width as the lands, cut with right-hand twist. This corresponds to the first models of the Navy Colt, the design being changed later to incorporate a left-hand twist. Some of the Nineteenth Century specimens are said to have had a gain twist — that is, increasing in pitch toward the muzzle — although the current production appears to be cut at a uniform rate throughout its barrel length.

Nominally, the Navy Colt, including current production, is caliber .36 — this being based upon 86 round balls to the pound, which would make it correspond to an 86-gauge shotgun, were there such an animal — although, in practice, almost any sort of leaden globule between about .368 and .400-inch in diameter can be fired with reasonable hopes of success and satisfaction.

The chambers of the cylinder measure about .375-inch in inside diameter and the ball must start its trip by being crammed down into this space, although there is a slight chamfer at the chamber mouth to accommodate lead balls of larger diameters.

Slugging the bore by carefully tapping a lead ball though it with a length of wooden dowel gave a trifle over 3/16-inch of land engagement on a ball that started out at about .400-inch diameter. When so handled, the expelled ball did not appear to have bottomed on the grooves, although it is likely that it would have done so under impetus of powder pressures.

Conical balls can be fired in the .36 Navy Colt. The oldtime logistics pegged these at fifty to the pound, which would work out to 140 grains apiece. Number 1 buckshot,

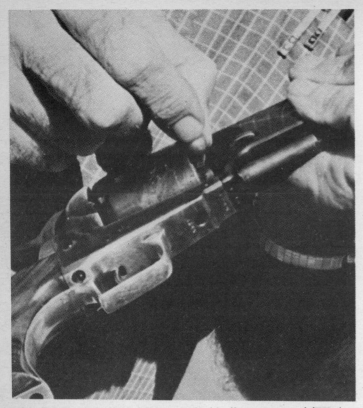

Round balls or – if preferred, conical bullets – are positioned into mouth of the bottom-most chamber, after charging with powder, after which they are seated by means of the rammer and loading lever before rotating the cylinder to put the next chamber into position for having same steps performed on it.

made by Lawrence, measures right around .400-inch and averages 87-90 grains. Some mould-cast balls, priced at $2.30 per hundred from a local gunstore, miked about .374-inch and weighed around 82-85 grains.

FFFg is the indicated granulation of black powder for use in the .36 Navy Colt and it should go without saying that nitrocellulose (smokeless) powder should not be used in it under any circumstances. The nipple diameter is such that the Remington number 10 caps fit perfectly.

Speaking of things not to do: Snapping the hammer on the uncapped nipple will burr and ruin the nipple quickly. Most people do not seem to know this, so you have to warn them against dry firing before letting them get their hands on a percussion firearm of any sort. The only safe policy is to warn everyone about this; if you assume the other guy is smart enough not to need warning, it's an excellent bet that you'll end up replacing at least one nipple.

Various approaches to powder measuring were used in the test firing. One of the Lee Loader measure kits was packed along and it was found that a number 108 scoop – the number indicates a volume of .108 cubic inch – worked quite well, leaving ample room for seating the round ball. Delivery with this dipper-type measure comes to 27.1 grains of FFFg black powder. Moving to the next larger size of Lee measure, the number 129, gave 31.8 grains of FFFg, which brought the charge just about level with the top of the chamber and made it somewhat difficult to ram the ball into the mouth far enough to clear the rear of the barrel during cocking. With a bit of care, the 129 dipper could be short-scooped, leaving about 1/8 to 3/16-inch of unfilled space at the top and this resulted in a workable charge of 28.5 grains, upon which the ball could

be seated easily.

The second measuring method involved Lyman's powder flask, intended for their caliber .36 black powder replica but equally well suited for use with the Navy Colt. This is a handsome production with a colorful antique patina on the copper flask and brass fittings. The technique for using it is simple, once you know how. Put a finger tip over the end of the spout, invert the flask, open the gate with the little lever, release the lever, up-end the flask and pour the contents of the measuring tube down into the mouth of the chamber. The operation is much quicker to perform than to describe. Average charge weight with the Lyman flask is 20.9 grains of DuPont FFFg, taken over ten consecutive charges.

The percussion revolver requires an application of grease over the top of the seated ball; serving at least two important functions as indicated earlier in this volume, but it deserves repetition. It reduces or eliminates lead-fouling of the bore and it prevents the uncomfortable adventure of having a second or third adjacent chamber set off accidentally by the firing of the one in line with the barrel. Further, it tends to soften and minimize the buildup of powder fouling in the bore. There are many kinds of preparations available for this purpose and priced accordingly. The lubricant used in the test was Sta-Lube type GM-21, a lithium base automotive grease containing molybdenum disulphide and priced at a rousing forty-nine cents for a one-pound can: enough for a copious quantity of shooting with percussion revolvers and there were no complaints with its performance.

Some highly self-respected authorities on the subject of firing black powder percussion arms have placed great stress upon the need for snapping a cap in each empty chamber, so as to clear the flash hole, prior to the initial loading for each shooting session. This is, undoubtedly, a sagacious procedure if you envision the possibility of having to stop a charging grizzly with a single fast shot. However, instances of being charged by a wounded paper target are quite rare. Visual examination of the flash holes showed every appearance of being adequately clear. So the first six rounds were loaded up without wasting any caps and, to no one's great surprise, all six fired at the first drop of the hammer. Had any of the chambers failed to fire, it was proposed to wait a decent interval, flick off the first cap and try with a second primer on the same nipple.

The photoscreen chronograph had been set up so as to permit measurement of velocity on each shot in conjunction with group testing. The obvious advantage over conventional, breaking-screen chronographs is that the latter do not permit easy sighting at a target and may produce some amount of deflection.

The charges thrown by the Lyman powder flask – with its measuring tube intended for the caliber .36 percussion revolver sold by Lyman – weighing a hair under 21.0 grains on the average, drove the 82-85-grain moulded balls forth at a rather leisurely 680 fps average velocity. Group size, for six shots at twenty-five yards was 8.257 inches wide by 6.482 inches high. Average muzzle energy came to 85 foot-pounds.

Moving on to the number 108 Lee dipper, with its average charge weight of 27.1 grains of FFFg, the velocity climbed to an average of 813 fps with the same projectile –

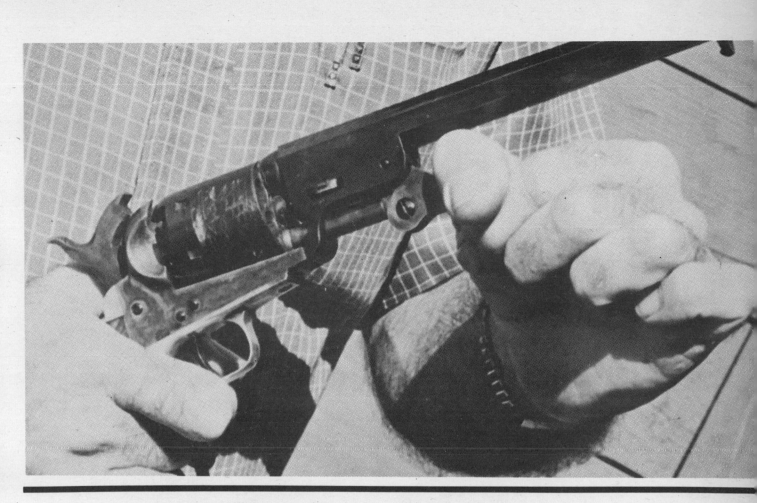

*With powder charge in place, ball is put into mouth
of chamber and loading lever is used to ram it home.*

good for 122 foot-pounds of muzzle energy — and the six-shot group came to a more respectable 3.702 inches wide by 2.379 inches high.

Short-dipping with the number 129 Lee measure, as described previously, raised the velocity to an average figure of 941 fps on 28.5 grains of FFFg and ciphered out to a muzzle energy of 164 foot-pounds. That will shade a few of the milder smokeless pistol cartridges such as the .25 auto (73 ft-lbs), .32 auto (145 ft-lbs), .32 S&W (90 ft-lbs), .32 S&W Long (115 ft-lbs) and the .38 S&W (150 ft-lbs).

True, the Navy Colt's ballistics may seem unimpressive when rated against the .44 magnum but the same could be said of most other handgun cartridges and the Navy Colt's big brother, the awesome Walker Colt Dragoon could defend the family honor much more tellingly in the heavyweight division. It is interesting to speculate upon the possibility that Colt might tool up for 20th-Century production of that legendary hoss-pistol but there's no word to that effect out of Hartford, as yet.

The heaviest charge delivered the highest output but the group size had expanded to 4.580 wide by 4.015 inches high, leaving the dipped load from the number 108 Lee measure as the apparent best combination for this particu-lar specimen. It should be noted that a four-by-four group is not particularly disgraceful for smokeless powder cartridges.

Certainly, it can be said that the re-emerging Navy Colt is the oldest design of handgun — perhaps you can make that "firearm" — being produced today by its original manufacturer. It is authentic Colt in every detail and it takes its glamorous final form from selected raw materials: steel, brass and wood, in the same place where the Immortal Sam'l. supervised production of the prototype, one hundred and twenty-six years ago.

The commemorative models are identified by stamping the appropriate name on the left side of the barrel. In addition, the Lee model has the round-back trigger guard while the Grant model has the square-back guard. Among the Navy Colts left over from the Nineteenth Century production, the square-back guard is encountered less frequently.

So the ever-growing group of black powder fans can bid a hearty welcome-back to this grizzled seafaring sixgun from 'way back down the road. And you can bet that many a collector/shooter is hoping that they've got someone prowling the back room at Hartford in quest of the tooling for the Paterson Model!

THE FINE ART OF FRONT-STUFFING SCATTERGUNS

CHAPTER 19

Black Powder Shotguns Do Not Enjoy The Intense Popularity Of Rifles And Pistols, But Their Acceptance Is Growing!

THE PAST FEW CHAPTERS illustrate the development of black powder arms and their application to today's replica firearms. Samuel Colt was one of the early developers and the company bearing his name has gone full circle coming back to produce — or actually to reproduce — one of the firearms on which his reputation was built.

But there is still another facet of black powder shooting that has changed even less over the past couple of centuries. This involves the muzzleloading shotgun.

Have you ever really wondered what it was like to hunt with a muzzleloading shotgun the way your great gran'pappy used to? Today it's so easy to swing on a rising covey of quail or a brace of cock pheasant and, without too much bother, bring down a double or even a triple with the modern pump guns or that marvel of marvels, the autoloading shotgun.

Hunting with muzzleloading black powder scatterguns was all but abandoned during the first half of this century. The late 1800s saw the introduction of the break-open breechloaders that were chambered for the early black powder shotshells. Shortly after break-open single and double barrel shotguns came into being, other developments came about that pushed the front-loading shotgun even further into the past. Among these later refinements

were smokeless powders, the pump and the autoloading shotgun.

Great grandfather, however, was usually quite content with his black powder smokepole. A flask of FFg powder, a pouch filled with the size shot best suited for the game he was seeking, wadding of some sort and a tin of percussion caps or a smaller flask filled with FFFFg powder to prime the pan if the gun happened to be a flintlock were all he needed for his day afield.

It's a good bet eventually you'll find an old photo or two in the family album showing some distant relative proudly showing off a great pile of ducks, geese or similar fowl. It's also another good bet that said relative probably is tenderly cradling his prized black powder scattergun in the crook of his arm in such a manner that the photo plays as much emphasis on the firearm as it does the taken game.

It is said that man's personality is clearly reflected in the armament that he chooses. If this is true, perhaps this is the reason that such shotguns were left propped in some forgotten corner or hung over a fireplace or rafter just to collect dust and rust, as their owners turned to such repeating shotguns as Winchester's Model 1897 pump. The arms scene changed rapidly during the last quarter of the 19th Century, no one wanting to be left out. If you didn't

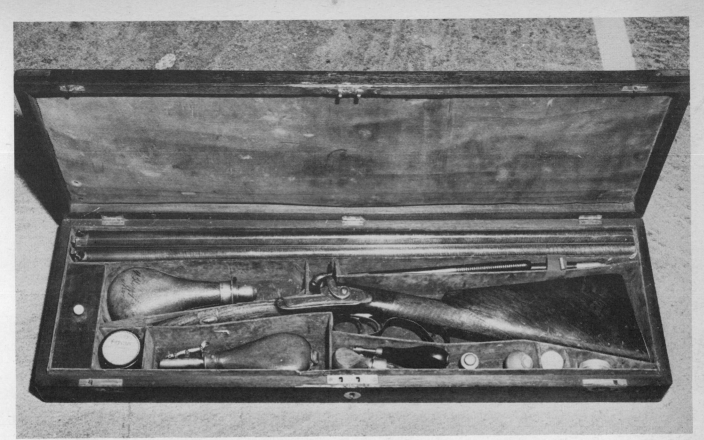

*Beautiful old original shotguns as this can be bought with little
harm done to shooter's budget. Barrels on old guns such as
this one are commonly of damascus twist steel and can be dangerous.*

CHART A

Gauge	Powder Charge	Wad Thickness	Charge Weight	
10	100 grains Fg	7/8 inch	1 1/4 oz.	Light
10	108 grains Fg	7/8 inch	1 1/2 oz.	Medium
10	120 grains Fg	7/8 inch	1 5/8 oz.	Heavy
12	70 grains Fg/FFg	3/4 inch	1 1/8 oz.	Light
12	84 grains Fg/FFg	3/4 inch	1 1/4 oz.	Medium
12	90 grains FFg	3/4 inch	1 5/8 oz.	Heavy
14	66 grains FFg	3/4 inch	1 oz.	Light
14	74 grains FFg	3/4 inch	1 1/8 oz.	Medium
14	85 grains FFg	3/4 inch	1 1/8 oz.	Heavy
16	60 grains FFg	5/8 inch	1 oz.	Light
16	66 grains FFg	5/8 inch	1 oz.	Medium
16	75 grains FFg	5/8 inch	1 1/8 oz.	Heavy
20	55 grains FFg	5/8 inch	3/4 oz.	Light
20	60 grains FFg	5/8 inch	7/8 oz.	Medium
20	69 grains FFg	5/8 inch	1 oz.	Heavy
28	55 grains FFg	1/2 inch	5/8 oz.	Light
28	60 grains FFg	1/2 inch	5/8 oz.	Medium
28	65 grains FFg	1/2 inch	7/8 oz.	Heavy
.410	34 grains FFg	1/2 inch	1/2 oz.	Light
.410	44 grains FFg	1/2 inch	1/2 oz.	Medium
.410	44 grains FFg	1/2 inch	5/8 oz.	Heavy

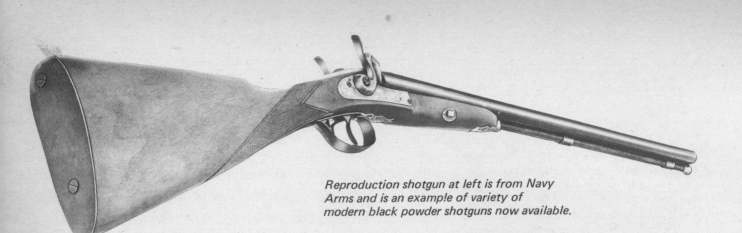

Reproduction shotgun at left is from Navy Arms and is an example of variety of modern black powder shotguns now available.

hunt with the latest of firearms, you just weren't with the times. Except for an occasional farm lad who couldn't afford anything better, shotgun shooters gave up the muzzleloading arm for the more reliable break-open singles, doubles and later the pumps and autos.

During the last decade, however, there has been growing interest not only in shooting arms of this type, but in hunting with black powder guns. Nostalgia certainly has played some role in the increasing number of muzzleloading hunters, but for many this interest stems from the real pleasure of hunting with arms of this type.

Cap and ball revolvers, single-shot pistols, rifles and muskets had received the majority of this attention with little going to muzzleloading shotguns.

As can be expected, the arms manufacturers and importers played upon the markets offering the greatest amount of sales and muzzleloading shotguns just don't fall into this category. Unlike the numerous well built Colt Army and Navy replicas, single-shot target pistols and Zouave musket reproductions, the number of modern-made shotguns is relatively small. Although there were quite a few well built originals, no exact reproductions of these are being offered currently. Instead today's front loading scatterguns are modern-made guns of the generally accepted designs.

Dixie Gun Works, Navy Arms, Mowrey Gun Works, Numrich Arms, just to name a few, all offer muzzleloading shotguns of some sort. With the exception of such guns as Mowrey's single-barrel 12-gauge shotgun, these guns are almost all made in one of three countries: Belgium, Italy or Spain. Unfortunately, some of these are cheap and lightly built guns that work fine initially, but result in a big headache in the end.

But if hunting with your lightning fast pump or auto has lost some of its appeal and challenge, give hunting with one of the muzzleloaders a try before condemning it. There's something about making a good hit on a fast rising pheasant, fleeing quail or running bunny with a flintlock or percussion caplock shotgun that adds to the pleasures of going afield.

As when hunting with the single-barrel designs, knowing that you may only get one chance, one shot, tends to make you concentrate more on making that first — and possibly last — shot count. There's nothing old fashioned about hunting with a muzzleloader, but there are certain steps that make shooting these guns simpler and increases their effectiveness greatly.

The first step toward hunting with this type of arm is to select one of the modern-made reproduction type arms or to locate a fine old original that is still in good serviceable

Handy to have around when figuring out loads is a dependable scale; this one is from Ohaus.

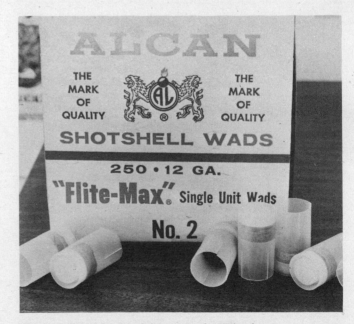

When available in the right gauge size, plastic wads such as these from Alcan make loading easy.

CHART B

GAME	GAUGE/LOAD	SHOT SIZE	MAX. RANGE WITH CYLINDER CHOKE
Small ducks	10 ga. medium	4, 5, 6	40-45 yards
	10 ga. light	4, 5, 6	30-35 yards
	12 ga. heavy	4, 5, 6	35 yards
	14 ga. heavy	5, 6	25-30 yards
Big ducks, geese	10 ga. heavy	BB, 2, 4	35-40 yards
	10 ga. medium	BB, 2, 4	35 yards
	12 ga. heavy	BB, 2, 4	35 yards
Pheasants	10 ga. light	5, 6	40-45 yards
	12 ga. heavy	5, 6	40 yards
	12 ga. medium	5, 6	35-40 yards
	14 ga. heavy	5, 6	35 yards
	14 ga. medium	5, 6	35 yards
	16 ga. heavy	5, 6	30 yards
	20 ga. heavy	5, 6	25-30 yards
Grouse, partridge	12 ga. medium	5, 6, 7½	35-40 yards
	12 ga. light	5, 6, 7½	25-30 yards
	14 ga. heavy	5, 6, 7½	35 yards
	14 ga. medium	5, 6, 7½	25-30 yards
	16 ga. heavy	5, 6, 7½	25-30 yards
	16 ga. medium	5, 6, 7½	20-25 yards
	20 ga. heavy	5, 6, 7½	25 yards
Quail, doves, pigeons, rails, snipe, woodcock	12 ga. medium	7½, 8	35-40 yards
	12 ga. light	7½, 8	25 yards
	14 ga. heavy	7½, 8	25 yards
	14 ga. medium	7½, 8	20-25 yards
	16 ga. heavy	7½, 8	20-25 yards
	16 ga. medium	7½, 8	20-25 yards
	20 ga. heavy	7½, 8	20 yards
Rabbits, squirrels	12 ga. heavy	4, 5, 6	40-45 yards
	12 ga. medium	4, 5, 6	35 yards
	14 ga. heavy	4, 5, 6	35-40 yards
	16 ga. heavy	4, 5, 6	35 yards
	20 ga. heavy	4, 5, 6	30 yards
	28 ga. heavy	4, 5, 6	20-25 yards
	.410 ga. heavy	5, 6	20 yards
Turkey, fox coyote, bobcat	10 ga. heavy	BB, 2, 4	40 yards
	10 ga. medium	BB, 2, 4	35 yards
	12 ga. heavy	BB, 2, 4	30-35 yards
	12 ga. medium	BB, 2, 4	30 yards
	14 ga. heavy	2, 4	25-30 yards
	16 ga. heavy	2, 4	20-25 yards
Deer, black bear	10 ga. medium	All loads made with either a bore sized round ball known as a pumpkin ball, a conical slug or buckshot.	40-60 yards depending on load.
	12 ga. heavy		
	12 ga. medium		
	14 ga. heavy		
	16 ga. heavy		
	20 ga. heavy		

The Harrington & Richardson Huntsman (top) is one of the few domestically produced muzzleloading shotguns presently on the market. Bottom double is imported by Dixie Gun Works.

and safe shooting condition. The latter could possibly have been lying around unfired for better than three-quarters of a century, so it is wise to really check these over before attempting to shoot them.

The outside appearance of a hundred year old original can be and often is deceiving at first inspection. The outside conditions of the gun can be near factory new and the gun could still be dangerous and unsafe to shoot. This is usually the end result of some long forgotten gunowner putting the arm away uncleaned, leaving the bore's metal at the mercy of the corrosive black powder foulings still in the barrel.

Another undersirable feature on many of the originals are the damascus twist steel barrels with which they commonly were fitted. Agreed, the pattern formed from the welds that hold the strip of steel together make an intriguing-looking arm, but they just aren't safe enough to warrant day-to-day hunting use. These welds also are more susceptible to corrosion by foulings left in the bore.

The best route to take is to purchase one of the better built modern black powder shotguns. These are much safer and in the long run will probably be more trouble free. When buying an original or gun of modern manufacture, there's one important thing to look for and that is quality. Collecting antique muzzleloading shotguns hasn't reached the level of interest of collecting original long rifles or early Colt and Remington revolvers and these guns can still be had for little less than what equals one month's grocery bill. If hunting, however, is to be the gun's main use, one of the new guns would probably be the wiser choice.

Nearly all of the old guns and a majority of the new ones are made with little if any choke constrictions in the barrel. Most of the originals were made well before anyone really knew just what choking would do to improve patterns. Even after its discovery, however, the barrels on muzzle-loading shotguns were rarely choked; due to the popular belief that any constricting of the muzzle would interfere with the loading. These cylinder bores mean that the patterns are going to be quite spread out and will be a far cry from that favorite trap gun of yours.

How the gun is loaded determines just how effectively these cylinder-bore patterns will take game. Today's components are actually far superior to what granddad had available to him; his usually being what he could make at home for the most part. Wads were usually made at home by cutting out the circular cardboard-like disks with the aid of a wad cutter. Commercial wads were available then, but not in the variety that we know today.

Although the one-piece plastic wad columns are easy to load, they usually don't give very favorable results when fired from a muzzleloading shotgun. The most effective and more reliable load is to use the commercially produced cardboard and felt wads, such as those available from Smith & Wesson-Fiocchi under the brand name of Alcan. These come in a variety of bore sizes and thicknesses.

Once these have been seated over the powder charge — not so firmly as to crush or compact the powder — a plastic shot cup can be placed over the wad. Available from a number of reloading component suppliers, plastic shot cups

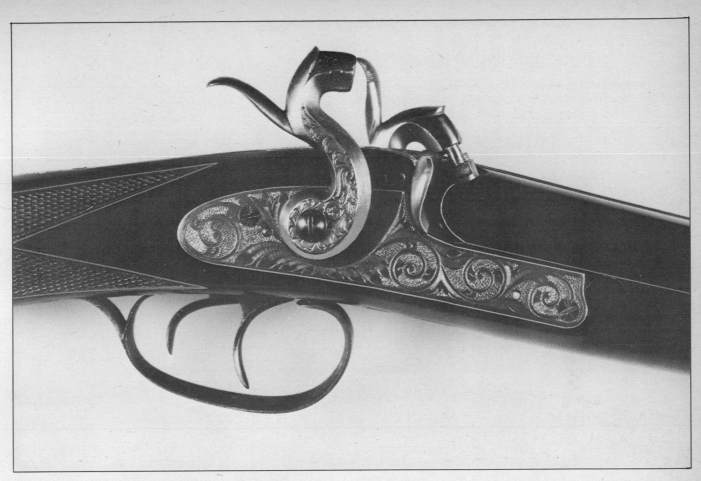

This close-up of the locks on the Replica Arms black powder double-barrel shotgun shows tasteful engraving.

help hold the patterns together and prevent the deforming of the pellets from scraping against the inside of the barrel walls as the load travels through the barrel. A tight fitting over the shot cardboard wad is used to keep the shot from rolling out the muzzle when the gun is being carried in a downward position.

What loads are best for what game? As the game's habitat varies, so will the range of the shot. As a rule, however, most shots taken with muzzleloading shotguns will be done at fairly close range so the gun can be loaded accordingly.

The key factor to successful hunting lies in matching the proper size of shot to the type of game being hunted. You've no doubt heard hunters explain how the larger the shot used the farther the effective range of the load. This is true to a certain degree, larger shot does hit with greater impact at the longer ranges, but without sufficient powder to propel it, the heavier shot is no better than a shot size two or three sizes smaller.

Here again we get back to increasing the powder charge and again we encounter the problem of having the pattern blown open by the excess pressures. About the only thing we can recommend is to start by using the starting loads shown in Chart A and work from there. Some of these loads, however probably will work better in one gun than another.

* For better results use plastic shot protectors in those gauges where available. The lighter loads normally will consistently give the best patterns.

It is only logical that you wouldn't load up with No. 2 shot, if quail were to be the afternoon's target, just as it would be equally foolish to drop in a charge of No. 7½s for big ducks or geese. True, it's nearly as easy to hit game with a muzzleloading shotgun as with a gun using modern smokeless powder shotshells, but that's not entirely the idea.

The idea is to hit them with something that will bring them down and keep them there. Chart B gives the proper size of shot to use on certain game species. This chart is to be used as a guide to follow, it doesn't mean that you can't kill geese with a load of No. 6s, because its been done before and probably will be done quite a few times more in the future. Instead, this chart should give you a good idea of what size shot and load is best suited for hunting a certain type of game.

An important thing always to keep in mind is that black powder shotguns are the underdog among hunting firearms. Due to their lack of choking and slight decrease in power, ranges naturally are going to be shorter.

But that's where the challenge lies: getting close enough for the shot and, when it presents itself, to make a good one-shot kill!

BUILDING THE MUZZLELOADING RIFLE

When completed from the furnished kit, the CVA long rifle is set on sandbags and initial test made for accuracy.

CHAPTER 20

THE KENTUCKY RIFLE has graceful lines, nice balance and was one of the favored arms of its time. However, at first glance, the Kentucky rifle kit from Connecticut Valley Arms is a lot of mysterious parts, each in its own little recess amid the Styrofoam packing. The caliber .45 barrel we received was in white and the stock was in two pieces, but there were enough bits of shaped brass to make up an authentic percussion replica.

Being caliber .45, the rifle would be legal for use in most states that hold a muzzleloader season for deer, though it would be below minimum standards in states requiring caliber .50 or higher for hunting elk.

With the time-consuming chore of getting the rest of this revision ready, we called in C.R. Learn, an individual with only two thumbs — one on each hand — who is an avid do-it-yourself practitioner.

The kit was turned over to him with instructions to get at it, and have it done for inclusion in these pages. The kit occupied a corner of Learn's workbench until he summoned the courage to open it.

He laid out the pieces according to their listing on the instruction sheet. Trepidation was eased as he discovered the barrel fit closely into the base and forend sections of the stock and only a small amount of sanding would be required. He still would have to remove a bit of wood from the places already inletted for the brass pieces.

"By the time I had all parts fit together as illustrated in the exploded view at the top of the instruction sheet, I had decided this project was not going to be as complicated as I had first suspected. It began to look more like it was going to be fun."

A beginner putting together his first rifle probably should be following the included instructions to the letter, but Learn felt it would be easier to use the basic directions and vary the procedure a bit. Where the instructions suggested putting the two pieces of the stock together first, he rationalized it would be more convenient to work with the shorter sections than trying to manipulate the three feet-plus of the complete stock. His first move was to place the L-shaped brass butt plate in its approximate position to see how much he would have to remove before it would fit properly.

"The tools I needed for this project were already in my workshop. Included were a small, motorized hand drill which makes inletting work go faster and means a neater job. I used the drill for the initial cutting work, then switched to a hand rasp for final shaping that would allow the butt plate, with its wide comb piece, to go in place. A good

With Today's Connecticut Valley Arms Kit, You Can Save Money While Giving Your Smokepole An Individual Look!

wood-to-metal fit takes time, but the rasp gave me better control over the amount of wood being removed."

The home craftsman soon had the butt plate matched to the stock and the two screws that would hold it in place seated. All that remained of this first step was to fit a long, thin, brass plate to the bottom of the stock, which was accomplished quickly with a flat rasp, and putting a slight groove in the butt plate to allow the bottom strap to fit without a gap. Holes for the three holding screws were predrilled and the screws twisted in to complete the job.

All of the heavy woodworking already has been accomplished by the kit manufacturers, so all the home assembler must do is some light inletting and stock finishing.

With the brass side plate in position on the left side of the stock, a slight widening of the recess was needed. Learn

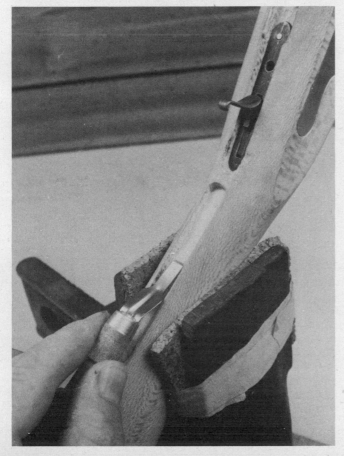

accomplished this quickly with the small drill and an inletting tool.

"The right side, where the lock holding the hammer would be positioned, was a bit trickier, as the trigger hadn't been prepositioned and I had to make room for the trigger to trip the arm that drops the hammer. Fitting in the lock did not require removing much wood; the inletting already done left just enough wood to make me work a bit without making a full-day chore out of it. This gave me the butt plate and bottom plate, the side plate and the lock already mounted. The next step would be the trigger assembly."

This required opening the trigger recess to seat the trigger plate, but this went quickly with the small drill and cutter tool. When the recess looked right, Learn placed the trigger unit in it and, gripping it tightly, tried the trigger to discover the hammer wouldn't drop. Wood needed to be removed from above the arm of the trigger lock.

"I worked at this with a combination of X-Acto blades and the cutter drill until, after several tries, the lock allowed the hammer to drop easily. Once the trigger unit was seated and working properly, I dropped a small locating pin into the trigger base and tapped it into the stock. This pin and the tang bolt that holds the base of the barrel would prevent any movement of the trigger unit."

Next came installation of the ornate brass trigger guard. This piece almost fit the factory inletting, but its recess

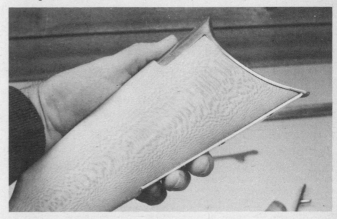

Left: Using small carving tools, inletting is done for trigger plate assembly as well as for the trigger guard. Above: Butt requires removal of a bit of wood for the brass butt plate to fit properly, it was discovered.

Brass and wood can be leveled by use of rasp to cut both. This affords a tighter fit; brass is polished later.

Area for lock plate is inletted on the right side of stock, then surface is sanded smooth. Area must be cut back enough so that the hammer is operable.

required a bit of cutting before it dropped into place with the top of the piece below the surface of the outer wood. The stock would have to be sanded down during final finishing, which would level the wood and metal to a single smooth surface.

The guard in place, Learn predrilled and set the three retaining screws. The forend fits to the base stock section on two steel rods, one on each side of the barrel channel in the base part of the stock. Holes for these were predrilled into the forend for a snug fit. A brass plate provides a seam between the two stock pieces, and this was slipped over the rods. To determine that the two sections were properly aligned, Learn placed the barrel in its channel with the sections held together. A slight amount of wood had to be removed before the two pieces would fit flush at the joint. Two tenons were welded along the bottom of the barrel — already inletted — to aid in holding barrel to stock. With a bit of shaving, the two stock sections and the barrel formed

a straight line.

"I removed the barrel and metal rods from the stock and began to mix a good, two-solution epoxy. When it was ready, I coated both rods and the holes they fit into, as well as both sides of the brass joining plate, with the epoxy. I placed the rods in their holes, fitted the brass plate over them, and pressed the two stock sections together until epoxy oozed from the joint. I coated the barrel with a wax parting agent, placed it in its groove, vised it to the maximum depth of its channel, and left the assembly to dry overnight.

"A good parting agent is a must if using the barrel as a guide, unless the kit assembler wants his barrel permanently glued to the stock. It is not necessary to have a guide, but I wanted to ensure a tight and straight fit."

Once the epoxy had cured properly, it was necessary to drill a hole for a tang bolt that extends through the grip part of the stock and engages the threaded base of the

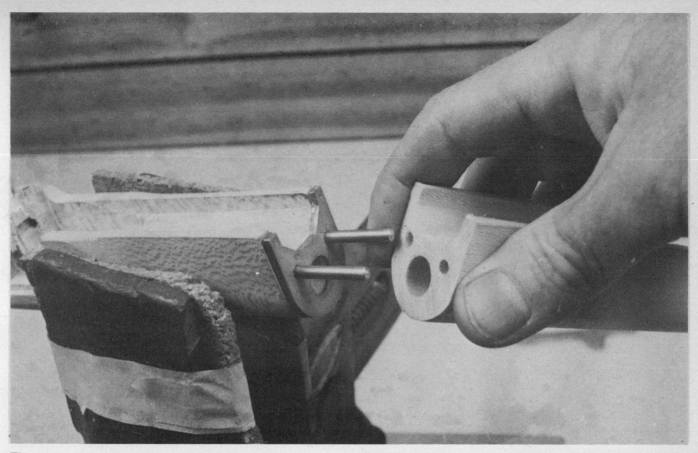

The two sections of the long stock were joined, using the furnished brass spacer and the steel dowel pins. The larger predrilled hole is for the gun's ramrod.

trigger plate to hold the barrel firmly.

To do this, Learn marked the top hole and removed the barrel, then removed the trigger guard and marked the hole in the trigger plate. The two holes had to be aligned through the stock. The tang bolt hole was to be drilled by starting at one of these marks and drilling through to the other. This was not a time for impatience. Following the instructions, he used a vernier caliper to mark a pencil line down the side of the stock and side plate. Learn checked the line to be certain it aligned with the upper and lower marks, then moved to a simple drill press: a hand drill that fits into a homemade table mount.

It was necessary that the drill bit be slightly larger than the trigger plate hole; thus, the tang bolt didn't have to be threaded through the stock. A right-angle square ensured that the drill bit was vertical to the stock, with the stock held tightly in a vacuum base vise. For added insurance, Learn used several extra clamps on the vise base.

"When I felt it was right, I started drilling. When finished, the mark I had made at the trigger base had disappeared. As a final check, I removed the stock from the vise and placed the barrel in its channel, making certain the base of the barrel was firm against the back of its inletted groove. Then I dropped the tang bolt through the new hole. It should fit snugly, but move freely all the way to the trigger plate. I threaded it home and the rifle was held together by this bolt from the base of the barrel, through the handgrip of the stock and into the trigger base plate."

For drilling the holes in the side of the forestock for the two tenon pins, Learn checked his drill index and selected a bit that would make snug holes for the diameter of these pins.

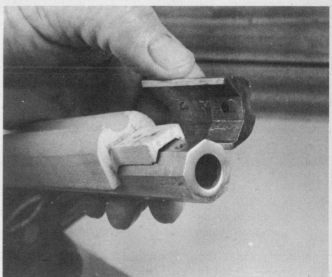

The brass tip cap must be fitted to the forend of stock. Cut the wood back to allow the cap to fit, then align it with the drilled and tapped holes for the brass screws.

To mark the proper spots on the stock, Learn first measured down the sides of the barrel with the vernier calipers to get the thickness of the barrel from top to bottom. This gave the position of the tenons on the barrel; adding a fraction allowed the pins to be placed more in the center of the tenon than toward the base, eliminating any danger of drilling into the base of the barrel.

"I marked the position of the tenons on the stock with a pencil, then placed the calipers on each mark and made corresponding marks on the tenons. I mounted the rifle in my bench vise and lined it up with the mounted drill,

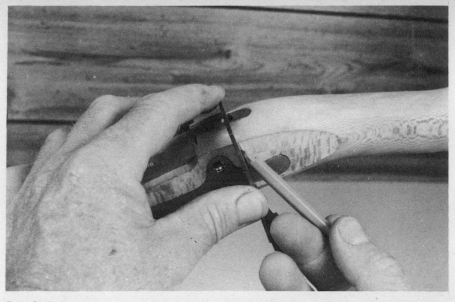

With the barrel fitted, tang formed to fit the stock, one must drill the tang bolt hole to mate tang to the trigger plate assembly. Mark line on side with the plates for drilling.

checking with an angle and a bubble level. Satisfied that all was aligned, I began drilling the first tenon. The same care on the second tenon paid off with perfect alignment."

Fitting the nose cap to the tip of the forestock involved aligning the cap with the bolt holes in the tip of the barrel and shaving a bit of wood from the shaped tip to allow a snug fit. Care is necessary not to take off too much wood as the retaining bolts are designed to go through the cap, through the wood and into prethreaded holes in the barrel. These bolts must be countersunk before they will screw all the way down.

The rifle now was completed, except for sanding and finishing the stock, blueing or browning the barrel, and adding the ramrod thimbles.

In finishing his rifle stock, the builder may elect to follow the traditional lines of the Kentucky rifle. This means rounding corners on all edges, with the exception of the side plate and the lock side. There is also some metal finishing to be done, but this can be accomplished by sanding metal and wood at the same time to get a smooth, integrated finish.

"In normal stock work, I usually remove all metal parts from a gun and work only on the wood. With the muzzle-loader, I already had some scratched brass, so I decided to take it down with the wood to make a clean-fitting union of wood and metal. Brass removes easily with a rasp and can be buffed and polished later.

"I removed the trigger guard as it would only get in my way and was already fairly flush with stock. I left the butt plate and bottom plate and the brass stock divider, which could not have been removed in any case, being epoxied on. I also removed the nose cap, but left the tenon pins in place until I removed the barrel when ready to stain."

Learn started stock shaping by rasping the forend at the tenon pins. This done, he removed the barrel, which left the stock with its brass fittings easier to work on. He turned his attentions to the butt and comb of the stock to shape the brass and wood into the traditionally flowing lines of the original Kentucky guns. Care was taken in working on the comb, because of the wide strip of brass that angles over the end of the stock from the butt plate. Moving to the upper portion where the tang bolt is inserted, he replaced

the barrel and made sure the wood and metal parts fit as closely as possible, then removed the barrel and set it aside.

The brass side plate should be almost flush with the side of the stock, but this area should be relatively flat, so care was taken not to round the edges with the rasp. The lock was removed to avoid marks on the metal. The rasp was held as flat as possible to avoid rounded edges on these two surfaces.

"The forend was simple to smooth; I just kept the rasp moving to round the edge of the barrel channel, but held

Starting with a small guide hole, check alignment of the drill, then drill hole a bit larger than tang bolt. Drill through stock. Brass side plate helps alignment.

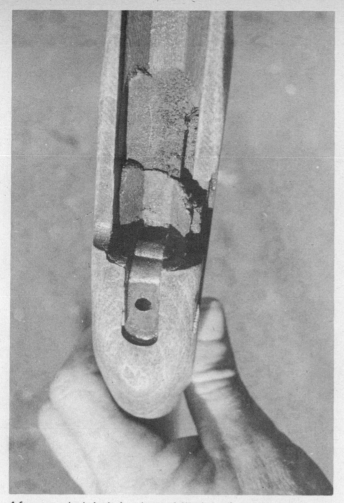

After tang bolt hole has been drilled, back section can be filled with wood putty, plastic wood or any similar material for a clean, solid fit into the barrel.

marks, using only light touches. The sanding block prevented dishing out the larger areas of wood. Checking the stock in strong sunlight, he found a few remaining rasp marks and used the strong sandpaper to remove them. Sandpaper of 120-grit was used to remove the sanding marks left by the coarser grade. This was followed by finishing touches with 0000 steel wool.

The Birchwood-Casey Muzzleloaders Barrel and Stock Finishing Kit contained a colonial red stock finish, but when tried on a piece of scrap wood, the color was too dark. Learn wanted the figure and grain structure of the wood to show. He settled for a can of Delft cherrywood stain. This stain is water soluble and cleans up easily after use.

"After removing all metal parts from the stock, I folded a clean rag as an applicator, stirred up the stain and dipped the rag in it. I applied the first coat heavily and quickly, following the grain of the wood. With the rag applicator, I could rub the stock down as I layered the stain. I covered the outside of the stock, the barrel channel and all internal areas, then set the stock aside to dry."

When checked an hour later, the smooth sanding job seemed to have disappeared. The water-base stain had lifted the hair of the wood grain and the stock felt rough again, which was exactly what was wanted. With 0000 steel wool Learn rubbed down the entire stock again. This removed the grain hair and put an added smoothness on the wood. It also lightened the shade of the stain.

"I took the first coat down until it was fairly light. I layered on the second coat, waited for it to dry and rubbed it down. This time I had removed most of the stain with the cloth applicator as I layered it down. The grain hair didn't lift as much. I set the stock aside for a few days to allow the stain to dry thoroughly."

The final phase was the stock finish. Learn decided to try the Tru-Oil type supplied with the finishing kit.

"Following the directions, I folded a piece of old flannel shirt into a square, tipped the bottle over on the pad and applied it to the stock. The Tru-Oil went on easily, and I didn't have any of the finish runs that come with too much haste. With the pad applicator, I worked the finish into the wood as I went. I had to keep moving because the solution dries rapidly. I also made sure I didn't leave any threads from the cloth pad in the finish."

While the first coat dried, all brass parts were cleaned and polished with a buffer mounted on an old washing machine motor. If a matte finish is desired, the polishing

this to a minimum. I took down some of the wood by the nose cap, since there was quite a ridge left when the cap had been taken down to fit the barrel. At the junction of the two stock sections, I rasped the brass joint flush with the wood," Learn reports.

With the majority of excess wood removed, he mounted 80-grit sandpaper in a sanding block and removed the rasp

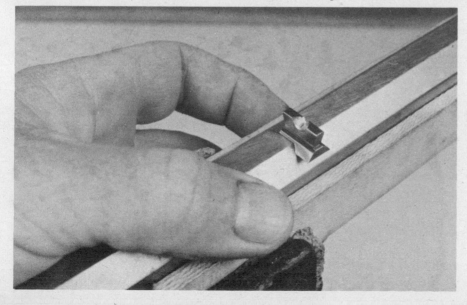

The barrel, still unblued, has been cleaned, sight slot lightly filed with a three-cornered file for snug fit.

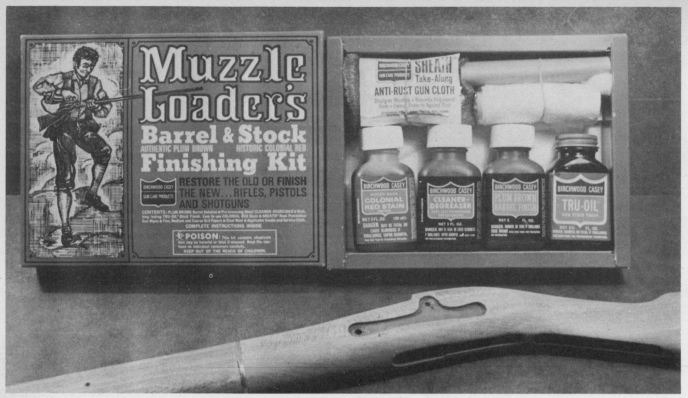

Connecticut Valley Arms also offers a Birchwood Casey stock and barrel finishing kit for simple, fast work. Kit includes stock dye or stain, Tru-Oil for the final finish, plus plum brown stains for finishing the steel.

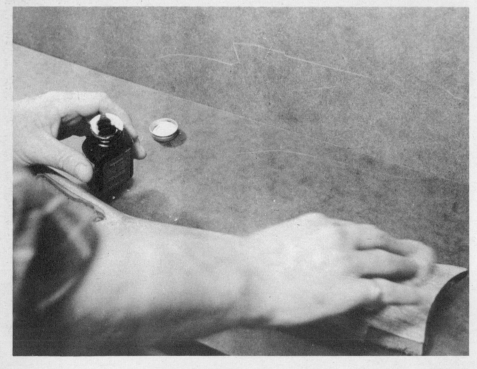

After final rubbing with 0000 steel wool, the stock is stained to the desired shade. After drying, Tru-Oil finish is applied with pad, fingers. The more it is rubbed, the deeper the resulting lustre on the wood.

can be done with steel wool. The buffer was used until each piece glistened.

After applying the second coat of Tru-Oil and allowing it to dry, 0000 steel wool was used to clean off the dust particles that had drifted onto the finish while still wet. A third coat finished the job. This procedure can be repeated until the builder has achieved the desired finish and luster.

"I reassembled the rifle and looked it over. When I had fitted the nose cap, I had neglected to countersink the three retaining screws. These screws blocked the channel in which

the ramrod would fit once I had installed the three brass thimbles that hold it."

Learn used a countersink bit to reposition the nose cap screws, then installed the ramrod thimbles. This is a simple matter of placing each band on the ramrod groove as the instructions direct and marking the stock where each screw hole will be drilled. Using a hand drill and the right size bit, he drilled from the barrel channel to the ramrod groove. Then he inserted the small brass screw, pulling the thimble tight with a small screwdriver. If the screws protrude into

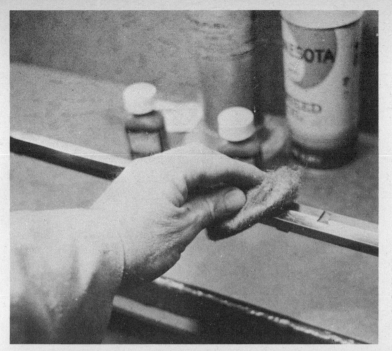

Left: Before applying brown finish, the barrel must be cleaned with 0000 steel wool, then with a degreasing solution supplied with the kit. Barrel then is heated and plum brown material applied. Below: The smaller metal parts can be heated in a small electric broiler. The heat is even and it makes parts easier to handle.

the ramrod groove, it is necessary to file them down slightly until the ramrod will pass through all three thimbles. The ramrod supplied was for field use and to complete the looks of the gun. A longer one can be ordered for firing on the range.

Instead of staining the ramrod, Learn sanded it lightly and used a propane torch to burn a series of stripes along its length, passing the rod through the flame and rotating it at the same time. The end result gave it a little different flare. He sanded it again, applied two coats of stain and a thin layer of gun oil, then polished it by rubbing. This method

left no layer of finish to flake off against the thimbles and fall into the barrel. The brass tips were polished with metal polish and 0000 steel wool.

"In the past, I had used only blueing compounds on the barrels of my guns, but I decided to try the steel dyes included in the Birchwood-Casey finishing kit. I was on equal footing with the rankest beginner as I got out the degreaser and the plum brown dye and started reading their directions," Learn says.

The first step was to clean the slots for the front and rear sights, using a small, three-cornered file. The sights

Top: Lock plate and hammer are case-hardened and normally aren't browned. Right: At proper temperature, small parts are dipped in brown solution. A set of hemostats or miniclaps will help in getting parts evenly coated.

then were installed by cleaning the burrs from the base of each and working slowly until the sight fit into the slot grooved into the top of the barrel. Once tapped home, the sights should not slip against finger pressure. A small plastic hammer will prevent breaking off the high brass blade of the front sight.

It also was necessary to clean out any filing residue around the drum that holds the firing cap nipple. Removing the drum makes it easier to buff the barrel. The drum, tenon pins, tang bolt and other steel parts were to be dyed separately.

To clean the barrel of scratches and lines, Learn chose a set of buffing wheels as being the easiest way. A draw file or a series of progressively finer steel wools will serve as well, but require more elbow grease. He checked the barrel for dents or gouges and found it to be in good shape, so started the cleaning process with the 120-grit wheel, jumped from it to the finer 240-grit wheel and finished off with a polishing sequence. At this point, the barrel is extremely vulnerable to moisture and can pick up rust from fingerprints. To prevent this, Learn donned light cotton gloves.

"I used the cleaner/degreaser solution to clean the entire

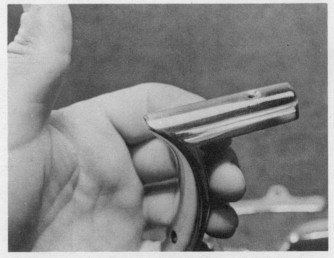

While the barrel is cooling, there is time to buff and polish the brass hardware. Butt plate has been cleaned, polished and is ready to be replaced on finished stock.

After browning, the rear sight is placed in the notch on barrel. In this case, it was centered with use of a Bushnell optical sighting system. As with the front sight, this one also was turned around by Learn later.

Left: After being cleaned, filed to fit, the front sight is placed in barrel slot. The sight later was turned around, as Bob Learn felt latter position afforded an improved sighting picture. Tip cap has been polished.

barrel of any wax, oil or other materials and found that it went on easily and had only a mildly offensive odor. Any good solvent, such as acetone or paint thinner could be used.

"I now needed some type of rack that would not dissipate during heating and coating. Coat hangers were not the answer. I finally clamped an old allen wrench in each of two bench vises with the hooks pointed up, and hooked the muzzle of the barrel over one and the tang bolt hole over the other. It was wobbly, but the barrel didn't need to be totally rigid.

"I used the propane torch as a heat source, moving it back and forth along the barrel to distribute the heat evenly. The instructions suggest using the water drop test to determine when the barrel is hot enough. This involves tossing a couple drops of water against the barrel. If the water steams away, the barrel is too hot. If the drops dance around on the metal, it is about right. I kept testing and when the water danced, I picked up the dauber, dipped it in the plum brown solution and ran it over the barrel. This solution contains nitric acid, which won't harm human skin, but care should be taken against letting it reach the eyes in the event of a splatter. A well-ventilated work area is mandatory as the fumes from this solution are rather pungent."

The next step was to apply light oil to bring out the color. The result was the messiest, most streaked barrel-coloring job in recent history.

Apparently the barrel was too cool, as the directions stated that the temperature was critical. After applying steel wool and elbow grease, our hero was ready to try again.

"This time, I heated the barrel until the water steamed off in a visible vapor. I set the torch aside and water-tested different areas of the barrel until it seemed to be a bit hotter than on my first try. I applied the solution along the length of one section of the six-sided barrel, turned it to cover the next section and repeated until the entire barrel was covered.

"I checked the tang and the end of the muzzle to be certain I had covered them and found that all parts had a deep, even color that I was happy with. I allowed the barrel to cool until it could be handled, then applied pure linseed oil to bring up the color. The brown had a nice depth and was even on the entire barrel."

To heat the smaller parts, Learn used a small electric oven he had rewired to make it run hotter. Parts were put on a metal tray covered with tinfoil and heated for staining. Rather than try to hold the hot parts and apply the dye to them, a pair of hemostats were used as dipping sticks with the parts clamped therein and dipped into the bottle of solution. It worked well and the parts were allowed to dry. When cool, each received a coat of linseed oil to make the color come up clearly.

"Once all parts were dry, it was a simple matter to assemble the rifle for the final time, lay it on the workbench and step back to admire my own cleverness. My final act was to remove the firing cap nipple drum from the base of the barrel and swab the barrel out with solvent and a clean patch. This removed wood shavings, metal filings and dust accumulated in the bore during assembly.

"Stan Hemenway had just finished a Numrich Arms rifle kit in caliber .50. We gathered up rifles and shooting necessities and headed for an isolated stretch of hills."

Learn's black powder shooting kit contained caliber .45 balls, patches, a powder flask with 30-grain measuring spout, patch lube, a can of caps and a magazine-type capper. He picked up a quantity of the recommended FFFg grade from a local dealer. Some shooters use a coarser grain powder, but it makes for a rougher clean-up job, and often compels the shooter to clean out the bore and cap nipple about every other shot.

"Following instructions, I started by tipping a 30-grain measure of powder down the bore, then spread a pre-lubed patch across the muzzle and laid a lead ball with the flat side or sprue facing upward. Using a fiberglass ramrod I had ordered with the loading kit, I pushed patch and ball down on top of the powder. The fit was relatively loose, so the flexible rod gave me no trouble. With a tight fit, a wooden

The CVA kit comes complete with all necessary instructions, but some of the tools, epoxies, et al., will be required from other sources.

For first test, .45 Kentucky rifle is fed a double load of FFFg black powder. Spout on flask drops 30 grains, but Learn wanted to determine if gun would handle 60.

Patch is greased using the patch lubricant furnished with the CVA kit. A dab was found sufficient for aid in lubricating the ball into barrel, sealing for first shot.

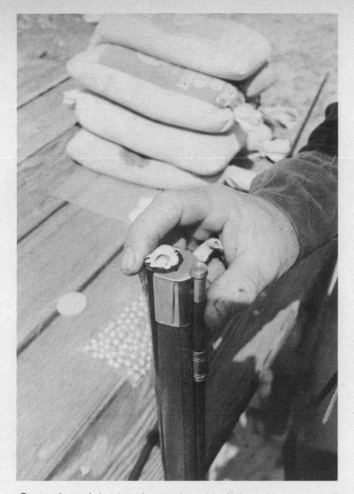

Greased patch is placed over the end of the barrel, a .443-inch round ball placed sprue up on patch. It is forced solidly against the powder charge with ramrod.

Blast from the black powder load rolls downrange, as the heavy smoke follows. Learn found the recoil to be less than with 12-gauge trap gun. Note shooting glasses.

starter is needed to force the ball into the bore, then the ramrod is used to seat it. The lubed patch rides smoothly against the surface of the bore and helps seal in the gases that will propel the ball when the powder is ignited."

Bob Learn cocked the hammer and slipped a firing cap on the nipple. He had been warned about placing the cap before loading and about keeping the bore pointed away from his body during loading. "I nestled the rifle against a high stump and sighted in on the cardboard box we had marked with an X as an improvised target. As the sight picture took shape, my finger curled naturally around the trigger and the shot went booming down the canyon."

To an experienced shooter, the process of cranking off a round does not vary much from rifle to rifle. Putting a hole in the box was made easier by the almost total lack of recoil, and Learn later learned this rifle could be fired all day with normal loads without beating the shooter's shoulder as with a contemporary rifle and modern loads.

As he fed a few more rounds through the tube, Learn noted the trigger needed tightening. It had too much play before the slack was taken up. The hammer had been bent slightly to one side, so it would strike the cap, but a few misfires indicated that it still needed some adjustment. The sights could be tuned a bit better. Learn headed back to his workshop for some fine tuning on his new shooter.

"Once the rifle was clean, I heated the hammer with a propane torch and bent it to the inside and forward. I placed a cap on the nipple and test-fired the mechanism to make certain the new angle and operation were correct.

"The rear sight is a simple dovetail while the front is a high brass comb. I may put on a different rear sight later, but my concern now was to adjust for a tight group on paper. The traditional way to accomplish this is to fire and correct, fire and correct and fire again. My method saves powder and shot. I pulled my Bushnell Bore Sighter out of a drawer and placed the caliber .45 mandril in the sighter unit."

Readings indicated the sights were off to the left, so Learn tapped the front sight a bit, then moved the rear sight until both were in center vertical alignment.

"Sights adjusted, I took the rifle out to the San Diego County Fish and Game Association range on Willow Glen Road. I set up my target halfway down their hundred-yard rifle course and sandbagged the rifle to place the sights at a level that would let me peer down the barrel without scrunching down.

"I loaded up the Kentucky rifle and placed a cap and triggered off my first shot. That round hit low and to the left. I fired a few more rounds. The group stayed in the lower left of the target, but was not as tight as I wanted. It takes time to build up the right load, but once this is done, the muzzleloaders shoot with accuracy. This shooting would kill a varmint, but not at over fifty yards. The muzzleloader is a one-shot rifle and I wanted that one shot to be right on every time.

"Any qualms about the recoil were totally gone even after I had doubled the powder charge to 60 grains. While the heavier charge was noisier, recoil was nil."

BUILDING THE CAP'N BALL SIXGUN CHAPTER 21

...Or Adventures In Building A Replica From Something Called Semi-Finished Parts!

Finished, the Dixie Gun Works' brass frame Remington cap and ball revolver is comparable to many of today's replica guns.

Aﬀer READING a number of tests on just about every type of black powder muzzleloader that is being produced today and perhaps trying some of them, one might find that he is interested in creating a black powder puffer that is strictly his own; something that he had a personal hand in creating.

With this thought, we cast about for a project that might intrigue the do-it-yourself type shooter. In checking a new catalog from Dixie Gun Works, I found that, among the new products, is a replica Remington brass frame cap and ball kit. And that's how I came to be in the gunmaking business!

A letter was sent to Turner Kirkland of Dixie Gun Works after I agreed to try my hand at gunsmithing. A week or so later I found a large and well packed box sitting on my desk when I arrived for work one morning. After a good ten minutes of sifting and digging through what must have been two, maybe three, editions of the Union City Gazette, I finally came to the conclusion that I had already found everything that was to be found from the then heaping pile of papers. Although, I must admit that I did occasionally take time to read a tidbit of news here and there, a fellow has to keep up on current events. One thing was for certain, though: Dixie Gun Works does an impressive packaging job. It would have been near impossible for any of the parts to be damaged in shipment.

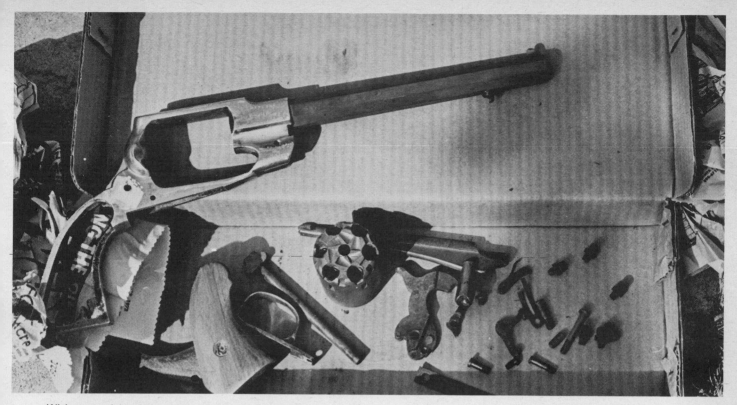

With exception of some minor finishing of the brass frame, but with barrel screwed in place, the kit arrived looking somewhat like it does above.

Taking a quick inventory of the parts included in the kit revealed that I was now in possession of a mould cast brass frame, a barrel of somewhere over seven inches long, a cylinder complete with six separate nipples, two well over-sized grip blanks, a brass trigger housing, a genuine steel loading lever and a handful of internal parts, that — hopefully — would allow me to fire the handgun once it was completed.

Deciding to perform most of the major operations first, I set all of the firing mechanism parts, the barrel, cylinder and loading lever aside.

Using a Dremel Moto-Tool with a 3/8-inch diameter cone shaped emery bit, I started in on the rough cast brass frame. This is the most time-consuming phase of constructing the kit. Care must be taken not to shave too much from the soft brass frame.

The rounded cone shaped emery bit is best for knocking down the rough surface from the areas of the frame that enclose the cylinder. For the squared-off portions of the frame, such as that found on the butt of the frame, I switched to a flat surfaced 3/4-inch diameter grinding point. The frame sported a crude ridge of built up brass in this area that was left from the mould casting. The flat sur-faced grinding bit makes removing this ridge quicker and easier, it also helps eliminate the possibility of accidentally giving this surface a beveled rounded edge, which would make the fitting of the grips to metal more difficult.

Before putting the final finish onto the frame, the threaded portion into which the barrel is inserted was heated slightly with a small torch and the barrel was firmly seated. If you decide to get one of these kits and do not have access to one of the small propane type torches, the barrel could possibly be seated with a chemical bonding agent such as Loc-Tite.

Next the grip blanks required minor inletting before they would fit onto the frame. This was accomplished with the Moto-Tool with a cutting wheel inserted.

With the wood stocks fastened to the frame, a medium-toothed wood file was used to remove excess wood from the grips. This was followed by a brisk sanding with 120-grit sandpaper and a lighter sanding with 300-grit sand-paper. Before finishing the grips with Birchwood Casey Tru-Oil, the grips received a final sanding with both 400 and 600-grit papers.

The Dremel Moto-Tool and the various bits that come with it make finishing of the rough brass frame much faster and easier.

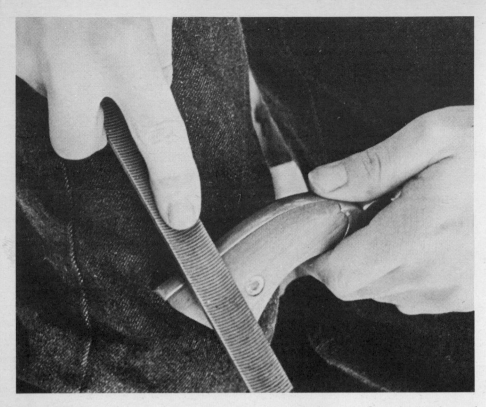

Over-sized walnut grip blanks are filed to nearly finished shape before using sandpaper for smooth finish. (Below) Naval Jelly removed the mottled finish and rust found on some of the parts in Dixie kit.

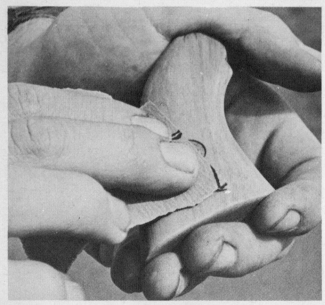

Sanding with the grain, the completely shaped walnut grip receives final sanding.

To give the wood a high gloss finish, the grips received four applications of the Tru-Oil finish. Between applications, which take approximately two hours to dry, the preceding application was rubbed down with 000 steel wool before the next coat was applied.

With the major operations out of the way, attention was turned to the parts that were to be blued. As the parts had been shipped, some were slightly pitted or not finished at all.

To remove the caked-on protective lubricant and mottled finish of some parts, they were soaked in Naval Jelly for approximately ten minutes. They were then washed in a hot soapy water solution to remove any oil that

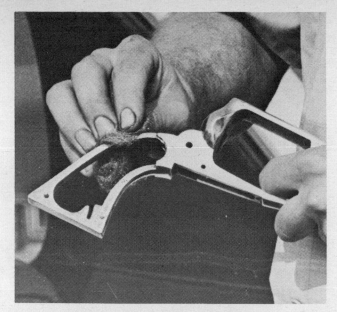

A fine grade of steel wool — 000 or 0000 — is used to remove the etched lines left by the bits of the high-speed Dremel Moto-Tool.

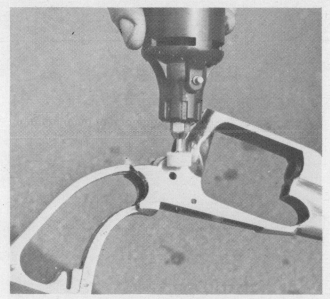

A high-gloss finish was easily obtained with the felt polishing cloth and tool's 30,000 rpm.

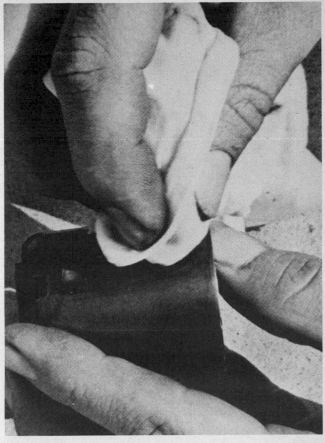

(Above) the 44/40 cold bluing is applied to degreased cylinder with clean cloth. Using nipple wrench, below, the revolver's nipples are securely tightened in place.

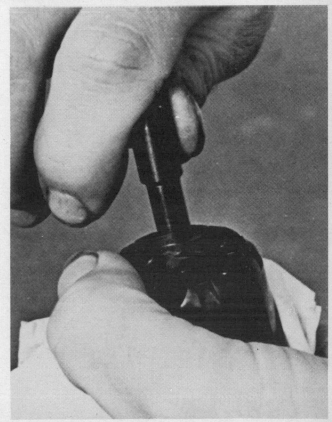

might have remained in the pores of the metal.

While the internal parts, cylinder and loading lever were soaking in the soapy solution, the area of the frame adjacent to the already fitted barrel was taped off with masking tape. The barrel was then cleaned with a dry cleaning solution known as Carbona, which has replaced the now-forbidden carbon tetrachloride.

After swabbing the barrel several times with Carbona, which was done outside where there was better ventilation, the barrel received a generous coat of 44/40 Instant Gun Blue. This bluing product begins to work as soon as it is applied to the metal surface and should be rinsed off as soon as the part or area being treated has received an application.

To give the metal a deeper finish, the first coat was worked down with 000 steel wool. The barrel was then

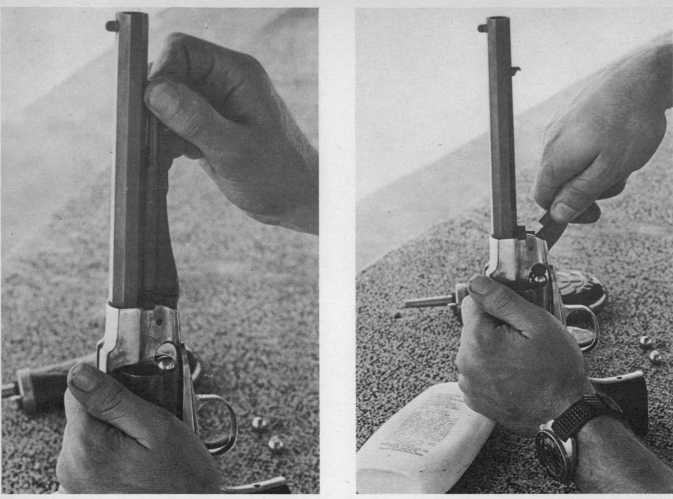

Left (above) The slightly oversized lead ball is placed over the chamber, then the cylinder is rotated until the ball is directly over the ball. (Right) Rammer then is pulled down to force the ball into the chamber, seating it on the powder.

Hodgdon's Spit Ball was the commercial lubricant that was in testing the black powder kit gun after its completion.

cleaned with the cleaning solution again and received an additional coat of 44/40, rinsed with clear water and dried. A coat of gun oil was applied to prevent the metal from rusting.

The remaining parts that were to be blued were also rinsed with clear water and allowed to dry. They then received the same treatment as the barrel. The result was a more than adequate bluing job.

To remove the heavily etched lines left in the frame by the emery and grinding bits of the Moto-Tool, I used 600 grit sandpaper. This also left lines in the brass that, although not evident to the touch, distracted from the revolver's appearance. To remove these, a heavy duty rubbing compound similar to that used by auto body shops to rejuvenate damaged auto finishes was used.

Several applications of the rubbing compound, applied in circular motions with a soft cotton cloth, gave the frame a smooth and glossy finish that was free from scratches. To give it an even higher gloss, the Moto-Tool with a felt polishing wheel inserted was used.

Now to put the revolver's working mechanism together! Really this isn't as difficult as it may sound. Even without instructions or a diagram to follow, I managed to assemble it in less than twenty minutes.

With the exception of the trigger and hammer, there are only two springs, four screws and two other internal parts.

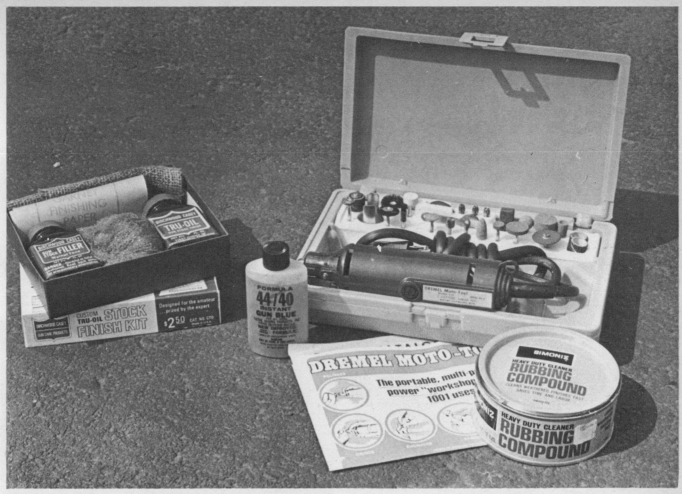

Utilized in construction of the Dixie Gun Works cap and ball kit were a Dremel Moto-Tool, Tru-Oil's stock finishing kit, 44/40 bluing mixtures and a commercial rubbing compound.

Using common sense and good judgment, anyone should be capable of figuring out what goes where.

The hammer is inserted through its slot in the frame and is worked downward until the lower end is extending from the lower part of the frame. There is a small threaded hole on the lower section of the hammer and this should fall below the lines of the frame.

Next to be installed is a small piece that has a small leaf type spring extending from it. This is the hand, the part of the mechanism that turns the cylinder during cocking. There is a narrow channel inside the frame and this is where the hand goes. The spring faces to the rear and the wedge shaped point protrudes through an opening in the area of the frame that is directly to the rear of the cylinder. The hand is fastened to the lower end of the hammer by the smallest screw in the kit and the whole assembly is held in place by one main screw.

Next to be installed is the cylinder bolt. This is located next to the trigger and both are actually installed at the same time. The cylinder bolt is inserted so that the small locking lug projects through the rectangular shaped port in the bottom of the frame. The cylinder bolt and trigger are fastened with the same screw. Tension is applied to both parts by the trigger and cylinder bolt spring. This fits directly over both and is fastened by a single short screw on the forward portion of the frame.

Next to be installed is the mainspring. This is sometimes difficult to get to slip right into place and often takes several attempts before popping into the correct position. This part rests on a tang located on the back side of the hammer, with the other end slipping into a slot that is provided in the frame. Supplying tension to the hammer, the mainspring is housed between the grips. With this part in place, the firing mechanism is completed.

The trigger guard then is fastened to the frame by inserting the notched rear section into place and then securing the forward section with a single screw.

The nipples then are threaded into the cylinder with the wrench provided. The hammer is placed at half cock and the cylinder is slipped into the frame. To secure it into position, the cylinder pin is inserted through the hole in the frame directly below the barrel. With this in place the loading lever is installed, this also holds the cylinder pin, preventing it from slipping forward.

The kit is now an assembled and shootable cap and ball handgun. Providing the builder uses a reasonable amount of care in building kit No. 140, as Dixie Gun Works has dubbed it, this revolver will handle any load that any of the numerous other preassembled revolvers are capable of firing. As with any black powder gun, however, smokeless powders should never be used. If you entertain any thoughts of getting this kit, or any other kit or assembled black powder gun, and have never fired one before, it is advisable that you get one of the black powder manuals that are now on the market, such as that available from Hodgdon Powder Company of Shawnee Mission, Kansas.

BUILDING THE DIXIE MUZZLELOADING SHOTGUN

CHAPTER 22

This Semifinished Kit Allows The Builder To Incorporate Design Ideas Of His Own

Ralph Walker admires the finished shotgun from Dixie Gun Works kit.

POPULAR ITEMS IN the Dixie Gun Works line are the wide variety of do-it-yourself gun kits. These run the gamut from a faithful reproduction of the flintlock Kentucky or Pennsylvania rifles to inexpensive and simple percussion kits that anyone can assemble. The various kits consist not only of Dixie Gun Works' own models but also those of other major companies currently producing kits and assembled black powder firearms.

There probably isn't a better shotgun repair expert in the country than Ralph Walker, who operates out of Selma, Alabama. He not only fixes them, but takes a lot of bobwhite quail during each season to prove he knows what it's all about.

But in recent times, Walker has become intrigued with the black powder field and has been experimenting with everything from chokes to loads. As a result, we decided he was the outstanding candidate to handle the do-it-yourself report on this firearm. So he was contacted and given a free hand.

"A couple of years ago Dixie offered a double-barrel percussion shotgun kit, which brought back many fond memories of my boyhood days when I first became interested in shotguns and used my grandfather's old double-barrel percussion shotgun on many hunting ventures," Walker says.

A phone call to Dixie about the new kit brought mixed news. Only one rough prototype was available at the time and they were waiting a sizable shipment of the refined version with orders already piling up. However, if we wanted to tackle the assembly of the rough prototype, they were willing to ship the gun. The refined version of the kit is now currently available and in sufficient quantity both as a kit and a finished product to meet consumer demand. It is only fair to point out that the kit received was a rough prototype and many of the details of construction described are no longer necessary, which makes the kit much easier to assemble with a minimum of tools.

Buying an authentic double-barrel percussion shotgun of even standard grade in good condition will leave little change from $200, and unless you know the owner, safety is always a question that must be considered. The old Damascus barrels may look good on the outside but quite often it is an entirely different story on the inside. Due to the ever-increasing value of the authentic guns, anyone desiring to shoot and hunt with a percussion firearm will do well to give careful thought to purchasing a modern reproduction from both a financial and practical point of view.

The Dixie kit leaves little to be desired in safety. The barrels are thick enough to withstand the heaviest of charges, are of modern steel and are silver soldered together. Using a bore micrometer to check the thirty-two-inch barrels, we found the left barrel measured .706-inch in diameter the full length for a cylinder bore without choke. The right barrel measures .706 bore diameter out to the last two inches at the muzzle where it measures .702-inch, which means an improved cylinder choke in a muzzleloader. Almost without exception, the authentic double-barrel percussion shotguns were straight cylinder bore in both barrels.

A heavy-threaded plug with a patent breech tang exten-

Barrel lugs of the patent breech are filed so there will be a snug fit into the breech tang when gun is completed.

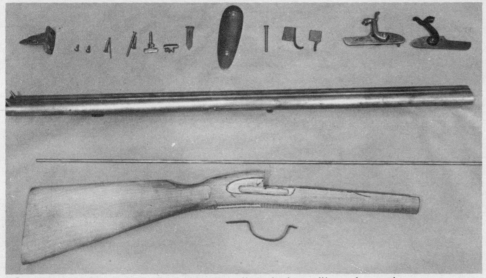

The parts included with the Dixie kit are well made, but still require work.

sion seals the rear of each tube. Considerable pressure is required to pull the plug up tight, thus creating a good gas seal. The percussion nipple screws down through the barrel and into the recessed breech plug, thus performing the dual purpose of locking the breech plug in correct alignment and directing the ignition at the rear of the black powder charge. While the barrels can be more easily cleaned by removing the breech plugs, this should be avoided as constant removal can cause wear and gas leakage.

The first step in construction consists of filing both the hooks of the breech plugs and their matching holes in the breech tang. This must be done carefully as the tang should require a slight amount of downward pressure for a correct fit after filing and polishing to assure a snug fit and eliminate any loose juncture of the two parts. This phase is completed by filing the square top ends of the tang to

match the contour of the rear of the barrels. A six-inch single cut file and a pillow file plus several grits of aluminum oxide cloth wrapped around the files for polishing are the only tools required.

The stock is about seventy-five percent semi-inletted and finished; this is a great asset in getting all of the parts and components in correct position. A small set of inletting tools and a bottle of inletting black will make the job easy. The tang must be inletted into the top rear of the stock first, so that the barrel and tang combination will lie smoothly in the preinletted top of the stock. Little work will be necessary for the barrels but the top tang section must be in proper position and fully inletted as this part is left blank on the stock. Hold the barrel and tang together, lower them into position and push back on the barrels until they butt against the stock. Now using a sharp-pointed

With breech plug removed from the barrel, it is noted that percussion cap nipple screws through the barrels and into the threaded breech plug, locking the plug in place. This assures proper alignment and means easy cleaning.

With breech plugs, nipples installed, lugs filed to the correct fit, the breech tang now fits snugly in place. Far side of tang has been filed to match barrel contour.

pencil, mark around the tang slightly angling the pencil point inward.

Remove the barrel and tang. Use the point of a sharp knife to make a downward cut about an eighth of an inch deep inside of your marked lines. Now switch to a one-eighth-inch flat chisel and cut away the excess wood between your cuts. Recheck the tang to see how you are doing. Go slow. Too often inletting is attempted as one full cut, with the result that too much wood is removed. Continue the process until the tang is inletted down deep enough so that the barrel and tang assembly will fit the stock well but leave the barrels slightly up on the ends. This final amount of inletting will come later. Remember that the patent breech must be snug at the rear and the barrels pulled down under slight pressure by the crosspin in the forend.

At this point the two locks are completely disassembled and each part carefully filed, stoned and polished to remove

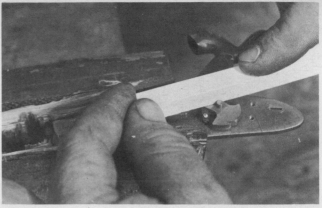

The locks are completely disassembled and each part is smoothed up with Arkansas hard stone for proper function.

all rough machining marks and burrs. This is a step often overlooked by the beginner. As with all mechanisms, the smoother the bearing surfaces, the less friction and the more efficient the operation of the mechanism. The locks of the Dixie kit are surprisingly smooth, and only light stoning and polishing are necessary. The sears of one lock were too soft and were case hardened using Kasenite, which is available from Brownell's, Incorporated, Montezuma, Iowa. Be sure that the sears are hard and that the engagement is solid, yet will allow easy function.

The locks are disassembled again, leaving only the hammer, hammer screw and tumbler attached to the lock plate. The removal of the other components will make the inletting of the lock plates to the stock easier and much simpler. Once the lock plates are correctly inletted, the other parts are reassembled to the lock plate and the necessary wood removed to allow their operation without binding. With the Dixie kit the location of the correct place to inlet the lock plates is simplified by the seventy-five percent preinletted stock and the metal-to-metal contact of the top front of the lock plates with the top tang. It is necessary to remove a small amount of metal from the locks to achieve a snug fit. With the prototype kit, it was also necessary to heat and bend the front of the hammers inward slightly for correct alignment with the nipples. Whenever this is required, the hammers should be bent slowly and then allowed to cool normally. Incidentally, this was done while a C clamp held the barrels down to the stock and another C clamp held the top tang in correct position. Finally, drill a crosshole for the lock plate screw, starting with a smaller diameter drill to allow for any adjustment required with the correct diameter drill. Pull the locks up tight and file off any excess on the end of the screw on the opposite lock plate that it passes through.

There are two ways to mount the triggers. Many of the older guns use a simple crosspin through the wood stock to position the triggers. The second method is to attach the triggers direct to the trigger plate. The latter system is best as it provides a more firm support for the triggers.

Both systems can be used with the Dixie kit. If the latter method is chosen, a three-sixteenths-inch hole is drilled through a small rod and a matching diameter trigger pin is made. A round file is used to cut a shallow depression in the trigger plate to position the drilled rod. Next the rod is silver soldered into place across the trigger plate and allowed to cool. After the ends are filed flush with the sides of the trigger plate, a jeweler's saw is used to make four cuts in the rod. These cuts remove a small section of the rod the same width as the trigger slots and, in effect, create three

Tang has been fully inletted into the stock, with the tang-to-trigger guard hole drilled for fit.

To inlet the lock, it first is stripped of all internal parts to simplify inletting, alignment. Parts are then replaced on lock, excess wood removed for freedom.

washers positioned on top of the trigger plate to support the trigger pin passing through them. The triggers are polished on each side until they will pass through the slots easily without binding. Next, three-sixteenths-inch holes are drilled in each trigger to receive the trigger pin. Finally, a small notch is filed on the bottom of each trigger at the rear to provide a stop and prevent them from passing or swinging down past the trigger plate. This in essence acts as a trigger stop downward. The notch also allows positioning the triggers far enough apart for the finger to pass between them when they are in the down position.

Then the assembled trigger plate component is inletted up into the stock until the tops of the triggers lightly touch the bars of the lock plate sears. Later these will be pulled up tighter in final assembly and filed until they just engage the sear bars without disengaging the cock notch. This

eliminates any return trigger spring and there is no slop in the trigger pull. By filing the top of the triggers, a snug fit can be achieved without tripping the sears. However, at this stage only light engagement is desired as the screw that connects the top tang with the trigger plate must be drilled, and it is always possible that a slight adjustment in the inletting of the trigger plate will be necessary. This is the reason for waiting for final trigger to sear bar fitting.

The next step is to drill the hole for the screw that connects the top tang to the trigger plate. This can be a bit tricky. Remove the trigger plate, hold it against the side of the stock in correct position and, with your pencil, draw a line down from the top tang to the trigger plate. If you insert the screw into the trigger plate at this point, you can draw the line much closer. Now locate the center of the top tang and drill a small hole down through the tang and stock. Install the trigger plate and use a small wire to check your alignment. Any deviation can be detected easily. Go to a larger drill, exerting pressure in the direction needed. Check again. Finally drill the full diameter hole or use a small round needle file to get the hole straight. The top tang and trigger plate should pull up good. Next use a larger diameter drill to recess the hole in the tang to accept the top tang screw head. It may be necessary to shorten the screw to pull the trigger plate up snug. Finally, drill a hole and install the wood screw used to hold the rear of the trigger plate.

The barrel wedge is the next order of business. As the wedge lug on the barrel already has its recess cut in the stock, the job is fairly easy. Use a pencil to draw a line around the stock in the center of the wedge slot. Now hold the barrels beside the stock in their relative position and make a cross mark on the line around the stock. Use a small drill first, taking care to drill exactly level. Install the barrels, pull them down tight and run the drill back through the hole. This will mark the slot in the wedge recess on the barrel and allow you to see how far you are off to one side or up and down. Using this information, make a series of parallel holes drilled through the stock. Now use a Dremel Moto-Tool with a dental burr to connect your drilled series of holes. Do not try to cut the slot in the wood to full size. Pull the barrels down with a C clamp and heat the wedge to a dull red color. Insert it in your hole and tap it on the rear with a hammer. This burns the hole through the stock lightly, charring the wood for a firm fit that will allow the barrel to be held down snugly. Polish the wedge after it has cooled. Any charred surface on the wood will be hidden when the stock is sanded and stained.

The butt plate goes on easily. The only trick involved is to drill the wood screw holes slightly deeper than required. With inletting black on the edges of the butt plate, use a wood rasp to fit the butt plate. When it is correct, the inletting black should make a full circle around the butt stock which indicates a solid fit. The reason for drilling the screw holes slightly deeper is to allow for final fitting and assure a snug fit. The sides of the butt plate will be sanded along with the stock in final stages, making it hard to tell where metal stops and wood begins.

With the gun assembled, but still in the white, test firing should be conducted to check the gun's performance. The prototype Dixie gun was rugged and withstood even heavy 3½-dram, 1½-ounce shot loads without any defects showing up, although this load is considered excessive and does not give the best performance. During the testing it was found that a load of 3¼ drams of powder behind 1¼ ounces of shot gave the best patterns at thirty yards, with the better patterns being made with No. 6 shot. By using a 12-gauge modern plastic shot protector wrapped in a paper-type cartridge, we obtained surprising results at forty yards with even 7½ size shot. A small note of caution should be made at this point. The use of plastic shot protectors and a paper cartridge holding shot protector, shot and powder should be used with caution in antique shotguns as the pressure seems to increase but gives no ill effects with the heavy-barreled Dixie shotgun. Start with the light loads and

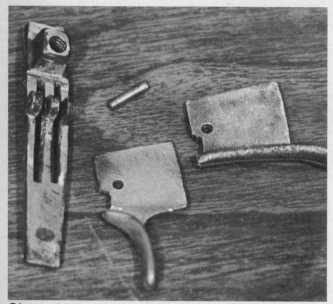

Disassembled trigger group has had tube cut away for clearance, holes located and drilled in the triggers. Walker used stock from his supply for trigger pin.

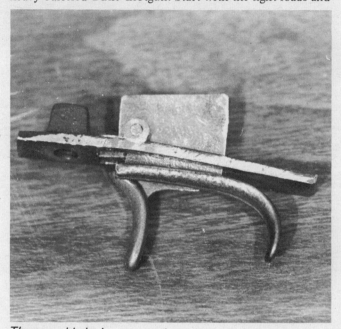

The assembled trigger group is ready for installation in the stock. Triggers are part of trigger guard instead of being installed with a pin through wood of the stock.

A jewelers saw is used to cut away sections of small metal tube that had been soldered to trigger guard. This allows triggers to fit. This makes the tube into three thick washers to support the trigger pin on which the twin triggers of the gun will swing.

In this rear view of the hammer section, it is evident that the excess wood has been cut away, hammers slightly bent so that they strike nipples correctly.

work up slowly. The cylinder bore barrel gave about ten percent less pattern density at all test ranges, while the choked barrel gave surprising results far in excess of what could be expected from an improved cylinder choke. This is probably due to less pellets being deformed as the shot does not have to pass through a chamber forcing cone as in a modern shotgun. As an experiment, Walker made up a .69 caliber Mini ball paper cartridge and, using makeshift sights, fired it though the cylinder bored barrel.

The results were surprising at fifty yards, resulting in several more test shots. As the modern 12-gauge slug is .69 caliber, several of these were made up in paper cartridges and better temporary sights installed. The cylinder barrel with modern 12-gauge slugs gave consistent three-shot groups in a five-inch circle at fifty yards, which is close to what most modern shotguns will do with the same slug. Due to the thick available barrel, considerable thought was given to actually cutting shallow rifling in the barrel. Another possibility was to insert a .45 caliber liner in the barrel. Both were discarded as it was decided to keep the gun as versatile as possible for both small and large game. However, it was decided to install a set of low sights on the barrels, front and rear, and sight in the barrel, while experimenting with loads. The idea was to take advantage of the Primitive Weapon season and the thick southern underbrush where buckshot and slugs are used to a great extent. Incidentally, the choked barrel gave its best performance with No. 1 buckshot with a sixty percent pattern at forty yards.

So, the breech plug on the cylinder barrel was removed

The barrel front lock wedge is in first position to pull down the barrels. End of the wedge must be filed and polished to blend in with stock's surface.

In this front view, all of the metal work has been done and stock is almost finished where shaping is concerned.

In sanding the stock, Walker used a piece of wood to back up the sandpaper rather than the palm of his hand. This prevents possible dips and waves in stock surface.

A half-round rifle is used to shape the stock around the lock plate, which should be slightly large to support the locks, but the grip is cut down for good hand fit.

and the sight installation began. The front sight came from an antique .22 of questionable ancestry and was silver soldered directly in the center of the top rib. Then Walker juggled another sight out of the junk box back and forth while bore sighting through the barrel at a seventy-five-yard target.

When the location was found, the position was scribed, then the sight filed smooth on top with a shallow V and the sight silver soldered into place. It was then a matter of reassembling the gun and returning to the range. As the sights are stationary, it was a matter of shoot and file, shoot and file to get the barrel zeroed in on the target. Using the 12-gauge modern slugs in a paper cartridge and after various tests on powder charges, the end results were a series of three-shot groups in a five-inch circle at seventy-five yards

which is fully adequate for deer, as most are taken at close range in the South.

The metal parts went into the bluing tank, as the gun was to be a working one. No attempt was made to reproduce an original. For those who prefer browning rather than bluing, there are numerous kits on the market that will give the old authentic brown finish. If you want a simple home solution, all you need is a saline solution, consisting of household salt and water. This is swabbed on and the parts placed in a high-temperature area and allowed to rust. Then scrub off the layer of rust with O steel wool, swab on more solution and keep repeating the process until a good coat of brown color builds up.

The kit's original stamped trigger guard was not used. Instead, an old damaged trigger guard of German silver was repaired and substituted. Quite often you can find parts and pieces of old guns that can be used on kits such as this to give them a personal touch. Dixie Gun Works offers a multitude of muzzleloading components that allow the kit builder to depart from the original plans and utilize his personal ideas. Originally, it was decided to remove the thimbles on the barrel and make brass ones, along with a wooden ramrod substituted for the metal ramrod that comes with the kit. This idea was abandoned after the gun performed so well with the shotgun slugs. However, the sling swivel link on the original thimble was removed and the swivels were not used. The swivels that come with the kit can be used if you want to use a sling or, with a little alteration, a set of Michaels Q-D swivels can be installed. Again, there are numerous variations possible with the kit.

Too often the sanding of a stock is rushed in the natural desire to complete the job. This is a bad mistake, for it literally ruins all of the effort put into building one of these kits. Before any bluing or metal finishing is done, the stock is thoroughly sanded with the metal parts installed. This system will naturally put minor scratches on the metal but it allows a metal to wood fit that cannot be achieved any other way. The scratches on the metal can be removed with fine grit aluminum oxide cloth or on the polishing and buffing wheels.

Another mistake is to use the palm of the hand to back up the sanding paper or cloth. This almost invariably results in dips, depressions and waves in the stock. The best method consists of nothing more complicated than wrapping the sanding paper or cloth around various-shaped wooden blocks for backing. On long stretches such as the sides of the butt stock, a small piece of 2x4-inch wood works fine to keep the lines and surface straight and even. Even before reaching the sandpaper stage, every effort should be made to clean up the scratches left in the wood while using the wood rasps. Regular metal files clog quite easily but are hard to beat in removing the scratches and the final shaping. One pass with a file cleaner removes all clogged sections on the metal files. Start with a rather heavy grit sandpaper and slowly work down to the fine grits. Remember to sand with the grain, not across the grain.

When the stock looks slick and smooth, it is time to whisker the stock. All that is needed is a small damp cloth and a heat source; even the kitchen stove will do fine. Lightly dampen an area of the stock about the size of your hand and hold the wood close to the heat source but keep the wood moving and far enough away to prevent scorching. The water evaporates and raises the grain until the surface feels like the whiskers on your face. Now using 000 steel wool, cut them off by going against the grain. Repeat this twice on the stock, and the surface will be ready to start the finishing process.

"There are numerous types of stains on the market but basically it is a choice between water-based stains and oil-based stains. Personally, I like the water-based stains and dilute them fifty percent more than the instructions suggest. Naturally, more coats are required but more control is obtained as some areas will require several extra coats to bring out the natural wood figure of the stock. After each staining application, allow the stock to dry and rub lightly with 0000 steel wool before applying the next coat. By gradually building up the shade, you can achieve any color desired and accentuate the best features of the wood grain.

G-96 stock oil was used after the staining. The first coat was applied heavily and rubbed down with 0000 steel wool after drying to fill the pores, although this stock required little if any filling of the pores. This was followed by thin applications of the oil, which were hand rubbed in thoroughly each time. This slow buildup of the coats will produce a deep mirror-like finish that really brings out the best in the wood. Too often sloppy, heavy coats are applied and the results are far from desirable. When finished, this specific stock with its mixture of walnut and oak stain topped with seven thin coats of oil gave a deep sheen that equaled the best of the old original stocks.

Perhaps the most interesting aspect of building the kit was the many possible deviations. The gun is rugged and made for hard usage but this does not mean that you have to follow the procedure used in building this specific gun. While every effort is made to eliminate the need for a massive gunsmithing tooling shop, sufficient material is left on the components to allow the builder to shape and contour the gun to his own ideas and needs. In these days of mass production, this is becoming a rare opportunity for the average gun buff without a complete gunsmithing shop at his disposal.

The rear sight is silver soldered to the top rib after the gun has been bore sighted. Small notch can be filed deeper and left or right to adjust it in final testing.

The front sight on the completed muzzleloading shotgun has been filed to the proper height after test firing. Thick barrels eliminate safety problems with heavy loads.

The salvaged trigger guard from an original muzzleloader was repaired and installed rather than the plain guard furnished with kit, thus giving gun an individual touch.

CHAPTER 23

TAILOR YOUR OWN MOUNTAIN MAN LEATHER

With Muzzleloading Buffs Returning To Old Ways, Here Are Ways To Nostalgia At Minimum Cost!

Californian Bob Learn is one of those individuals with a garage full of odds and ends and an inquiring mind, who isn't happy until those items of his collection have been put to some practical use.

We really think he was born 150 years too late and would prefer to have been a true mountain man. Meantime, with his beat-up Stetson and a scraggly beard, he works at developing the image from those aforementioned odds and ends. Here's how he does it:

THE WHOLE THING started with the first buck I managed to down while on a backpacking hunt a number of years ago in Colorado. Next, I took a heavy doe in New Mexico and last year, it was a good buck again in Colorado. Still, it took several years of backpacking and hunting to get the material together for a buckskin shirt.

You can buy buckskin in most leather shops or split cowhide that resembles buckskin, but there is no substitute for making your own hides into a garment for your personal use.

As the hides were returned from the tannery, they were packed away until I felt there was enough material to make a shirt.

the sewing machine. Sewing isn't one of my main hobbies, but it can be therapeutic. We tend to think of women as being the expert stitchers but there are many men who can sew a mean seam, too. My first encounters with men at sewing machines were with the Navy parachute riggers. They not only repaired parachutes but made many items like bags, tarps and other needed materials that couldn't be purchased.

One of my friends, Andy Drollinger, is a six-foot-plus grizzly bear-type man who sits at a machine for hours, sewing backpacks, trail tarps, backpack back bands, turning nylon materials into all sorts of useful items.

The first thing one needs to start this project is a good

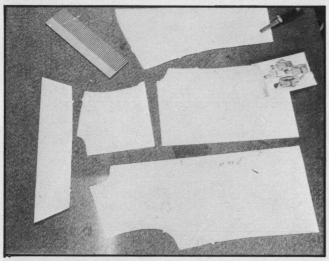

Cardboard templates from the modified Simplicity pattern laid out. The five pieces are for the front, two for the back, one sleeve, and one collar is all it takes to start.

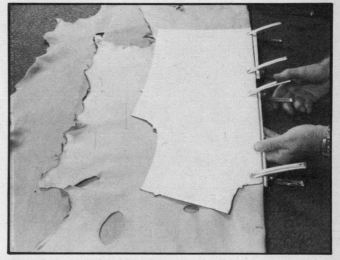

To be doubly certain the leather doesn't slip while you're cutting, clamp it with small clamps to the cutting board. Whatever is used for clamps must be strong to avoid slips.

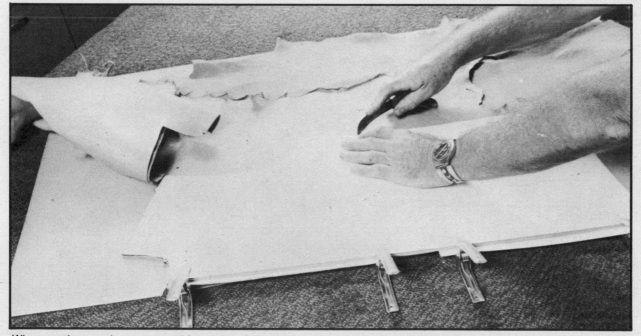

When cutting, apply pressure with one hand near the cut to be certain the leather stays perfectly aligned with the pattern and use a sharp knife. There is no second chance, mistakes are permanent.

Now a shirt doesn't sound like much but when you start using the hides with all the skinning cuts I put in the first buck, plus broadhead slices, you can't use all of the thin leather.

While I waited for the final buck I needed, I practiced on

sewing machine. My wife has a beauty but she laid down the law that I wasn't to touch her machine with my heavy threads, materials and least of all leather.

An ad in a local newspaper listed a portable machine in good condition. For $15, I purchased an old White rotary

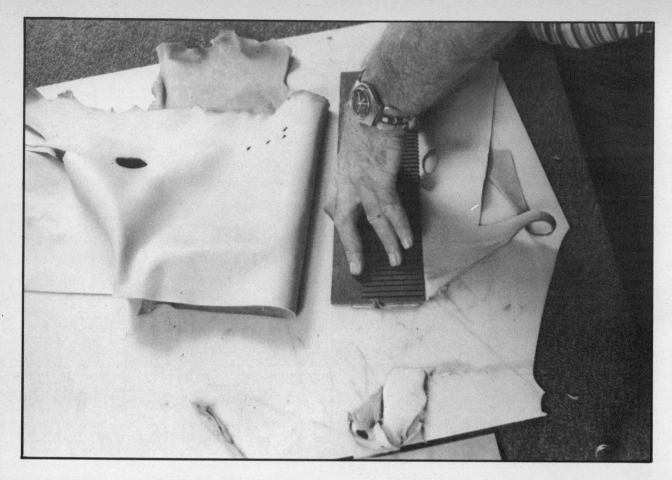

After cutting out the major portions of the pattern, some small pieces of buckskin will probably be left over. Using the fringe pattern, check to see if these small pieces can be used as fringe to avoid wasting buckskin.

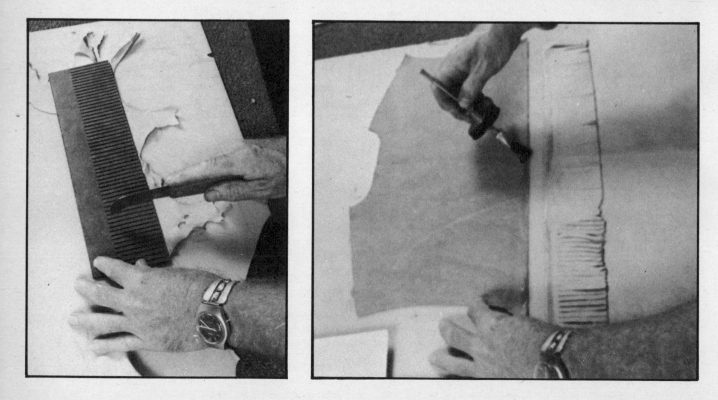

Left: The homemade fringe cutter works well, however, care must be taken as buckskin slips easily and doesn't cut as well as cowhide. Right: Glueing pieces together before sewing goes a long way toward preventing slips in machine.

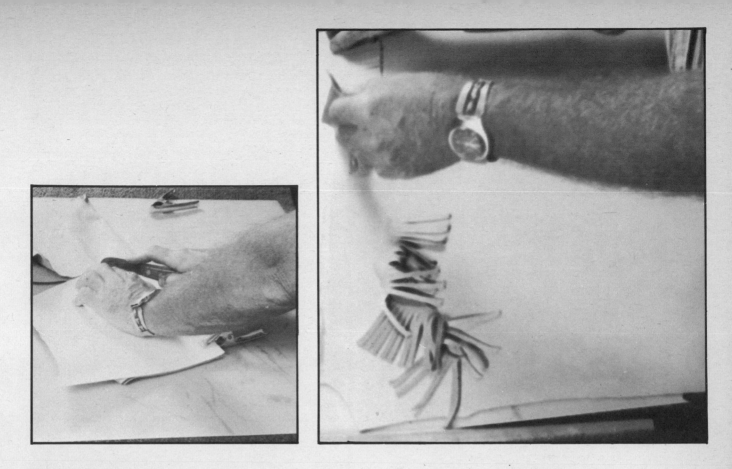

Left: A small section of hide is used for cutting the folded upper back area. When making this part of pattern allow extra for seam overhang. Right: Attach fringe to upper back leaving upper back seam over top of fringe.

machine that had been converted to an electric motor from the old treadle system. This machine has a shaft on the needle section that is at least a quarter inch in diameter. Nothing stops it from stitching except too much material passing under the foot. I had it cleaned, oiled and some springs replaced for another $15. It hasn't failed since.

After learning to operate the gadget without sewing my fingers in the process, I had to find a pattern that would fit me — and my abilities. Sitting in a shop to look over patterns with the gals may be interesting to some extent, but it's not exactly my thing. I delegated this to the wife and, after some months, she came up with a pattern that proved terrific. We could have made our own pattern, of course, but that could be more complicated than I would want.

What she found was a Simplicity pattern — number 8950 — for a man's shirt. It will provide three different styles but I was interested in the slipover version with long tails, since the buckskin would be worn outside.

My wife used the pattern to make several standard shirts for me and each time modified the pattern as only women know how. When she had the shirt fitting well, hanging right and refined to a simple operation, I took over and made a light cardboard template from the pattern.

The pattern is printed on flimsy paper, not exactly what I thought I could work with in the shop. One could use heavy Kraft paper for a first modification, but I plunged and used medium weight show card stock for a workable pattern that has held up well after several operations.

While waiting for the last deer hide to come back from the tannery, I worked on the pattern using rip-stop nylon to make some windbreakers, perfecting my technique with the sewing machine. But there will be more about that later. These turned out great and even fit!

When the last hide came in, I laid all three out on the table for checking. There was enough leather overall, but there was no way I could get two huge, one-piece sleeve sections cut from the leather available. I had to modify the modification. I halved the size of the big, wide sleeve pattern. You use the sleeve pattern twice by turning it over. Normally, there are only four pieces to my pattern — a sleeve, front, back and collar pattern. By reducing the size of the sleeve template, I would have some leather left over. The back was sectioned to allow the addition of fringe across the back.

After the pattern was modified, I used denim with which to experiment. I cut the material with my modified pattern and it went together as it should to fit the way I wanted. I shortened the sleeve length and the front and back sections to prevent wasting leather that would have to be cut off anyway.

With the pattern, all I needed was the guts to cut into that beautiful buckskin and not make any mistakes; there was just enough leather for one cut per pattern section. There could be no goofs. To be doubly certain, I laid the pattern on the leather and checked to obtain the maximum area for each hide.

After determining I had enough material, I washed the buckskin in a bucket of tap water and mild detergent. This removes some of the dyes. By stretching the hides on a section of plywood and stapling them to dry, I would have little shrinkage. It goes against my thinking to wash leather but that is the way to start.

While the leather dried on the plywood frame, I made a template from masonite with which to cut the fringe. I took my bench saw, my finest veneer blade and made two-inch cuts into the masonite one quarter of an inch apart. From a section of masonite about twenty inches long, I cut over fifty sections. This fringe cutting guide was tested on a piece of scrap buckskin trimmed from the hide when placed on the plywood frame. It worked fine and the fringe was even.

After all the hides were dry, the cutting session started. The hides already had been selected specifically for back, front and sleeves, so it was merely a matter of cutting them out now. I used a section of thin plastic as a backup cutting board. This material is hard, but it doesn't dull the blade as much as masonite and it will lie flat with no warping problems. I placed the pattern on the leather and checked for surface cuts and nicks by moving it from side to side to obtain the best areas.

When cutting the front and back sections, fold the leather, and even though the pattern is small, make an even double cut with the fold. The leather was folded and checked for holes. The pattern was held to the leather with small clamps to prevent any sliding. Sections of cardboard were used on the back of the leather to avoid clamp marks.

A sharp knife is a must for this project, and a carpet or linoleum knife is excellent. It is thin, holds an edge and the curved cutting point will fit into a tight area. Also, when the tip of the blade is on the leather, one can make precise cuts and not cut over or run over.

Each of the pattern sections was worked in the same way. The half sleeves were placed on the leather and I even remembered to reverse the other side to make them match. The back pattern was modified to allow for the overlap and stitching.

All parts were cut out before any sewing started. The sections looked good, with no bad cuts. There was one small hole on the front by the left shoulder, but you might say it gave it character. I folded a piece of scrap leather and ran it through the sewing machine so that I could adjust the tensions to obtain a good stitch. I used some twisted nylon thread of 22 denier that is really tough. I sewed a piece of leather about ten inches long, turned it over and the stitch was locking perfectly. To test the thread's strength, I took a pair of pliers and with force pulled the stitched thread out full length without breaking it. That is tough thread!!

There are several reasons for putting fringe on a leather jacket or shirt. First, it's for looks but it also serves as a drain for the water, if you get it wet. Without fringe, the water will stay in the seams and dry slowly. The fringe more or less wicks the water off and your shirt will dry faster. The fringe also will help to break up the pattern of the shirt for camouflage purposes. I intended to use this shirt for hunting, after it darkened down, so the fringe would help.

The cut leather was sorted to find areas that were big enough to use for fringe. The fringe template was placed on them and cut with the carpet knife. I cut four sections of fringe and found it was enough.

The first step in the sewing operation was to sew the two sections of the back together with the fringe in the middle. I placed the bottom of the back on the plastic, applied rubber cement to the upper edge and placed the fringe with the solid section on top of the cement. More cement went onto the fringe base and finally the upper section was put in place. With the upper section going on last, water would shed off the seam rather than run into it. An advantage of using rubber cement is that one can check the sections and, if wrong, remove and change them. Once sewn, this becomes a rework job. But don't use too much cement, as it is needed only for temporary holding.

The triple layer of buckskin was moved to the old White

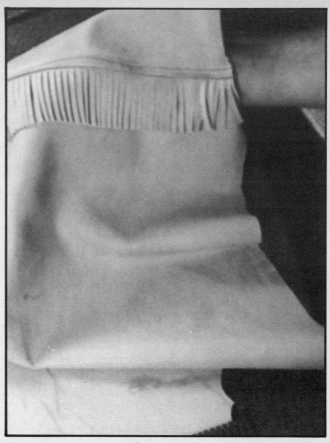

Note double stitch used on fringe. Actually, it was done more for the appearance, than for any extra strength that might be provided. Single stitching will suffice.

To make facing for the front neck area you need two one-inch wide strips, the length of slit you want. Sew first to front of shirt, then roll inside and sew them again.

sewing machine and inserted under the foot. It was just about all the old machine could take. I helped the feed system by working the leather into the needle and moving slowly so as not to run off or make a sewing goof.

The back was stitched in one direction, reversed and

sewn back to make a double seam. This is the only place where the stitches show and I got them almost even.

Next, the two sleeve sections were sewn with an inside seam. I put the hair side of the leather together to stitch from the flesh side.

The front needed a slit cut down the front to allow the shirt to slip over the head. I had found that six inches allowed enough to fit over my head.

Using two pieces of leather 1½ inches wide and just a little longer than the cut, flesh side up, I turned them back and sewed down the edges as close to the fold as possible. This gives a reinforced slit and looks better than just the raw edge of the leather.

All sewing on the shirt, with the exception of the back yoke, was done from the rough flesh side. With all seams inside, all that shows is the one seam across the back.

Make certain the leather is faced correctly or you can end up with one flesh and one hair side, which doesn't match.

The upper seams are next, joining the front and back panels at the shoulder. Again, I used rubber cement sparingly and checked before moving to the sewing machine to double stitch all seams.

After the front and back panels are together, insert the collar and sew it on. I placed the collar on the shirt, checked it again and stitched it down. I had a bit of leather left over, but that could be cut off; you can't add. I am fussy about the way the seam fits on the neck, since it can rub, if done wrong.

With the two sleeves ready to be sewn at the shoulders, check that the little aligning arrows match before starting to sew. I cemented, checked and moved to the machine.

Sewing is on a bit of a curve here, so one must take care. Don't get any leather bunched beneath the needle, keep it out of the stitching area and go slowly. Check from time to time and, after stopping, leave the needle in the leather.

With both sleeves sewn at the shoulder, all that remains is to sew down the sleeves and the sides of the front and back.

When ready to sew the sleeves down the final seam, this is the time to add the sleeve fringe. Place the precut fringe on the sleeve. One can goof at this point, so take it slow and be certain.

The fringe can go on with the smooth side forward or back. Check for this by folding the sleeve over the front. I made mine with the smooth side forward. When my arm crosses the front of the shirt, the rough or suede side is against the smooth front section for contrast. One can do it this way or reverse the process so that the smooth is on smooth. Make the base section of the fringe wide enough so that it can be stitched solidly to the seam.

I varied the sewing procedure on the sleeve and side sections a bit. I started at the underarm junction and sewed from there to the end of the sleeve, then reversed and sewed back to make three overlaps at the underarm section.

In sewing back from the end of the sleeve, continue down the side and sew the front and back panels together. I sewed back up to double stitch and made a fourth seam at the underarm junction. Do the same on the other side and the shirt is finished as far as sewing is concerned. However, there is still the fringe to cut and buttons to add.

After sewing the last sections under the arm, I turned the shirt right side out and looked at it. The fringe had come out right and was long enough. All seams were clean

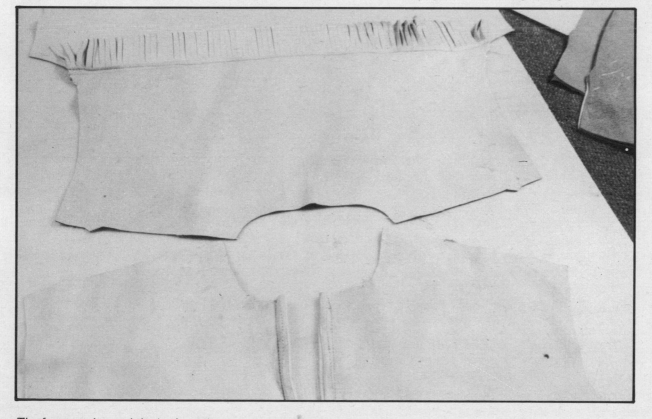

The front section and the back section are now ready to be joined, they are joined at the shoulder area so be certain that both pieces of material are facing the same direction. Remember to glue before sewing to avoid slips in machine.

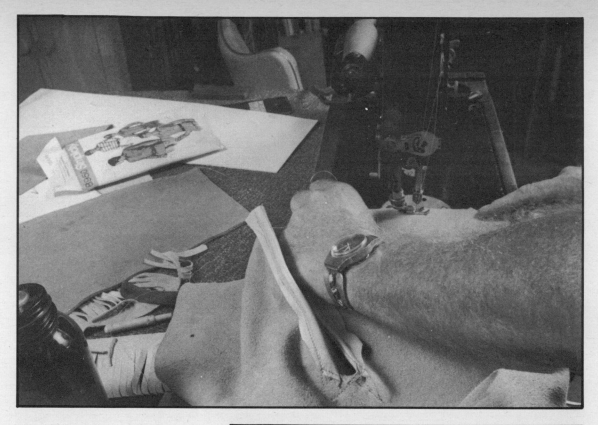

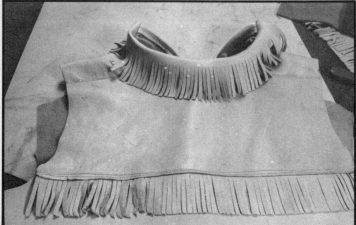

Above: Sew collar to sewn sections of back and front. Right: The collar can be fringed as in the pattern or left alone as you perfer.

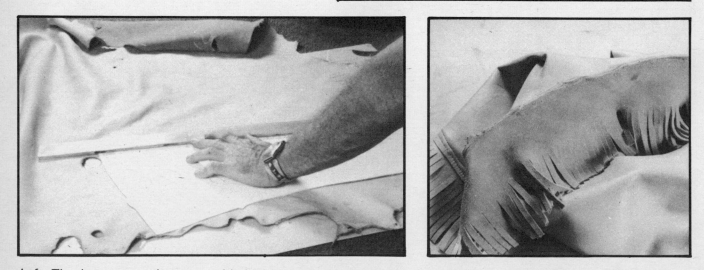

Left: The sleeve pattern that comes with the Simplicity unit is huge. This was modified and cut in half so smaller areas of leather could be used. Right: Sew two sections of sleeve together, the upper edge and lower, fringing on the lower.

with no extra holes from a bad needle runover. Leather doesn't hide needle marks like cloth.

The final test was to see how it fit. The front and back sections were a bit uneven, but later were trimmed to match. I used the fringe template to fringe the collar edge, the front and back sections, taking care not to cut through the seam on the sides of the shirt. All threads had been tied off when removed from the machine, so there never should be any loose threads to unravel on this shirt.

I had taken sections of deer antlers and cut them on a band saw. These made unique buttons and also utilized more of the game. The horn buttons were cut, polished and two holes drilled for the thread. A heavy needle and No. 16 thread were used to attach four buttons at the closure and two to hold down the collar.

The shirt looks good, fits even better and will last for many years. The thread will last as long as the leather, which will darken.

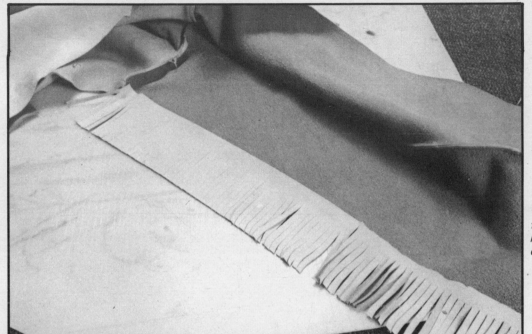

You have an option with the fringe, you can have rough side in or out, it depends on what you like.

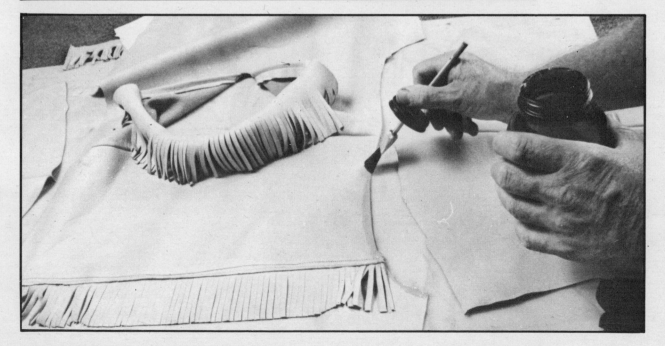

The sleeves are cut in four sections from leather that will give the best color, with no holes or other imperfections. This modification of the Simplicity pattern will allow you to use more of the leather.

If You're Going To Play The Mountain Man Role, You Have To Protect Your Muzzleloader As They Did

Completed gun case and possibles bag compliment each other. Instructions for make both are outlined here.

CARRYING YOUR MUZZLELOADER to, from and in the field won't hurt it, but it does help to have a good rifle wrap to cover it both in transit and for storage after cleaning. There are many materials from which you can make a cover. The new nylon materials are excellent. They are tough, colored and offer a great variety of weaves, but in this instance, leather is the only material involved.

One needs a big chunk of leather for this project, not in size but in length. The wrap can be made from pieces by sewing more sections but the full-length piece keeps a clean line in the leather cover.

This is one instance wherein a pattern is more trouble than just laying out the leather and going to it with knife or scissors. The rifle is placed on the length of leather after finding one that is long enough and wide enough to allow cutting direct from the hide on the cutting board. If smaller pieces are used, a pattern would be necessary.

The length of leather was folded over the rifle and one inch added for the seams. There was a taper on the rifle from the curve of the butt section to the barrel, so we allowed extra material for this section and the cocking lever on the side plate. This lever protrudes and you must allow for it or the final fit won't work.

Fold the leather over the complete rifle and take it up until the shape of the leather matches the shape of the rifle.

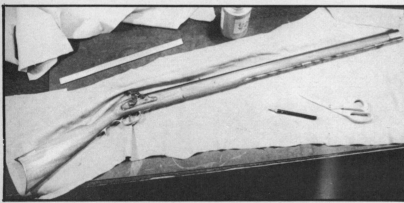

The case for the muzzleloader requires about five square feet of leather. The rifle is laid on the leather to determine the best position. (Below) Rifle positioned, the leather is pulled over and allowance made for sewing the seam. Allow enough slack so the hammer won't rip leather later.

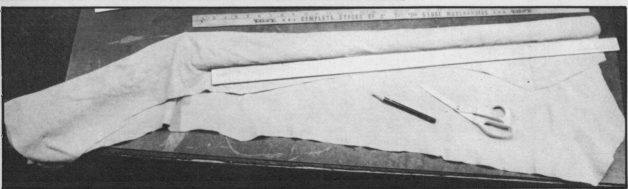

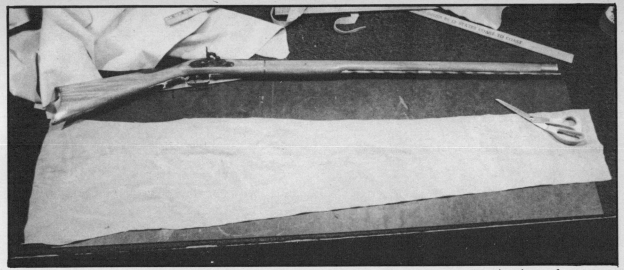

Using stainless steel scissors to cut the leather, make sure of taper. Tip should be narrower than base of case.

Using the bare edge of the short side, mark the leather at that point with a marking pen. Cutting can be done with a knife or scissors.

Move the rifle underneath the leather until you are certain of the fit, then make the cut a bit wider for the seam. That is the simple way to do it.

With shorter hides or less leather, you can make patterns to cover the barrel section and a pattern to cover the stock section, matching these by sewing. It just takes a bit more time.

After the cuts have been made on the hide, turn it with the surface you want outside when finished, face up on the table.

Such a unit for a muzzleloader should be fringed to conform to the early mountain man or Indian motifs. The fringe for this unit was made by utilizing the lower section of leather cut from the main case section. Simply mark the length and start cutting fringe. The fringe can be tapered to the case contour. On the case we made, the fringe ranges from eight inches, decreasing to about two inches along the carrying section, continuing to the end at the buttstock. A fringe cutter made for other projects didn't work with the longer fringe. A pair of stainless steel scissors was used instead.

The fringe should be on the outside, so again lay out the main body of the cover, apply rubber cement along the

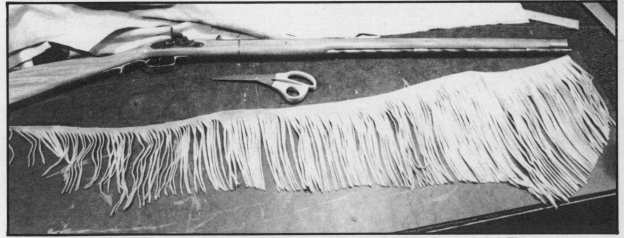

Above: Fringe for sheath is cut from scrap remaining after the basic case shape has been cut. This was cut from the lower leather of the pattern. If piece isn't large enough, fringe can be cut from another section. (Below) Rubber cement is smeared on lower edge of the case and on inside fringe edge before making bond.

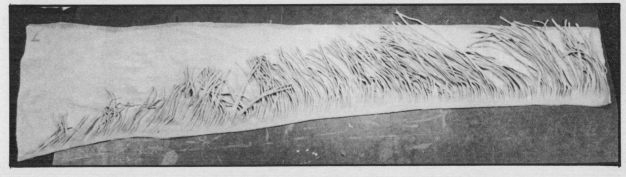

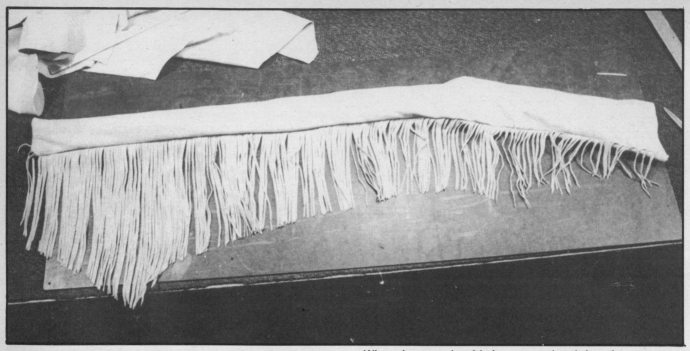

When the opposite side is cemented and the edges sewn, one has three thicknesses of leather. Using good needle, any home sewing machine should handle the job. When the case is turned right side out, fringe drops in place.

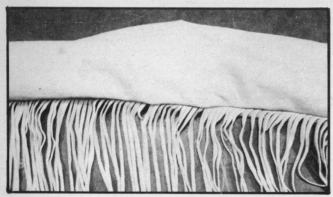

Hammer sticks up and appears bunglesome, but there isn't much one can do for better appearance with this type of sheath. If made in sections, leather may contour better.

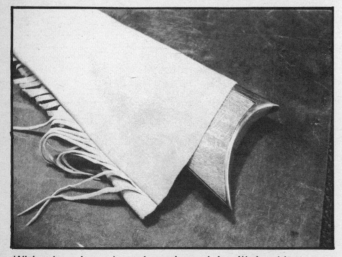

With edge trimmed evenly at the end, it still should be long enough to cover butt of the rifle. In this case, stock has been drawn out to illustrate trimming method.

lower edge and to one edge of the fringe base. When it has dried for a short time, start at the barrel or small end of the cover and lay the fringe on the cemented section. Place the fringe inside the cover.

Cement the outer side of the fringe base and the other side of the case cover. When sufficiently dry bring the edges together; they will set nicely as you sew. For sewing this light leather, pick a good thread — dacron or polyester, the toughest you can find — then find a needle that will work with that thread. We used an 18-gauge needle for sewing these three thicknesses of leather. Modern machines might not take this heavy sewing, but the old treadle-converted White rotary machine eats it up as fast as you can feed the leather through it.

If using a lighter machine for leather projects, you can buy special needles. They have chisel points rather than the round point used for most sewing.

Sew the small end of the case together, then it is merely a long stitch down the full length of the case. We did it twice with backstitching on both ends since the base where the rifle is inserted will undergo the roughest treatment. The project is finished when the case is turned right side out. The fringe hanging as it is supposed to, you have a functional yet decorative rifle wrap for a few dollars and little time. The most time is spent in fringe cutting.

Some muzzleloaders prefer what is termed the primitive system and either hand-stitch or lace the case. To lace or whipstitch with leather, do it from the outside where the stitch will give the added effect.

Incidentally, this particular project took about five square feet of leather.

You can elaborate by beading the case, dye it different colors or paint Indian pictograms on the surface.

Those who aren't intrigued by leather and fringe but do want a cover for that rifle can follow the same procedure with a good flannel material. This will protect the rifle from dust and careless fingerprints, costing only a few dollars.

The Needs For Muzzleloaders Afield Are Broad, So You Need A Possibles Bag For Any Possible Contingency

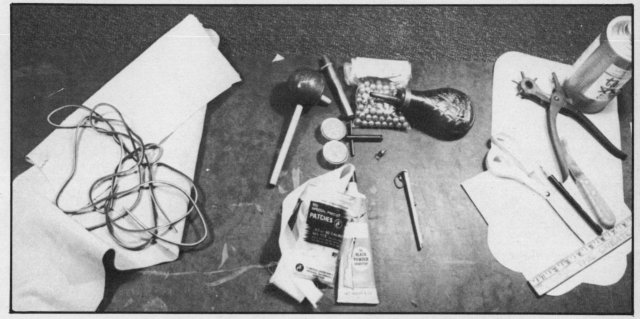

Materials needed for the possibles sack include light leather and either lacing leather or thread. In center are some of the items that might be carried in sack. Tools needed to make the sack include a ruler, punch, cement, scissors and, of course, some type of pattern.

BLACK POWDER BURNERS can be a ball, but when one goes into the field for plinking or small game, he needs a small boy to carry all the materials required to feed and maintain the boomsticks.

"My nipple seems to be fouled. Got a nipple pick?" Stan Hemenway queried as he waited for the barrels of his rifle to cool before reloading and trying for a long shot.

"That's possible," Bob Learn replied, as he swung a gray leather pouch bag from his right side and reached into the sewn compartment that held his pick and other items. "Possibly I have it my possibles sack."

Learn had looked at some possibles sacks hanging on the pegs in a gun shop, but they looked too polished, too clean and commercial for his taste. "Good workmanship and good leather, but not my style," Learn recalls.

After consideration, a bright red shoulder purse he had made to match a pair of his wife's then-new shoes looked perfect as the pattern for a possibles sack. In his shop, he cut a new modified pattern using the purse as a guide. The muzzleloader's possibles sack can be made from a light or medium canvas, but most avid black powder buffs feel the only material for the muzzleloading units is leather. Earlier, Learn had located some split cowhide at a good price and bought fifty square feet for such projects. This would be used for his possibles sack.

The first item of business is to make a pattern. Decide the size possibles sack you want and lay it out on some stiff cardboard or, better yet, show card stock. The latter cuts easily and is stiff enough to make a good line edge.

"I wanted mine to be nine inches square for the main bag," Learn explains. "The front section was drawn nine inches square on show card stock with a carpenter's square and marking pen.

"I didn't want the bottom corners at right angles, so I took a lid from a one-pound coffee can — the plastic slip-

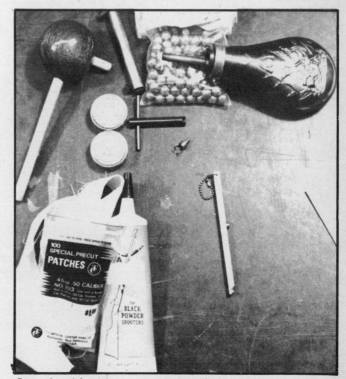

Part of sack's ultimate contents include a ball starter, caps, lead balls, patch material, along with lube, cap retainer and black powder flask equipped with a measure.

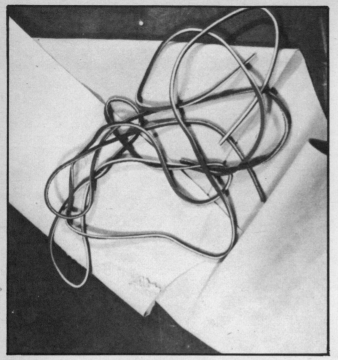

For those who prefer the primitive look, a leather punch can be used to make the lacing holes for the strands.

over type — and used it for a curve to round the corners by lining it up on the bottom and sides, marking the curve for rounded base corners." Learn wanted the back section to have the same nine-inch square base, but it had to have a flap to cover the opening as the sack is carried in the field. This is accomplished by extending the length to sixteen inches. That gives you a seven-inch flap over the front of the sack. Using the coffee can lid, round all four corners.

You can sew or lace these two sections together and have a small, compact sack for short trips, but Learn made his bag larger by adding a strip of leather called a gusset and stitching it between the front and back sections. Vary the width of the gusset and the size of the bag is varied in proportion.

Learn inspected the 1½-inch gusset in his wife's bag and decided it was too small. He cut a gusset pattern from scrap paper three inches wide and placed it with the show card pattern to see how it would look. A bit too big, the paper was cut to 2½ inches in width and stapled to the front and back of the other pattern segments to see how it would look. By working with the so-necessary paper or board patterns, one can make all the decisions before cutting leather, thus avoiding expensive errors.

To make this possibles sack easier to work with, Learn cut a section of card stock six inches long and two inches wide as pattern for an inside pocket. It would be sewn inside to hold needed items. This, he felt, would hold

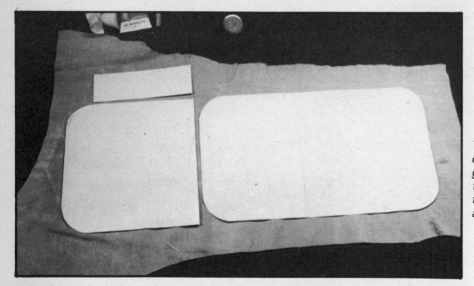

The paper pattern is cut to desired dimensions, then laid on leather to get the best cuts. Long section is the back combined with the fold-over front. Second largest is the front and small section is inside pocket.

The small pocket is sewn into the cut-out back section before the rest of the unit is assembled. This pocket will hold 200 caps, nipple wrench and cleaning jag.

rummaging to a minimum.

The patterns were moved to a piece of the gray split cowhide and positioned. Leather often has some bad sections where the skinner worked too close, thus causing the leather to tear easily. Learn moved the pattern about until he found solid, clean areas, then marked the pattern out with his marking pen.

"The leather cut easily with a pair of new stainless steel scissors and they made the job a fast one. When cutting the gusset section, I merely took a long area on the skin and cut it as long as the skin would allow, as I also needed a shoulder strap the same width as the gusset.

"After cutting all the parts and laying them out on the Masonite board I use for these projects, I decided to add some fringe. Fringe not only is decorative, but it wicks off water if you get in the rain," says Learn.

The fringe was cut with the stainless shears using sections of scrap left from the sack cutting.

The front section was turned with the good leather side up, the gusset the same way and the two units cemented together with a good rubber cement. This serves two purposes: it holds the leather together while you sew it and it seals the seams after they are sewn.

After curing, the cemented sections were placed together and pressed firmly. Rubber cement allows you to remove a

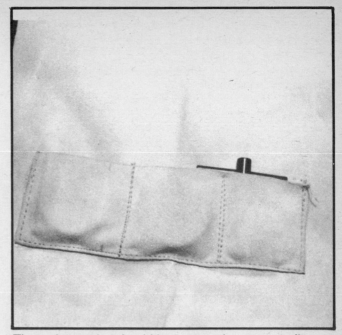

The pocket section should be sewn so that contents fit snugly. There is room for other items in right pocket.

The best type of fringe is the edge of the piece from which matching piece has been cut. The contour will help in fitting and sewing the two pieces.

When ready to assemble, the fringe is placed on the back side of the sack, the exterior side up. The stitching lines should indicate correct side.

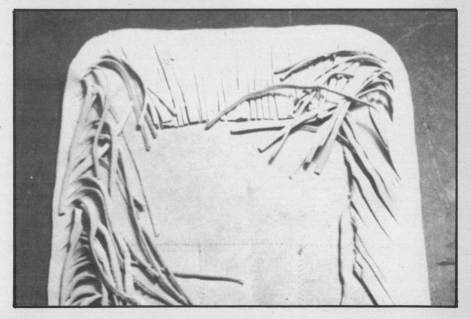

191

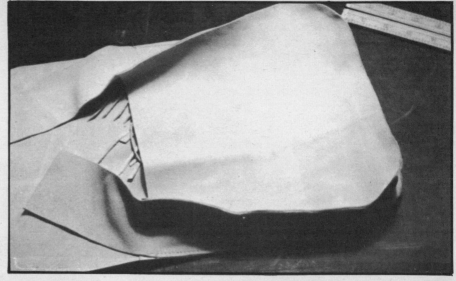

Fringe and gusset have been cemented in place. By using rubber cement, it is possible to correct any mistake. Final sewing is all that remains.

Below: With the seams sewn, the sack is turned right side out. Last step is to sew a leather carrying strap.

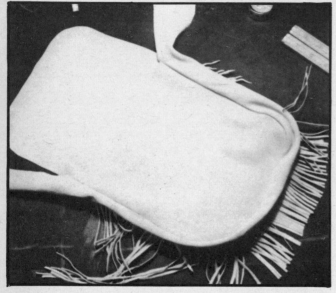

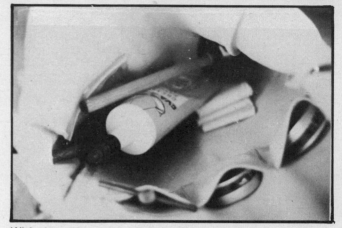

With the wide mouth, the possibles bag affords its maker quick access to his needs for black powder shooting. The side pockets segregate larger items for easier finding.

bonded area and replace it, if the position isn't right. The cemented gusset front was placed on Learn's old treadle sewing machine and sewn in a matter of seconds. For the real frontier primitive route, you can lace or stitch the bag with latigo or other strips of leather lacing. Sewing is faster and there won't be any holes later as might happen with a loose lacing system.

After sewing the front to one edge of the gusset, the bottom of the front and back are marked in their middles and aligned, the back section being placed on top of the bag for alignment checking.

When satisfied with the alignment, remove the back section and place the fringe after being cemented, along with the edge of the back gusset, against the back section. If you place it on the outside, it will be inside when you finish, as you turn the bag inside out when completely sewn.

While waiting for the fringe cement to cure, place the six-by-two-inch strip on the inside of the back section and position it for height and cement that on the edges. This should be sewn in before the fringe/gusset sewing; it is easier. Learn sewed the mini-pocket into the back, then made two more lines of stitching. This gave him a small compartmented section on the back side upper section of the sack that will hold two cans of caps along with the nipple wrench and some strip material to hold the wrench in place.

With the back section sewn to the gusset, the fringe flopped inside, the possibles sack is finished with the exception of the carrying strap. As mentioned, this was cut 2½ inches wide and full hide length to match the width of the sack gusset. The result was a strap about 3½ feet long by 2½ inches wide. This was cemented and laced, the latter mainly for effect, to the back section of the gusset. The sack was turned right side out and the fringe fell at the back of the sack as it should. The sack was placed on the right side, the strap run over the left shoulder and around in front and held at different heights for ease of getting material in and out of the sack. When it hung right for Learn's arm length, he laced it, using some of the cut strips for the scrap leather.

"My possibles sack proved handy in the field. I now have all my caps, patch grease, patches, tools and other needed items in a convenient sack that is light to carry and out of the way when I fire the rifle."

Carrying Your Loads Into The Field Can Be Simplified With This Simple Project!

A BULLET POUCH is needed in the field in which to carry the bullets, so they will not roll in the bottom of the possibles sack. This was made simply and rapidly with a tear-drop design, using a butter dish for the pattern. The dish was laid on paper and the base pattern cut. This was folded to make certain the sides were even, then the paper pattern was placed on a bit of leather scrap.

This bullet pouch has a three-inch base tapering to a two-inch mouth. This size proved perfect for holding an even one hundred balls, more than one normally needs in the field. Pick the side of the leather you want to face out and cement the edges. When it has seasoned, press the sides together and stitch.

When the stitching is finished, turn the bullet pouch inside out and add a leather drawstring at the top by cutting or punching holes and inserting a leather strap. The chore is simple and makes transportation of balls simple, loading faster. You can reach into the narrow mouth and pull out one ball at a time or roll them out for a series of shots.

This bullet pouch can be made in a few minutes from scrap leather.

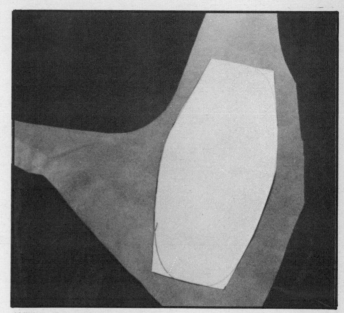

With scraps left from possibles sack project, Bob Learn used butter dish for a pattern, outlining shape on paper, then cutting to size on the remaining leather.

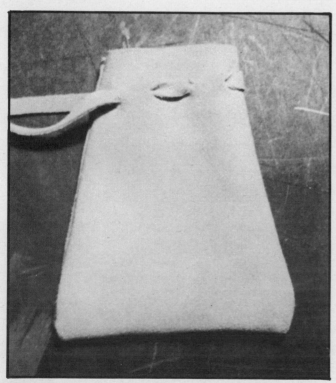

The finished ball bag made from scrap leather holds 100 .45 balls. Leather punch was used for holes for the string. Another string of opposite draw would help.

Filled, the bag is best carried in the possibles sack, as it would prove too heavy if slung from your belt.

EXPERIMENT IN BLACK POWDER

CHAPTER 24

Michigan's First Muzzleloading Buck Hunt Offered A Scientific Touch To Efficiency!

Mike Hogan was one of the few Michigan black powder hunters to get a buck during the state's first season of muzzleloader hunting. He used a .50 Hawken replica. (Below) His rifle leaning against a nearby tree, the hunter attaches tag to his buck's antler as required.

A DOE CAME first, moving into an area of cutover white cedars. She was at a distance of about one hundred yards, followed by a smaller animal, which was probably her offspring. Then, there was a good buck coming behind the youngster.

Mike Hogan shouldered his rifle and was about to take a shot when he saw three more deer approaching — all bucks! Their racks showed up well against the blanket of snow that covered the landscape. One was a spikehorn and the other two looked like they carried six-point racks.

These animals were moving parallel to one another rather than in single file. None were as big as the first buck but their appearance was somewhat distracting. Hogan forgot about shooting.

As he was regaining his composure, the biggest whitetail whirled on those in the rear and charged. Not willing to challenge him, the lesser animals retreated. Without breaking stride, the big fellow turned to rejoin the doe.

Normally, the last day in November marks the end of firearms hunting for whitetails in Michigan. But this Fall of 1975 was different. A special ten-day hunt for muzzleloading rifle enthusiasts opened December 5. Bucks were the only legal game.

This first black powder season was designed as experimental. No one knew how many individuals would be interested in such a season, what problems might be encountered or what impact the additional pressure would have on the deer herd. The hunt was held to learn.

Richard P. Smith, who hunts the Michigan country, is familiar with what happened and we asked him to give us a rundown on that first black powder deer season in his home territory:

The impetus for a special hunt didn't arise suddenly. The drive, spearheaded by the Lansing Muzzleloading Gun Club, was supported by other groups throughout the state. Members of the Lansing group, avid black powder buffs all, began their drive for a special hunt in the early 1970s.

The Michigan Department of Natural Resources also supported the hunt, with officials fairly confident the impact on whitetails from the season would be minimal.

Their judgment was affected to a significant degree by the timing of the hunt. Michigan's regular firearms season runs from November 15 through November 30. During that period, most surplus bucks would be harvested.

Those remaining would be super cautious and hunter shy. Nonetheless, black powder enthusiasts were pleased. The special season gave them a chance to be in the field when they wouldn't be competing with conventional firearms hunters.

The added opportunity to hunt deer also served as incentive for individuals new to muzzleloaders to try their hand. And it was one more chance to score, if a hunter hadn't done so previously. Michigan allows a hunter to take only one whitetail per calendar year, regardless of the armament used. Projectiles were restricted to round balls, .44 caliber and larger.

Black powder arms were new to Hogan. He had failed to collect a buck in November, so he decided to give the added season a try. One of his hunting partners, Paul Myron, loaned him his muzzleloader, a .50 caliber Hawken. Myron wouldn't be able to use it, as he had scored with a modern weapon. Paul Myron briefed Hogan on the use of the rifle and they sighted it in for one hundred yards.

It was the third day of the black powder hunt. Myron knew of an area where a logger had cut some cedars. The leaves of white cedar are a preferred late fall and winter food of whitetails in Michigan. Theorizing animals would be feeding on the downed tops, the hopeful pair headed there.

A cold day, there was six to eight inches of snow on the ground. Myron put Hogan on a stand, then walked around trying to drive game to his partner. Plenty of tracks and droppings were in the vicinity.

Paul Myron eventually worked his way into the downed cedars. Deer began popping up everywhere, fifteen altogether. In the confusion, he managed to identify two of the animals as bucks — a spike and one with a rack.

However, none of the whitetails headed toward Hogan, so Myron repositioned his buddy and tried another push. This time, the neophyte saw some of the deer but they were too far away.

The cold had gotten the best of Hogan, who had to walk around to warm up. The amateur hunter thought he might have a better chance for a shot if he sneaked up on the deer, so he circled downwind of where they had disappeared and followed their trail.

He was within thirty feet of a good buck when it saw him. Before he had a chance to shoot, it moved off with another whitetail. It didn't appear spooked, though. The hunter moved a few steps ahead to see better.

As Hogan stood pondering the situation, the procession of six deer, including four bucks, came into sight. After the biggest buck chased the others away, he and the doe disappeared into some thick saplings.

When they came back into his line of vision, he was ready to try a shot. The range was about seventy-five yards. The buck stopped with only his head and neck visible. Hogan aimed for the deer's head.

At the shot, the buck spun in a tight circle, then dropped. The .50 caliber ball had hit under the buck's eye. Eight evenly matched points graced the animal's rack.

John Falk from L'Anse, a small upper Michigan town on Lake Superior, was just as new to hunting with a muzzleloader as Hogan. The day before the special season, he bought a .50 caliber Hawken from a local sporting goods store. It took him five shots to sight in.

He spent every day of the first week in the field, concentrating his efforts around apple orchards. Deer visited them to dig for frozen apples buried in the snow.

Falk saw plenty of whitetails, but all were does, until the evening of December 12. He was on a stand at the edge of an orchard by late afternoon. There was about a half-hour of daylight remaining when he heard a deer behind him.

One of the biggest bucks he'd ever seen walked into the open. After a well-placed shot, the eight-point, 185-pound whitetail was his first buck.

Falk and Hogan were among the few lucky muzzleloading hunters during Michigan's first black powder hunt, but the techniques they used illustrate how others can score in future seasons.

It is important to understand something of the habits of

As is usually the case, getting the buck out of the woods often can be a more difficult chore than finding him for that fatal telling shot.

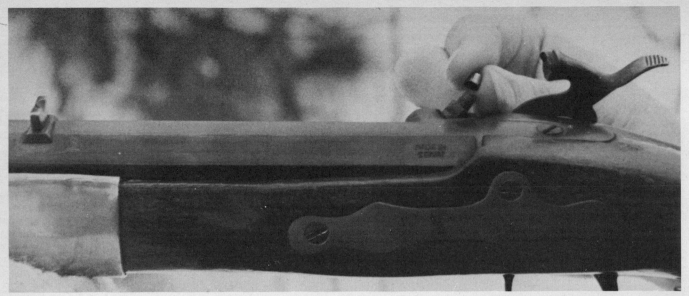

Percussion cap is placed on the nipple of the CVA model used by Bruce Wood. Nipples are kept dry in rain, snow.

whitetails at that time of year in the area hunted. Both men took their bucks in the northern part of the state, the Upper Peninsula. More often than not, that region has snow by December.

With snowfall, deer begin moving toward wintering areas called yards. At the same time, the animals' diets change.

Before snow covers the ground, they graze on grasses and remnants of crops in farmer's fields, as well as on the tips of sprouting trees. After snow covers food close to the ground, woody plants are all that remain.

In active or recent logging areas, tons of deer feed are accessible in the form of treetops. Naturally, whitetails con-

Smith carefully measures out a charge of black powder, which he has predetermined as best load for his rifle. (Left) John Falk kneels beside his first buck, an eight-point whitetail taken with a .50 caliber Hawken load.

centrate in the vicinity of cuttings, so these are prime spots to hunt during that time of year.

Whitetails will go for the tops of any type of hardwoods, but white cedar is a preferred food species.

Anyplace cedar is being cut in December, there will be plenty of deer. Hemlock is another variety Michigan deer favor; they don't derive much benefit from either spruce or balsam.

Foresters can be a big help in pinpointing logging sites to hunters. In most cases, however, operations can be located by driving roads that are plowed through woods. Snow soon clogs back roads that aren't being used. The sound of chainsaws can be heard for long distances on quiet mornings, giving hunters a clue as to loggers' whereabouts. Some cutting is done on private property, so be sure to ask permission before hunting an unfamiliar area.

Apples, where available, are an exception to a whitetail's strictly woody diet once snow covers the ground. The animals go out of their way to dig up the frozen fruit. Seemingly, they can smell them through the snow. Apparently, the starchy food is desired to help build up their fat reserve for the long Winter ahead.

Upper Michigan is dotted with apple orchards. Many of them mark the sites of old homesteads that have long since been abandoned and in ruins. Here again, scouting is necessary to locate orchards.

All orchards aren't visited by deer during December. Those located in or near winter yards get the heaviest use. Department of Natural Resources biologists can be helpful in directing interested individuals to traditional yards.

In addition to hunting near feeding areas, black powder hunters in the Upper Peninsula of Michigan have a chance to intercept whitetails along trails the deer use leading to winter range from their summer quarters. The animals use the same trails every year. An exceptionally heavy snowfall will trigger a massive movement on these migration routes.

"A partner, Bruce Wood, and I tried to work that angle to our advantage last December. Where we hunted the weather was warmer than normal. The end result was rain, rather than snow," Smith recalls.

"We were in Dickinson County, one of the southern counties in the region. In counties farther to the north — Baraga, Marquette, Houghton and Alger — where I had hunted before, it was colder and they got snow instead of rain.

"At any rate, the deer weren't using migration trails to any extent that first week. My partner and I saw a few animals but they were all bald. There was a turnabout the last couple days, though.

"On December 13, I was hunting alone, watching one of the more heavily traveled migration trails. When I had arrived there at daylight, there were quite a few fresh tracks on it.

"The deer have to be moving today," Smith thought to himself, as he hurriedly got in position twenty-five yards to the side and downwind of the trail. He saw about a dozen animals that day. He had a good look at all of them and every last one was anterless.

"That illustrates how much game can be seen along these routes when deer are using them. Had one of the animals I saw been a buck, I would have chalked up my first black powder kill. Maybe it will be different next year."

Migration trails can't be mistaken for anything else. They are well-worn ruts in the snow packed down by hundreds of whitetail hooves. By cruising the borders of a known yard, the pathways often can be seen crossing roads. The severity of the weather and amount of snow dictate how much they will be used.

Deer will travel on migration routes just about any hour of the day. Peak use, however, is from nine or ten in the morning until three or four in the afternoon. As a general rule, it is a good idea for hunters to be in feeding areas early and late in the day and along travel routes in between.

As a result of that first experimental hunt, a ten-day black powder season has been established for December.

Obviously, the first hunt turned out as expected. Not many deer were bagged, but hunters enjoyed extra hours of quality recreation. Most of the bucks that were taken carried respectable racks, so December seems to be a prime time to collect a bragging-size buck.

With the coming of snow, some of the big racked bucks that hide out through November are forced to head toward yards, which makes them vulnerable to hunters. Additionally, with the coming of Winter, Old Moss Horn has to work a little harder to get a full day's rations, also increasing his vulnerability.

Patched ball was started down the barrel of .45 caliber replica muzzleloader by Wood. This rifle was built by Wood from one of the kits from Connecticut Valley Arms. Round balls were only legal projectiles in first season.

CHAPTER 25

BLACK POWDER IN AFRICA

From left: African hunter Lew Games, Jim Carmichel and Turner Kirkland pose with the elephant taken by Kirkland, using antique muzzleloading double rifle.

H OW ABOUT MAKING a trip to Africa with me and hunting elephants with a muzzleloader?" Jim Carmichel was talking to Turner Kirkland, president of the Dixie Gun Works during a Chicago National Sporting Goods Association show.

After a few minutes of deliberation, Kirkland responded

with a "why not?" Carmichel had hunted with Hunter's Africa, an outfitter headed by professional hunter Lew Games, several times before and volunteered to make all the arrangements for Ernest Tidwell, Dixie's vice-president, and Kirkland.

Several months later, Carmichel reported that he had set the dates for the hunt for the following June, allowing a whole year to prepare for the trip. However, as most well-planned hunting trips have a way of doing, the time for departure seemed to arrive without time to prepare the gear they would need, especially the rifles the two black powder buffs were planning to use.

"With less than two weeks before we were to arrive at Victoria Falls in Rhodesia, where we would team up with Carmichel and Lew Games, Tidwell and I set about to working up suitable hunting loads for the two double-barreled percussion elephant rifles we were taking with us. At anywhere from 175 to 300 grains of FFg black powder

The heavy, thirty-one-inch Damascus twist barrels have poly-groove rifling, with ten rounded lands and grooves. In addition to the stationary close-range rear sight aperture, there are three folding sights marked for one-hundred, two-hundred and three-hundred-yard ranges. The sights are set on a wide, flat, solid rib that is marked W.G. RAWBONE, MAKER, CAPE TOWN. The only other markings on the gun are W.G. RAWBONE stampings on each lock plate and PRAHA stamped into a small, rectangular brass plate inset on the breech plug area of the rib. The lock plates, hammers, trigger, trigger guard and tang are colorfully case hardened. These metal parts are elaborately scroll engraved and the twist barrels have a beautiful, eye-pleasing pattern to them.

Completely modern, the percussion 6 gauge was specially made for Kirkland about ten years ago in Liege, Belgium. "Ever since I purchased the big Rawbone rifle at the London arms show, I had thought about going to Africa

Turner Kirkland Proves Muzzleloader Efficiency Against The World's Biggest Game!

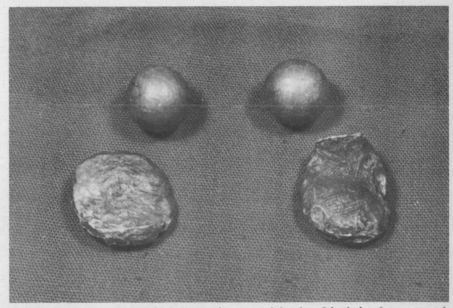

Round balls of soft lead for the 4 gauge measure .880-inch diameter, but recovered slugs from elephant had expanded to 1.75-inch diameter.

for each shot, it didn't take long to burn up a few pounds of powder," Kirkland recalls.

"Experimenting with various powder charges and patched ball sizes in both the 4 gauge I was planning to use and the 6 gauge Tidwell would be toting along, we fired the guns so much that the impact area behind our targets looked more like the impact zone for heavy artillery than for something that had been fired from the shoulder. Those big 725-grain, 6-gauge balls and 1030-grain, 4-gauge balls ripped some mighty huge holes in the dirt backstop."

At an arms show in London about fifteen years ago, Turner Kirkland had come across a gun and, after some swift talking, had managed to persuade its owner, Anthony Foley, to part with it for $100. Since then, he has thumbed through countless firearms publications trying to shed more light on the gun's manufacture, but to date has not been able to find any information on the gun or its maker.

and hunting with a muzzleloader. I had the 6 gauge made with the intentions of using it for a back-up gun if something went haywire with the century-old Rawbone. For ten years that African hunt failed to materialize and when Tidwell and I boarded the plane at Memphis, Tennessee, it was hard to realize that I was finally on my way."

As planned, they flew to Victoria Falls, but not without first stopping in Monrovia, Liberia, Senegal, Libya, Ghana, Nigeria and Johannesburg, South Africa. When they unloaded from the ancient prop plane used on the last leg of the trip, Jim Carmichel was there to meet them.

"From Victoria Falls, we traveled 180 miles across flat savannahs into Botswana, where we were to hunt. It was a tiring trip and it was a welcomed relief to enjoy a good meal and hit the sack early that evening.

"Sunrise on the African veld has to be unlike sunrise anywhere else in the world. One minute dawn is a faint gray line on the distant eastern horizon, silhouetting the sparsely growing acacia trees; the next minute, the sun already has risen to mid-morning position. June is a winter month in the southern hemisphere and the early morning temperatures were right around thirty-five degrees.

"Although Carmichel and Games opined they thought it would be a good idea to test the muzzleloaders for accuracy before leaving camp, I'm sure they were just anxious to see the big guns being fired. Before leaving on the trip, Tidwell and I had managed to keep the 4 gauge's round-ball projectiles well within the six-inch bull's-eye of a regulation fifty-yard, slow-fire muzzleloading target.

"After a few rounds with the big gun, Carmichel decided that the accuracy could be improved with a little work on the loads we were using."

Sticking with the 300 grains of FFg Kirkland had felt were suitable, Carmichel experimented with various thicknesses of patching and finally managed to shrink the groups some, but not enough to make any real difference. However, he worked wonders with the Kentucky percussion rifles brought along for antelope.

Carmichel felt the rifles were hitting too high, so he took a file to the rear sight and knocked it down low enough that he was able to keep the majority of his shots well within the black bull's-eye at ranges of seventy and eighty yards. Incidentally, these .45 caliber muzzleloaders are basically the same rifle that Kirkland first introduced in 1955, shortly after cleaning out his father's coal bin and founding Dixie Gun Works. The big difference between the two rifles are the buttstocks: the original had a straight typical Kentucky comb; the rifles they had with them in Africa featured the curved, Roman nose shaped buttstocks similar to the originals that had come from the Pennsylvania gunsmith shops.

"With most of the morning spent testing our rifles, we waited until after lunch before going out. Driving across some of the worst roads I've ever been on, we traveled only about ten miles from camp, then returned. The native spotters, trackers and skinners were complaining about not having any fresh meat in camp. The whole purpose of the afternoon hunt was to bring back camp meat, but the fleet-footed game we did manage to spot usually was well out of range, even for Carmichel's scoped Ruger Model 77 in 7mm magnum. We returned empty-handed."

Early the next morning the hunters loaded up the percussion elephant rifles and headed off in the opposite direction from which they had gone the previous afternoon. About a half hour from camp, they spotted their first elephant.

"The young bull was stripping leaves from the limbs of a low tree and didn't even know we were anywhere around. Games maneuvered the four-wheel drive Toyota within a hundred yards of the elephant and even without using our binoculars we could distinguish that his ivory was on the small side. As unnoticed as we had slipped up on the animal, we slipped away without disturbing him.

"The warming sunlight felt good on my chilled fingers and on the back of my neck. By ten o'clock the temperature had risen to near eighty degrees and was more like what I had expected," Turner Kirkland says.

They were cruising along a dirt trail that was little more than two tire ruts across the dry soil and sand, when one of the spotters pounded on the cab top and started jabbering away in his native dialect. Games slammed on the brakes and nearly threw everyone out of the land cruiser. Climbing on top of the Toyota, he studied something through his binoculars for a few minutes, then looked down and said, "There's a pretty good bull about three hundred yards away. Get your rifle and let's go take a closer look."

On foot, they covered the first two hundred yards without much trouble. The elephant was busy feeding and was facing away from them. A ten or twelve-foot acacia tree provided perfect cover to within sixty yards of the feeding bull.

Behind the security of a thick bush, the hunters paused to size up the situation. Lew Games inched forward to plan their next move. A few minutes later, he returned and explained that the bull was a fair animal, big bodied and sporting tusks of around fifty pounds each.

Moving to the right at an angle, Kirkland was able to keep in the bull's blind spot as he continued to feed. Less than forty-five yards away, someone must have snapped an unseen twig. Hearing the sudden, unnatural sound, the elephant swung his head around and shook his massive head

Ernie Tidwell combined supplying camp meat with trophy hunting with Kentucky-style replica marketed by Kirkland's Dixie Gun Works firm.

Locally prepared jerky was the staple of their noon snack, as the hunters ranged far afield in pursuit of elusive elephants they sought with muzzleloaders.

and vigorously flapped his huge ears.

"We had already decided that the big muzzleloader would be most likely to deal a lethal blow with a well-placed shot into the lung area, figuring that the extremely thick, porous bones of the skull would greatly reduce penetration. The towering bull momentarily froze and stared directly at us; I was sure he was about to charge. Instead, he turned and offered the broadside shot for which I had been waiting."

"Shoot now! Shoot now!" the guide whispered. The heavy rifle was still at Turner Kirkland's side, but he hardly noticed its eighteen-pound bulk as he swung it into shoulder and automatically aligned the bead on the elephant's rib cage. He squeezed the trigger and the gun belched fire and smoke. He knew it was a good hit even before the smoke had cleared.

"Shoot again," urged Games, as the elephant lengthened his stride. The bull had covered less than five yards when the second shot sounded. By the time the huge cloud of smoke cleared, the elephant was in the brush and out of sight.

"Until then, I had been as cool, calm and collected as the proverbial cucumber. Then I realized I was starting to tremble and my mouth was as dry as cotton. I just stood there looking into the brush where the elephant had disappeared."

The trail of broken limbs and splotches of blood was an easy one to follow. Games was afraid the elephant would cross over into Rhodesia, since they were practically on the border. If it did, the hunters wouldn't be allowed to cross over and put in a finishing shot.

Tidwell reported that from the truck he had watched the bull stumble at the first shot and he said it showed signs of being hit hard as it crashed through the brush. Following the blood trail, the elephant was found four hundred yards away and unable to travel any farther. A close shot from twenty yards put the animal down for keeps.

Examination of Kirkland's first shot revealed it had been perfectly placed in the lung area. The whole left shoulder was covered with blood and air bubbles around the bullet hole assured that the 1030-grain soft lead ball had penetrated into the lungs. The second shot had been too high, hitting nearly eighteen inches above the first.

Both shots had penetrated around twenty inches and the soft .880 diameter round balls were badly deformed. In fact, both had expanded so greatly they were flattened into small lead disks measuring 1.75 inches across and .40 inches in thickness. The tough hide probably accounted for much of this expansion, since the first shot completely missed any bones and yet was flattened just as badly as the second hit, which had struck a heavy rib bone. Balls cast from heavily tinned lead or from lead with some antimony content would most likely have penetrated deeper; their extra hardness would have minimized expansion.

On the way back to camp that afternoon, the hunting

The only markings on Kirkland's 4-gauge elephant rifle are a line reading, "W.G. RAWBONE MAKER CAPE TOWN," and the word, "PRAHA," stamped in area above breech plug.

party spotted another nine elephants, but they were either immature bulls or cows.

The group hunted another week at Nunga camp along the Rhodesian border without spotting a single elephant of near trophy size. Using a Ruger Model 77, Ernest Tidwell managed to take a beautiful sable that was just a fraction under record book size and Carmichel had dropped a big wildebeest with the 6-gauge double rifle.

"Games decided our chances of finding an elephant for Carmichel and Tidwell would be much better at another of his camps located along the Chobe River and bordering northern South West Africa. It was a long and grueling 330-mile trek across the dry and parched savannahs and we had to make it in two days of traveling, stopping about halfway at the village of Kasane, headquarters for Hunter's Africa. Occasionally we managed to get the Toyota up to a top speed of around twenty-five miles per hour. Most of the time, though, we crawled along at speeds of ten to fifteen miles per hour. All of us were bushed by the time we pulled into Saile camp, near where the Kwando River empties into the Chobe.

"We spent the next morning sighting in our .45 caliber Dixie Kentucky rifles, mainly because we still were tired from the long drive of the two previous days. A short drive through the grassy plains near camp produced a few long-range shots for our muzzleloaders, but we failed to connect."

Some distance from camp was located a large concentration of game. Large numbers of lechwe, eland and an occasional warthog were almost always in sight, but getting within muzzleloader range of the wary animals was a different story. As they were about to head back to camp, Carmichel spotted a group of lechwe feeding about three hundred yards from the narrow dirt trail.

"Each grabbing a Kentucky rifle from the gun rack, Carmichel and Tidwell went after them. Stalking to within seventy yards, Carmichel dropped a big ram with a well-placed shot through the chest cavity. Tidwell hadn't gotten off a shot and, when the same group of lechwe was spotted a quarter-mile down the trail, he slipped within one hundred yards of the nervous animals and dropped a nice ram with a solid hit in the spinal column."

During the next few days the party managed to down a variety of African game with both muzzleloaders and center-fire high-powered rifles. They hadn't spotted any elephants, but had found enough signs to assure that they were in the area. Tidwell used a Winchester Model 70 in .458 Winchester magnum to take a Cape buffalo and was so impressed with the powerful cartridge's knockdown ability, he decided to use it when his turn came to down an elephant.

Loaded with 72 grains of IMR3031 behind the big, 500-grain solid Hornady bullet, the handloads develop a muzzle velocity of right around 2150 feet per second and nearly 2½ tons of muzzle energy. Although the massive 200 to 300-grain powder charges fired in the 6 gauge probably produce muzzle energies in the same neighborhood, the soft lead round balls don't hold up long enough for proper penetration.

Time was running out and neither Carmichel nor Tidwell had taken their elephant. All three had taken lechwe, impala and wildebeest with the .45 caliber muzzleloading rifles. Tsessebe also had fallen to Kirkland's front-loader, while the other two added eland, sable, Cape buffalo, kudu and zebra to their list of trophies.

With only a few days left, Lew Games decided to concentrate on getting the two elephants needed before filling the antelope license. He decided to travel some distance from camp to an area that usually had a good concentration

Most of the tusks have been worn away on the big elephant taken by Carmichel in one-shot kill.

of elephant. It would be a three-hour drive and an early start was necessary.

Less than a half-hour from camp, one of the spotters excitedly pointed off into the brush and started jabbering away in his native tongue. Games slid the land cruiser to a stop and explained that the spotter had glimpsed elephants through an opening in the brush. There were three fairly respectable bulls, one sporting ivory in the sixty-pound class.

Carmichel handed Tidwell his Winchester .458 magnum and, with Games packing his custom Remington 700 in the same caliber, the three of them worked closer for a better look and to plan a stalk that would put them within reasonable rifle range.

The elephants were only about 150 yards from the Toyota, but the thick brush made it all but impossible to see the huge animals. Stalking upwind, the group of hunters were able to move undetected to within seventy yards, but the elephants kept moving and it was necessary to make a second stalk before Tidwell could shoot.

Holding for the lower portion of the ear which leads directly into the brain, he squeezed off the chambered round. At the report, the elephant sunk to his knees in the classical manner that elephants are supposed to go down. Deciding that there might not be another chance for an elephant, Carmichel quickly took the rifle from Tidwell and was about to drop the second largest of the trio when the downed elephant stumbled back to his feet.

"Hit him again," Carmichel shouted as he handed the rifle back to Tidwell. But before he could touch off a second shot, the three elephants ambled off into the thick brush. Peter, a native tracker, shinnied up a twelve-foot acacia tree and reported that he could see the elephant down and apparently quite dead about five hundred yards away, but his two comrades were standing guard over their fallen companion.

From a downwind approach, the three hunters eased through the brush until they could see the big animals fairly well. It was apparent that the remaining two bulls were aware of the death of their companion and reacted by tearing up the brush around the downed elephant. One of them even pushed down a ten-foot acacia tree and was ripping it apart when Carmichel slipped in for a shot.

It was a dangerous situation, with both elephants grieving their companion's death and running around in an unexplainable manner. Games was cautious not to let Carmichel get himself into a position that he might not be able to get out of. Flipping the safety of his Remington 700 off, he stood ready just in case one of the elephants charged.

Resting against a tree trunk, Carmichel held for the lower portion of the ear when his elephant turned broadside. The rifle bucked from the stout recoil and the bull crashed to the ground. For a moment the remaining member of the trio crashed through the nearby brush and made several false charges, flapping his huge ears and holding his head high in a menacing gesture. Finally he wheeled around and disappeared into the thick brush. The hunters could hear him crashing through the low bushes and scrub, then it was quiet.

The two elephants lay less than twenty yards apart. The three hunters moved in for a closer check. Tidwell had just climbed atop Carmichel's bull when all of a sudden he made a fast dive for the ground. The elephant was still alive and he had felt its heart beating. Another .458 into the top of the head did the trick.

"The next few days were spent chasing what few species of antelope we needed to fill our licenses. We had taken a lot of game with both muzzleloaders and center-fire rifles, but nothing matched the excitement of slipping within forty-five yards of the world's largest land animal and taking him with a muzzleloading rifle that was made in South Africa over a hundred years ago," Turner Kirkland contends.

CHAPTER 26

THE LORE OF LEAD

Lyman mould for .672" round balls, together with 12-gauge plastic wad assemblies is used in firing this antique bronze cannon with bore of that size.

Facts And Figures On A Metal Without Which Shooting Might Have Been Delayed For Centuries!

Although round balls and Minie projectiles can be bought in most of the common sizes, apparatus to make them yourself is neither overly expensive nor difficult to use with highly satisfactory results.

Lᴇᴛ ᴜꜱ ᴘᴀᴜꜱᴇ briefly to give thanks for the existence of lead. For that humble metallic element has simplified the gunner's problems down through the centuries since the invention of firearms; aiding the shooting arts to an extent that few appreciate properly.

There's an old folk saying to the gist that, "you never miss the water till the well runs dry." In much the same manner, you start recognizing the many useful virtues of lead right about at the time you begin trying to find an adequate substitute for it. This has become quite evident in certain areas of waterfowling, due to the fact that lead shotgun pellets remain on hard bottoms beneath shallow water to be ingested by the bottom-feeding species of ducks. This, in turn, causes the loss of serious quantities of the birds, due to lead poisoning.

The best replacement for lead shot that has been found to date has consisted of pellets formed from soft iron or steel. Sadly, it's far from satisfactory. The steel is so much

harder that it tends to be rough on the bores of shotguns and it's quite a bit lighter than lead, volume for volume, so that pellets of the same diameter won't travel as far or retain their velocity as well. In order to get comparable performance, steel pellets must be of larger diameter and that automatically decrees that you can't get as many pellets into the same amount of space and this, in turn, cuts down seriously on your chances of making an effective hit.

This discussion has little concern with steel shot as a replacement for lead but it is mentioned by way of pointing out the admirable virtues of that heavy gray metal. What are these virtues? It is available in generous quantities and at relatively modest cost. It is heavy and dense, that is, it has a high specific gravity — of which, more later. It is easy to form into desired shapes since it has a low melting point. It is comparatively soft, which makes it adapt easily to the shape of the lands and grooves of a rifled barrel, without danger of damaging the rifling. Being soft, it has consider-

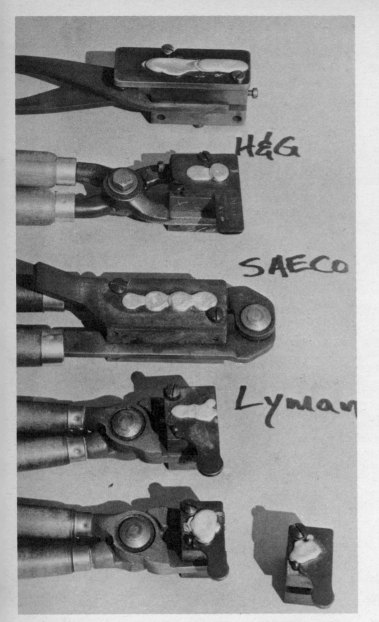

Moulds are made with various numbers of cavities to expedite production. Three lower moulds, by Lyman, have 1, 2, and 4 cavities. Saeco also has a hardness tester for measuring this in samples.

able capability for upsetting — flattening — at the time of impact so as to increase its striking effectiveness.

Lead has been known and used since ancient times. Unlike copper, it is rarely if ever found in the native state as a fairly pure metal. However, lead ores and the technique for smelting them have been a part of mankind's technology for over two thousand years.

The old Romans were well acquainted with lead, calling it by the name of plumbum, from which stems the modern chemist's symbol for that element, Pb. Likewise, this is the root-word for other terms such as plumbing — in which lead was and still is used extensively — plumb bob and so on.

Specific gravity is the term used to denote the comparative weight of a given volume of a material in relation to an equal volume of water. In the example of lead, it's about 11.37 times as heavy as an equal volume of water. To fairly precise specs, that makes a single cubic inch of lead scale out at 0.4105 pounds or 2873.5 grains, since there are 7000

grains in one avoirdupois pound. To establish comfortable familiarity with the avoirdupois weight system, it can be noted that is the same one in which your bathroom scale is graduated.

If you have a good supply of pencils and scratch paper, plus patience and curiosity, you can work out the weight for a round lead ball of any given diameter with the information given here. The final bit of data — if your third-grade arithmetic is getting rusty — is that you determine the volume of a sphere by multiplying the diameter cubed times .5236. To take an easy example, a caliber .50 round ball would be .5 x .5 x .5= .125; this, times .5236 gives us .06545 cubic inch as the volume. Since lead weighs 2873.5 grains per cubic inch: 2873.5 x .06545 = 188.070575 grains as the probable, approximate weight for the caliber .50 round ball.

Admittedly, predicting the weight to a millionth of a grain is a bit more precision than that for which most of us might feel a burning need, but it's handy to have the basic information available, where you can find it when needed.

In actual practice, the textbook figures often don't work out quite that closely. For one thing, you can encounter a rather broad band of disparity as to the exact specific gravity of lead in the first place. The quoted figure of 11.37 as the specific gravity, along with 0.4105 pounds as the weight of one cubic inch of lead, is taken from an excellent work entitled Complete Guide to Handloading, by the late Philip B. Sharpe. My high school chemistry textbook, circa 1936, pegs the specific gravity of lead at 11.24 times the weight of water. A periodic chart of the atoms, appearing in The Random House Dictionary of the English Language, offers the figure of 11.4 as its entry for the sweepstakes.

I once quizzed a friend who works for the Bureau of Standards, in Washington, D.C., as to his explanation for such apparent paradoxes, pointing out that you can find about the same number of figures for the specific gravity and melting point as the number of reference works you consult. He looked harried for a moment, shrugged and said, "The heck of it is, every time you try to work it out, you come up with a slightly different answer."

I rather doubt if the Bureau of Standards would care to consider that an official pronouncement, but I offer it as a sort of pre-explanation if you find that other reference sources do not agree with the figures quoted here.

As metals go, lead is a friendly sort of soul, happily entering into partnership with numerous other elements to form compounds. It is most cordial toward oxygen and it will oxidize rapidly upon exposure to air, regardless of temperature. As it turns out, this dull, gray coating of lead oxide is extremely durable and resistant to the effects of weather and climate. It would not be too far off the mark of characterize lead as "the self-painting metal." Iron, as all of us are ruefully aware, oxidizes into the familiar red coating of rust, but this loosens and falls away, exposing fresh interior metal to further oxidizing so that, after a time, there's nothing left but rust. It's this durable trait of lead that has preserved century-old musket balls and Minie projectiles so they can be turned up in an amazing state of preservation in sites such as Civil War battlefields. Likewise, it's the source of the duck-poisoning problem previously mentioned.

We have noted that lead melts easily; the approximate melting point being 621 degrees on the Fahrenheit scale or 327 degrees Centigrade. Most combustible materials will burn at a flame temperature which exceeds the melting point of lead by a comfortable margin, qualifying that useful metal as one of the most convenient of all casting materials.

Lead, as we've noted, combines chemically with several

NAME OF ELEMENT	CHEMICAL SYMBOL	SPECIFIC GRAVITY	MELTING POINT °F	°C
Aluminum	Al	2.70	1218	660
Antimony	Sb	6.62	1168	630.5
Arsenic	As	5.72	1550	817
Barium	Ba	3.5	1550	817
Bismuth	Bi	9.8	522	271.3
Cadmium	Cd	8.65	321	610
Copper	Cu	8.96	1981	1083
Gallium	Ga	5.91	86	30
Gold	Au	19.3	1945	1063
Iron	Fe	7.86	2774	1536
Lead	Pb	11.4	622	327.4
Mercury	Hg	13.58	-38.4	-39.5
Osmium	Os	22.6	4892	2700
Silver	Ag	10.53	1762	961
Tin	Sn	7.30	450	232
Zinc	Zn	7.14	786	420

NOTE: Some of the entries in this chart are obviously unsuited for use in bullets, but they were included as being of possible interest. For example, if osmium were cheap and plentiful, with a lower melting point, it would make a wonderful bullet!

other elements. Likewise, it mixes physically with most of the other metals having melting points in the same thermal neighborhood. Tin and antimony are the two metals most frequently used in producing alloys with lead, although bismuth, cadmium and zinc will combine if you give them a chance.

Practically any metal — offhand, I can think of no exception — when alloyed with lead, will result in a mixture that is somewhat harder than the pure lead was in the first place. Properly mixed lead alloys can serve useful purposes when working with the more modern and sophisticated firearms designed for use with smokeless (nitro) powders. However, it is the general consensus that the most pure and soft grade of lead that you can get will give you the best performance out of the beloved old black powder muzzleloaders and their modern-made counterparts to which the book at hand is dedicated.

Which brings up the question: What are the sources for pure, soft lead, suitable for producing muzzleloader projectiles? One obvious approach, though far from the most economical, is to go to a plumber's shop and buy as many pounds of pig lead as you need. Depending upon current prices, as well as the good tradesman's generosity or lack of it, virgin pig lead can span a cost range from around thirty to sixty cents per pound.

In earlier years, lead pipes were used widely in domestic plumbing. Sadly, this has been changing with the shift to the use of galvanized iron, copper and — more recently — plastic pipe. At one time, most plumbing shops had a pile of salvaged lead pipe somewhere about the place and many of them would sell you any reasonable quantity at well below the going price of virgin metal: i.e., fresh from the mines and refineries. Plumbers continue to use lead for joining sections of cast iron soil pipe: They pack the joint with oakum fibers, pour molten lead into it and beat around the joint with a hammer and caulking iron to assure a watertight seal.

Some shops will melt down scrap pipe to obtain further supplies of soft lead for pouring joints, but most prefer to buy virgin pig lead, due to the rising hourly scale of the trade, which tends to absorb any saving of money via the salvage operation.

So you still may be able to find plumbers who rip the

occasional batch of lead pipe out of older houses in the process of replacing plumbing systems and they may be willing to sell it to you for about the same price as they'd get from the local scrap dealer. Once it gets into the hands of the scrap dealer, it seems to be gone. At least, I've yet to find one who would part with this sort of treasure at any realistic price level.

Scrap lead pipe may be found joined together in the form of various Ys and Ts by means of plumber's wiping solder. This is an alloy consisting of about 67 percent lead and 33 percent tin. Since you don't want tin in your muzzleloader mixture, it's best to cut the wiped joints off and set them aside before melting down the sections of plain pipe. Don't throw the joints away, as they can be used in casting bullets for smokeless powder loads. If you have no use for them, they can be swapped for soft lead from a shooting buddy who casts for the more newfangled ordnance!

Lead pipe will average about the same degree of purity as commercial pig lead: approximately 99.6 percent lead, with the remainder consisting of insignificant quantities of zinc, silver, arsenic, antimony, tin or even a trifle of gold. However, these impurities do not harden the lead to any serious extent and they can be disregarded. Most of the other metals turn up amid the lead ore in varying quantities and are separated at the refinery to the extent that it may be necessary and/or commercially economical to do so.

So the unwritten law among bullet casters is, "always be kind to plumbers," because you never know when they might provide you with needed raw material at friendly prices ranging clear down to free, which is the friendliest price of all! Much the same observation applies to telephone company lineman, who can be valuable sources of scrap telephone cable sheathing.

The common estimate of purity on cable sheathing is around 98.5 percent, which still is quite sufficiently pure for the purposes of black powder aficionados. However, the solder used in joining sections of cable sheathing contains

This photo of a Lyman mould illustrates principle of such devices. Sprue cutter has just been driven over and solidified ball is ready to be tapped out.

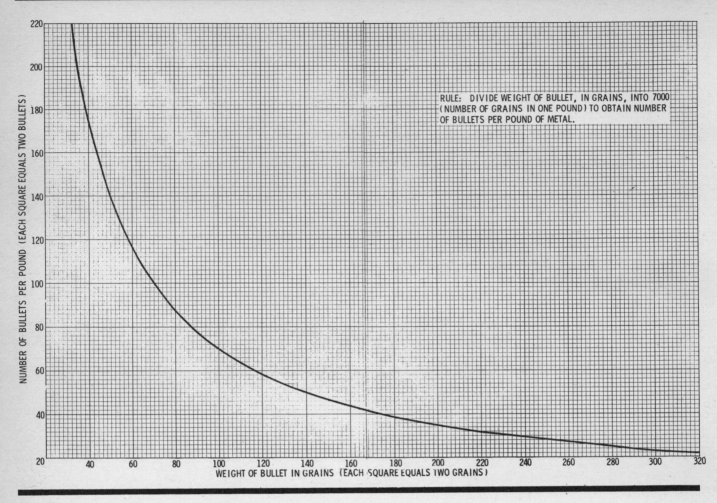

RULE: DIVIDE WEIGHT OF BULLET, IN GRAINS, INTO 7000 (NUMBER OF GRAINS IN ONE POUND) TO OBTAIN NUMBER OF BULLETS PER POUND OF METAL.

This handy chart tells how many bullets of a given weight one can cast from a pound of lead or alloy.

some insidious and obnoxious ingredient which, if it gets into your melting pot, even in small amounts, makes it all but mandatory to consign the entire batch of metal for use in such non-critical applications as gluing weights or boat anchors. Whatever the stuff is, it makes the mixture pour with the consistency of corn meal mush, even at quite high temperatures. So you quickly learn to clip and trim away all of the cable sheathing solder and put it aside for careful disposal where it won't get mixed in with the choicer metals.

Lead pipe, cable sheathing and commerical pig lead are the primary sources of metal sufficiently soft for the purposes under present discussion. Should you gain access to large amounts of jacketed bullets, such as from the fall-out area of a range, these can be smelted down and the jackets skimmed away as they float to the surface and the resulting cleaned metal will be suitably soft and pure. It's not a practical source unless low-cost labor is available. Nor are the unjacketed lead bullets found on most civilian target ranges of much use for making soft lead bullets, since most of them will have been hardened through the addition of gosh-knows-what by the previous caster for use in smokeless powder loads.

Battery plates contain a considerable quantity of antimony, up to eleven percent or so; moreover, they can have little pockets of trapped acid which can erupt with explosive violence when you go to smelt them down.

Wheel weights vary widely as to content, typically around 90 percent lead; most of the rest is antimony and a bit of tin may have gotten into some of them. There is no practical way for the individual to refine this metal back into reasonably pure lead. Much the same applies to the various alloys used in the printing trades.

One further category of available metal must be mentioned: scrap metal of unknown composition, meltable and more or less lead-like in appearance. Such finds can and do turn up in every conceivable form and the question is one of determining if the metal is sufficiently soft and pure for use in projectiles for muzzleloaders.

Happily enough, almost everyone possesses a testing device which can yield a valid clue as to whether it's soft lead or not; it's known as a thumbnail. Put on a little pressure and try to scribe a line in a smooth area of the metal being tested. If your nail can leave a mark of detectable depth, exposing the beautiful, silvery glint of unoxidized lead, then it's a fairly safe bet that the metal does not contain enough impurities to disqualify it for your purposes.

One further quick and simple test is easy to carry out. Some time when you happen to luck onto a really super-

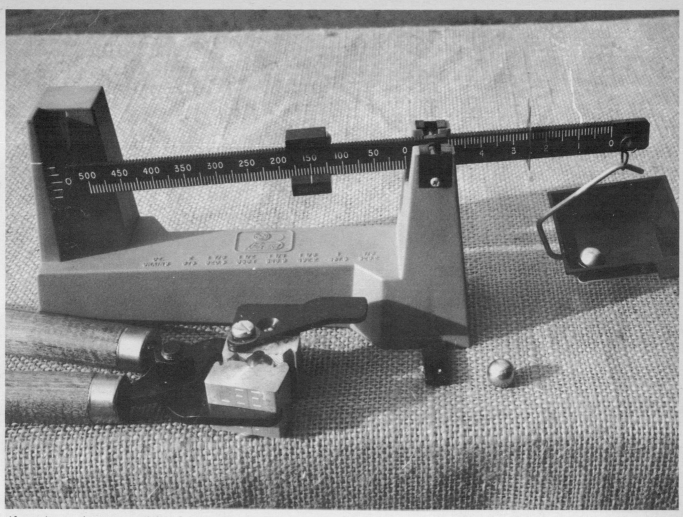

If you know the exact weight of a pure lead ball from a given mould, another ball from the same mould, of unknown alloy can be weighed as test.

Some shooters buy reclaimed lead that has been cast into pigs, but which is adequate for bullet making.

grade batch of pure lead, so luxuriously soft that you can almost spread it on bread with a table knife, try to cast up one perfectly filled sample out of each of your moulds. Set these samples aside, or weigh them carefully on an accurate powder scale and record the weight for each mould where the data will not get lost — which is no minor feat, in itself! Then, as you acquire hunks of metal of dubious parentage or analytical content, it becomes a simple operation to cast up a sample from one of the moulds you've pre-checked with the dead-soft lead. When you get a ball or bullet that's filled out as completely as was the original test specimen, toss the new sample on the pan of your scales and compare its weight to that of the one known to have been pure lead.

Since all of the metals apt to be present in lead as impurities have specific gravities well below that of lead, the less pure alloys will produce samples having identical volume but perceptibly lighter weights. The evaluation procedure just described will not indicate whether it's tin, antimony or what-have-you that's present, but it does provide a useful yardstick as to the amount of impurities on a percentile basis. If your test sample weighs within a few grains of a pure lead casting out of the same mould, it's an excellent bet that it's pure within any fairly charitable definition of the word. However, you can expect to be astonished at the weight-loss possible because of impurities. This can run to ten percent or more, although anything that tests much more than three percent weight-loss probably will not pass your initial thumbnail test.

CHAPTER 27

CASTING THE STARS OF YOUR SHOOTING SHOW

A Thoughtful Look At The Projectiles You Can Buy Or Make And How To Sort Out Which Is Which!

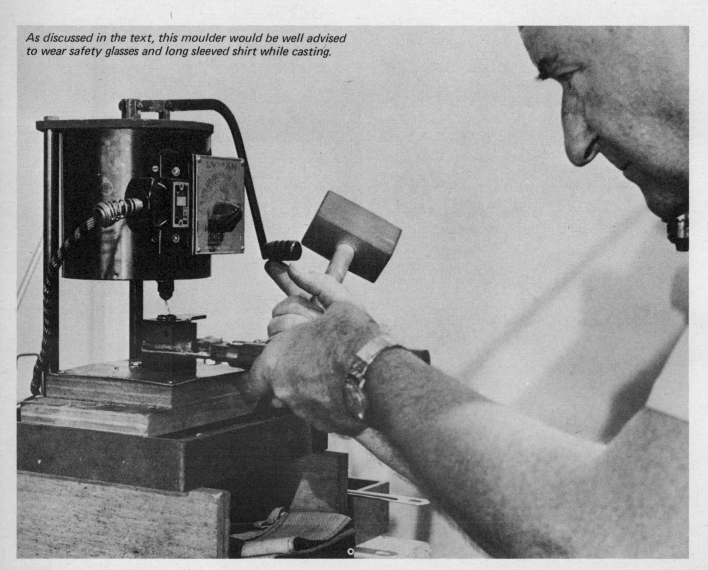

As discussed in the text, this moulder would be well advised to wear safety glasses and long sleeved shirt while casting.

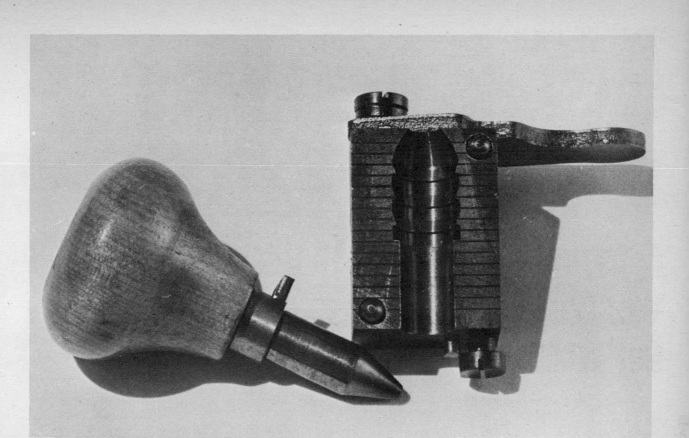

Moulds for Minie balls require the separate base cavity forming punch, which makes them more expensive to produce and prevents furnishing as multi-cavity types.

LET US START by considering a few basic safety precautions before we begin discussing operations concerned with the melting and casting of lead. It is sound good judgment to form the habit of wearing eye protection — such as safety glasses or a face shield — when working with melted lead. Dress sensibly, which means long-sleeved shirts, if temperatures make this bearable, with the minimum area of unprotected hide being exposed to the hazards of spills and spatters.

Lead has certain toxic properties, as do some of the other metals with which it may be mixed. It is well to wash your hands thoroughly after handling lead and before eating, with appropriate cautions about how you handle cigarettes, cigars, et al., when working with lead, either in the molton or solidified state. Melted lead gives off sufficient aerial contaminants to make the provision of adequate ventilation necessary if exposure is frequent and/or extended. Zinc and cadmium, when melted or vaporized, are much more toxic than lead in this respect. Dust-fine particles of lead are suspended in the air after firing, so that ventilation can be required for indoor ranges, as conditions may indicate.

It is particularly important to isolate any lead-melting activities, such as casting, cleaning, et al., from any of those flammable materials employed in shooting such as powder, primers, caps and the like. A tiny spatter of molten lead, falling into an open container of black powder spells instant catastrophe and this is worth avoiding at almost any cost!

In bringing up such gloomy topics, I do not mean to discourage you from exploring the interesting and rewarding field of bullet casting but, rather, to help assure that you will enjoy this absorbing pastime without falling prey to its occasional hazards. All it really takes is a moderate ration of common sense.

For example: On a night long ago, common sense should have kept me from filling a large old frying pan nearly to the brim with melted-down hunks of lead pipe, which I was cleaning up and pouring into pig moulds for future use. Certainly, common sense should have blown the whistle when I went to pick it up by its use-worn wooden handle which, under the strain of about forty-odd pounds, slipped on its shank and abruptly decanted quite a bit of the lead over the top of the gas range, onto the linoleum of the floor, with a goodly dollop of the fiery stuff ending up inside the loose-fitting bedroom slippers I happened to be wearing (common sense, we were talking about: remember?). This discolored patch of the linoleum reminded me of my folly for as long as we lived in that house, as did my long-suffering better half!

For the record, an old frying pan on the kitchen stove works well enough — if you can live with the gamy odors arising from reclaimed plumbing pipes — but the secret is to clamp down tightly with a large pair of Vise-Grip pliers on the edge of the pan opposite the handle before attempting to lift and pour from your jury-rigged smelting pot.

As noted in the foregoing discussion, almost any fuel produces flame temperatures high enough to top the required 621 degrees F, with some to spare. However, you

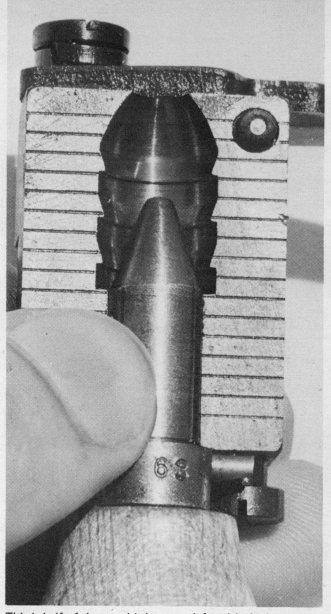

Lyman moulds are identified by a design number, first three digits of which indicate diameter. The 672 is serial for the day's production assuring that the two halves both match.

This is half of the mould shown at left, with the bottom punch held in place to show how it forms the base cavity.

could hold a ten-pound pot of lead over a cigarette lighter all day and nothing would happen. Your heat source must generate enough BTUs of thermal energy to offset heat lost from the metal by means of radiation, convection and conduction or you'll never raise it beyond the melting point.

I've used blowtorches, camp stoves, kitchen ranges powered by wood, gas and electricity, plus assorted gas and electric hotplates for melting down lead, with varying degrees of success and satisfaction. The handy little propane torches, such as Pratt & Lambert or Bernz-O-Matic, can be used to good advantage during the initial melting phase of the operation to hasten the lead into a liquid state.

If you've started out with several lumps, pigs or odd-shaped pieces of lead in a clean pot, it will take a long while before it starts to melt. This is because the lead only touches the metal of the pot at a few small points. Once the metal has melted, it is in contact over a much larger area

and the rate of heat transfer is much more rapid and efficient. For this reason, it's best to start with small amounts of lead until you get a shallow layer of molten metal across the bottom, after which you can feed in the larger pieces.

Try to leave your melting pot with a small layer of metal at the bottom, so that things will go more quickly the next time you fire up for a session. Any excess can be ladled out and poured into pig moulds for future use, leaving a half-inch or so in the pot.

Several suppliers offer handy little pig moulds, well made of cast iron. These turn out a pig shaped like an oblong, truncated pyramid, about three inches long, 1½ inches wide and three-quarter inches thick, weighing a pound or a bit over. If desired, the four-trough mould can be filled brim-full, producing an ingot that weighs around six pounds, which can be broken up into the four small

This is the Lyman mould designed for producing 12-gauge slugs for use in shotguns, including muzzleloading designs.

Ohaus Minie mould, design number 58-275-M turns out a caliber .58 projectile which weighs 275 grains in soft lead.

pieces at your convenience.

You may find that one-pound pigs are a bit small for volume production. I did and made the happy discovery that the top half of an old GI messkit makes the greatest pig mould of all time. Usually made of stainless steel, it's durable and lead won't stick to its shiny surface. Depending upon how deeply you fill the messkit top, it yields two kidney-shaped pigs weighing upward of six pounds apiece or, if poured full, it solidifies into an oval blob that can be broken into two sizeable chunks with the aid of a small hatchet and a chopping block. The messkit pigs are just the right size for feeding into the top of those small electric melting pots which represent the pinnacle of going first class, so far as the bullet caster is concerned.

Several firms have produced electric lead melting pots over the years and some of these continue in business: Lyman and SAECO being two noteworthy examples. At the lower end of the price range, there are utility pots, open at the top for feeding and ladling, with their temperature being regulated by the slightly more primitive technique of plugging or unplugging the cord, as necessary.

A notch higher up the melting pot peck-order of luxury, we find the open-topped pot with an adjustable, thermostatically controlled heating element which will cut in and out to maintain any pre-set temperature from about 550 to 800 degrees F. You still have to dip the lead out of the top with a ladle but it maintains a uniform temperature at the chosen point and that is extremely helpful in producing the best possible bullets.

Whether you're melting your metal in an electric, open-topped pot or an old skillet, you quickly develop a practiced roll of the wrist that backs the lower surface of your ladle across the dull, gray skim of oxidized metal on the surface so as to dip from the pure, coin-bright supply of metal beneath.

After the metal has melted, drop in a small piece of beeswax, about the size of your smallest fingernail, and stir the metal to flux it. This causes the metal to combine into a uniform mixture and brings dross and impurities to the surface where they can be skimmed off and discarded. An old spoon works well for this purpose. After that point, don't try to remove the thin film of new oxide that forms immediately as the bright metal is exposed. Leave the film alone to protect the rest of the metal from the air and, thereby, cut down on oxidation.

It should be noted that the beeswax or other material used as a flux may catch fire and flare up above the melted metal. It depends upon whether or not the metal temperature exceeds the wax's flash point. Bear this possibility in mind and take care not to have flammable material in the area within three or four feet from the top of your melting pot. If it doesn't flare up, it will smoke furiously.

The slickest deals of all are those electrically operated, thermostatically controlled melting pots with a lever on the side to open and close a small valve on the bottom. When open, molten metal is delivered through an outlet nozzle

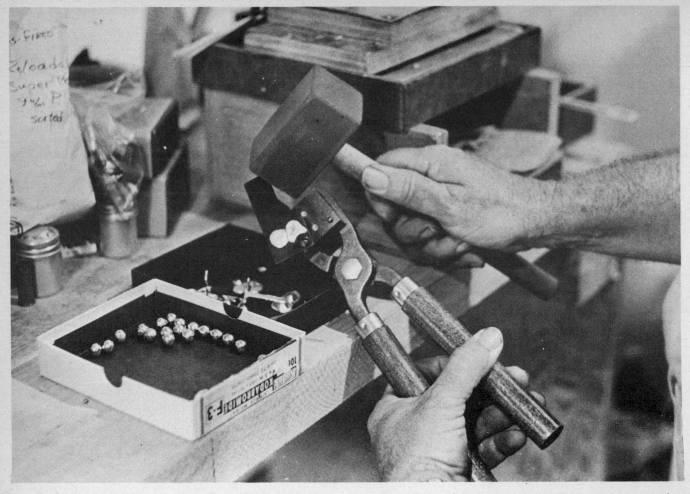

A non-marring mallet is used to knock the sprue cutter over and the sprue is dropped into a separate box for return to pot.

having a tapered outer surface. This moves the lead from pot to mould without contacting the air and reduces oxidation loss to a minimum. Likewise, the rigs are extremely convenient to use.

Here, you have a choice between holding the tapered opening on the sprue-cutter of the mould against the conical delivery nozzle, thereby delivering the metal into the mould at a small head of pressure; or you can hold the mould an inch or less beneath the spout and "air-pour" instead of using the "pressure-pour" technique. Neither method is necessarily best for all purposes and it may take a little experimenting to find which to use for the given mould or design.

The Lyman or Ohaus dipper, with its front hood and tapered snout, permits the pressure-pouring approach in much the same manner. You fill your ladle, hold the mould on the side with your left hand, position the snout in the hole of the sprue-cutter and rock the assembly upright to pour in the metal. It works perceptibly better than air-pouring in several instances.

Form the habit of either mounding up the metal on top of the sprue-cutter slightly — if air-pouring — or leaving the spout in contact for a few seconds, if pressure-pouring. This tends to bypass the formation of air pockets in the upper part of the ball or bullet which might otherwise be caused by shrinkage of the metal as it cools.

Lead, in the soft and pure state that's best for muzzle-loader projectiles, is something less than the caster's dream metal, it must be conceded. In fact, it tends to be a trial to

the patience and a challenge to the perserverance. Even if you crank up the temperature to around the 700-mark or so — unless otherwise stated, all temperatures in this discussion are Fahrenheit — it's often hard to fill the mould smoothly and avoid little wrinkles in the finished casting. This poses a minor problem in the case of round balls, but it's worse when casting hollow-based projectiles such as Minie balls.

The first thing to do is to remove any rust-preventive oils that may have been applied to the mould at the factory or at the close of the previous casting session. Most moulds are made of iron or steel alloys which seem to rust if you look at them or even so much as think about them. Accordingly, an effective rust-preventing coating is mandatory.

Most moulds will not cast smoothly until they have been heated up to a considerable extent. Normally, they'll reach this point after some six or a dozen fillings, depending upon the size of the cavity, the temperature of the molten metal and such factors. The heating process can be hastened by careful use of a propane torch flame on the interior surfaces of the opened-apart mould blocks. Likewise, this helps to burn away any remaining trace of oil or solvent. If preheating the blocks in this manner, take precautions to keep the flame moving so as to heat the blocks evenly, preventing them from warping.

When using one of the electric pots, it may be practical to place the mould on top of the pot, with its blocks over the lead supply, as the pot comes up to temperature and melts the metal. This can be helpful in preheating — if you

214

SHOT				BUCK SHOT		
NUMBER	DIAM. IN INCHES	APPROX. PELLETS IN 1 OZ.		NUMBER	DIAM. IN INCHES	APPROX. PELLETS IN 1 LB.
• DUST	.04	4565				
• 12	.05	2385		4	.24	340
• 11	.06	1380				
• 10	.07	870				
• 9	.08	585		3	.25	300
• 8	.09	410				
• 7½	.095	350				
• 7	.10	290		1	.30	1.75
• 6	.11	225				
• 5	.12	170		0	.32	145
• 4	.13	135				
• 2	.15	90				
• AIR RIFLE	.175	55		00	.33	130
• BB	.18	50				

The chart at left, giving specifications on the various sizes of shot, is from Remington Arms Company, shown at actual size, and applies to their shot production. Specs may vary with the other manufacturers. Below: After casting, it's important to sort out the defective castings such as these. They can be returned to the pot with sprues.

take care that the mould does not fall into the hot metal.

With moulds such as those for Minie balls, a propane torch or similar flame can be applied carefully to the metal of the lower punch which forms the base cavity of the bullet, helping to eliminate wrinkles and gaps in the skirt of the completed casting.

Make it a practice to drop the sprue and the balls or bullets — even if imperfect — into some sort of shallow cardboard box or similar container and, as necessary, pour the scrap back into the pot from the box. Do not drop the bullet from the mould directly back into the molten metal, since this is apt to cause spattered drops of metal to adhere to the exposed inner faces of the blocks. These would prevent the necessary tight closing of the block halves and would cause unsightly fins around the bullet at the juncture of the blocks.

In addition to guarding against corrosion, the iron, brass, aluminum or other material used in making bullet mould blocks must be handled gently to prevent damage. Never use the tip of a screwdriver, ice pick, scratch awl or similar

Since round ball moulds have no bottom punches, as do the Minie designs, they can be made for producing more than one ball at a filling, such as this Ohaus double-cavity mould.

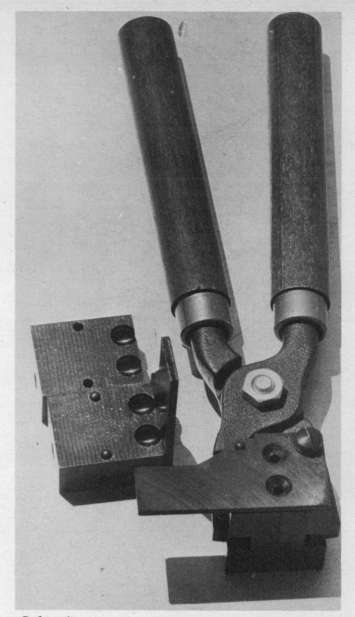

device to jab the bullet free from the blocks as this will quickly ruin the relatively soft metal from which the mould is made. On extended production runs, make it a firm habit to check the holding screws which fasten the blocks to the handles or tongs; do this every one hundred bullets.

Selection of the proper size of ball or diameter of Minie bullet is discussed elsewhere in this book. The following listing is intended to assist the reader in choosing which of the several manufacturer's moulds he may wish to purchase. (Addresses appear in the directory section at the rear of the book.)

Lee Precision Manufacturing offers a catalog of their shooting products, free upon request. Items of special interest to the shooter of muzzleloaders include:

Single cavity bullet moulds, complete with handle and aluminum blocks, diameters of .296, .308, .311, .319, .323, .336, .350, .375, .378, .380, .390, .395, .424, .433, .440, .445, .451, .454, .457, .470, .490 and .495-inch.

Lyman Gun Sight Corporation offers a complete catalog of their shooting products, free upon request. Items of interest to the shooter of muzzleloaders include:

Diameters available in Lyman round ball moulds include the following: .235, .244, .300, .308, .311, .313, .319, .323, .330, .340, .345, .350, .358, .360, .370, .375, .378, .380, .389, .395, .400, .410, .420, .424, .429, .433, .437, .440, .445, .451, .454, .457, .465, .470, .490, .495, .498, .500, .526, .535, .550, .560, .562, .575, .648, .662, .672, .678, .690, .715 and .735-inch.

Diameters available currently in Minie balls, with weights as noted, include: .445 (250 grains); .533 (410); .557 (475); .575 (400); .575 (460); .575 (505); .575 (315); .577 (570); .580 (520); .580 (535) and .685 (730).

Dixie Gun Works, Incorporated, offers a 362-page catalog at $2.00 per copy, devoted to muzzleloading shooting supplies, which include certain proprietary lines of bullet moulds, some of which have metal handles, integral with the blocks and shaped similar to those of tin snips. These do not have a sprue-cutter, requiring that the sprue be trimmed off after cooling. They can be furnished in almost any conventional diameter in increments of .001-inch but the catalog notes that delivery is slow and recommends consideration of other makes of moulds that they stock, such as Lyman.

Herter's, Incorporated, offers a 653-page catalog of their items for shooters and others, the price being $1.00 per copy. Their listing of round ball and Minie moulds is quite similar to that of the Lyman line.

Before discussing the technique of bullet and ball production, let's review the steps covered previously. Pure, soft lead is obtained and, if necessary, cleaned of its non-metallic impurities by stirring, fluxing and skimming. As possible and practical, it is made up in sizeable batches so that a considerable quantity will be of uniform softness and specific gravity, thus assuring consistent performance out of the gun. After mixing and cleaning, it is cast into pigs of convenient size for future use. Such pigs can be marked — using a scratch awl, or by an established code such as Roman numerals stamped with a small cold chisel — as to its content or properties.

Pig lead is melted in a suitable pot or furnace — even a small pot over a wood campfire or fireplace will serve, as countless pioneers could testify — and brought to a temperature of about 700 degrees F. Lacking thermostatic controls for the purpose, this temperature will have been reached when lead poured into the mould will begin producing satisfactory castings.

The molten lead is poured into the top of the mould, through the hole in the sprue-cutter, if the mould is so provided. A small surplus is mounded over the opening, or the nozzle is kept in contact with the cutter plate so as to

produce a slight head of pressure during the few seconds required for the lead to solidify within the mould.

After the metal hardens, the sprue cutter is driven over by means of a few judicious whacks of a mallet made of non-marring material, so as not to damage the mould. A hardwood stick of appropriate size works well, as does a wooden or plastic mallet. For many years, I used an old screwdriver with a plastic handle until an apprentice caster allowed the plastic to droop into a pan of hot lead and the plastic vanished amid some spectacular pyrotechnics. My present pet mallet has a block of polyurethane plastic on a wooden handle; the head material is resilient, non-marring, yet fantastically tough. You can drive finishing nails into wood without leaving a mark on the plastic, yet it won't damage a mould in the course of producing bullets by the thousands.

The trimmed sprue is dropped into a separate catch-box for later return to the pot, along with any sub-standard balls or bullets. A small pair of pliers on the bench is convenient for handling hot castings. I keep an old pair of welder's gloves in the storage compartment of the base I built for my Lyman Mould Master furnace, along with the stirring stick, an old tablespoon for skimming off impurities and a 3/16-inch screwdriver for tightening or changing blocks.

Most bottom-delivery pots, such as the Lyman, SAECO or Herter's, have more room between the base and the spout than you really need. Lyman makes a mould guide that clamps to the upright columns, being adjustable to position the mould precisely under the spout. The trouble is, this gets in the way when you're working with the moulds having a base stem on a wooden handle, such as those for the Minie balls. I fastened a couple of slabs of three-quarter-inch scrap plywood together to slide under the spout as a rest when working with those moulds which have no base punch and handle. Spilled lead stuck to the wood, so I covered the top with a piece of sheet aluminum, to which lead won't adhere. It removes in a jiffy for casting with hollow base mould designs and, after a good many years of extended use, I still consider it the most practical accessory for this purpose.

After the trimming of the sprue — an operation not to be confused with William Shakespeare's play of nearly the same name! — the mould is moved over the catch-box for the finished bullets and the handles are spread apart to separate the two halves of the mould block. Often, the ball or bullet will drop out freely at this point. If it remains in one half or the other, a few careful taps on the side of the tongs, ahead of the pivot pin, should dislodge the bullet to drop into the box.

Since the balls or bullets are quite hot when they come from the mould and, as a result, soft and vulnerable to damage, it pays to drop them onto a fairly yielding surface. I use a shallow cardboard box — the ones for sheet film or photo paper are perfect for this — and, if necessary, I cut a sheet of one-quarter-inch corrugated cardboard to put across the bottom of the box. From time to time, I raise

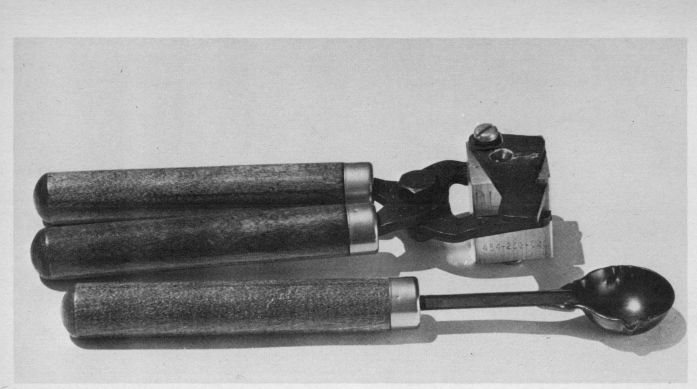

Lee moulds, here with same firm's dipper, feature blocks of aluminum which heat up quickly and resist rust and corrosion.

the near edge of the tray to let the cooler castings roll to the front end, so that the fresh ones won't land on top of earlier production to the damage of both. An old towel, shop rag or piece of scrap carpet can be used as a landing pad for the bullets, if preferred.

As the catch box fills up with balls or bullets, they can be poured — with appropriate care — into some other container for further processing, so as to make room for more new castings in the box. Then, when you feel ready for a break in the routine, you can address yourself to inspection of the cooled batch, tossing all of the imperfect specimens back into the sprue box for re-melting. Unless your standards as to accuracy are pretty carefree, it pays to be rather critical and ruthless in scanning the output, rejecting any that are wrinkled or not completely filled out, since metal and casting time are less expensive than the risk of a shot missed because of imperfect bullets.

A powder scale can be used to good effect as a means of inspection. Adjust the weight poises so that it will balance the beam on center with typical balls or bullets. You may have to weigh a dozen or so to establish the typical average weight. After that, any bullet that doesn't lift the end of the pointer should be rejected for the obvious reason that it has wrinkles, rounded corners or a concealed air pocket. The last defect is impossible to detect by any other method.

Lyman makes a series of slug moulds for all of the popular shotgun gauges. These are closely similar in design to the moulds for Minie balls. The blocks are single cavity, but are made to fit the Lyman double cavity handles. At one time, they offered a set of male and female dies for swaging the rifling grooves onto the sides of slugs from these moulds. However, extensive testing turned up the surprising fact that the rifling marks on the side of the shotgun slugs made scant difference in their accuracy in comparison to slugs fired as they came from the mould, without the rifling marks.

It turns out that the reason a shotgun slug flies nose-foremost is not due to any spin imparted by passage of the rifled slug up the barrel or through the air; rather, it's stabilized by the fact that the center of its weight is up near the nose, with the lighter skirts at the rear of the slug serving much the same function as the vanes on an aerial bomb, the fletching on an arrow or the feathers on a badminton bird.

Since most muzzleloading shotguns have straight bores, unchoked at the muzzle, a Lyman slug mould of the appropriate gauge may well prove a useful accessory to broaden the versatility of the tradition-soaked smoothbore. You can expect to expend some time and effort in tracking down the most accurate powder charge, but that can be a fair percentage of the fun.

As with other muzzleloader projectiles, dead-soft, pure lead is the best material for casting the shotgun slugs and you may find it something of a challenge to produce perfect specimens of these consistently, since they're a bit more stubborn and cantankerous to use than the Minie moulds — and those are tough enough! However, it can

Aligning grooves for Lee blocks can be seen here.

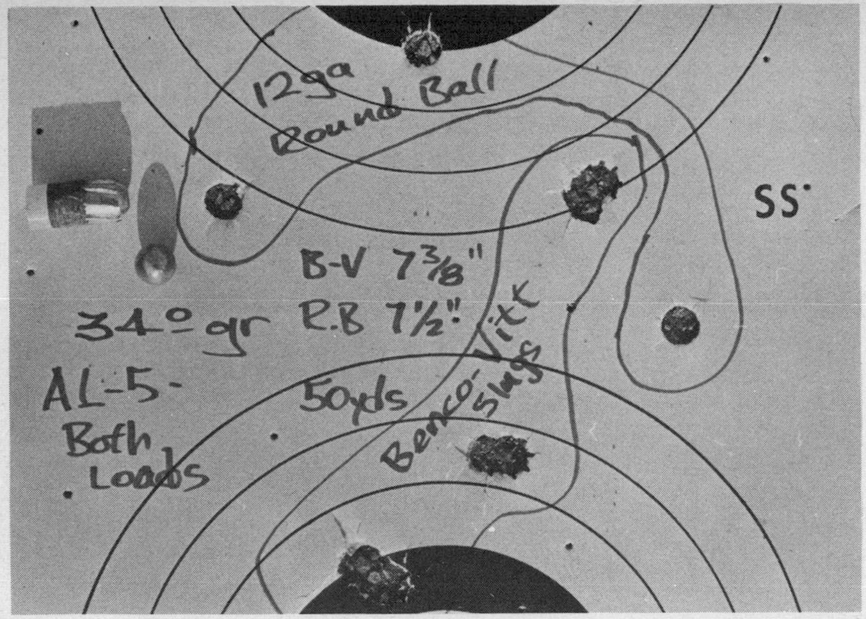
12ga
Round Ball
SS
B-V 7 3/8"
34 gr R.B 7½"
AL-5-
Both
Loads
50yds
Benco-Vitt
Slugs

Round lead balls in 12-gauge Alcan Flite-Max wads, shown at right, are capable of reasonable accuracy in smoothbores, equaling groups from a factory-made slug at 50-yards.

make an interesting project to tackle and the potential rewards are well worth the effort.

As has been noted elsewhere, firing a round lead ball from a smoothbore musket produces some amazingly random groups, measurable in feet rather than inches. In high probability, this is due to the fact that the ball, in whizzing up the bore, rubs harder on one side than the other and, as a result, picks up a considerably amount of rotation in some direction other than in line with the axis of the bore. As it emerges from the muzzle, let's assume for purposes of discussion that it's spinning in a horizontal plane, clockwise, as viewed from above. This means that the left side is traveling faster in relation to the passing air than is the right side. This uneven distribution of air resistance will tend to make the ball curve to the right, in the direction of least resistance. It's the same basic principle that makes it possible for a baseball pitcher to throw a curve ball. And, next shot, it may spin and veer in the opposite direction, vertically, up, down or in any of an infinite number of diagonals. Hence, the morning-glory configuration of the groups delivered by such arms.

However, there is a solution to this problem of obtaining fair accuracy with round balls out of smoothbore barrels, provided they happen to be dimensioned in diameters close to those of the more popular shotgun gauges. The answer lies in putting the round ball down into one of the plastic wad assemblies, as supplied for reloading conventional shotshells. The thin but tough plastic sleeves at the front of such wads, intended to protect the charge of shot as it goes up the barrel, likewise protects a round ball and, at the same time, keeps it from picking up any significant amount of crosswise spinning motion.

As a result, it becomes possible to maintain some reasonable semblance of accuracy with round balls. The potential will vary with the given gun, of course, but keeping hits in an eight-inch circle at fifty yards is not uncommon and it may prove possible to better that by a bit.

CHAPTER 28

*This Muzzleloading Classic
Heals Old Wounds While
Increasing Black Powder Interest!*

N
S
SKIRMISH

A CHILLING MAY rain cascaded from dark storm clouds as five men, attired in the drab gray uniform of the Confederate Army, marched onto the small Maryland clearing, stepping in rhythm to the tune of Dixie. From the opposite side of the clearing, carrying their Civil War style .58 caliber muskets and wearing the blue uniform of the Union Army, five Yanks moved on line across the same clearing.

At a range of twenty-five yards, both teams stopped, brought their muskets to their shoulders, aimed ever so cautiously and fired.

Had the time and place been nearly a hundred years before, this same incident at the Berwyn Rod and Gun Club probably would have become a part of history as the Battle of Berwyn, the Siege of Berwyn or perhaps even Berwyn Run. The truth is, neither of the two rifle teams actually was aiming and firing at the other. Instead, the shooters were firing at some thirty balloons, fifteen each, that had been attached to the twenty-five-yard target frames.

As the smoke of that first volley cleared, it was clear that the Norfolk Gray Backs had proved themselves the deadlier of the two teams, taking five of their targets with their first five shots, while all fifteen balloons stared back at the Berwyn Bluebellies.

Both teams then reloaded as fast as possible and sent another volley on its way, then another, and another, until the cry of "cease fire" echoed across the clearing. The Confederate team had won the first event easily.

Firing at standard match type targets from the fifty-yard line, the Confederate team also managed to walk away with the honors in the second and final event of the day. There were no bitter feelings, however. This had only been a friendly shooting match between two musket teams that had decided to make things a little more colorful by wearing uniforms of an an era when the North and South had met on less friendly terms.

Since that first meeting of North and South in May of 1950, the number of participating shooters has grown from the original two five-man teams to more than 2,000. Also spawned that day was the North/South Skirmish Association, which now is the overseeing organization of the twice-a-year event.

Representing over 150 regiments that had comprised the majority of the original units that had participated in the Civil War, these dedicated black powder shooters flock to rustic Fort Shenandoah, Virginia, twice each year to participate in a few days of marksmanship competition. A walk through the parking lot will show license plates from nearly

Good times and rain seldom go hand in hand, but these members of the Washington Blue Rifles don't seem overly upset about the damp conditions, while they practice the manual of arms, which is part of competition.

Even this wild assortment of clothing would have conformed to regulations during the Civil War. Quite often uniforms of the times matched even worse.

Replicas of the Remington Zouave share the rack with well preserved Civil War Springfield as this unit sits waiting for its turn to fire.

every state in the Union — even those that had not taken part in the first original North/South skirmishes of the mid 1800s.

Even so, shooters without units or regiments get to shoot; everyone shoots, as a team or individually. For shooters without a team with which to participate in the team matches, volunteering is allowed when one of the teams suddenly comes up a man short. It's not unusual to see someone from the West Coast firing with a unit from Georgia, Mississippi or Tennessee. Then there are always the individual competitions, where the lone shooter can display his expertise with one of the charcoal burners.

Safety becomes a prime factor when this many shooters get together. All events are scheduled, thus limiting the number of shooters on the line at any given time. To make things even more safe, all loading is done by the numbers, or at least on the command to load.

A large number of the musket shooters prefer to use homemade paper cartridges instead of going through the bothersome measurement of powder charges from flasks or horns. There are several preferred ways to make these cartridges, but one of the most simple methods is to use a small paper or cardboard tube as the body or casing.

The paper hull can be formed by rolling up heavy stock brown wrapping paper or cutting cardboard tubing of the right diameter to the desired length. The tube should be small enough in diameter to allow it to be almost inserted down the muzzle — but not quite, for obvious reasons.

One end of the tube is sealed off. Cartridges made out of brown wrapping paper may be merely tied off with string and those utilizing cardboard bodies can be sealed by plugging one end with a cardboard insert.

A measured amount of powder then is dropped into the tube, with the Minie ball large enough in diameter to plug the open end of the cartridge. Usually this ball has a tight fit and is inserted to the first or second lubricating ring. The finished cartridges are most likely to be carried in leather cartridge boxes that hang from the shoulder by a wide leather strap or are fastened to the belt.

To load, all the shooter has to do is reach down, grab

Cannoneers move away from cannon as fuse is lit. North/South Skirmishes include competition even for these beastly bored black powder shooters.

Officials of the North/South Skirmish Association watch closely as individual shooters compete. Targets are clay pigeons attached to the target frame.

These two shooters alternate, as one fires the other glasses through scope. Individual shooters without a team can occasionally fill in on short team.

Timer and safety officer monitors the firing line.
Some volunteering is permitted if a man does not
have a team to shoot with or one is short a man.

one of the cartridges, pull the Minie ball from the mouth of the cartridge with his teeth, dump the powder charge down the muzzle, drop in the lead ball, run it home with the rod, slip on a percussion cap and he's ready to fire. It is hardly poetry in motion, but experienced shooters can go through the entire loading procedures in less than twenty seconds.

Jeff Davis, with Generals Grant and Lee would probably turn in their graves, if they could witness what takes place when the gray and blue uniforms start to mingle at Fort Shenandoah for the semi-annual shootouts. It's a good time for all. Troubles are left at home with the roof that needs fixing, screens that need repairing and the doors that need painting. When the carpenter from Indiana, the farmer from Missouri or textile worker from Alabama slips on his regimental colors, it's time for some serious shooting.

At first glance the Virginia camp grounds resemble a Boy Scout jamboree, especially with all the uniforms being proudly displayed. Except for a few well intentioned jeers about the time someone's original unit got lost behind enemy lines or the day that one regiment whipped the daylights out of another, it is difficult to realize that all this fun is the result of what originally had been a war within this country.

Instead of harboring information and giving only name, rank and service number, a visiting shooter seems to take pride in sharing his shooting experiences, boasting of his personal little tricks that might give him an edge over his competition. A few even go so far as to give away secret recipes for patch lubricant that have been handed down by forgotten ancestors.

More often than not, these passed-on homemade lubricants end in disaster with a gooey cartridge box or a fouled bore. Many of these concoctions spew forth odors that are strong enough to clear the sinuses of a dead man or at least bad enough to get you — and your pot of goodies — run out of the basement by your wife.

Although it wasn't around at the battles of Shiloh, Bull Run or even Gettysburg, one of the most widely used lubricants at the North/South Skirmish matches is Crisco vegetable shortening. Also growing in popularity are such ready-made lubricants as Hodgdon's Spit Patch for cap and ball revolvers and Spit Ball for muzzleloading rifles and muskets.

There are undoubtedly mixed feelings at the sight of an authentic Harper's Ferry or an original Smith carbine being put through the rigors of continuous competition. Die-hard collectors tend to weep over such sacred items actually being put to the purpose for which they were designed.

There are now numerous well made replicas on the market that are actually better built than the originals. Utilizing stronger steel as well as better construction, most of these reproductions are capable of withstanding powder charges that would probably result in damage to an original. Before any replica is allowed in actual match competition, however, it first must be approved by the North/South Skirmish Association.

The .58 caliber Remington Zouave reproduction being offered by Navy Arms is an example of a quality replica. The original, with its 33½-inch rifled barrel, was the most accurate rifle of its time. Since accuracy is the name of the game when Rebs and Yanks assemble at Fort Shenandoah, its not unusual to see even entire teams armed with the Navy Arms copy.

Competition is divided so that individual matches are held on Saturday and the team matches on Sunday. Typical individual competition consists of fifty and hundred-yard match targets for musket and carbine shooters and twenty-five and fifty-yard targets for the handgun shooters.

Team competition, with eight men comprising a team, varies from one match to another. It is admissable for a regiment to host as many as four eight-man teams. Most units, however, have only an "A" and "B" team.

To give spectators something to view, some of the targets are made of objects that not only break but disintegrate when contact is made with one of the .58 caliber slugs — or whatever hits it. These targets may consist of the standard clay pigeons or perhaps clay flower pots. Reasoning behind this is simple; a spectator can see, without a doubt in his mind, when a competitor has scored a hit.

One of the most popular strings of fire consists of a board suspended in a frame as the target. A vertical line is drawn down the center of the board, serving as the point of aim. The object is to hit the line in such a manner that the impact of the slug splits the board down the middle.

Other targets consist of the standard silhouette, water-filled beer cans or even styrofoam cups, with variations running from match to match. All events are timed and the team utilizing the shortest amount of time to hit or break all of its targets is the winner.

After a busy day of shooting, a good portion of the evening is spent in cleaning the black powder guns. There are numerous cleaning solvents that do a fine job of turning a powder-fouled bore into the bright and shining cylindrical drilling it had been before the day's shoot. BlakSol and Bucheimer's black powder solvent are two of the commercial solvents that have won wide acceptance, but for many shooters there in no replacement for the old favorite standby — hot, soapy water.

Regional shoots of the North/South Skirmish Association are held from spring through summer, into fall, whenever there are enough shooters to participate. Black powder shooters are a minority when compared to the number of shooters comprising such shooting sports as trap, skeet and benchrest competition. The dates for the Nationals varies from year to year, but is always divided into two matches, the Spring and the Fall Nationals.

Nostalgia probably accounts for the reason why a large number of the North/South Skirmish Association members drive thousands of miles, just to slip on a blue or gray uniform that could probably withstand a little repair work, just to see all of his efforts go up in a puff of FFFg smoke, as the Minie makes its way to the target.

Then again, maybe they're just true Americans wanting to relive our American heritage.

The length of hair and beards of these shooters add to the authenticity of the uniforms worn by these shooters of the 17th Virginia Infantry, Joe Leisch, Jr. (left) has played Lincoln on TV often.

Battery H of the 4th Artillery Memorial Regiment drills with this well-preserved mountain howitzer. Text discusses the procedures for target work with such guns.

CHAPTER 29

A NEW APPROACH TO BLACK POWDER CANNONEERING

For Indirect Fire, A Knowledge Of Basic Math Is A Requirement!

IF YOU'RE A Civil War buff — or if you just like to shoot historic cannon and replicas — there's a lot of fun to be had shooting them as our grandfathers rarely if ever could: in indirect fire. Indirect fire means that you shoot over the horizon at a target not visible from the gun position. It's the way artillery is habitually fired these days, and the only way that full use can be made of the range and accuracy of the guns. If you get a kick out of blasting away at a target several hundred yards away and seeing an occasional good solid hit, you have yet to live! Wait till you can lob a shot over the hill into your favorite meadow from 1500 yards away and do the same thing.

This homemade replica of old style gunner's quadrant is used to establish angle of elevation of gun.

When one is experimenting with such a concept, it is best to go to someone who knows what it is all about. We told Claud S. Hamilton, an old cannoneer from way back, what we intended to do in this chapter and he was kind enough to lend his expertise.

Gunnery is not a complicated business, and particularly not with vintage cannons. We'll need a suitable place to shoot, away from houses, roads and farm animals, an area which can be seen and controlled from an observation post. By controlled, we mean that you can post it to warn away trespassers, physically block roads and paths into it and watch it to insure that you cease firing should your other safety measures prove insufficient.

We'll need to use the plot plan or surveyor's drawing of the property which usually goes with the owner's deed. If the owner of the farm doesn't have a copy handy one usually can be obtained at the county seat. The first thing to do is to study the lay of the land and the plot plan to become familiar with where the boundaries are. While we're doing this we'll pick out by inspection and mark on the plot plan the places where we plan to put the cannon and the target.

We should try to locate the target in a large, safe area about four or five hundred yards on a side. To keep things practical and safe we'll try to hold the range from the gun position to the target to 1500 to 2000 yards or less.

On the plot plan using the gun location as the apex, we draw in red a large, wedge-shaped slice extending out along each side of the chosen impact area and then close it off with an arc beyond the target. Next we mark the selected observation post (OP) on the plot plan. Then, using the given directions of the land boundaries and a protractor we measure the azimuths of the gun-target and OP-target lines. Since we also must know the scale of the firing chart we are making, we determine that by measuring in inches the lengths of several boundaries and then computing the yards to the inch ratio resulting.

The last step at this point in the preliminaries is to take a sheet of thin graph paper (better yet, glazed acetate, if available). Convert the grid on it to the scale of the plot plan so that you can read it in yards, then cut a disk large enough to just cover the safe impact area. This we'll call our target grid; more about how to use it later.

We are going to need a chart table; a card table will do but something a little bit sturdier would be better. For it, we need a wood or composition top to which the plot plan can be taped or pinned, and into which we can stick pins without bending or breaking them. Then, naturally, we'll need some ordinary pins, a protractor, a good ruler and some wooden stakes in two sizes. We need some about six feet long and one foot long. And don't forget the magnetic compass and plumb bob!

With the gear at the selected gun position, we use a short stake to mark the exact location over which the center of the gun trunnions will be placed. We may have to level the ground a little where the wheels will rest; it is important that the trunnions be level when the gun is in position.

Set up the chart table over the gun stake with the marked gun location exactly over the stake. This we'll do using the plumb bob hanging beneath the table. Placing pins in the gun and target locations, and using the magnetic compass, rotate the table carefully until the pins marking the

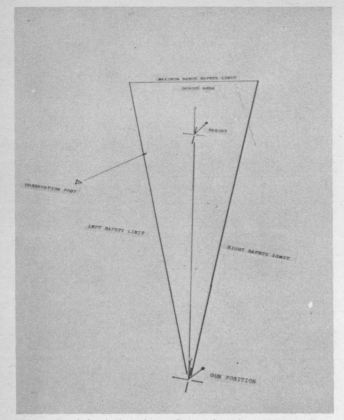

Using a land deed plot plan, a firing chart is constructed by marking gun, target and observation post locations, with the danger area indicated by red or orange lines.

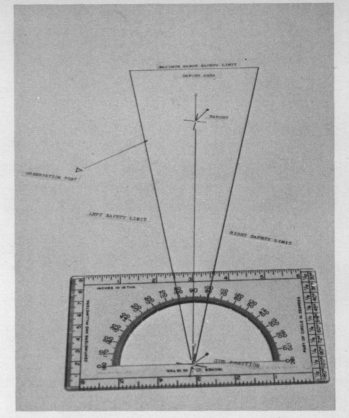

Azimuths of the gun/target and observation post/target lines are measured, using a protractor and the known directions of the boundaries of the danger zones.

gun-target line are on the correct azimuth as measured on the plot plan. Sight along these two pins while your partner takes two stakes and drives them firmly into the ground along the line they form. Use a white stake and a black one; put one in about fifty paces from the gun and the other about half that distance. In this way, we have marked the gun-target line on the ground just as it is on the firing chart.

Repeat this operation, placing pins in the right and left-hand corners of the safe impact area and sighting on them from the gun location pin. These mark the right and left safety limits, so use red stakes that are quickly and easily recognized.

It really doesn't make too much difference what sort of cannon you plan to shoot so long as it is serviceable and small enough to handle easily. Let's assume you have a six-pounder cannon on a field carriage available, and that you are familiar with your gun and its impedimenta. We assume that you probably use cement filled cans for projectiles, and that these are of uniform weight and dimensions so that they fill the bore snugly. We'll also need to be able to measure powder accurately.

Remember that one of the first things we did was to draw on the plot plan a red wedge-shaped area including the safe impact area and extending all the way back to the gun position. That was to emphasize that this whole area must be kept clear and considered a danger zone. With the tools we're using we don't want to fire over the heads of people or over valuable property even after we know a good bit about the cannon that we don't know now.

We need communications between the gun position and someone who will man the OP. A surplus field telephone hookup with field wire will do but a C-B radio is a lot less trouble to put in. Once this is in place and working, we're ready to bring in the gun. It will be placed directly centered over its marker stake and pointed carefully over the black and white target stakes.

Now comes the problem which requires judgment and care. Indirect fire is usually done at elevations of twenty to thirty-five degrees. This makes high velocity ricochets unlikely and permits us to get over whatever intervening mask there may be between gun and target. It also permits us to use a relatively light propelling charge. What charge and elevation should we begin with?

Unfortunately, our grandfathers who used these cannons in anger rarely if ever fired them in this way and no firing tables for them have survived so far as we can determine. We have seen one Table of Fire for a six-pounder gun which indicates that, with six-pound round shot and a 1¼-pound powder charge, the gun would shoot over 1500 yards at five degrees elevation. That's much too high a velocity for what we want. Based upon experience, and without consulting ballistic tables for spherical shot, Hamilton feels that load would carry 4500 to 5000 yards at about thirty-five degrees elevation.

To begin with at least, he recommends using a one-half-pound charge. This won't give half the velocity; we all know powder and projectiles are not quite that simple, but it will keep us in the ball park for safety.

Since range increases up to about thirty-five degrees elevation, let's agree to start at twenty degrees which ought to clear the mask and still hold the range down to within our safe area. It would probably be a good idea to paint the

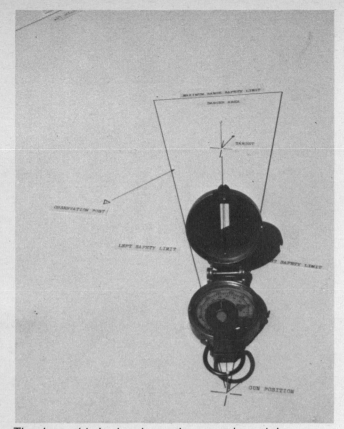

The chart table is placed over the gun stake and the chart is then oriented, using a magnetic compass, with appropriate compensation for possible compass error.

The location of the first shot is plotted and marked with a pin when the observer reports, "Doubtful, 400 right." A target grid converts observer data into scale dimensions.

projectiles white or bright yellow so as to make them easier to see on the ground and in grass.

We had no problem laying, or pointing, the gun for deflection (horizontal direction, azimuth) using the black and white stakes, but how to lay for elevation? Simple. Let's make a gunner's quadrant of the same general sort used when these guns were new. Take a straight piece of wood about two feet long and to this attach a quarter circle of some soft metal or wood. The quarter circle should be at least four inches from the apex to the circular rim; the larger it is the easier it will be to use accurately.

Use the same protractor we've used so far to carefully mark off graduations in degrees about the circular rim. If you make fine cuts with a razor blade against a hard ruler, you can later wash the surface with diluted black paint so the fine cuts will show more clearly. Then mark off your degrees starting with zero at the point away from the wooden stick and ninety degrees next to the stick. Punch a tiny hole and, using fine black thread, hang a weight so that it will hang from the origin of the disk out across the graduated edge. When the stick is placed in the cannon muzzle along the bottom of the bore, the weighted thread will hang down giving you the angle of elevation of the tube. If you wish, you can restrict this exercise to marking off the first forty degrees or so; we won't be using elevations greater than thirty-five degrees.

Check communications to be sure the range is clear, then fire the first shot. Next we'll get a call from the OP sensing the hit, and here's where that little circle of graph paper we made comes into its own. The target grid, as we called it, is centered over the target and the target pin replaced in its

center. Then we rotate it to the azimuth of the observer-target line, in other words so that it is showing a grid in one-hundred-yard increments, right and left, over and short as the man on the OP sees it. Using this device, when the observer tells us what he sees we can immediately plot it on our firing chart.

Let's suppose that, seeing the first shot, the observer comes to life on the C-B radio and says: "Doubtful, four hundred right." This means that the shot fell too far to the right for him to judge whether it was over or short of the target, and that he estimates the distance to the right to be four hundred yards.

Since we have no better data to go on, we place a pin in the target grid four hundred yards to the right of the target and at target range. Now, since the gun usually jumps back out of position with each shot, there will be no problem in placing the chart table once again directly over the gun stake. Since the shot fell to the right as the observer saw it, we want to go left. Sighting along the gun pin and the pin in the place where the shot fell, line up on the black and white target stakes. Then move these stakes and realign them with the gun pin and the target pin; this shifts the gun-target line on the ground to the left by the appropriate angle. When the gun is moved back into position and we're ready to do that now, it will point in the new direction.

As far as range is concerned, looking at the plot we see that the four hundred right reported by the observer really translates to nearly four hundred yards increase in range. Keeping the powder charge constant we'll get this by increasing elevation, but how much?

The old Table of Fire for the six-pounder gun showed a

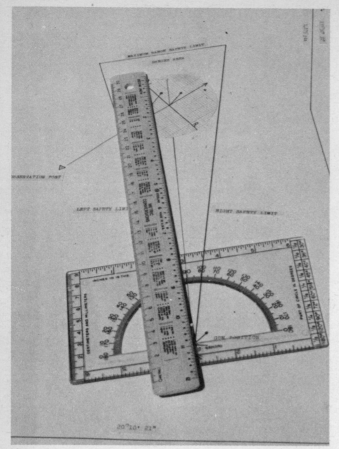

Here, the second shot — reported as "Doubtful, 200 left " — is being marked, using the translucent paper grid.

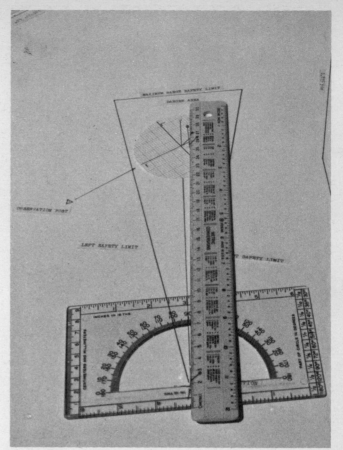

A third shot falls close enough for the observer to report it as "50 over, 50 right " and hit is recorded.

change in elevation of one degree to be good for about 240 yards in range. This isn't very valid, since the charge we're using is different as are the elevations at which we're firing. However, it's the best data we've got to go on at this time, so let's say that with our reduced charge it will take about twice the elevation change to get the same range change. This isn't accurate but it is reasonable. So, to add four hundred yards range we'll add four degrees elevation and command the gunner, "Elevation twenty-four degrees." We're ready for the second shot.

We radio the OP, "On the way," and shortly comes back the reply: "Doubtful, two hundred left." Not bad for a bunch of beginners! We go through the same drill once again. Set up the chart table over the gun stake and, using gun and shot pins, sight on the black and white target stakes. Then realign the stakes, this time to the right, on the gun-target pin line. Bring the gun back into position.

We're beginning to accumulate some useful knowledge about the cannon which we'll improve on as we go along. We thought that we gave the observer four hundred more yards range last time by adding four degrees elevation. From what he says, and the plot, we can see that he actually got nearer to six hundred yards more range for a four-degree increase, or 150 yards per degree. Once again, his "two hundred left" comes to a needed range change of about minus two hundred yards. To keep things in round numbers we announce to the gunner, "elevation twenty-three degrees."

We follow this same procedure, drawing closer and closer to the target until, watching your firing chart plots, you see that a one-hundred-yard range bracket has been split (looking at it from the gun-target line, not the observer-target line).

At this point you may want to fire two groups of three rounds each and see what results you get.

If the observer reports a clear preponderance in one direction — that is, two overs and a short, or three overs — you may wish to make a minor adjustment in your data for the second three. With luck you may just get a target hit! With the gun laying equipment we have, there's not too much point in trying to further refine your firing data.

Having finished this mission, you can use the same method to fire on other targets in the safe area. The data developed with respect to the value of one degree's elevation in range in yards should be recorded for future use, but with certain reservations. Any gun is subject to many internal and external variables, particularly in indirect fire. The weather plays a big part in what you get on the ground. Temperature, humidity, air density and winds aloft all have their effect. So do differences in batches of powder you use and in projectiles, and the way you load and ram. Don't think that you are going to be able to come back tomorrow and set the exact same data on the gun and get an immediate target hit — you won't, but you will be a lot closer than we were when we started out!

Something to keep in mind for this sort of a shoot is that it is not at all necessary that the gun and the target not be intervisible. You can do your shoot exactly as described with the gun crew able to see the results of their shooting (and your gunnery) as long as they don't conspire to point the gun at the target visually every time. Shooting at a visible target has a lot to commend it. Serving a gun without being able to see what's happening soon leads to a bored gun crew and you'll have to scratch for volunteers.

There's something about the roar and smoke of a black powder cannon that does things for the real buff, but when that palls, indirect fire as described in this chapter can do much to retain interest of a group.

If you think that you'd really like to get into this indirect fire bit seriously and find out just what your gun can do, you can't do it with the equipment talked about so far. Depending upon how carefully you made your gunner's quadrant, it's a safe bet you're reading much better elevations than the accuracy with which you can lay your gun for horizontal direction. Old cannons are notorious for the poor quality of their sights and many found today don't have any at all.

If you're really serious, you'll have to plan a program of overall improvement: improve the quality of your ammunition, its fit to the tube and the uniformity of weight round to round; refine your powder-measuring accuracy for loading. But mostly, you must improve your fire control instruments. You may wish to make a new and much larger gunner's quadrant which will make your readings possible to half a degree and even finer. You must do something about sights for your gun which will permit close and consistent laying on the aiming stakes. If you are mechanically inclined, good sights can be made relatively simple.

The easiest idea that comes to mind is simply to mount a good, vertical blade on your muzzle (properly centered with the bore, of course) and a good peep at the breech. With these you lay for direction before elevating the gun to the firing elevation. Level trunnions are critically important! It might even pay for you to rig your plumb line to a frame in front of and above the gun and track the plumb line up and down to assure the trunnions are level.

A variation sight system has the same blade front sight but replaces the peep at the breech with a vertical bar having a number of peep holes cut through which you can lay for direction after the gun is at firing elevation. This is better, but more difficult to make and may be fragile. If it is not absolutely "true" when you install it and kept that way, forget it.

Other variations can be tried, such as mounting a rear sight on a band welded to one of the trunnions, to go with a blade front sight appropriately offset from the muzzle and long enough to take care of a variety of elevations. Once again, this requires accurate initial installation work and tends to be fragile in service.

The elevation data and powder charges discussed here are purely hypothetical and we don't recommend that you go blindly out and try them. They are intended only as a guide.

If you are in doubt as to a charge to use in your gun for this type of shooting, the best course of action is to try a reduced charge such as that described in direct fire on targets you have used previously, gradually increasing the elevation and observing the effect upon range. Once you have safely reached the twenty to thirty-degree elevation range without shooting out of your safety limits, you are ready to try indirect fire safely, and you've probably accumulated some excellent data on your gun to boot.

A SCOPE CAN COPE!

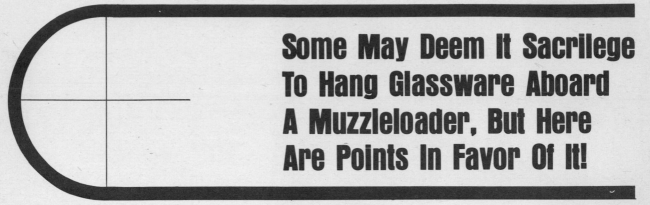

Some May Deem It Sacrilege To Hang Glassware Aboard A Muzzleloader, But Here Are Points In Favor Of It!

CHAPTER 30

Prodigious output of smoke, fumes and high-velocity particles dictate scope mounting well forward, as here.

THERE ARE TWO schools of thought that seem to form in regard to the collecting and use of the artifacts from the past and this most definitely includes the field of muzzle-loading firearms.

There are the purists, the traditionalists, who avow that if it was good enough for their more remote ancestors, it shall be equally good for them, for ever and ever, world without end, amen.

The opposing school of contention may point out that, if this philosophy were to be carried to its natural limits, then all progress should have been suspended by moratorium as of the day that first pithecanthropus erectus picked up a hunk of granite with which to whap a sabertooth atwixt the eyes. If we're to accept the thesis that weapon improvements are a no-no, they contend, then we should draw the line at binding a stick to the rock with lengths of vine so as to make an axe out of it!

The furor waxes thick and furious when it reaches areas such as the use of optical — telescopic — sights in conjunction with black powder antiques and replicas. Those preoccupied with the sacredness of tradition say that Dan'l Boone didn't use a scope on his trusty flintlock so, by jing, they aren't going to use one, either. Their opposing counterparts respond by yelling "heil," right in the furor's face and deck out their coal-burning artillery with modern scopes, callous as to the unesthetic effect of the resulting anachronism. "It's renegade, but it's right," is their rallying cry!

Actually, as it turns out, telescopic sights for firearms are not really all that disgustingly newfangled. They have been materializing upon the shooting scene in some sort of primitive and rudimentary form since some time well prior to the War Between the States. Again, as is the case so often in such matters, the earliest origins of optical sights are cloaked in the foggy mists of misinformation and controversy. It is impossible to assert with positive confidence that, for example, the scope sight was invented on Tuesday morning, the 10th of May, 1757, by one Alois Weilbacher in the picturesque village of Braunfogel, high in the Swiss Alps. It just as well could have been some other time, some other place, some other guy; in fact, it is superlatively probable!

This much can be hypothecated with reasonable confidence and plausibility: From all of the data which has been handed down to the present day on the personality traits of Dan'l Boone, Davy Crockett, Jim Bridger, et al., it seems likely to at least sixteen decimal places that, had scope sights been available in their day, they would have had them mounted atop their rifles and would have used them with immense satisfaction.

Which may — or, again, may not — settle the matter of whether or not such sights are moral and ethical. What remains to be established is the question, are they or are they not practical?

And, as the old lady said when she kissed the cow, that's something else again. The crux of the problem stems from the vast, thick clouds of smoke, fumes and miscellaneous murk which go a-boiling about the immediate adjacency when a shot is set off in most designs of flintlock or percussion firearms. What happens when these cubic yards of

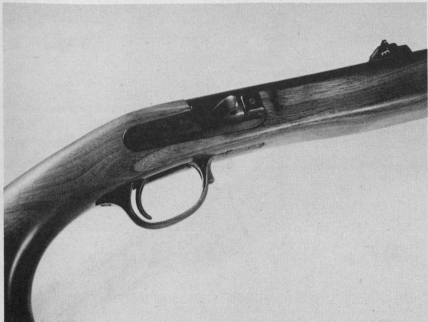

Rear-mounted scope on the rifle above will entail serious problems with deposits of powder residues on its lens. The Esopus Pacer .45 rifle at left has an enclosed cap, nipple and straight-line hammer, making it well adapted for addition of scope sight.

crud and corruption condense across the exquisitely polished surfaces of a scope lens?

That's quite correct: The scope becomes more or less opaque in short order and a scope with opaque lenses is just about as useful and practical as the addition of the sunshine vitamin to rat poison.

In fact, the design of the breechwork may be such that small hot particles of powder residue and/or priming compound are impacted against the glass surface with sufficient force to leave pockmarks in it which defy your most tender solicitude in cleaning up the lens for another try. It is quite possible that you have had an unwary hand in the wrong place at such a time, in which case, you're thoroughly familiar with this particular problem.

However, scope sights do offer some notable advantages to the shooter, especially to those shooters whose eyes are not getting a bit younger with the passage of the decades. Trying to achieve a simultaneous focus upon rear sight, front blade and target can be a real challenge under ideal circumstances. But if you're reaching that stage of life where your eyes are fine but your arms are just too short, the rear sight tends to become nothing but a hazy blur, offering no more than token assistance in aiming.

Here, a scope can be a friend in need. The actual magnification of the target image is of no more than secondary importance. What counts is the fact that the crosshairs and the point at which you're aiming are all incorporated into the same plane of focus and you're working with just one sharp picture. Even if your eyes have wandered off into some non-standard focal length of their own choosing, the objective lens of the scope usually can be adjusted to compensate for the aberration. It's almost as handy as having your auto's windshield ground to your optical prescription, though it may croggle your friends if they grab up your rifle for a hasty shot.

There are certain black powder rifle designs that are much better suited to the installation of scopes than are most of the rest. These are the ones in which the fuss and commotion of ignition is not in close proximity to the logical mounting place for the scope, i.e., atop the barrel and near the breech end of it. Typical examples of such designs would include the Hopkins & Allen rifles, with their hammer located underneath the barrel and driven by a trigger guard which doubles as a mainspring. Then, there's the Esopus Pacer .45 rifle, with its hammer and cap nipple located in a recess in the receiver on the side of the action

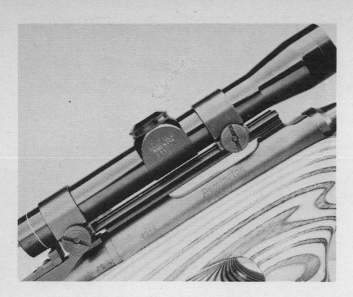

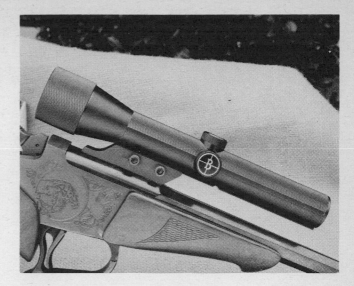

Here are three modern scope sights that are well suited for mounting some distance forward on the barrel. Above left, the M8-2X by Leupold-Stevens; top right, the Bushnell Phantom in 1.3X – also available in 2.6X – and, at right, the 1.5X Puma scope by Thompson/Center.

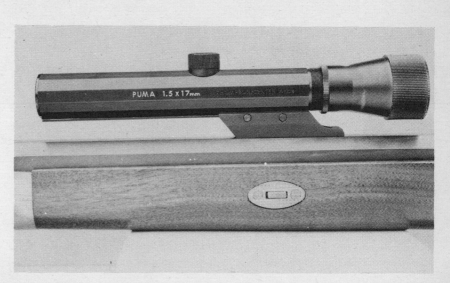

above the trigger and well out of the way of a scope. The break-action Harrington & Richardson Huntsman rifles, with their cap nipples tucked away in the area that would be the chamber of a breechloader, are adaptable for scoping in much the same way.

Those who essayed — with varying degrees of success and satisfaction to mount a scope on the more common, top-ignition rifle designs usually took the hopeful step toward a solution to their lens-fogging problems by locating the scope well forward on the barrel, several inches away from the nipple or flash-pan. This was more or less helpful, depending upon the smoke-spewing traits of the given rifle. However, it presented another problem in that most scopes are designed to provide an eye relief of not much over three inches between the aiming eye and the rear or objective lens of the scope.

If you back off farther than that distance, the image, as seen through the scope, shrinks down into a tiny area in the center of the glass, hardly more than a half-inch across and it becomes a time-consuming challenge to find the target by squinting through the optics.

There have been accessory eyepieces, by means of which the eye relief of a conventional scope could be extended to permit their use when mounted well forward along the barrel. Such devices have not proved overly popular with the buying public and, as a result, have not remained on the market in general supply for very long.

One reason that most shooters are disinclined to attempt modification of standard scopes for purposes of increasing the eye relief is that there are several scopes that are designed expressly to provide a longer eye relief. These have been appearing on the market in increasing variety in the last ten years or so.

Many such scopes were developed initially for use on handguns, with eye relief on the order of eighteen or twenty inches. One of the earliest to appear was a small unit made in Germany, known as the Nickel scope. Small and light in weight, it had no provision for internal adjustments as to elevation or windage, relying upon adjustments in the mount for these. The field of view was quite narrow and there was but little magnification of the image, but the crosshairs of the reticle were seen by the aiming eye as being in the same plane of focus as the target and this was acclaimed as quite helpful by many shooters.

One aspect of scoping handguns should be noted, however, and that's the way they seem to accentuate your

The late Al Goerg was a tireless pioneer and advocate of scope sights for muzzleloaders and handguns, here with a predatory seal.

Hunting the steep slopes of Waimea Canyon, on Kauai Island, Goerg regretted the lack of carrying strap on H&A's Heritage Model rifle.

amount of wavering and wobbling across the target when fired from unsupported or offhand positions. Actually, you don't waver much more with a scope than without one, but the oscillations are a lot more apparent than when aiming with iron — open — sights.

I first encountered examples of the Nickel scope around 1948 and cannot say how long they had been around at that time. By the middle and latter '50s, various American scope makers were adding models with extended eye relief to their lines. Redfield had their "FrontIER" line — the last three letters stood for "Intermediate Eye Relief" — Leupold had their fine little M8-2X unit and Bushnell began importing their Phantom pistol scopes in 1958.

These designs were intended for use at about an arm's length distance from the eye and ingenious shooters began mounting them on various problem rifles, as well as upon the handguns for which they had nominally been designed. Such impromptu grafting projects included the old, lever-action Model 94 Winchester carbine — heretofore impractical for scoping by reason of its top-ejection of spent cases — and any number of muzzleloading rifles, plus a few front-feeder handgun designs.

One of the most intrepid, indefatigable and innovative workers in the field of scoping guns that had never been fitted with such sighting systems before was the late Al Goerg — lost in a plane crash while hunting Alaska in the fall of 1965. During that era, Goerg scoped air rifles, innumerable types of handguns, muzzleloading rifles and stopped barely short of slingshots; he might have gotten around to those, had fate been more kindly.

By conducting the initial installations — often jury-rigged with vast ingenuity — and then working the bugs out of the setup, going on to prove the practicality of the

Goerg had left the hooded iron front sight in place on the H&A and its scope was mounted to permit use of open sights if emergency were to rise.

With grouping capability on the order of six minutes of angle, Goerg felt a bit undergunned for the vast reaches of Waimea Canyon, but he vindicated his choice, as usual!

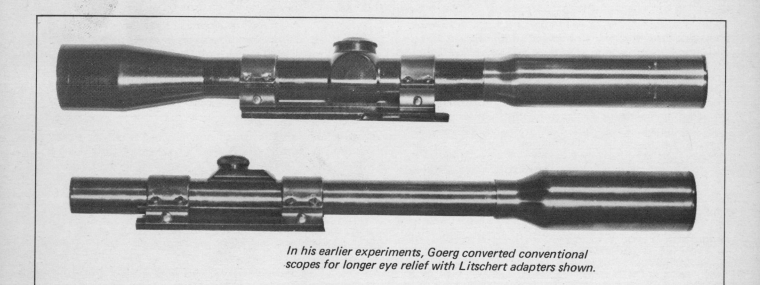

In his earlier experiments, Goerg converted conventional scopes for longer eye relief with Litschert adapters shown.

Not a true scope sight, since this particular one lacks lenses, tubular sight is authentic example of equipment used by sharpshooters on both sides in the Civil War. A few had lenses.

Limited reach of black powder rifle made it necessary to approach game by patient stalking and climbing of steep slopes.

combination via successful hunting in the field, followed by enthusiastic accounts of the entire procedure in the firearms press, Goerg did a great deal toward popularizing the broader application of scopes in hunting and target shooting. The impact of his work upon present-day attitudes and practices can hardly be over-estimated.

One such safari was typical of the many conducted by Goerg. He had mounted a J2.5 Weaver scope on a Heritage Model Hopkins & Allen — the modern replica as sold by Numrich — using a pair of Weaver number 39 bases and the same firm's top scope mount. Due to the underhammer design of the H&A, he had been able to locate the scope well to the rear of the barrel, so as to afford comfortable and conventional eye relief.

Preliminary sighting-in and target tests with the rifle indicated that its patched .45 round ball was capable of delivering groups on the order of six inches at one hundred yards, when powered by 70 grains of FFFg powder. Chang-

ing to FFg granulation opened up the groups to around twenty inches at the same distance and, oddly enough, shifting back to FFFFg powder focused things right back to the six-inch diameter again.

Ordinarily FFFFg would not be considered for use as the primary powder charge for a muzzleloading rifle, being intended chiefly for the priming charge in flintlocks and, perhaps, for the smallest handguns. However, Goerg had not contented himself with sallying forth to strafe some rockchucks in his native Pacific Northwest with the new lash-up. Instead, he had flown to Hawaii and was intent upon bagging a goat on a private hunting preserve in Waimea Canyon, in the high country of Kauai Island.

Arriving with a supply of powder that was sparse to the verge of non-existence, Goerg attempted to replenish his flask, only to find that availability of black powder in that corner of the world was close unto nil. Frantic scouring

From about fifty yards, the Heritage Model fired its .45 ball with more than ample force for a one-shot kill.

turned up the one lone can of FFFFg and, after determining that the Hopkins & Allen could perform capably with the stuff, the remaining quantity was husbanded carefully for employment in the actual hunt.

Goerg noted, in writing up the ensuing adventures, that the open expanses of terrain suggested that he would have been better advised to bring one of the flattest-shooting modern magnum rifles in place of his faintly diffident black powder replica. His H&A had a cone of fire spanning some six minutes of angle when, it appeared, one-twelfth of that

dispersion would have held more optimistic hopes of success. His hunting companions, residents of the area, were armed with modern rifles in the .270 Winchester class and tended to look in askance at Goerg's unlikely choice.

The lay of the land was vertical, or nearly so, to a predominant extent, requiring long interludes of hand-and-foot climbing. This prompted the reflection that the absence of a sling or carrying strap consituted something of a major handicap, equally as much a problem as the comparative limitations of the rifle as to range and grouping ability.

However, while midway up a precipitous slope, Goerg paused and, after a bit, one goat showed a cautious exposure of head. While debating the odds in favor of landing a hit on the tiny area presented, a second goat appeared, almost completely exposed to view and at a distance the hunter estimated at fifty yards.

Holding the top of the post reticle well up on the goat's shoulder, Goerg squeezed off his one and only round — since reloading procedures would have been even slower than usual on his precarious perch — and, as the blue smoke billowed and eddied about him, he knew he had scored by the sound of the goat, rolling bonelessly down the rocky canyon wall.

The .45 ball had struck precisely at the point of aim, on the shoulder and had penetrated completely through the goat, exiting on the far side for a clean and instantaneous kill. All that remained was to dress down the carcass and pack the hindquarters and backstraps back to camp in a plastic sack which had been carried in Goerg's pack against just such a moment of need.

Upon his return, after displaying the proof of his success Goerg felt gratified and somewhat vindicated to observe that the rest of the hunting party had come to regard his primitive artillery with respect that was considerably different from their good-natured chaffing of the same morning. It was, he felt, one more small victory in his one-man campaign to win recognition and appreciation for the rifles of an earlier and simpler day — and for the concept of employing telescopic sights in conjunction with them.

One of the simplest and most satisfactory avenues for assembling a scoped muzzleloader takes the form of the Thompson/Center Hawken replicas. Available in a choice of .45 or .50 barrels, with option of percussion or flintlock ignition, it is an easy operation to replace the open, adjustable rear sights furnished on these rifles with one of the Thompson/Center Puma scopes, offered by the firm for use on their single-shot breechloader pistols which feature interchangeable barrels in a wide assortment of calibers.

Installation is but a matter of tapping out a roll pin and removing the factory rear sight after loosening a couple of screws that fasten it to the barrel. The mount for the Puma scope screws into place on the barrel, using the same holes as the open iron rear sight, putting the rear surface of the lens a good five and one-half inches away from the nipple or priming pan.

Magnification of the Puma's optical system is 1.3X and the eye relief is just right to afford a comfortable sighting picture when mounted on the Hawken. All that remains is to convince yourself that the practical aspect of the installation outweighs any disturbing effect it may have upon your innate sense of the fitness of things and your own visualization of the proper image of the muzzleloader shooter and huntsman.

Once your own misgivings are reconciled, it should not prove unduly difficult to still the jeers of your contemporaries by the same method Goerg used with repeated success, namely by bringing home the bacon and flashing it in their faces.

239

CHAPTER 31

BIRTH OF A MUZZLELOADER

Or How Thompson/Center's Black Powder Line Originates And Gets Made

The somewhat stylized Hawken was Thompson/Center's first venture into the field of muzzleloading firearms.

A later design, which has found a ready market with the black powder buff, is T/C's Patriot pistol.

BACK IN 1962, Warren Center, then head of research for a gun company, and Ken Thompson got together and came up with a concept in handgunnery called the Contender.

They've done fine with that gun with its interchangeable barrel capability, but black powder guns have come to overshadow the firearm that started their business.

"I made a drop block rifle and a black powder rifle and took them to a National Sporting Goods show. At the same time, Bill Ruger showed up with his single-shot rifle and Ken Thompson and I felt that two single-shot rifles might be more than the market would bear. We decided to produce the black powder rifle, the Hawken."

Thompson Center's Hawken, Seneca and Renegade rifles all are built on the same basic concept. The company uses quality investment castings to eliminate a large chunk of the traditional machining and finishing which drives the costs of producing a quality rifle to the limit of many shooters' ability to pay.

Of the black powder rifle's design, Center says simply, "We made it for the hunter. I can't picture myself walking around the woods with a forty-two-inch barreled rifle. There's nothing original in the whole gun except the use of coil springs. Flat springs wouldn't last ten minutes." The rifles are among the few today which feature double set triggers as standard equipment.

The Hawken, in .50 caliber, was introduced in December 1970, and in November 1972 the firm brought out its black powder, .45 target pistol, the Patriot. Less than a year later, in August 1973, the Seneca, a 6½-pound New England-styled rifle appeared on the scene, then in November 1974, the .54 Renegade made its debut.

Of the black powder rifles, Center's favorite is the Seneca. It is light; only 6½ pounds. But with the .45 barrel and a 230-grain, .45 caliber Maxi-Ball, the rifle is more than adequate for deer.

"The design of the Maxi-Ball," Center shakes his head, but smiles, "was a terrible thing." The Maxi-Ball is a

Under the watchful eye of an experienced machinist, two barrels for Renegade rifles are button rifled in the Thompson/Center plant, where all manufacturing is done.

In keeping with the great amount of handwork that is done on each Thompson/Center muzzleloader, each breech plug is hand fitted to individual rifle by craftsman.

uniquely shaped flat based, conical bullet adapted for use in .35, .45, .50 and .54 caliber muzzleloading rifles.

"I'd heard a lot about the Minie ball, but I could not get them to group. We tried twenty-one different moulds and ended up, in exasperation, with one that used driving bands like an artillery shell.

"Then we began looking for the right lubricant. We used everything we could lay our hands on from beeswax to tallow and they were too stiff. Each time we went out to test one of the lubes, accuracy was unacceptable.

"Then somebody suggested trying Hodgdon's Spit Patch. I would never have suspected that would do it, but we tried it anyhow. It did the trick. The Maxi-Ball design was shooting into a tight group."

Determining the twists for the rifle barrels was another matter. Traditionally muzzleloading rifles have been built with twists suited for round balls, in the neighborhood of one turn in sixty inches. That's slow and in comparison the twist of pitch of the T/C black powder bores, 1:48 is fast indeed.

"I didn't know anything about twists in black powder barrels," Center admits. "We tried twenty-two different pitches; 60, 50, 48, you name it, and couldn't see much difference, so we picked the one which was slightly better

with the Maxi-Ball. Most of the people who buy our rifles do shoot Maxi-Balls."

Accuracy of the Maxi-Ball has been well established from coast to coast. Center tells of a shooter in California who has been cleaning up black powder shoots with a .45 caliber Hawken and Maxi-Balls. And in New Hampshire, the only argument in the turkey shoot circuit is whether the guy with the .50 caliber Hawken is going to beat the guy shooting a .45 caliber Hawken. And it's quite a contest because both are using Maxi-Balls. Round ball accuracy in the 1:48 barrels is also superb.

The Hawken is offered in both .45 and .50 calibers in either flintlock or caplock versions. The Seneca, available only in caplock, comes in either .35 or .45 caliber. With these two rifles accounting for a large segment of the black powder rifle market, why did Thompson/Center introduce the Renegade?

Center says bluntly, "There was a hell of a demand for a bigger caliber black powder rifle. We wanted to make a rifle that would sell for less money, meet the hunters' demands for delivered energy, and still maintain our standards of quality."

The eight-pound Renegade rifle with a twenty-six-inch barrel uses a .54 caliber 400-grain Maxi-Ball that, at the muzzle, generates more than 2000 foot-pounds of energy, more than 400 foot-pounds greater than the venerable .45/70 cartridge. By the firm's own admission, the Renegade isn't fancy. There's no brass furniture. But the essentials — a barrel held to .002-inch tolerance, adjustable double set triggers and the coil spring lock — all spell accuracy.

To build accurate rifles at a reasonable price, the company has to be able to produce precision parts inexpensively, a natural for Ken Thompson's tool and die company.

The process of investment casting begins with a metal mould that has been machined out in the shape of a particular part, say a frame for the Contender, for example. Under pressure, hot wax is injected into the mould and, when the wax has cooled, the mould is opened, revealing a wax copy of the frame.

With more hot wax, these duplicates are soldered to a waxen core and the whole works is dipped into a ceramic slurry which drys and hardens to a shell around the wax casting. After several dippings, the shell is strong enough to withstand the heat and pressure of molten metal.

Then the ceramic shell is heated and the wax inside melts, and runs into a recovery tank to be used again. This leaves a void to be filled by molten steel in the foundry.

In the room with the metal furnaces, the ceramic moulds are heated to incandescence and filled with liquid steel. After the steel cools, the ceramic mould is broken revealing steel frames spiraling around a center core.

It's rough and still needs much machining and finishing, but the investment casting process replaces most of the gross machining steps that would convert a bar of steel stock into a frame. The process replaces most of the waste which accompanies those machining steps. In addition, it takes less time and when you add that to the savings in materials, it totals less cost.

In its rough state, the frame passes through a series of milling, grinding and machining operations.

Ceramic moulds, filled with molten metal, are cooling before being broken open to expose rough trigger guard.

Customer service manager Tim Pancurak examines the lock plates for Seneca rifle which have been investment cast.

Each rifle stock is sanded by hand, using a compressed air power sander. This Renegade muzzleloader stock will be finished in a special facility developed strictly for the purpose by Thompson/Center research staffers.

While the metal parts are moving from the wax room through the foundry to machining and finishing, on the other side of the plant, walnut boards from Missouri, Kansas and other Midwestern states are being cut into rough stock blanks.

Using a Mastercarver, a milling machine for wood which shapes twenty-four rifle stocks to the contours of a metal master at one time, the blanks are readied for inletting. Templates guide cutters who inlet the stocks. After an initial sanding, the unfinished stocks and the metal parts for a gun come together for the first time.

After furnishings are fitted to each stock, the metal parts and the stock are given the same numbers and the stock is sent to a separate plant to be finished. Because finishing the stocks requires strict temperature and humidity control, T/C helped one of its former employees establish a company to handle finishing of all T/C stocks.

As the stocks are finished and the metal parts receive final polishing and blueing, barrels for the black powder rifles are being bored, rifled and contoured in the Rochester plant. Made from 4140 steel, the barrels arrive at the plant as round bar stock.

This wasn't always so. In the beginning T/C bought their barrels from Douglas, but as the demand for Hawkens increased, it became less and less feasible to buy already rifled blanks which had merely been bored, but the demand for T/C rifles finally dictated that the barrels had to be made in the plant.

Skilled craftsmen fit the deeply blued steel, highly polished brass and softly finished walnut together into the final product.

What the future holds for Thompson/Center is clear up to a point. Shooters are expressing interest in a target model black powder rifle complete with false muzzle, a precision bullet mould and other paraphernalia which accompanies the guns which shooters of the Ned Roberts ilk used so well a century ago.

"We've talked about it several times," Warren Center says, "but they've just got to be better made than our production rifles to warrant being called target rifles. That means we would have to set up a special division to insure the kind of quality and production tolerances that could mean noticeably improved performance over our current levels. Possibly in the future we'll give it a try."

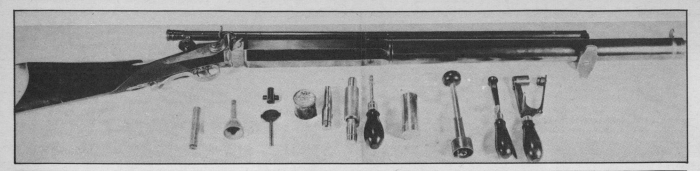

CHAPTER 32

SLUG GUNS ARE ACCURATE

"To Make A Perfect Score, You Must Deliver A Perfect Bullet From A Perfect Barrel With A Perfect Charge And A Perfect Hold!"

As evidenced by this group of national winners from an earlier era — 1954 — slug gun shooters come from all walks of life, are all ages, with accuracy in common.

The supreme moment for the slug gun shooter is a score such as this. Fired in 1953 by Bill Furst with iron sights at 100 yards, the group measures 1-9/16 inches.

THE "GOOD OLD DAYS," has been a favorite subject of every generation; escape backwards to the time when: "...the pace was slower and we were faster."

Perhaps we all indulge in this form of escapism at times; but we still want the wonder drugs available, like the plumbing inside and some of us even enjoy the boob-tube. A day's leisurely shooting with the muzzleloading slug-gun is real escapism, though. It's heady stuff to sit at your bench and fire ten shots into one ragged hole, a not unusual procedure for a slug-gun. These are specialized, big bore — .42 to .70 caliber — target rifles, capable of magnificent accuracy; probably only surpassed by our modern, center fire, .22 caliber benchrest rifles.

Their great weight (20 to 70 pounds), numerous accessories, detailed cleaning and loading procedures, delicate scope sights and the hours of work required to produce a few perfect bullets make slug-gun shooting a highly specialized technique.

Amplified as such shooting may seem, slug-guns saw duty during the Civil War. The best marksmen on both sides welcomed this scope sighted rifle for sharp-shooter duty and generals, even at ranges of over one mile, were included among its victims. The cross paper patch slug-gun, with its two-piece swaged bullet is a purely American development.

Soon after the introduction of the percussion ignition system, circa 1815, a search for something better than round ball accuracy and range began. By 1830 the superiority of the oblong bullets was firmly established. This accuracy quest seems to have been more intent in America, and by 1835 we were using the acorn, picket and sugar-loaf bullets. All were cast, then swaged and all used a round cloth patch. Due to their short bearing surfaces, they were difficult to load uniformly, making it rare to hold con-

sistent groups. However, they did give better all around performance than the round ball.

In 1848 Captain C. E. Minnie of France combined several oblong bullet developments into a stable, hollow-base cylindro-ogival military bullet which had instant acceptance; it later became immortalized as the "minny-ball," used by both sides in our Civil War.

An Englishman named Whitworth, in 1855, perfected a hexagonal bullet which fitted into a matching bore to give fine accuracy out to 1,000 yards and beyond. It once made a ten shot, 8¼-inch center-to-center group at five hundred yards, yet the Whitworth system failed of popular acceptance because the bullets were expensive, the bore and chamber wore rapidly and fouled excessively making the unit unfit for either military or civilian service. Then, too, unfortunately for Mr. Whitworth, breechloaders were rounding the corner.

The records are not clear and exact on the date and point of origin of the slug-gun, although 1840 is considered as the era and either New England or New York State as the place. Walter Grote of Canton, Ohio, gives the nod to Edwin Wesson of Massachusetts as the creator. He was the elder brother of D. B. Wesson, co-founder of Smith & Wesson.

Walt and Ellyn Grote have been enthusiastic slug-gun collectors and shooters for over thirty years. Theirs is probably the finest private collection of these gilt-edge match guns in the U.S. In addition to the gun collection, they have many original technical records and shop notes of famous gunsmiths, including Norman Brockway. Walt has won the big championships and set a number of national records, which still stand, with these bench guns.

William Billinghurst, Rochester, New York, was known

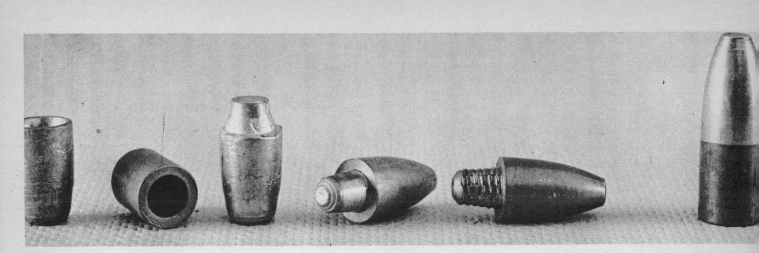

To build a two-piece bullet of the type favored by slug-gun champs, first cast the soft lead base; swage the base; cast the hard point; swage the point; serrate stem; assemble finished bullet that's cavity free.

world wide as a fine gunsmith. He advertised in 1835 that he made rifles: "— on the most improved principles with which few are acquainted." He, too, produced a slug-gun circa 1840.

Nelson Lewis of Troy, New York, probably made more slug-guns than any other man. He bought cast steel barrels from Remington; Bill Hart made his moulds and swages and John Wolfe did his engraving. Lewis was particular about fitting the bullet to the bore of the gun and field testing it before delivery to the buyer. Each of his guns came with complete bullet making and loading instructions, a standard practice among slug-gun makers even today. Norman Brockway died in July, 1936 at age 95. Since 1867, he had

been not only one of the world's master rifle makers but also an expert shot.

Horace Warner of Hartford, Connecticut, and H. V. Perry of Jamestown, New York, were dominant figures in this specialized rifle field from the mid-1840s to the early 1890s, not only as master craftsmen but also as bitter competitors in target matches. Warner liked to use the double end rest while Perry rested on the muzzle, holding the gun butt against his shoulder, the accepted form today.

Most of the matches in those years were fired at ranges measured in rods and forty rods or 220 yards was the favorite. One time Warner built a .69 caliber, seventy-pound rifle

Precission is the key word to successful slug-gun shooting. Mechanical bullet starter, two part bullet, paper patches, loading ring, false muzzle and special barrel muzzle are all a part of the equipment that the slug-gunner utilizes.

for himself. This gun used 275 grains of Fg black powder to push 1750 grain (four ounces) bullet. He kept this gun under wraps only bringing it out for special matches such as the one he fired against Perry at Warren, Ohio, in 1881. It was to be a string measure, fifty-shot match of forty rods. After forty-five shots, Warner's string was only 26½ inches, Perry was so far behind, he gave up. In a string measure event, the distance from the center of the bullseye to the center point of each shot is measured and added, the lowest total wins. Warner averaged less than six-tenths of an inch off center per shot.

Walter Grote bought this gun and won many matches with it; however, managing a seventy-pound bench rifle on a hot day at an exposed firing point is work, so he sold it.

George Ferris, D. H. Hilliard, Jacob Harter, George Gingerich, Horace Fox, and Meredith Wolfe were some of the master gunsmiths featuring this American development.

Today the art continues in the capable hands of modern masters: Lloyd Resor, Union City, Indiana; Edward Ellis, Detroit, Michigan; Robert Morris, Hagerstown, Indiana, and Harold Fuller of Cooper Landing, Alaska. If you get a new slug-gun or an old one that won't shoot tight groups, Milo Taylor of Long Beach, California, can make new moulds and swages for it.

Harry Pope, America's greatest barrel maker and champion target shooter of the pre-WW II period, was a graduate of the Massachusetts Institute of Technology, co-founder of the Pope-Hartford Automobile Company, and studied manufacturing methods for a year in Europe, yet rifle barrels and their shooting were his true love and for all his sixty active years he was dominant in this field. He said: "To make a perfect score, you must deliver a perfect bullet from a perfect barrel with a perfect charge and a perfect hold."

The slug-gun comes closer to letting you do this than any other gun and its two-piece bullet is the most important of these components in obtaining this superior accuracy. The bullet can be perfect. It is loaded in the best manner yet devised, for as it sits there, gently pressed against the powder charge, it has been through the barrel once, thus "taking" the rifle without stripping or deforming in any way.

The flat-bottomed base of these two-piece bullets is made of pure lead; the point is an alloy of lead and tin, ranging from soft at 20:1 to hard at 8:1, depending upon your shooting tests. The base has straight or slightly tapered sides and is a little shorter than the point so that the centers of form and gravity are the same or at least close.

Any bullet, when in the barrel, is tightly gripped by the lands and compelled to rotate around its center of form. Once out of the barrel it will rotate around its center of gravity and if these two centers are not the same, the bullet may take a spiral flight path.

In these two-piece bullets, both parts must be well swaged to give correct shape and eliminate internal cavities. Then both parts are assembled and firmly swaged together so there is no chance of shifting or separating in flight, as either fault would cause wobble or yaw. The print on the target will indicate such trouble.

The majority of shooters use a bullet the base of which bears lightly on the lands without a patch. It bears so lightly it can be blown through the bore with one puff of air but it won't fall through by itself. It should be tapered so that the bearing surface stops just short of the joining line; such a bullet holds perfect alignment in the barrel when loading and will give one-hole groups.

The general form and proportions of the bullet were determined a long time ago but the exact dimensions must be determined by experimentation to find out what your gun "likes." High density for wind bucking is not extremely critical today, because most of the competition is at 100 and 200 yards; if tight groups at 300 and 600 yards are required, the sectional density can be regulated by varying the base length.

Care always is taken to fire a match with bullets of the same weight. These two-piece bullets are tiresome things to make, as fifty good ones takes me two days. The national championship record holder, Ed Ellis fired a blazing 250-22X in 1957. After the match he gave me one of his bullets.

We have been told that Ellis and his shooting partners Ed Ballots — senior and junior — have switched to one-piece bullets which they can knock out, at the rate of twenty-five or thirty an hour, however the 1957 record remains un-equaled.

A final comment on the bullet; Water is not compressible but lead is. Considerable pressure is generated in the swaging process and sometimes these bullets will "grow" in storage. If the bullets to be used in a match are over one week old, some shooters drop them in the final swage and hit them one light tap before the match.

It has been proven repeatedly, that a bullet produced from cold lead in a precision swage is a more nearly perfect bullet than can be made in any other way but when stored, changes may occur, so be sure to check them.

The "perfect" powder charge and the "perfect" hold can be acquired by a little experimental practice, but the barrel is tricky to change by lapping, so short of reboring and re-rifling, you are stuck with it.

A rifled bore is more accurate than a smooth bore merely because the rotation it gives turns the bullet into a gyroscope. The perfection of this gyroscope action depends upon the speed of rotation, density and form of the bullet.

This Billinghurst under-striker slug gun of .32 caliber features a detachable stock and full length Malcolm scope. Built about 1865, it is sometimes known as a buggy rifle.

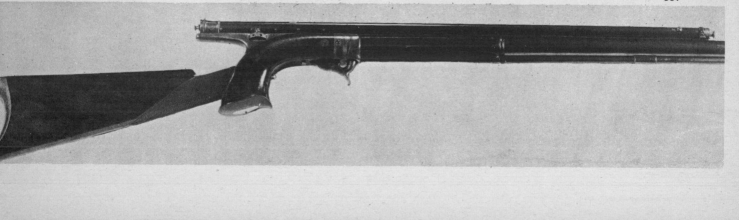

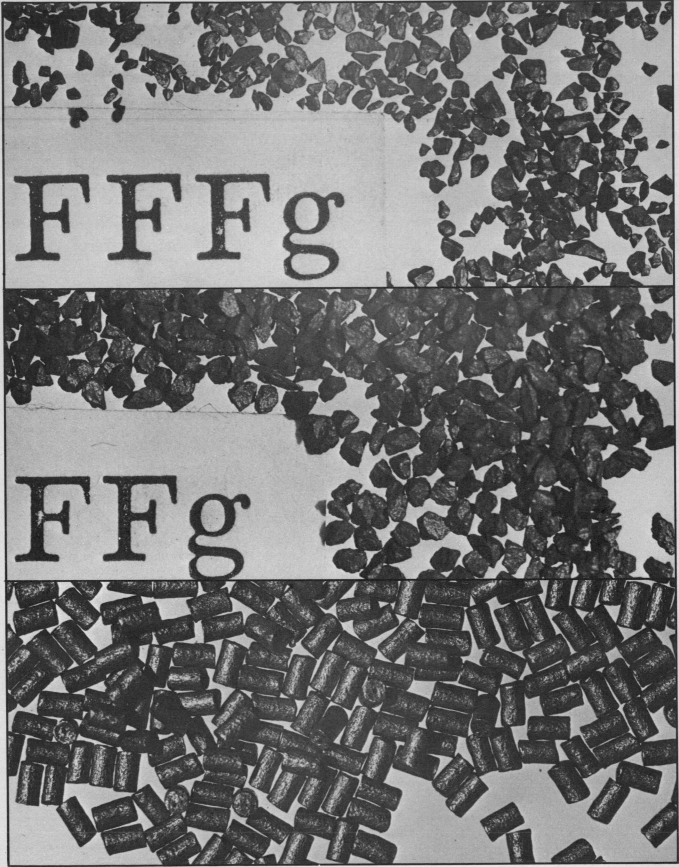

Photos are of the same magnification; the difference between FFFg (top and FFg (middle) is easily distinquished; smokeless powder at bottom.

The Rowland-Pope Ballard action gun featured a figured walnut stock with an inset fancy patch bow, movable finger rest and a wire set trigger.

Col. Berdan gave a spectacular demonstration in 1861 with a thirty-five-pound scope-sighted slug-gun. He fired on a "man target" at two hundred yards, ending the show by having spectators call where they wanted the next shot — "in the left eye, tip of the nose," then hitting that exact spot.

For several years Southern California slug-gun shooters met each Wednesday at the San Gabriel Valley Gun Club range in Fish Canyon. Here experiments were conducted and theories tested. This is a busy range, always open to the public, but a ten-bench section is reserved for the muzzle-loaders. Before the hunting season, the sportsmen come to refresh themselves on the fundamentals of safe gun handling and good marksmanship. Some check the sight setting on "Old Betsy," others sight in that new beauty that set Happy Hunter back $300 or more. In an hour or two he is holding them in the black, he is pleased, he relaxes, his money was well spent, for this is good hunting accuracy. Now he becomes aware of loud booms and clouds of white smoke further down the range. He finds some "nuts" with great heavy guns, all kinds of gear and equipment performing endless cleaning and loading operations to get a shot off every ten minutes — this is amusing and sometimes from lack of understanding, he is inclined to laugh. He asks a general question: "Will those things shoot straight?"

We all keep quiet, silently giving Milo Taylor the floor as he replies, "Oh, I can keep them in the black most of the time. How are you shooting?" Frequently he has a bet before two more minutes have passed. "Five shots,

benchrest at 100 yards for $1." The hunter has two chances to beat Milo: Slim and none. Milo fires a high ten, performs the usual routine and fires number two — a low ten. Now ten minutes or so have passed and the hunter has completed his five shots. He moves over to a spotting scope and takes a look at Milo's paper and watches the third ten go in at the left of center and Mr. H. begins to turn green as the "dawn" breaks — he is beginning to suspect a major problem. Sometimes, at this point the money is returned, depending upon how much "braying" is going on, but Taylor always finishes the string by putting number five in the middle of the carton.

Now the not so happy hunter and his pals inspect these guns and their operation with interest. They doubtlessly mention this event from time to time and we are sure that when they come upon a slug-gun another time, they gaze upon it with respect.

On another one of these Wednesday sessions the late Elmer Herman made an extraordinary shot. Herman was just settling down to squeeze one off, when he said: "There is a fly on my target, in the white at one o'clock. Watch me hit it."

We all swung our guns around so we could watch through out own scope sights. (These twenty-power scopes show a house fly very clearly at one hundred yards.) Herman fired and a bullet hole appeared where the fly had been. When the targets came in, we examined the area around the hole and sure enough it was splattered. With what other gun can you shoot house flies at one hundred yards?

TWO CENTURIES OF BLACK POWDER

CHAPTER 33

Muzzleloading benchrest rifle used in test was fitted with Tower lock above. Reverse side is shown in photo at right.

What Happens With Muzzleloaders Had Been Theoretical, Until 7000 Frames Per Second Told The Story

Cameraman Elmer Herman looks through Fastex camera while Warren Barnes sights down rifle barrel; mirrors reflect firing sequence to camera.

HAVING STARTED HIS shooting education at the age of 8, Bob Furst has been shooting — and investigating — firearms for more than sixty years.

His first rifle he remembers as the most beautiful ever built. It was a Marlin 1897 takedown .22 with three folding Marble sights and a twenty-four-inch octagonal barrel.

"The peep sight on the tang folded down so the leaf sight on the barrel could be used," he recalls. "The front sight had an ivory bead in the open position or when the bead was down, a pinhead on a post with a protecting ring was up.

"I've owned hundreds of fine guns since that wonderful

summer of 1908, but none any better than the little Marlin.

"Occasionally, my grandfather would drop by to observe our shooting progress and to say, "Always be careful. A gun is dangerous without lock, stock or barrel."

"I didn't know exactly what he meant; I knew what the barrel and the stock were but that lock bit threw me, but in those days a boy of eight didn't horse around with or ask dumb questions of grandfathers. I think he was misquoting, but I didn't know that then. The old boy was sharp and spry for his seventy-odd years and he could take that .22 rifle and make it sing, so I had great respect for him.

"The locks on most modern guns are not a definite thing

251

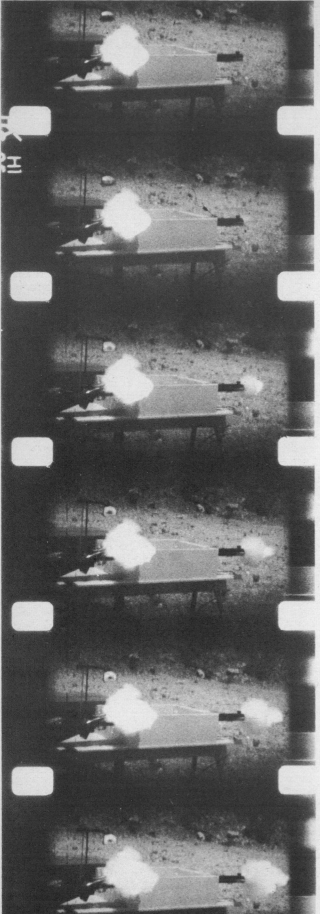

Direct path of flash from percussion cap to powder in chamber makes this Wiechold-Range-King one of best caplock designs. Below, Furst's operation at work, shot from flintlock has just broken the front mirror; replaced after each shot.

Sequence at left demonstrates the speed of camera being used. In frame one the powder in flash pan has ignited, but there is no evidence of the shot leaving the flintlock's muzzle until frame three.

you can take out as a unit and study as you can the locks of a muzzleloader. In fact, I didn't pay much attention to locks until the muzzleloading phase of target shooting bit me about twenty years ago. Then locks became definite, important things. I never have collected muzzleloaders as a hobby. I bought a gun because I wanted a shooter, a good target gun; so I bought and tested many guns and either kept them or traded or sold them off, in the process of getting my equipment together."

Sometimes it was impossible to find an antique to meet his specs; then he would have one made. At times it would be a new gun from the ground up or maybe all new except for the lock which might be a venerable item of more than 100 years. In any event, he would end up with a fine target gun that will permit somebody to enjoy this hobby one hundred or more years from now when many of the current crop of prize antiques no longer will be serviceable.

"The ideal situation for me would be to have one gun with which to fire all matches. It certainly would simplify things and make the whole hobby more fun for me. I am close to such an ideal condition, with Buttercup, my free-

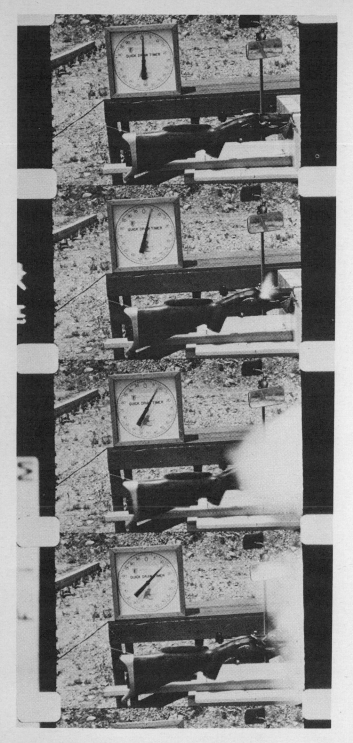

Taken at 24 frames per second, clip above shows the hammer falling with clock reading .01 seconds in frame one. At .04 seconds in frame two, the pan is ignited, gun has fired in frame three, the clock reading .085 seconds. Fair estimate of firing time author judges to be from .055 to .075 seconds.

style, flintlock, fifteen-pound rifle.

In discussing the ignition time of flintlock versus caplock guns with the experts, opinions varied so, while Fursts' "eyeball" observations only added to my confusion. So he felt it necessary to make a careful study of the subject. Having spent four years in Hollywood in the late Twenties making feature length moving pictures and since his son Bill, in addition to being an avid target shooter, makes his living as a professional photographer, they decided on a movie test of the two types of locks for our own information.

"It all started out as a simple experiment, using one Bolex 16mm camera. This unit operates at a normal speed of twenty-four frames per second; the film can be speeded up to sixty-four frames per second which slows down the action two and two-thirds times slower than normal. I thought this would do the job but sixty-four fps were not fast enough to find out what we wanted to know.

"Bill did some recruiting and we finally made the test with three view cameras, two Bolex movie cameras and one Wollensack Fastax camera complete with cameraman Warren Barnes, who was experienced not only with the camera but with the accompanying electronic gear. We had a Quick Draw Timer and Jim Quinn covered the whole production with his 35mm color slide camera. The three movie cameras used color film, the still cameras black and white. All cameras photographed each firing. The Fastax camera used a special color film that is kept refrigerated. We ran thirteen of these one hundred-foot good reels of 16mm film through the Fastax that day and only got two good ones. Luckily one was of a flintlock shot and the other a caplock shot. Our troubles are of no interest to this account. The quality of our high speed shots were disappointing to me but Bill and Warren assured me it was better than most high speed stuff. It certainly gave us the information we sought.

"When choosing the guns to be tested, we deliberately selected the fastest or what we believed (and still do) to be the fastest firing caplock rifle: A Weichold Range-King with an understriking action. The short hammer fall, and short, straight path for the ignition-fire to follow, may be seen in one of the illustrations. The flintlock rifle selected belonged to Vaughn Wiley and was completely modern made except for the Tower lock which was one of the late Elmer Herman's best. The lock shows its age but it was in perfect mechanical condition. Elmer tuned-up both guns and was in charge of the loading and firing operations. To be sure the gun was fired, when the Fastax camera was going at full speed, the trigger was pulled by a solenoid actuated from the programming device under the Fastax operator's control."

The gun was loaded and mounted in the cradle, the mirrors were aligned, the gun was primed and the solenoid was plugged into the control panel or programming device; now the Fastax cameraman was in charge of the whole deal. He checked to make sure the range was clear (we almost got Quinn twice), gave the Bolex cameramen a five-second countdown; then started the cameras at minus-three and at "blast," he hit the start button. A lot of things happened all at once. The film started through the camera and after .43 seconds it had built up to a speed of over 6,000 frames per second and the trigger was pulled. The hammer fell, striking the frizzen and the powder in the pan ignited. The film was now going at the rate of 7,000 frames per second as the gun fired. All this took place in the space of one second.

"The high speed camera so extended the time of firing that it permitted us to see and study wonders the eye alone could never catch. What a pleasure it would be to show this

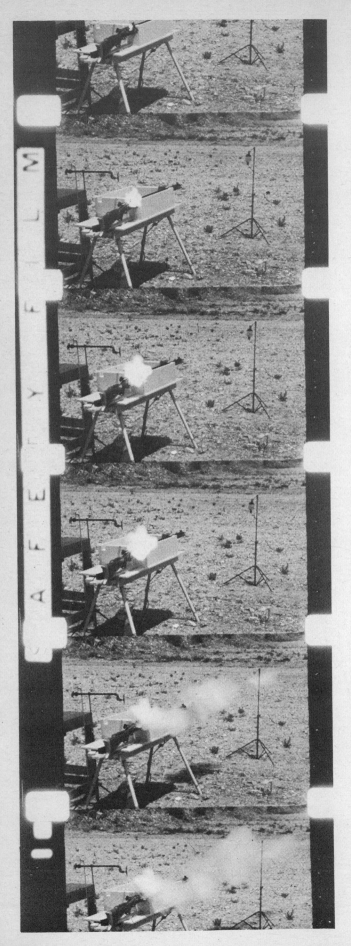

The series of shots at the left show the bullet actually breaking the mirror. Camera has already recorded shot.

picture to a man like Joseph Manton of England or LePage of France who were masters in advancing the perfection of the flintlock action in the late 1700s. I wonder what interpretations they would put on what they would see? The findings of this experiment showed that the caplock fired (time taken from the start of the hammer fall to first sighting of fire at the muzzle) in .022 second (twenty-two thousandths of one second). The flintlock fired in .055 second.

"Even though this caplock rifle fired 2½ times faster than the flintlock rifle, I think the firing time of a conventional caplock rifle, with lock in the side of the gun and the hammer falling down on a nipple, exploding a cap, whose fire must travel around a ninety-degree angle to get into the powder chamber, would slow down almost to the .055 second speed of this Tower lock.

"The way the flintlock guns have been winning open matches over caplock guns in recent years leads me to believe they may be more accurate than we have been giving them credit for and possibly for reasons we don't even suspect.

"This first hi-speed movie investigation of ours, like most movie productions, exceeded the budget several times. Even so, we are starting to plan for the "second round" with improved backgrounds at the lock and muzzle, larger mirrors, two clocks in every shot and several other refinements which will make the picture worthwhile for showing at club meetings, etc., especially after dialog and sound have been dubbed in.

"My biggest disappointment with this hi-speed movie was the fact that one could not see the bullet coming out the muzzle from the side view. The only view of the bullet is the one the mirrors give you from the front as the bullet smashes into the front mirror and powders it.

"We are studying flintlock actions and their performance, overall life of the piece of flint itself, shaprening interval as well as potential improvements in the handling of the flint-lock target rifle and maximum results possible. Concurrently with the study of the flintlock phases, such items as speed of twist, depth of rifling and the strange phenomenon of the difference of the quality of the explosion in the chamber of a caplock rifle as opposed to a flintlock rifle are being considered.

The Fastex cameras were manually started four or five seconds
before the actual shot. In frame one the camera is going as
the solenoid automatically pulls the flintlock's trigger.

PYRODEX: NEW FODDER FOR MUZZLELOADERS

CHAPTER 34

This Shooting Concoction Marks A Milestone In Black Powder Shooting!

To QUOTE FROM the label on the Pyrodex can, it "is not a black powder. However, it does smoke and it is designed and intended for use in certain black powder firearms." There is a report that one ingredient was added to Pyrodex for the express purpose of making it smoke more profusely when fired. It allegedly was felt the smoking capability would have a pronounced effect upon the sales appeal.

Black powder shooting has enjoyed tremendous growth in recent years, but not without its problems. In fact, one problem stems from the mushrooming interest in the use of black powder.

Unlike the modern nitro powders, black gunpowder will explode with considerable vigor, even if it is not confined. Nitro powders burn rapidly if ignited, but require confinement to accelerate their burning rate into the category of an explosive.

Black powder is rated as a Class A explosive, while nitro powders are designated Class C flammable solids. Many governmental bodies, from the Federal Department of Transportation on down have jurisdiction over the transportation, storage, sale and use of explosives. This creates complexities in getting the black powder from manufacturer to distributor to dealer to ultimate consumer.

Most transportation systems decline to handle black powder or any other Class A explosive. In many localities, there is a low limit to the number of pounds that can be stored or possessed, either by a dealer or a private citizen. The upshot is that black powder becomes expensive and difficult to find on dealers' shelves.

The logical solution was the development of a nitro-type propellant designed for use in muzzleloading guns.

Pyrodex currently is marketed in two grades, designated RS and P. Pyrodex RS is intended for use in rifles and shotguns, and has general burning properties comparable to FFg black powder. Pyrodex P is for use in pistols and can be compared to the FFFg grade.

To be successful as a muzzleloader propellant, a powder must be extremely easy to ignite; but, if it becomes too easy to ignite, it edges into the properties of Class A explosives, ending up having no advantage over black powder.

Pyrodex manages to walk the tightwire at a minor sacrifice in matching the versatility of black powder completely. It is just sufficiently difficult to ignite that it qualifies as a Class C flammable solid in shipments of up to one hundred pounds per shipment, when packed in one-pound cans.

The slightly greater difficulty of ignition requires the use of a hot percussion cap for reliable ignition and rules out the use of Pyrodex in flintlock guns, even if a priming charge of FFFFg black powder is employed.

Pyrodex is designed to be loaded bulk for bulk, the same as FFFg black powder. It is not intended to be loaded weight for weight with any other propellant. Pyrodex is about twenty percent less dense than black powder. A charge of Pyrodex will weigh about 80.0 grains if it duplicates the volume occupied by a 100.0-grain charge of black powder. When loaded bulk for bulk with FFFg, Pyrodex duplicates the black powder velocities and pressures within close specifications.

Pyrodex is distributed by Hodgdon Powder Company, Shawnee Mission, Kansas. Hodgdon credits Dan Pawlak as the co-inventor of Pyrodex.

Hodgdon stresses the importance of seating the projectile firmly on top of the powder charge and only full charges should be used when loading cap and ball revolvers. With a reduced charge, it may not be possible to seat the ball deeply enough into the cylinder to compress the powder; this could result in a hangfire.

Pyrodex produces less fouling buildup than black powder and Pyrodex fouling does not show the tendency to increase with successive shots. While it may become difficult to load a patched ball into a rifle after five shots with black powder, there is no appreciable increase in loading difficulty after fifteen or more shots with Pyrodex.

This is both a benefit and, potentially, a liability. For many years, the more knowledgeable black powder shooters have preached and practiced cleaning the bore after each shot for two reasons. First, a clean barrel shoots better. More important is the fact that the chance of a spark or a hot spot in the barrel could set off the powder charge as the gun is being reloaded.

Hodgdon's Spit-Ball grease, Spit-Patch lubricant and Spit-Bath solvent, developed for use with black powder, are compatible with Pyrodex. Spit-Ball is used as a packing around the seated projectiles in the front of cap and ball revolver chambers, lubricating and preventing chainfires. Spit-Patch is applied to the cloth patch used with round balls for muzzleloading rifles and Spit-Bath is the recommended cleaner and solvent for cleaning muzzleloading guns, whether fired with black powder, Pyrodex or both.

A Hodgdon technical bulletin lists loading data for use in percussion rifles, shotguns and pistols. Quoted velocities range as high as 1930 fps for 40.0 grains of Pyrodex RS behind the .395-inch round ball in the caliber .40 Dixie rifle from Dixie Gun Works. Shotgun velocities run from 1025 to 1190 for 1-1/8-ounce charges in the 12 gauge. With Pyrodex P in Ruger's Old Army, 32.0 grains of powder drives a .457-inch ball out at 986 fps.

Pyrodex data obtained from pressure guns are listed, also. Top figures are out of a caliber .50 rifle, with a .490-inch round ball ahead of 100.0 grains of Pyrodex RS, delivering 2049 fps muzzle velocity at 7400 lead units of pressure. Judged from the quoted performance specs, the potential of Pyrodex is by no means diffident.

Pyrodex is not as corrosive as black powder. In the technical bulletin from Hodgdon, however, it is stressed that guns require cleaning after being fired with Pyrodex and should be treated with a suitable rust preventive before being stored.

In the interest of science, we decided to take two approaches with the new powder. We designated Dean A. Grennell to check it out in a standard muzzleloader, with Texan-type Hal Swiggett doing a similar test in a black powder cartridge rifle. Grennell reports: "Our primary test gun was a Parker-Hale Model 1858 Enfield. This is the two-band, sometimes called the Navy rifle, in caliber .577." Made in England by Parker-Hale, it is distributed in this country by Jana International of Denver, Colorado.

Except for the addition of the Parker-Hale name, this Enfield is an impressively accurate and meticulous duplication of the rifle that saw extensive use by both sides in the Civil War, as well as in other military actions across the globe in the middle of the Nineteenth Century.

"By prearrangement, we met with Ray and Jackie Taylor, operators of The Flintlock Sporting Goods in Anaheim, California. At that time, our total supply of the new powder consisted of one can of Pyrodex RS, but we took along a stainless steel Ruger Old Army, planning to incorporate it into the trials, even if we had to make allow-

ances for using the coarser RS granulation," Grennell says.

The Taylors brought other needed items including one of the three-band Model 1858 Enfields and some massive .577 Minie balls, which Jackie proceeded to daub with Thompson/Center's Maxi-Lub lubricant as a necessary prelude to firing.

Taylor swabbed excess oil from the bore, using a cleaning patch in the slotted end of the polished steel ramrod supplied with the Enfield. Then he seated a Navy Arms No. 1081 wing musket cap on the nipple, pointing the muzzle at a soiled cleaning patch he had placed on the ground, and snapped the cap. This verified that the flash hole through the nipple was free and clear, as was the bore.

To be certain the rifle didn't have a charge of powder and a ball seated, before clearing the nipple, Taylor had run the ramrod down the bore, marking the location of the muzzle with his thumb, then laid the ramrod against the side of the barrel, verifying that it extended clear back to the breech plug.

Taylor contends the big muskets, such as this Enfield tend to do their best work with Minie balls, rather than with patched round balls. It was designed originally to fire a 570-grain Minie ball ahead of 70.0 grains of FFg black powder. As used by USA and CSA forces, the bullet was somewhat lighter, about 505 grains, and the powder charge was reduced to 60.0 grains of FFg, giving a muzzle velocity of about 1050 fps. The specified load developed a muzzle energy of about 1237 foot-pounds.

Taylor used a powder flask to fill an adjustable measure, pouring the powder from the measure into the barrel. Again, there are sound safety reasons behind this procedure. Should there be any spark or smoldering remnant left in the barrel, it cannot set off more than the single measure of powder. Were one to load the powder directly from the flask into the muzzle, such a spark could set off the entire contents of the flask.

The Minie ball, greased with Maxi-Lub, was held between thumb and forefinger and started into the muzzle with the aid of a few taps from a small mallet. Taylor stressed the importance of keeping the muzzle from coming into line with the face, head or other items of anatomy during loading sequence.

The Minie ball started in the muzzle, he used the ramrod, which has a cavity in one end that matches the contour of the nose of the ball to seat the hollow base of the bullet firmly against the powder charge.

If there is perceptible air space between the top of the powder and the base of the bullet, ignition may be faulty,

The Pyrodex can carries the same legend on both granule sizes. Note information on the bottom of the label which explains its use, but designates it is not black powder.

Oehler chronograph recorded 1822 fps for 80 grains of Pyrodex by volume, when a Speer .490 round ball was shot out of a Thompson/Center .50 Hawken during the tests.

Dan Pawlak is set to fire through chronograph screens to test velocity and pressure with sophisticated equipment. Pressure remains constant with Pyrodex no matter how often rifle is fired without cleaning. Velocity increases after fouling shot, then remains constant without any cleaning, according to the findings resulting from field testing.

resulting in a hangfire or misfire; the bore might be bulged at the base of the bullet if the powder does ignite. Naturally, some discretion is indicated. One must not seat the projectile with such force as to distort the soft lead of the bullet. The lead must be pure and soft, if maximum accuracy is to be obtained.

Seating another of the Navy Arms No. 1081 wing musket caps on the nipple completed the loading procedure and Grennell took the offhand stance, aiming at a target on the fifty-yard line. The big hammer dropped, the Enfield emitted its curious *whummpf!* sound effect and 570 grains of greased soft lead set forth for the paper amid billowing clouds of white smoke. Taylor commented that the Pyrodex smoke didn't smell quite the same, but that it was close enough to the aroma of authentic black powder to serve any reasonable purpose.

"I fired several more rounds out of the Enfield. The sights put the big projectile creditably close to the point of aim without further adjustment. Although the muzzle deflected upward by a good many degrees with each shot, the recoil was by no means uncomfortable, nor was the muzzle blast painful to my ears," according to Grennell.

The Enfield enjoyed a reputation as the outstandingly accurate rifle in service during its era. Its barrel was of steel,

rather than the wrought iron used in most rifles of domestic make and the rifling had a pitch of one turn in forty-eight inches, with deep rifling at the breech, tapering to shallow rifling at the muzzle. The original Enfields were extremely strong for their day and the modern replicas are stronger than the originals. They can be fired with loads as heavy as 125.0 grains of FFg black powder behind a 570-grain Minie, producing muzzle velocities of about 1250 fps and corresponding energies of about 1978 foot-pounds.

The four wing-shaped flanges on the musket caps served two purposes in that they helped in removing the spent cap and indicated the open end when it became necessary to load in the dark. Mindful of the need of a hot percussion cap, the current line of caps marketed by Navy Arms Company — made in Germany by Dynamit Nobel Troisdorf — seem to be the hottest of those currently available.

"Taylor produced a tin of Navy Arms No. 1075 caps and we proceeded to load up and fire several six-shot groups out of the stainless Ruger Old Army percussion revolver. Despite the use of the Pyrodex RS, nominally intended for rifles and shotguns, we experienced no problems in firing the Ruger. Taylor seated a greased felt wad over the powder, followed by the round lead balls, rather than the approach of applying grease over the top of the seated balls,

Bruce Hodgdon, whose firm is marketing the black powder substitute, lets off a shot while testing an 80-grain load of Pyrodex under a Speer .490 round ball. Because of slow ignition, powder is not good in flintlock arms.

explaining that the treated wads served the same purpose of preventing chainfires and tended to produce somewhat better accuracy.

"Pyrodex more than lived up to its advance billing. It does not seem likely that it will replace black powder completely, since it's not suited for use in flintlocks, but it performs in satisfactory fashion out of percussion guns. It seems probable Pyrodex will attract additional devotees to the ranks of muzzleloading buffs, by reason of the reduced amount of fuss and bother connected with handling it and

cleaning up after using it. Guns fired with Pyrodex clean in about one-quarter the time needed for cleaning after firing black powder."

Meantime, down in San Antonio, Hal Swiggett was taking his own approach to our investigations.

"Deer season was upon us at that time, so I trundled out my heavy-barreled Navy Arms Remington rolling block replica chambered for the time-honored .45-70 cartridge," he recalls.

Meager information supplied stated Pyrodex should be

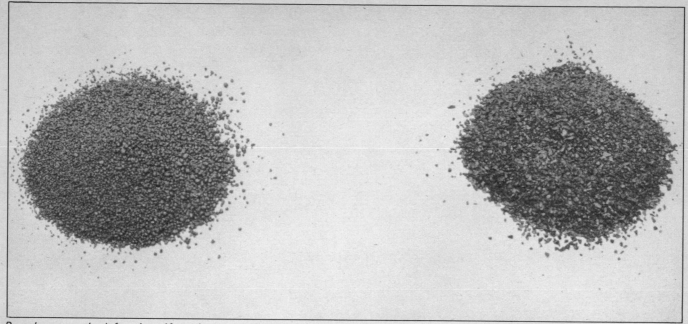

Pyrodex — on the left — is uniform in granulation in comparison with real black powder, Gearhart-Owen FFFg.

used as FFFg by volume, but if weighing, to use eighty percent of the normal FFFg black powder charge. Even though it isn't necessary, I've always weighed black powder charges in metallic cases. Since eighty percent of 70 grains comes out to 56 grains on my computer, I dumped said amount into a .45-70 case — and came up with a full case.

Lopping off enough to comfortably seat a bullet, Remington's 405-grain jacketed soft-point, the remainder was weighed and tipped the scale at 52 grains even."

Half a dozen cases were stuffed in this manner just to see what would happen. At the range, the first shot printed exactly in the same spot for which the rifle was sighted in, with factory ammunition at the standard one hundred-yard distance. The other five were fired and Swiggett had a nice 2¾-inch group for the six shots.

"Back at the loading bench I stuffed a box of twenty cases in the same manner and took myself deer hunting. Oh yes, after shooting those six I fired two smokeless powder cartridges to clean the barrel, and put the rifle away.

"On the second day of the hunt, a sleek little eight-pointer stood in the same spot too long for his best interests. The big 405-grain flat-nosed slug whopped his heart clean out of his chest. I mean it exploded that heart in the same manner one comes to expect from modern high-intensity cartridges. At seventy-eight steps for the shot, strange things were happening.

"I called Bob Hodgdon, gave him the load and asked for information on what was happening. In due time, I received data stating my 52 grains of Pyrodex under the 405-grain bullet was producing 1306 feet per second. For all practical purposes velocity was identical to factory smokeless ammunition.

"Continuing with that load, the remainder of that box, plus twenty more rounds were fired over a period of about three weeks. Three more groups were shot at one hundred yards. The tightest was 2½ inches and the lousiest was 3½ inches. The other stayed with that first one at 2¾ inches.

"And I still haven't cleaned it, though I do confess to watching it rather closely. Each day, after use, two smokeless cartridges were fired to burn out whatever might have been left in the barrel of a damaging nature. Not billed as a

no-cleaning-after-use item in any sense, it does come mighty close as it turns out.

"Phil Chase of Connecticut Valley Arms visited the YO Ranch where I do a lot of my testing. He had along three or four rifles in .50 caliber. We fired one of his rifles eight times without cleaning and found the eighth ball not a bit harder to shove down the barrel than the first," Swiggett recalls.

This test came about on the spur of the moment. Science was served by Chase sticking his finger in the muzzle after the first shot to see how dirty it was. Likewise after the second and third shots. Since that third ball didn't go down any harder than the first, he decided to shoot a few more rather than clean the gun as he had been doing after every third shot.

When the eighth ball slid down as if in a clean barrel, he saw no use to continue and quit for the day.

"Since then, I've shot thirty-two rounds through my Thompson/Center .45 Seneca, using a measure set on 55 grains at one sitting without cleaning the barrel until finished. About this 55-grain setting for my powder measure: don't forget most measures are calibrated for FFg black powder. If you are not accustomed to using FFFg in rifles and shotguns, don't forget it is denser than FFg; use a scale to set your measure initially.

"My Seneca likes 65 grains of FFg, so to get the 3F equivalent I went to my scales and ended up setting the measure on 55 grains which, in turn, gives me the eighty percent needed for Pyrodex at this same setting."

Swiggett's setting of 90 grains on the measure gives him about 80 grains by weight of Pyrodex and this same volume of FFFg has been serving him well for years. This figures out to about 100 grains of FFg, which he considers a right and proper load for the Thompson/Center .50 Hawken.

With a round ball or Maxi, he uses the same charge for both. His handgun flask has a 30-grain spout for FFFg black, so he uses it as is with Pyrodex and has had no trouble.

"My Thompson/Center .50 Hawken put out sixty-one shots without cleaning and seemed to be producing the same accuracy when finished as it always has with the

Neal Knox (right), one of the backers of Pyrodex, looks on as inventor Dan Pawlak checks equipment for testing.

barrel cleaned after each three shots.

"In both these instances I stopped shooting only because it was all the lead round balls available at the time.

"I don't encourage anyone to leave any front-loading gun in an uncleaned state but, from my own experience, it can be done. For how long I don't know, but I tried three weeks with one rifle and, when cleaned, it showed no signs of any rust whatever."

In the little information supplied only days before this is being written, the distributor says: *Pyrodex burns cleaner and produces less fouling build-up than black powder.*

Although fouling is left in the barrel, and must be cleaned before the gun is stored, the fouling — unlike black powder fouling — does not increase with successive shots, and does not affect ease of loading, pressure or velocity after the initial shot. Therefore it is not necessary to clean the bore between each shot as with black powder. In our tests, we find that Pyrodex gives greater accuracy if the bore is not cleaned between each shot.

"In other words, I found out by accident and blunder what was known to be fact by the manufacturer all along.

"I have a cute little CVA Philadelphia Derringer .45 which was fired with Pyrodex. I shot the little gun three times using Lyman's Patch Lubricant, then loaded it without cleaning and carried it four days. No sign of any rust was in evidence and the pistol fired instantly when called upon. After that fourth shot the little Derringer again was loaded with 30 grains by volume of Pyrodex and left for a week. It fired perfectly with no trace of rust anyplace. It was cleaned after that fifth shot and put away.

"Accuracy has been phenomenal for me using Pyrodex, because I'm so used to shots going wide with black powder after three or so without cleaning. When they could be shoved down a barrel, that is. Some guns won't perform unless cleaned after each shot. With this new powder, those days are gone forever.

"It is a real pleasure to pull back the hammer, set the trigger, touch it off, wait for the smoke to clear and see another hole right beside the others, regardless of how many shots have been fired without cleaning.

"When Bob Hodgdon supplied the information on my .45-70 load of 52 grains, by weight, of Pyrodex under the 405-grain Remington JSP bullet, he also included information on three other loads. My load gave 1306 feet per second as mentioned. Using Hornady's 500-grain bullet with 50 grains of Pyrodex produced 1153 fps. Hornady's 350-grain bullet over 56 grains gave 1449 fps and the light 300-grain Hornady bullet over 58 grains of Pyrodex romped along at 1555 fps."

BLACK POWDER DIRECTORY

ANTIQUE ARMS DEALERS

F. Bannerman Sons, Inc., Box 126, L.I., Blue Point, N.Y. 11715

Wm. Boggs, 1243 Grandview Ave., Columbus, Ohio 43212

Ellwood Epps Sporting Goods, 80 King St., Clinton, Ont., Canada

Farris Muzzle Guns, 1610 Gallia St., Portsmouth, Ohio 45662

A. A. Fidd, Diamond Pt. Rd., Diamond Pt., N.Y. 12824

N. Flayderman & Co., Squash Hollow, New Milford, Conn. 06776

Fulmer's Antique Firearms, Detroit Lakes, Minn. 56501

Herb Glass, Bullville, N.Y. 10915

Gold Rush Guns, P.O. Box 33, Afton, Va. 22920

Goodman's for Guns, 1101 Olive St., St. Louis, Mo. 63101

Griffin's Guns & Antiques, R.R. 4, Peterboro, Ont., Canada

The Gun Shop, 6497 Pearl Rd., Cleveland, O. 44130

Heritage Firearms Co., 27 Danbury Rd., Rte. 7, Wilton, Conn 06897

Holbrook Arms Museum, 12953 Biscayne Blvd., N. Miami, Fla. 33161

Ed Howe, 2 Main, Coopers Mills, Me. 04341

Jackson Arms, 6209 Hillcrest Ave., Dallas, Tex. 75205

Jerry's Gun Shop, 9220 Ogden Ave., Brookfield, Ill. 60513

Wm. M. Locke, 3607 Ault Pk. Rd., Cincinnati, O. 45208

John J. Malloy, Briar Ridge Rd., Danbury, Conn. 06810

Charles W. Moore, R.D. 2, Schenevus, N.Y. 12155

Museum of Historical Arms, 1038 Alton Rd., Miami Beach, Fla. 33139

National Gun Traders, Inc., 225 S.W. 22nd Ave., Miami, Fla. 33135

New Orleans Arms Co., Inc., 240 Chartres St., New Orleans, La. 70130

Old West Gun Room, 3509 Carlson Blvd., El Cerrito, Cal. 94530

Pioneer Guns, 5228 Montgomery, Norwood, O. 45212

Powell & Clements Sporting Arms, 210 E. 6th St., Cincinnati, O. 45202

Glode M. Requa, Box 35, Monsey, N.Y. 10952

Martin B. Retting Inc., 11029 Washington, Culver City, Calif. 90230

Ridge Guncraft, Inc., 234 N. Tulane Ave., Oak Ridge, Tenn. 37830

S.G. Intl., P.O. Box 702, Hermosa Beach, CA. 90254

San Francisco Gun Exch., 74 Fourth, San Francisco, Calif. 94103

Ward & Van Valkenburg, 402-30th Ave. No., Fargo, N. Dak. 58102

M. C. Wiest, 234 N. Tulane Ave., Oak Ridge, Tenn. 37830

Yeck Antique Firearms, 579 Tecumseh, Dundee, Mich. 48131

GUNS & GUN PARTS, REPLICA AND ANTIQUE

Antique Gun Parts, Inc., 569 So. Braddock Ave., Pittsburgh, Pa. 15221 (ML)

Armoury Inc., Rte. 25, New Preston, Conn. 06777

Artistic Arms, Inc., Box 23, Hoagland, IN 46745 (Sharps-Borchardt replica)

Bannerman, F., Box 126, Blue Point, Long Island, N.Y. 11715

Shelley Braverman, Athens, N.Y. 12015 (obsolete parts)

Carter Gun Works, 2211 Jefferson Pk. Ave., Charlottesville, Va. 22903

Centennial Arms Corp., 3318 W. Devon, Chicago, (Lincolnwood) ILL. 60645

Colt, 150 Huyshope Ave., Hartford, CT 06102

Connecticut Valley Arms Co., Saybrook Rd., Haddam, CT 06438 (CVA)

Cornwall Bridge Gun Shop, Cornwall Bridge, CT 06754 (parts)

R. MacDonald Champlin, Stanyan Hill, Wentworth, N.H. 03282 (replicas)

David E. Cumberland, 3509 Carlson Blvd., El Cerrito, CA 94530 (Replica Gatling guns)

Darr's Rifle Shop, 2309 Black Rd., Joliet, Ill. 60435 (S.S. items)

Dixie Gun Works, Inc., Hwy 51, South, Union City, Tenn. 38261

Early & Modern, P.O. Box 1248, Studio City, Ca 91604

Ellwood Epps Sporting Goods, 80 King St., Clinton, Ont., Canada

Golden Age Arms Co., 14 W. Winter St., Delaware, OH 43015

Hawes Firearms Co., 8224 Sunset Blvd., Los Angeles, Calif.

Ithaca Gun Co., Ithaca, N.Y. 14850

Kindig's Log Cabin Sport Shop, R.D. 1, P.O. Box 275, Lodi, Ohio 44254

Edw. E. Lucas, 32 Garfield Ave., Old Bridge, N.J. 08857 (45-70)

Lyman Products for Shooters Route 147, Middlefield, NY 06455

R. M. Marek, Rt. 1, Box 1-A, Banks Ore. 97106 (cannons)

Markwell Arms. Co., 2414 W. Devon Ave., Chicago, Ill. 60645

W.L. Mowrey Gun Works, Inc., Box 711, Olney, Tex. 76374

Navy Arms Co., 689 Bergen Blvd., Ridgefield, N.J. 07657

Numrich Arms Co., West Hurley, N.Y. 12491

Potomac Arms Corp., P.O. Box 35, Alexandria, Va. 22313

Richland Arms Co., 321 W. Adrian St., Blissfield, Mich. 49228

Riflemen's Hdqs., Rt. 3, RD 550-E, Kendallville, IN 46755

S&S Firearms, 88-21 Aubrey Ave., Glendale, N.Y. 11227

Sturm, Ruger & Co., Southport, Conn. 06490

Thompson-Center Arms, Box 2405, Rochester, N.H. 03867

Rob. Thompson, 1031-5th Ave., N., Clinton, Ia. 52732 (Win. only)

Ultra-Hi Products, 150 Florence Ave., Hawthorne, N.J. 07506

Tingle, 1125 Smithland Pike, Shelbyville, Ind. 46176 (muzzleloader)

Trail Guns Armory, 2115 Lexington, Houston, TX 77006 (muzzleloaders)

C. H. Weisz, Box 311, Arlington, Va. 22210

Wescombe, 10549 Wilsey, Tujunga, CA 91042 (Rem. R.B. parts)

MUZZLE LOADING BARRELS OR EQUIPMENT

Luther Adkins, Box 281, Shelbyville, Ind. 47176 (breech plugs)

Armoury, Inc., Rte. 25, New Preston, Conn. 06777

Barney's Cannons, Inc., 61650 Oak Rd., South Bend, IN 46614 (ctlg. $1)

Dan Barr, Rte. 1, Thornville, OH 43076 (hunting bag)

John Bivins, Jr., 446 So. Main, Winston-Salem, N.C. 27101

Jesse F. Booher, 2751 Ridge Ave., Dayton, Ohio 45414

G. S. Bunch, 7735 Garrison, Hyattsville, Md. 20784 (flask repair)

Pat Burke, 3339 Farnsworth Rd., Lapeer, Mich. 48446 (capper)

Challanger Mfg. Co., 118 Pearl St., Mt. Vernon, NY 10550 (Hopkins & Allen)

Caution Tool Co., Scout Rd., Southbury, CT 06488

Cherry Corners Gun Shop, Rte. 1, 8010 Lafayette Rd., Lodi, Ohio 44254

Cornwall Bridge Gun Shop, Cornwall Bridge, CT 06745

Earl T. Cureton, Rte. 6, 7017 Pine Grove Rd., Knoxville, Tenn. 37914 (powder horns)

John N. Dangelzer, 3056 Frontier Pl. N.E., Albuquerque, N. Mex. 87106 (powder flasks)

Ted Fellowes, 9245 16th Ave. S.W., Seattle, Wash. 98106

Firearms Imp. & Exp. Corp., 2470 N.W. 21st St., Miami, Fla. 33142

Golden Age Arms Co., 657 High St., Worthington, Ohio 43085 (ctlg. $1)

A. R. Goode, R.D. 1, Box 84, Thurmont, MD 21788

Green River Forge, 4326 120th Ave. S.E., Bellevue, WA 98006 (Forge-Fire flints)

Virgil W. Hartley, 1602 S. Hunter Rd., Indianapolis, IN 46239 (ML pouch)

Hornady Mfg. Co., Box 1848, Grand Island, Nebr. 68801 (round lead balls)

International M. L. Parts Co., 19453 Forrer, Detroit, MI 48235

JJJJ Ranch, Wm. Large, Rte. 1, Ironton, Ohio 45638

Art LeFeuvre, 1003 Hazel Ave., Deerfield, Ill. 60015 (antique gun restoring)

Kindig's Log Cabin Sport Shop, R.D. 1, Box 275, Lodi, OH 44254

Les' Gun Shop (Les Bauska), Box 511, Kalispell, Mont, 59901

Lever Arms Serv. Ltd., 771 Dunsmuir, Vancouver 1, B.C., Canada

J. Lewis Arms Mfg., 3931 Montgomery Rd., Cincinnati, Ohio 45212 (pistol)

McKeown's Guns, R.R. 1, Pekin, IL 61554 (E-Z load rev. stand)

Maryland Gun Exchange Inc., Rt. 40 West, RD 5, Frederick, MD 21701

Maywood Forge, Foley, MN 56329 (cannons)

Jos. W. Mellott, 334 Rockhill Rd., Pittsburgh, Pa. 15243 (barrel blanks)

W. L. Mowrey Gun Works, Inc., Box 711, Olney, Tex. 73674

Muzzle Loaders Supply Co., Rte. 25, New Preston, CT 06777

Numrich Corp., W. Hurley, N.Y. 12491 (powder flasks)

R. Parris & Son, R.D. 5, Box 61, Gettysburg, Pa. 17325 (barrels)

Penna. Rifle Works, 319 E. Main St., Ligonier, Pa. 15658 (ML guns, parts)

Fred Renard, Rte. 1, Symsonia, Ky. 42082 (ML)

H. M. Schoeller, 569 So. Braddock Ave., Pittsburgh, Pa. 15221

Shiloh Products, Inc., 37 Potter St. Farmingdale, NY 11735 (moulds and furnace)

C. E. Siler, 181 Sandhill School, Asheville, N.C., 28806 (flint locks)

Thos. F. White, 5801 Westchester Ct., Worthington, O. 43085 (powder horn)

Lou Williamson, 129 Stonegate Ct., Bedford, TX 76021

MISCELLANEOUS

Breech Plug Wrench, Swaine Machine, 195 O'Connell, Providence, R.I. 02905

Cannons, South Bend Replicas Inc., 61650 Oak Rd., So. Bend, IN 46614 (ctlg. $1)

Capper, Muzzle-Loading, Pat Burke, 3339 Farnsworth Rd., Lapeer, Mich. 48446

Flat Springs, Alamo Heat Treating Co., Box 55345, Houston, Tex. 77055

Nipple Wrenches, Chopie Mfg. Inc., 531 Copeland Ave., La Crosse, Wis. 54601

Powder Horns, Thos. F. White, 5801 Westchester Ct., Worthington, O. 43085

Powder Storage Magazine, C & M Gunworks, 4201 36th Ave., Moline, IL 61265

Rust Bluing/Browning, L.B. Thompson, 568 E. School Ave., Salem, O. 44460

Salute Cannons, Naval Co., Rt. 611, Doylestown, Pa. 18901

Shooting/Testing Glasses, Clear View Sports Shields, P.O. Box 255, Wethersfield, Conn. 06107

Shooting Glasses, Bausch & Lomb, Inc., 635 St. Paul St., Rochester, NY 14602

Shooting Glasses, Bushnell Optical Corp., 2828 E. Foothill Blvd., Pasadena, CA 91107

Shooting Glasses, M. B. Dinsmore, Box 21, Wyomissing, Pa. 19610

Shooting Glasses, Mitchell's, Box 539, Waynesville, Mo. 65583

Shooting Glasses, Ray-O-Vac, Willson Prods. Div., P.O. Box 622, Reading, PA 19603

MUZZLELOADING ASSOCIATIONS

(Each includes a magazine with the membership)

National Muzzle Loading Rifle Association, Box 67, Friendship, Indiana 47021. $6.00 a year.

National Rifle Association, 1600 Rhode Island Ave., N.W., Washington, D.C. 20036. $10/year.

Western States Muzzle Loaders Association, 414 E. Grand Ave., El Segundo, California 90245. $4.50 a year.

North-South Skirmish Association. Address inquiry to Chas. M. Hunter, 6214 - 29th Street, N.W., Washington, D.C. 20015.

The American Mountainmen, P.O. Box 259, Lakeside, California 92040. $4.00 a year.

TODAY'S BLACK POWDER FIREARMS

The black powder firearms being manufactured today cover a broad range of quality and prices; they vary from faithful replicas of the originals of the century or more ago to new innovations with semi-modern design and Space Age materials.

The majority of today's muzzleloaders are imports and, because of the nature of the business, many of them are available from more than one source. Because of realistics such as mass buying, general overhead, et al., prices may vary from one importer's line to that of another. The names of the pieces may change in advertising or even the legend stamped into the steelwork, but the design otherwise well may be identical. The major number of foreign manufacturers proof their guns; look for these proofmarks in purchasing a firearm. If it is missing, tend to go in another direction. There have been some black powder replicas that were made strictly as decorator pieces and which should not be fired. These, of course, should have no proofmarks.

The catalog section that follows is divided into four sections, covering single-shot handguns, revolvers, rifles and muskets and shotguns. Prices shown may increase in time.

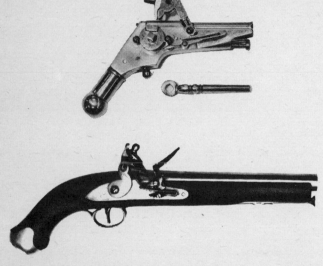

DIXIE WHEELOCK COURIER PISTOL
Caliber: 36.
Barrel: 4", half octagon, half round; flared muzzle.
Weight: 1¼ lbs. **Length:** 7" over-all.
Stock: Metal.
Sights: None.
Features: Replica of 1580 Courier Pistol. Frame and hammer of brass, engraved. Steel barrel. Comes complete with spanner. Imported from England by Dixie Gun Works.
Price: **$175.00**

TOWER FLINTLOCK PISTOL
Caliber: 45, 69.
Barrel: 8¼".
Weight: 40 oz. **Length:** 14" over-all.
Stock: Walnut.
Sights: Fixed.
Features: Engraved lock, brass furniture. Specifications, including caliber, weight and length may vary with importers. Available as flint or percussion. Imported by The Armoury, F.I.E., Hawes, C.V.A., Centennial, Dixie, Navy/Replica.
Price: ....**$23.00 to $57.95.**
Price: Kit form, flintlock (CVA) **$43.95**

NAVY ARMS SCOTCH PISTOL
Caliber: .577".
Barrel: 7".
Weight: 28 oz. **Length:** 11" over-all.
Stock: All brass.
Sights: None.
Features: Flintlock action. Duplicate of original Blackwatch pistol. Highly polished steel. From Navy Arms.
Price: **$125.00**

CHARLEVILLE FLINTLOCK PISTOL
Caliber: 69.
Barrel: 7½".
Weight: 48 oz. **Length:** 13½" over-all.
Stock: Walnut.
Sights: None.
Features: Brass frame, polished steel barrel, brass buttcap and backstrap. Replica of original 1777 pistol. From Navy Arms.
Price: **$125.00**

HARPER'S FERRY 1806 PISTOL
Caliber: 54.
Barrel: 10".
Weight: 40 oz. **Length:** 16" over-all.
Stock: Walnut.
Sights: Fixed.
Features: Case hardened lock, brass mounted browned bbl. Replica of the first U.S. Gov't.-made flintlock pistol. Imported by Navy/Replica.
Price: **$95.00**

Kentucky Percussion Pistol

Similar to above but percussion lock. Imported by Centennial, The Armoury, Navy/Replica, F.I.E., Hawes, Jana, C.V.A., Dixie, EMF, Century, Markwell.

Price: . . . . $26.95 to $90.00
Price: In kit form . . . . $35.95 to $54.95

KENTUCKY BELT PERCUSSION PISTOL

Caliber: 45.
Barrel: 7″, rifled.
Weight: 29 oz. **Length:** 12″ over-all.
Stock: Walnut.
Sights: Fixed.
Features: Engraved lock, brass furniture, steel ramrod. Available as flint or percussion. Imported by The Armoury, Markwell Arms.

Price: . . . . $22.95 to $55.49.
Price: Kit form . . . . $27.95 to $30.80

KENTUCKY FLINTLOCK PISTOL

Caliber: 44, 45.
Barrel: 10⅛″.
Weight: 32 oz. **Length:** 15½″ over-all.
Stock: Walnut.
Sights: Fixed.
Features: Case hardened lock, blued bbl.; available also as brass bbl. flint Model 1821 ($95.00, Navy). Imported by Navy Replica, EMF, The Armoury, Century, Centennial, F.I.E., Dixie, C.V.A., Hawes, Kassnar.

Price: . . . . $40.95 to $89.95
Price: In kit form, from $24.95

COLONIAL PISTOL

Caliber: 44 (.451″ bore).
Barrel: 7″, octagonal, rifled.
Length: 12″ over-all.
Stock: Walnut.
Features: Case-hardened lock, brass furniture, fixed sights. Available in either flint or percussion. Imported by CVA.

Price: Percussion $36.95
Price: Flint $40.95
Also available in kit form, either flint or percussion. Stock 95% inletted.
Price: . . . . $26.95 to $32.95

HARPER'S FERRY MODEL 1855 PERCUSSION PISTOL

Caliber: 58.
Barrel: 11¾″, rifled.
Weight: 56 oz. **Length:** 18″ over-all.
Stock: Walnut.
Sights: Fixed.
Features: Case hardened lock and hammer; brass furniture; blued bbl. Shoulder stock available, priced at $35.00. Imported by Navy/Replica.

Price: $95.00
Price: With detachable shoulder stock $125.00

DIXIE OVERCOAT PISTOL

Caliber: 39.
Barrel: 4″, smoothbore.
Weight: 13 oz. **Length:** 8″ over-all.
Stock: Walnut-finish hardwood. Checkered p.g.
Sights: Fixed.
Features: Shoots .380″ balls. Breech plug and engraved lock are burnished steel finish; barrel and trigger guard blued.

Price: Plain model $26.95
Price: Engraved model $34.50

DIXIE DUELING PISTOL

Caliber: 44 to 50 cal. (varies with each gun).
Barrel: 9″, smoothbore, octagon.
Weight: 1¼ lbs. **Length:** 15¼″ over-all.
Stock: Maple, checkered.
Sights: Fixed.
Features: Shoots round ball or shot.

Price: $79.95

DIXIE BRASS FRAME DERRINGER

Caliber: 41.
Barrel: 2½″.
Weight: 7 oz. **Length:** 5½″ over-all.
Stock: Walnut.
Features: Brass frame, color case hardened hammer and trigger. Shoots .395″ round ball. Engraved model available. From Dixie Gun Works.

Price: Plain model $32.50
Price: Engraved model $37.50

BLACK POWDER SINGLE SHOT PISTOLS—FLINT & PERCUSSION

DIXIE LINCOLN DERRINGER
Caliber: 41.
Barrel: 2", 8 lands, 8 grooves.
Weight: 7 oz. **Length:** 5½" over-all.
Stock: Walnut finish, checkered.
Sights: Fixed.
Features: Authentic copy of the "Lincoln Derringer." Shoots .400" patched ball. German silver furniture includes trigger guard with pineapple finial, wedge plates, nose, wrist, side and teardrop inlays. All furniture, lockplate, hammer, and breechplug engraved. Imported from Italy by Dixie Gun Works.
Price: **$99.50**
Price: Kit (Not engraved) **$49.95**

PHILADELPHIA DERRINGER PERCUSSION PISTOL
Caliber: 41.
Barrel: 3⅛".
Weight: 14 oz. **Length:** 7" over-all.
Stock: Walnut, checkered grip.
Sights: Fixed.
Features: Engraved wedge holder and bbl. Also available in flintlock version (Armoury, $29.95). Imported by C.V.A., Markwell Arms, The Armoury,
Price: .... **$18.37 to $39.95**
Price: Kit form **$25.25**
Price: Kit form (C.V.A.) .... **$21.95 to $24.95**

DIXIE PHILADELPHIA DERRINGER
Caliber: 41.
Barrel: 3½", octagon.
Weight: 8 oz. **Length:** 5½" over-all.
Stock: Walnut, checkered p.g.
Sights: Fixed.
Features: Barrel and lock are blued; brass furniture. From Dixie Gun Works.
Price: **$49.95**

BUCCANEER DOUBLE BARREL PISTOL
Caliber: 36 or 44 cal.
Barrel: 9½".
Weight: 40 oz. **Length:** 15½" over-all.
Stock: Walnut, one piece.
Sights: Fixed.
Features: Case hardened and engraved lockplate, solid brass fittings. Percussion or flintlock. Imported by Hawes Firearms, The Armoury.

CLASSIC ARMS NEW ORLEANS ACE
Caliber: 44.
Barrel: 3½", rifled or smoothbore.
Weight: 16 ozs. **Length:** 9" over-all.
Stock: American walnut.
Sights: None.
Features: Solid brass frame (receiver). Cleaning/ramrod under barrel. Available complete or in kit form. Kit is 90% complete, no drilling or tapping, fully inletted. Made in U.S.A. From Classic Arms International. Add $2.00 for rifled bore.
Price: Complete **$44.95**
Price: Kit **$29.95**

CLASSIC ARMS "SNAKE EYES"
Caliber: 36.
Barrel: 3", double barrel.
Weight: 24 ozs. **Length:** 6¾" over-all.
Stock: American walnut.
Sights: None.
Features: Solid brass barrels and receiver. Also comes in kit form, 90% complete with only 14 pieces. Made in U.S.A. From Classic Arms International.
Price: Complete **$49.95**
Price: Kit **$34.95**

CLASSIC ARMS "DUCKFOOT"
Caliber: 36.
Barrel: 3½", three barrels.
Weight: 32 ozs. **Length:** 10½" over-all.
Stock: American walnut.
Sights: None.
Features: Steel barrels and receiver, brass frame. Also comes in kit form, 90% completed, no drilling or tapping. From Classic Arms International.
Price: Complete **$49.95**
Price: Kit **$34.95**

BLACK POWDER SINGLE SHOT PISTOLS—FLINT & PERCUSSION

SINGLE SHOT PERCUSSION TARGET PISTOL
Caliber: 44.
Barrel: 10" octagonal.
Weight: 42 oz.
Stocks: Walnut.
Sights: Bead front, rear adj. for w. and e.
Features: Engraved scenes on frame sides; brass backstrap and trigger guard; case hardened frame and hammer. Imported by Dixie, EMF.
Price: **$77.95**

TINGLE BLACK POWDER M1960 PISTOL
Caliber: 40, single shot, percussion.
Barrel: 8", 9", 10", or 12" octagon.
Length: 11¾ inches. **Weight:** 33 oz. (8" bbl.).
Stocks: Walnut, one piece.
Sights: Fixed blade front, w. adj. rear.
Features: 6-groove bbl., easily removable for cleaning; 1-in-30 twist.
Price: **$74.95**

Markwell "Loyalist" Target Pistol
Similar to the Thompson/Center Patriot pistol except has different lock. Available as complete gun or as kit, from Markwell Arms.
Price: Complete **$91.95**
Price: Kit **$66.95**

THOMPSON/CENTER PATRIOT PERCUSSION PISTOL
Caliber: 45.
Barrel: 9¼".
Weight: 36 oz. **Length:** 16" over-all.
Stock: Walnut.
Sights: Patridge-type. Rear adj. for w. and e.
Features: Hook breech system; ebony ramrod; double set triggers; coil mainspring. From Thompson/Center Arms.
Price: **$125.00**
With accessory pack (bullet mould T/C patches, adj. powder measure, short starter, extra nipple and nipple wrench).
Price: **$152.50**

BLACK POWDER REVOLVERS

CLASSIC ARMS ETHAN ALLEN PEPPERBOX
Caliber: 36.
Barrel: 3", four smoothbore barrels.
Weight: 38 ozs. **Length:** 9" over-all.
Stock: American walnut.
Sights: None.
Features: Replica of the first double-action pistol. Steel barrels, brass receiver. Also comes in kit form, 90% completed. From Classic Arms International.
Price: Complete **$54.95**
Price: Kit **$39.95**

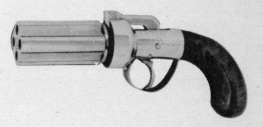

WALKER 1847 PERCUSSION REVOLVER
Caliber: 44, 6-shot.
Barrel: 9".
Weight: 72 oz. **Length:** 15½" over-all.
Stocks: Walnut.
Sights: Fixed.
Features: Case hardened frame, loading lever and hammer; iron backstrap; brass trigger guard; engraved cylinder. Imported by EMF, Navy/Replica, Jana.
Price: ....$100.00 to **$130.00**

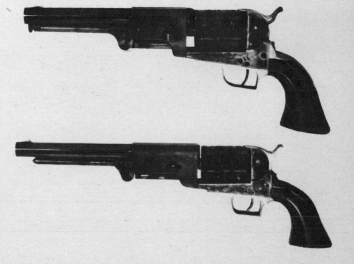

SECOND MODEL DRAGOON 1848 REVOLVER
Caliber: 44, 6-shot.
Barrel: 7½".
Weight: 64 oz. **Length:** 14" over-all.
Stocks: One piece walnut.
Sights: Fixed.
Features: Case hardened frame, loading lever and hammer; engraved cylinder scene; safety notches on hammer, safety pin in cylinder. Imported by Navy/Replica, EMF. First and Third Models also available.
Price: **$125.00**

COLT 3RD MODEL DRAGOON REVOLVER
Caliber: 44 (for .457" round ball), 6-shot.
Barrel: 7½".
Weight: 4 lbs., 2 oz. **Length:** 14" over-all.
Stock: Oiled walnut, one piece.
Sights: Blade front, fixed V-notch rear.
Features: Brass backstrap and trigger guard. Color case hardened frame, hammer and loading lever. Blue barrel and cylinder engraved with original Ranger and Indian scene. Serial numbers resume at 20,901 where manufacture stopped in 1860. From Colt.
Price: **$284.95**

BABY DRAGOON 1848 PERCUSSION REVOLVER
Caliber: 31, 5-shot.
Barrel: 4", 5", 6".
Weight: 24 oz. (6" bbl.). **Length:** 10½" (6" bbl.).
Stocks: Walnut.
Sights: Fixed.
Features: Case hardened frame; safety notches on hammer and safety pin in cylinder; engraved cylinder scene; octagonal bbl. Imported by Navy/Replica, F.I.E., EMF.
Price: .... **$38.15 to $95.00**

1850 WELLS FARGO PERCUSSION REVOLVER
Caliber: 31, 5-shot.
Barrel: 3", 4", 5", 6".
Weight: 22 oz.
Stocks: Walnut.
Sights: Fixed.
Features: No loading lever; square-back trigger guard; case hardened frame and hammer; engraved cylinder; brass trigger guard and back-strap. Imported by Navy/Replica, EMF.
Price: **$95.00**

COLT 1851 NAVY PERCUSSION REVOLVER
Caliber: 36, 6-shot.
Barrel: 7½".
Weight: 40½ oz. **Length:** 13" over-all.
Stocks: Black walnut.
Sights: Fixed.
Features: Color case hardened frame; barrel and cylinder blued. Silver plated trigger guard and backstrap. Naval Scene engraving by W. L. Ormsby on cylinder. From Colt.
Price: **$200.00**

1851 NAVY-SHERIFF
Same as 1851 Sheriff model except: 4" barrel, fluted cylinder, belt ring in butt. Imported by American Import, Replica/Navy, Hawes, Richland, Armoury.
Price: .... **$50.00 to $100.00**

LYMAN 1851 NAVY
Same as standard model except 36 cal. only, has square-back trigger guard, nickel plated backstrap, color case hardened frame **$129.95**
Gun and kit (includes .357" single cavity round ball mould with handles, six spare nipples with wrench, Hodgdon's "Spit Ball" and Lyman's "Black Powder Basics" manual). **$124.95**

POCKET MODEL 1849 PERCUSSION REVOLVER
Caliber: 31, 5-shot.
Barrel: 4", 6".
Weight: 26 oz.
Stocks: Walnut finish.
Sights: Fixed.
Features: Round trigger guard; Colt stagecoach hold-up scene on cylinder. Imported by Navy/Replica, EMF.
Price: **$95.00**

NAVY MODEL 1851 PERCUSSION REVOLVER
Caliber: 36 or 44, 6-shot.
Barrel: 7½".
Weight: 42 oz. **Length:** 13" over-all.
Stocks: Walnut finish.
Sights: Fixed.
Features: Brass backstrap and trigger guard; engraved cylinder with navy battle scene; case hardened frame, hammer, loading lever. Imported by Centennial, The Armoury, Navy/Replica, Hawes, Valor, Century, F.I.E., EMF, American Import, Dixie, (illus.) Richland.
Price: Brass frame .... **$31.50 to $66.60**
Price: Steel frame .... **$40.95 to $100.00**
Price: Kit form (Centennial and Dixie) .... **$30.95 to $44.95**
Price: Engraved model (Dixie) **$52.95**

1851 SHERIFF MODEL PERCUSSION REVOLVER
Caliber: 36, 44, 6-shot.
Barrel: 5".
Weight: 40 oz. **Length:** 10½" over-all.
Stocks: Walnut.
Sights: Fixed.
Features: Brass back strap and trigger guard; engraved navy scene; case hardened frame, hammer, loading lever. Available with brass frame from some importers at slightly lower prices. Imported by The Armoury, Navy/Replica, Hawes, Markwell Arms, Richland, EMF.
Price: Steel frame .... **$41.95 to $100.65**
Price: Brass frame .... **$34.95 to $54.95**

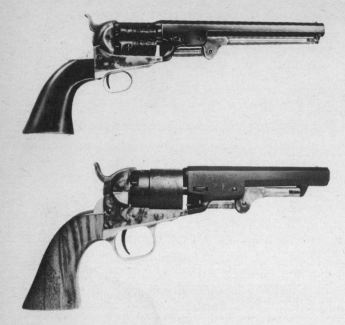

ARMY 1851 PERCUSSION REVOLVER

Caliber: 44, 6-shot.
Barrel: 7½".
Weight: 45 oz. **Length:** 13" over-all.
Stocks: Walnut finish.
Sights: Fixed.
Features: 44 caliber version of the 1851 Navy. Imported by Valor, The Armoury, Richland.
Price: .... $33.50 to $65.00

1853 POCKET NAVY MODEL REVOLVER

Caliber: 36, 6-shot.
Barrel: 4½", 5½", 6½".
Weight: 26 oz. **Length:** 12" over-all (6½" bbl.).
Stocks: Smooth walnut.
Sights: Fixed.
Features: Shortened version of std. Navy model. Case hardened frame, hammer and loading lever; brass backstrap and trigger guard. Imported by Navy/Replica Arms, Armoury.
Price: $95.00

NEW MODEL 1858 ARMY PERCUSSION REVOLVER

Caliber: 36 or 44, 6-shot.
Barrel: 6½" or 8".
Weight: 40 oz. **Length:** 13½" over-all.
Stocks: Walnut.
Sights: Fixed.
Features: Replica of Remington Model 1858. Also available from some importers as Army Model Belt Revolver in 36 cal., shortened and lightened version of the 44. Target Model (Centennial, Hawes, Iver Johnson, Navy/Replica) has fully adj. target rear sight, target front, 36 or 44 ($74.95-$152.45). Imported by Navy/Replica, Century, F.I.E., Hawes, C.V.A., Valor, American Import, Iver Johnson, Jana, The Armoury, Centennial, Markwell (brass frame), Richland, EMF.
Price: .... $49.95 to $128.25
Price: Kit form $46.95
Price: Nickel finish (Navy Arms) $125.00
Price: Stainless steel (Navy Arms) $165.00

LYMAN 44 NEW MODEL ARMY REVOLVER

Caliber: 44, 6-shot.
Barrel: 8".
Weight: 40 oz. **Length:** 13½" over-all.
Stock: Walnut.
Sights: Fixed.
Features: Replica of 1858 Remington. Brass trigger guard and backstrap, case hardened hammer and trigger. Solid frame with top strap. Heavy duty nipples. Includes .451" single cavity mould block. From Lyman Gunsight Corp.
Price: $129.95

LYMAN 36 NEW MODEL NAVY REVOLVER

Caliber: 36, 6-shot.
Barrel: 6½".
Weight: 42 oz. **Length:** 12¼" over-all.
Stock: Walnut.
Sights: Fixed.
Features: Replica of 1860 Remington. Brass trigger guard and backstrap, case hardened trigger and hammer. Solid frame with top strap. Heavy duty nipples. Includes .375" single cavity mould blocks. From Lyman Gunsight Corp.
Price: $129.95

1860 ARMY PERCUSSION REVOLVER

Caliber: 44, 6-shot.
Barrel: 8".
Weight: 40 oz. **Length:** 13⅝" over-all.
Stocks: Walnut.
Sights: Fixed.
Features: Engraved navy scene on cylinder; brass trigger guard; case hardened frame, loading lever and hammer. Some importers supply pistol cut for detachable shoulder stock, have accessory stock available. Imported by Navy/Replica, Centennial, The Armoury, Hawes, Jana, Dixie, Lyman, Iver Johnson, Richland, EMF.
Price: .... $44.95 to $129.95
1861 Navy: Same as Army except 36 cal., 7½" bbl., wt. 41 oz., cut for stock; round cylinder (fluted avail.), from Navy/Replica $100.00
Lyman 1860 Army gun and kit (includes single cavity round ball mould with handles, six spare nipples, nipple wrench, Hodgdon's "Spit Ball" and Lyman's "Black Powder Basics" manual). $139.95

1861 NAVY MODEL REVOLVER

Caliber: 36, 6-shot.
Barrel: 7½".
Weight: 2½ lbs. **Length:** 13" over-all.
Stocks: One piece smooth walnut.
Sights: Fixed.
Features: Shoots .380" ball. Case-hardened frame, loading lever and hammer. Cut for shoulder stock. Non-fluted cylinder. From Navy/Replica Arms, Iver Johnson.
Price: $100.00
Price: With full fluted cyl. $100.00

BLACK POWDER REVOLVERS

RICHLAND 44 BALLISTER REVOLVER
Caliber: 44, 6 shot.
Barrel: 12".
Weight: 2¾ lbs.
Stock: Two-piece walnut.
Sights: Fixed.
Features: Barrel and cylinder blued, frame and trigger guard are brass; hammer and loading lever are color case hardened. From Richland Arms.
Price: **$78.00**

GRISWOLD & GUNNISON PERCUSSION REVOLVER
Caliber: 36, 44, 6-shot.
Barrel: 7½".
Weight: 44 oz. (36 cal.). **Length:** 13" over-all.
Stocks: Walnut.
Sights: Fixed.
Features: Replica of famous Confederate pistol. Brass frame, backstrap and trigger guard; case hardened loading lever; rebated cylinder (44 cal. only). Imported by Navy/Replica, Markwell Arms.
Price: . . . . **$60.00 to $72.03**
Price: Kit form (Markwell) **$57.57**

HIGH STANDARD GRISWOLD & GUNNISON REVOLVER
Caliber: 36, 6-shot.
Barrel: 7½".
Weight: Approx. 40 oz. **Length:** 13¼" over-all.
Stocks: Smooth walnut.
Sights: Fixed.
Features: Brass frame and trigger guard, rest blued. Reproduction of Confederate versions of Colt 1851 Navy. Comes with Georgia White Pine presentation case and brass plate depicting Georgia state seal.
Price: **$145.00**

HIGH STANDARD LEECH & RIGDON REVOLVER
Caliber: 36, 6-shot.
Barrel: 7½".
Weight: Approx. 40 oz. **Length:** 13¼" over-all.
Stocks: Smooth walnut.
Sights: Fixed.
Features: Steel frame with satin nickel finish. Brass trigger guard and backstrap. Comes with deluxe walnut presentation case and reproduction Civil War belt buckle.
Price: **$145.00**

1862 POLICE MODEL PERCUSSION REVOLVER
Caliber: 36, 5-shot.
Barrel: 4½", 5½", 6½".
Weight: 26 oz. **Length:** 12" (6½" bbl.).
Stocks: Walnut.
Sights: Fixed.
Features: Half-fluted and rebated cylinder; case hardened frame, loading lever and hammer; brass trigger guard and back strap. Imported by Navy/Replica, Armoury.
Price: **$95.00**
Price: Cased with accessories **$125.00**

SPILLER & BURR REVOLVER
Caliber: 36.
Barrel: 7", octagon.
Weight: 2½ lbs. **Length:** 12½" over-all.
Stock: Two-piece walnut.
Sights: Fixed.
Features: Reproduction of the C.S.A. revolver. Brass frame and trigger guard. Also available as a kit. From Dixie, Navy/Replica, Richland.
Price: . . . . **$69.95 to $75.00**
Price: Kit form . . . . **$39.95 to $44.95**

DIXIE "WYATT EARP" REVOLVER
Caliber: 44.
Barrel: 12" octagon.
Weight: 46 oz. **Length:** 18" over-all.
Stock: Two piece walnut.
Sights: Fixed.
Features: Highly polished brass frame, backstrap and trigger guard; blued barrel and cylinder; case hardened hammer, trigger and loading lever. Navy-size shoulder stock ($40.00) will fit with minor fitting. From Dixie Gun Works.
Price: **$62.50**

RUGER 44 OLD ARMY PERCUSSION REVOLVER
Caliber: 44, 6-shot. Uses .457" dia. lead bullets.
Barrel: 7½" (6-groove, 16" twist).
Weight: 46 oz. **Length:** 13½" over-all.
Stock: Smooth walnut.
Sights: Ramp front, rear adj. for w. and e.
Features: Stainless steel standard size nipples, chrome-moly steel cylinder and frame, same lockwork as in original Super Blackhawk. Also available in stainless steel in very limited quantities. Made in USA. From Sturm, Ruger & Co.
Price: Blued **$125.00**
Price: Stainless steel **$167.50**

BLACK POWDER MUSKETS & RIFLES

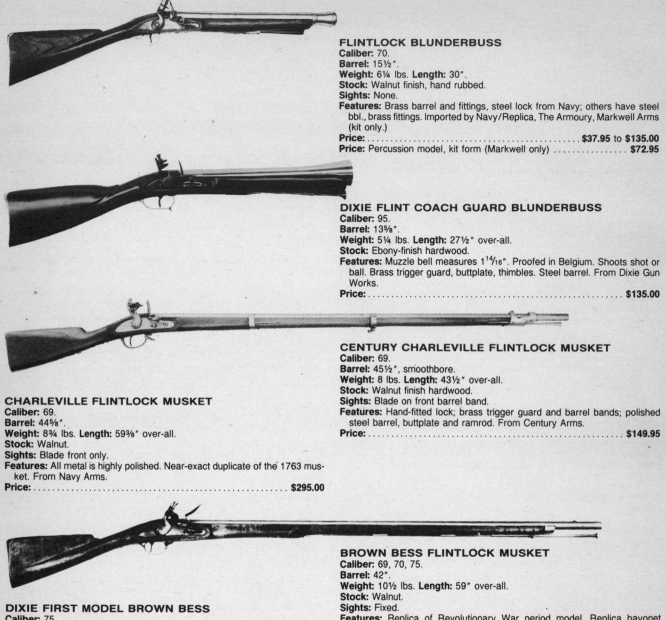

FLINTLOCK BLUNDERBUSS
Caliber: 70.
Barrel: 15½".
Weight: 6¼ lbs. **Length:** 30".
Stock: Walnut finish, hand rubbed.
Sights: None.
Features: Brass barrel and fittings, steel lock from Navy; others have steel bbl., brass fittings. Imported by Navy/Replica, The Armoury, Markwell Arms (kit only.)
Price: .... $37.95 to $135.00
Price: Percussion model, kit form (Markwell only) $72.95

DIXIE FLINT COACH GUARD BLUNDERBUSS
Caliber: 95.
Barrel: 13⅝".
Weight: 5¼ lbs. **Length:** 27½" over-all.
Stock: Ebony-finish hardwood.
Features: Muzzle bell measures 1¹⁴/₁₆". Proofed in Belgium. Shoots shot or ball. Brass trigger guard, buttplate, thimbles. Steel barrel. From Dixie Gun Works.
Price: $135.00

CENTURY CHARLEVILLE FLINTLOCK MUSKET
Caliber: 69.
Barrel: 45½", smoothbore.
Weight: 8 lbs. **Length:** 43½" over-all.
Stock: Walnut finish hardwood.
Sights: Blade on front barrel band.
Features: Hand-fitted lock; brass trigger guard and barrel bands; polished steel barrel, buttplate and ramrod. From Century Arms.
Price: $149.95

CHARLEVILLE FLINTLOCK MUSKET
Caliber: 69.
Barrel: 44⅝".
Weight: 8¾ lbs. **Length:** 59⅜" over-all.
Stock: Walnut.
Sights: Blade front only.
Features: All metal is highly polished. Near-exact duplicate of the 1763 musket. From Navy Arms.
Price: $295.00

BROWN BESS FLINTLOCK MUSKET
Caliber: 69, 70, 75.
Barrel: 42".
Weight: 10½ lbs. **Length:** 59" over-all.
Stock: Walnut.
Sights: Fixed.
Features: Replica of Revolutionary War period model. Replica bayonet ($12.00) available. Carbine version (30½" bbl., 7¾ lbs.) also available from Replica/Navy only. Can be purchased as kit ($175.00). Imported by Navy/Replica, Lyman.
Price: Replica/Navy version $325.00
Price: 69 caliber $250.00
Price: Lyman $295.00
Price: Kit form (Navy) $195.00

DIXIE FIRST MODEL BROWN BESS
Caliber: 75.
Barrel: 42", smoothbore.
Weight: 10 lbs. **Length:** 59" over-all.
Stock: Walnut finished.
Sights: Fixed.
Features: Brass furniture with bright barrel, lock and ramrod. Lock marked "Grice 1762" with crown and "GR" underneath. Original Brown Bess bayonets $25.00. Imported from England by Dixie Gun Works.
Price: $450.00

DIXIE SECOND MODEL BROWN BESS
Caliber: 74.
Barrel: 41¾" smoothbore.
Weight: 9½ lbs. **Length:** 57¾".
Stock: Walnut-finish hardwood.
Sights: Fixed.
Features: All metal finished bright. Brass furniture. Lock marked "Tower" and has a crown with "GR" underneath. From Dixie Gun Works.
Price: $250.00

Lyman "Brown Bess" Musket
Musket with Shooting Accessory Kit (includes .715" round ball single cavity mould with handles, 6 strips .015" round ball patching, 8 oz. squeeze tube of Lyman patch and ball lubricant and "Black Powder Basics" manual
Price: $275.00

BLACK POWDER MUSKETS & RIFLES

CENTURY TOWER MUSKET
Caliber: 72.
Barrel: 38½", polished steel.
Weight: 10¾ lbs. **Length:** 55½" over-all.
Stock: Walnut.
Sights: Fixed.
Features: Brass buttplate, trigger guard and thimbles; baynot lug; lock plate stamped with British crown. From Century Arms.
Price: **$149.95**

ULTRA-HI MINUTEMAN MUSKET
Caliber: 67.
Barrel: 32", smoothbore.
Weight: 8¼ lbs. **Length:** 49" over-all.
Stock: Walnut-stained hardwood.
Sights: Blade front only.
Features: Polished steel barrel, brass patch box and nose cap. Flintlock only. From Ultra-Hi Products.
Price: **$130.00**

CENTURY LONG TOM MUSKET
Caliber: 56.
Barrel: 51".
Weight: 7¾ lbs. **Length:** 67¾" over-all.
Stock: Walnut finish hardwood.
Sights: Bead front only.
Features: Polished steel barrel and ramrod; 2-piece lock; buttplate, trigger guard and barrel brass plated. American eagle seal on lockplate.
Price: **$94.95**

ULTRA-HI KENTUCKY RIFLE
Caliber: 45 (.453").
Barrel: 32½", octagon.
Weight: 8 lbs. **Length:** 50" over-all.
Stock: Walnut-stained hardwood.
Sights: Brass blade front, fixed iron rear.
Features: Hand engraved patch box, trigger guard and lock plate. Available in percussion or flintlock. From Ultra-Hi Products.
Price: **$150.00**

CENTURY "KENTUCKY" DELUXE RIFLES
Caliber: 45 (.453" bore).
Barrel: 36" octagon.
Weight: 6½ lbs. **Length:** 50" over-all.
Stock: Walnut finish.
Sights: Fixed.
Features: Brass nose cap, thimbles, buttplate and patch box. Case-hardened lock and hammer. Imported by Century Arms.
Price: Flintlock **$119.95**
Price: Percussion **$119.95**
Price: Matched pair (one of each) **$235.00**

PENNSYLVANIA LONG RIFLE
Caliber: 36 or 45.
Barrel: 39" octagonal.
Weight: 10½ lbs. **Length:** 55" over-all.
Stock: Full-length tiger striped maple, traditional Pennsylvania form.
Sights: Brass blade front, open notch rear.
Features: Solid brass engraved furniture (crescent buttplate, patch box, fore-end cap, etc.) From The Armoury.
Price: Flint or percussion form **$179.95**

CVA KENTUCKY RIFLE
Caliber: 45 (.451" bore).
Barrel: 34¼", rifled, octagon (⅞" flats).
Length: 50" over-all.
Stock: Dark polished walnut.
Sights: Brass Kentucky blade type front. dovetail open rear.
Features: Available in either flint or percussion. Nipple wrench included. Imported by CVA.
Price: Percussion **$104.95**
Price: Flint **$107.95**

DIXIE FLINT SWIVEL BREECH RIFLE
Caliber: 45.
Barrel: 32", octagon.
Weigth: 11½ lbs. **Length:** 48½" over-all.
Stock: Curly maple.
Sights: Fixed.
Features: Wood panelled barrels rotate for second shot. Single trigger. Brass furniture. From Dixie Gun Works.
Price: Flintlock **$450.00**
Price: Percussion **$325.00**

KENTUCKY FLINTLOCK RIFLE
Caliber: 44 or 45.
Barrel: 35".
Weight: 7 lbs. **Length:** 50" over-all.
Stock: Walnut stained, brass fittings.
Sights: Fixed.
Features: Available in Carbine model also, 28" bbl. Some variations in detail, finish. Kits also available from some importers. Imported by Navy/Replica, Centennial, The Armoury, Century, Dixie and Challenger, F.I.E., Hawes, Kassnar.
Price: .... **$59.95 to $165.00**

Kentucky Percussion Rifle
Similar to above except percussion lock. Finish and features vary with importer. Imported by Jana, Centennial, Navy/Replica, Firearms Import & Export, The Armoury, Century, Challenger, Dixie, Connecticut Valley, Valor, Hawes, Kassnar, Markwell Arms, EMF.
Price: .... **$54.95 to $229.95**
Price: Kit form .... **$68.95 to $77.78**

DIXIE STANDARD KENTUCKY RIFLE
Caliber: 45.
Barrel: 40", six land and grooves, 1 turn in 48".
Weight: 10 lbs. **Length:** 56½".
Stock: Chestnut colored maple.
Sights: Brass blade front, Kentucky-type rear.
Features: Trigger guard, buttplate, patchbox and thimbles are brass. Double set triggers available ($8.50 extra). Color case hardened lock. From Dixie Gun Works.
Price: Percussion **$260.00**
Price: Flintlock **$270.00**

DIXIE PENNSYLVANIA PERCUSSION RIFLE
Caliber: 45.
Barrel: 40", octagon.
Weight: 10 lbs. **Length:** 55".
Stock: Maple, Roman nose comb.
Sights: Fixed, Kentucky open-type.
Features: Brass patchbox, wide buttplate, color case hardened lock, blue barrel. From Dixie Gun Works.
Price: Flint **$290.00**
Price: Percussion **$282.50**
Price: Engraved model, flint or percussion (limited) **$299.95**

INTERARMS PENNSYLVANIA LONG RIFLE
Caliber: 45.
Barrel: 39".
Weight: 7¾ lbs. **Length:** 56" over-all.
Stock: Full cherrywood stock.
Sights: Blade front, drift-adj. rear.
Features: 8-groove, button rifled, octagon barrel. Stock furniture in bright brass. Made by Mowrey Gun Works, available from Interarms.
Price: **$475.00**

KENTUCKIAN RIFLE & CARBINE
Caliber: 44.
Barrel: 35" (Rifle), 27½" (Carbine).
Weight: 7 lbs. (Rifle), 5½ lbs. (Carbine). **Length:** 51" (Rifle) over-all, carbine 43".
Stock: Walnut stain.
Sights: Brass blade front, steel V-Ramp rear.
Features: Octagon bbl., case-hardened and engraved lock plate. Brass furniture. Imported by Dixie.
Price: Rifle (illus.) or carbine, flint or percussion ......**$135.00** to **$145.00**

CENTURY PERCUSSION MUSKET
Caliber: 69.
Barrel: 37", part octagon, part round.
Weight: 7½ lbs. **Length:** 54" over-all.
Stock: Walnut finish hardwood.
Sights: Bead front.
Features: Polished steel barrel, lock plate, hammer, barrel bands ramrod and trigger. From Century Arms.
Price: **$89.95**

DIXIE PERCUSSION MUSKET
Caliber: 66.
Barrel: 37", smoothbore.
Weight: 8 lbs. **Length:** 54" over-all.
Stock: Walnut-finish hardwood.
Sights: Fixed.
Features: Made from old original parts but with new Belgian-proofed barrels. Shoots shot or .650" ball. Also available as flintlock.
Price: Percussion **$93.00**
Price: Flintlock **$96.50**

CVA MOUNTAIN RIFLE
Caliber: 45 or 50.
Barrel: 32", octagon; 15/16" across flats.
Weight: 8 lbs. **Length:** 48" over-all.
Stock: Polished European walnut, oil finish.
Sights: German silver blade front, screw-adj. rear for e., dovetail.
Features: Engraved percussion lock with adj. sear engagement; hooked brooch with two barrel tenons; rifled 1 in 60"; double set triggers; German silver patch box, tenon plates, pewter-type nosecap; browned iron furniture.
Price: Either caliber **$159.95**
Price: Kit form **$109.95**

BLACK POWDER MUSKETS & RIFLES

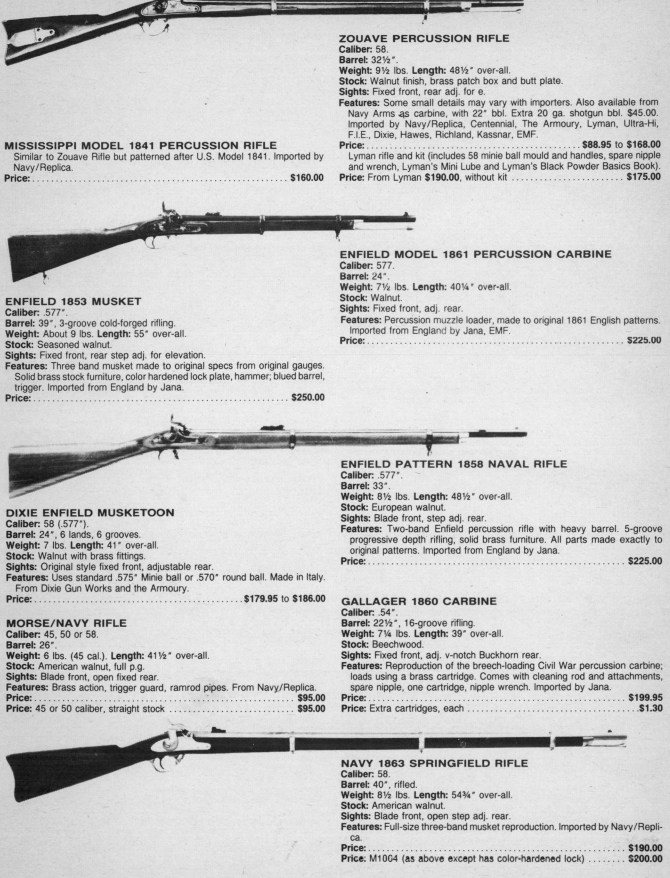

MISSISSIPPI MODEL 1841 PERCUSSION RIFLE
Similar to Zouave Rifle but patterned after U.S. Model 1841. Imported by Navy/Replica.
Price: **$160.00**

ZOUAVE PERCUSSION RIFLE
Caliber: 58.
Barrel: 32½".
Weight: 9½ lbs. **Length:** 48½" over-all.
Stock: Walnut finish, brass patch box and butt plate.
Sights: Fixed front, rear adj. for e.
Features: Some small details may vary with importers. Also available from Navy Arms as carbine, with 22" bbl. Extra 20 ga. shotgun bbl. $45.00. Imported by Navy/Replica, Centennial, The Armoury, Lyman, Ultra-Hi, F.I.E., Dixie, Hawes, Richland, Kassnar, EMF.
Price: .... **$88.95** to **$168.00**
Lyman rifle and kit (includes 58 minie ball mould and handles, spare nipple and wrench, Lyman's Mini Lube and Lyman's Black Powder Basics Book).
Price: From Lyman **$190.00**, without kit **$175.00**

ENFIELD 1853 MUSKET
Caliber: .577".
Barrel: 39", 3-groove cold-forged rifling.
Weight: About 9 lbs. **Length:** 55" over-all.
Stock: Seasoned walnut.
Sights: Fixed front, rear step adj. for elevation.
Features: Three band musket made to original specs from original gauges. Solid brass stock furniture, color hardened lock plate, hammer; blued barrel, trigger. Imported from England by Jana.
Price: **$250.00**

ENFIELD MODEL 1861 PERCUSSION CARBINE
Caliber: 577.
Barrel: 24".
Weight: 7½ lbs. **Length:** 40¼" over-all.
Stock: Walnut.
Sights: Fixed front, adj. rear.
Features: Percussion muzzle loader, made to original 1861 English patterns. Imported from England by Jana, EMF.
Price: **$225.00**

DIXIE ENFIELD MUSKETOON
Caliber: 58 (.577").
Barrel: 24", 6 lands, 6 grooves.
Weight: 7 lbs. **Length:** 41" over-all.
Stock: Walnut with brass fittings.
Sights: Original style fixed front, adjustable rear.
Features: Uses standard .575" Minie ball or .570" round ball. Made in Italy. From Dixie Gun Works and the Armoury.
Price: .... **$179.95** to **$186.00**

MORSE/NAVY RIFLE
Caliber: 45, 50 or 58.
Barrel: 26".
Weight: 6 lbs. (45 cal.). **Length:** 41½" over-all.
Stock: American walnut, full p.g.
Sights: Blade front, open fixed rear.
Features: Brass action, trigger guard, ramrod pipes. From Navy/Replica.
Price: **$95.00**
Price: 45 or 50 caliber, straight stock **$95.00**

ENFIELD PATTERN 1858 NAVAL RIFLE
Caliber: .577".
Barrel: 33".
Weight: 8½ lbs. **Length:** 48½" over-all.
Stock: European walnut.
Sights: Blade front, step adj. rear.
Features: Two-band Enfield percussion rifle with heavy barrel. 5-groove progressive depth rifling, solid brass furniture. All parts made exactly to original patterns. Imported from England by Jana.
Price: **$225.00**

GALLAGER 1860 CARBINE
Caliber: .54".
Barrel: 22½", 16-groove rifling.
Weight: 7¼ lbs. **Length:** 39" over-all.
Stock: Beechwood.
Sights: Fixed front, adj. v-notch Buckhorn rear.
Features: Reproduction of the breech-loading Civil War percussion carbine; loads using a brass cartridge. Comes with cleaning rod and attachments, spare nipple, one cartridge, nipple wrench. Imported by Jana.
Price: **$199.95**
Price: Extra cartridges, each **$1.30**

NAVY 1863 SPRINGFIELD RIFLE
Caliber: 58.
Barrel: 40", rifled.
Weight: 8½ lbs. **Length:** 54¾" over-all.
Stock: American walnut.
Sights: Blade front, open step adj. rear.
Features: Full-size three-band musket reproduction. Imported by Navy/Replica.
Price: **$190.00**
Price: M1004 (as above except has color-hardened lock) **$200.00**

BLACK POWDER MUSKETS & RIFLES

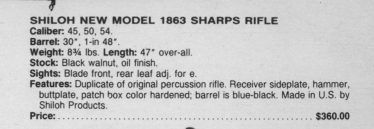

SHILOH NEW MODEL 1863 SHARPS RIFLE
Caliber: 45, 50, 54.
Barrel: 30", 1-in 48".
Weight: 8¾ lbs. **Length:** 47" over-all.
Stock: Black walnut, oil finish.
Sights: Blade front, rear leaf adj. for e.
Features: Duplicate of original percussion rifle. Receiver sideplate, hammer, buttplate, patch box color hardened; barrel is blue-black. Made in U.S. by Shiloh Products.
Price: **$360.00**

Shiloh New Model 1863 Sharps Carbine
Shortened, carbine version of the 1863 rifle. Has 22" barrel, black walnut stock without patch box, single barrel band. Weighs 7¾ lbs., over-all length is 39⅛". Made in U.S. by Shiloh Products.
Price: **$330.00**

ULTRA-HI HAWKEN RIFLE
Caliber: 50. (.503").
Barrel: 28", octagon with ¹⁵/₁₆" flats; hooked breech.
Weight: 8½ lbs. **Length:** 48" over-all.
Stock: Walnut stained cherrywood.
Sights: Blade front, read adj. for w. and e.
Features: Engraved lock plate. Coil mainspring. Brass furniture, single trigger. Available in percussion or flintlock. From Ultra-Hi Products.
Price: **$190.00**

HOPKINS & ALLEN HERITAGE RIFLE
Caliber: 36, 45, 50, 58.
Barrel: 32".
Weight: About 9½ lbs. **Length:** 49" over-all.
Stock: Walnut stock and fore-end.
Sights: Blade front, u-notch rear adj. for w. and e.
Features: Under-hammer action; all metal brightly polished. No patch box on 58-cal. gun. From Challenger Mfg. Co.
Price: Heritage models **$149.95**
Price: Forager models (45 or 50 cal., 25" bbl.) **$144.95**
Price: Buggy Deluxe (36 or 45 cal., 20" bbl.) **$139.95**

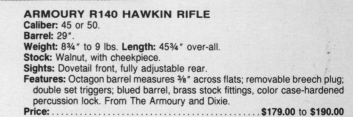

ARMOURY R140 HAWKIN RIFLE
Caliber: 45 or 50.
Barrel: 29".
Weight: 8¾" to 9 lbs. **Length:** 45¾" over-all.
Stock: Walnut, with cheekpiece.
Sights: Dovetail front, fully adjustable rear.
Features: Octagon barrel measures ⅜" across flats; removable breech plug; double set triggers; blued barrel, brass stock fittings, color case-hardened percussion lock. From The Armoury and Dixie.
Price: ....**$179.00 to $190.00**

Markwell Super Hawken
Similar to the Lyman Plains Rifle except in 50-cal. only, different lock and patch box. Available complete or as kit. From Markwell Arms.
Price: Complete **$149.95**
Price: Kit **$109.95**

MARKWELL HAWKEN RIFLE
Caliber: 45.
Barrel: 28".
Weight: 7 lbs. **Length:** 43½" over-all.
Stock: Dark polished walnut.
Sights: Blade front, open read adj. for w.
Features: Brass patchbox, trigger guard, buttplate and furniture; color case hardened lock, rest blued. From Markwell Arms.
Price: **$119.95**
Price: Kit form **$89.75**

MARKWELL SUPER KENTUCKY RIFLE
Caliber: 45.
Barrel: 33½", octagon.
Weight: 9 lbs. **Length:** 48" over-all.
Stock: Walnut-stained hardwood.
Sights: Blade front, u-notch rear.
Features: Hooked breech system; adj. double-set triggers; brass furniture and patch box. From Markwell Arms.
Price: **$141.95**
Price: Kit **$109.95**

HAWKEN HURRICANE
Caliber: 45 or 50.
Barrel: 28", octagon.
Weight: 6 lbs. **Length:** 44¾" over-all.
Stock: American walnut.
Sights: Blade front, open fixed rear.
Features: American made. Curved buttplate, brass stock furniture. From Navy/Replica.
Price: 45 or 50 cal. **$195.00**
Price: Hawken Hunter (58 cal.) **$195.00**
Price: Hawken kit **$125.00**

THOMPSON/CENTER HAWKEN RIFLE

Caliber: 45 or 50.
Barrel: 28" octagon, hooked breech.
Stock: American walnut.
Sights: Blade front, rear adj. for w. & e.
Features: Solid brass furniture, double set triggers, button rifled barrel, coil-type main spring. From Thompson/Center Arms.
Price: Percussion Model .. **$205.00**   Flintlock Model **$215.00**

THOMPSON/CENTER RENEGADE RIFLE

Caliber: 54.
Barrel: 26", 1" across the flats.
Weight: 8 lbs.
Stock: American walnut.
Sights: Open hunting (partridge) style, fully adjustable for w. and e.
Features: Coil spring lock, double set triggers, blued steel trim.
Price: **$165.00**
Price: With accessory pack (includes 20 maxi-balls, maxi-lube, adjustable powder measure, bullet starter, nipple and nipple wrench) **$177.35**

THOMPSON/CENTER SENECA RIFLE

Caliber: 36, 45.
Barrel: 27".
Weight: 6½ lbs.
Stock: American walnut.
Sights: Open hunting style, square notch rear fully adj. for w. and e.
Features: Coil spring lock, octagon bbl. measures $^{13}/_{16}$" across flats, brass stock furniture.
Price: Rifle **$205.00**
Price: Rifle with accessory kit (includes bullet mould, patches, powder measure, short starter, extra nipple & nipple wrench) **$232.50**

H & R SPRINGFIELD STALKER

Caliber: 45 or 58.
Barrel: 28" round.
Weight: 8 lbs. (45 cal.), 7½ lbs. (58 cal.). **Length:** 43" over-all.
Stock: American walnut.
Sights: Blade front, rear open adj. for w. and e.
Features: Action similar to Civil War Springfield. Supplied with solid brass ramrod with hardwood handle and nipple wrench. Blue-black finish.
Price: **$185.00**

H & R DELUXE SPRINGFIELD STALKER

Same as standard model except has hand checkered p.g. and fore-end, better wood, hand polished American walnut stock **$265.00**

LYMAN PLAINS RIFLE

Caliber: 45 or 50.
Barrel: 28", 1-48" twist.
Weight: 8¾ lbs. **Length:** 45" over-all.
Stock: European walnut.
Sights: Blade front, fully adj. rear.
Features: Double set trigger, hooked breech system, brass stock furniture, patch box. Imported from Italy by Lyman.
Price: Rifle only **$225.00**
Price: Rifle and kit (includes single cavity .440" dia. round ball mould, handles, nipple wrench, ball starter, Lyman's patch lube, patches and Lyman's "Black Powder Basics" book **$240.00**
Price: Lyman Accessory Shooting Kit **$30.00**

DIXIE PLAINSMAN RIFLE

Caliber: 45 or 50.
Barrel: 32", octagon.
Weight: 8 lbs. **Length:** 47½".
Stock: Cherry wood.
Sights: Brass blade front, buckhorn rear.
Features: Bolster-type breech plug with blow-out screw, brass stock furniture.
Price: 45 or 50 caliber **$175.00**

BUFFALO HUNTER PERCUSSION RIFLE

Caliber: 58.
Barrel: 25½".
Weight: 8 lbs. **Length:** 41½" over-all.
Stock: Walnut finished, hand checkered, brass furniture.
Sights: Fixed.
Features: Designed for primitive weapons hunting. 20 ga. shotgun bbl. also available **$45.00**. Imported by Navy/Replica.
Price: **$160.00**

DICKSON BUFFALO HUNTER RIFLE/SHOTGUN

Similar to standard Buffalo Hunter except: over-all length 42", no checkering, 26" bbl. 58 caliber, imported by American Import.
Price: **$165.50**

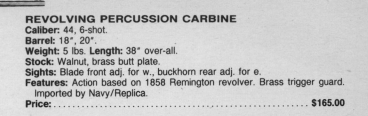

REVOLVING PERCUSSION CARBINE
Caliber: 44, 6-shot.
Barrel: 18″, 20″.
Weight: 5 lbs. **Length:** 38″ over-all.
Stock: Walnut, brass butt plate.
Sights: Blade front adj. for w., buckhorn rear adj. for e.
Features: Action based on 1858 Remington revolver. Brass trigger guard. Imported by Navy/Replica.
Price: **$165.00**

YORKSHIRE RIFLE
Caliber: 45.
Barrel: 36″, rifled, 7⁄8″ octagon.
Weight: 7½ lbs. **Length:** 51¾″ over-all.
Stock: Select maple.
Sights: Blade front, open U-notch rear.
Features: Adj. double set triggers. Brass front and rear sights, trigger guard, patch box, buttplate and fore-end. Case hardened lock plate. From Dixie and Richland.
Price: Percussion . . . .**$144.00** to **$150.00**
Price: Flintlock . . . .**$153.00** to **$159.95**

RICHLAND MICHIGAN CARBINE
Caliber: 45.
Barrel: 26″ octagon, 7⁄8″ flats.
Weight: 5¾ lbs. **Length:** 41⅜″ over-all.
Stock: Hand finished maple.
Sights: Blade front, open fixed rear drift adj. for w.
Features: Color case hardened lock plate; brass patch box, buttplate, trigger guard, fore-end tip and sights; adjustable double set triggers. From Richland Arms.
Price: Percussion **$158.00**
Price: Flintlock **$167.00**
Price: Kit form **$112.00**

INTERARMS ALLEN & THURBER REPLICA
Caliber: 45, 50, 54 or 58.
Barrel: 32″, 8-groove rifling, octagon.
Weight: 10¼ lbs. **Length:** 48″ over-all.
Stock: Walnut with curved brass butt plate.
Sights: Open, adj. for w. & e.
Features: Polished brass furniture, brass fore-end, ramrod. Made by Mowrey, available from Interarms.
Price: Complete **$243.00**

INTERARMS A. & T. BICENTENNIAL
Caliber: 50.
Barrel: 32″.
Weight: 10¼ lbs. **Length:** 48″ over-all.
Stock: Cherrywood stock inlayed with Liberty Bell medallion.
Sights: Blade front, open rear adj. for w. and e.
Features: Nickel-chrome buttplate, fore-end, action housing and trigger guard; gold plated trigger. Stock medallion is struck from minthouse coin dies. Two models—"1 of 100" and "1 of 500". Made by Mowrey Gun Works, available from Interarms.
Price: One of 100 . . . . **$285.00**
Price: One of 500 . . . . **$261.00**

INTERARMS GEORGIA TREE GUN
Caliber: 45, 50, 54, 58.
Barrel: 22″.
Weight: 7¼ lbs. **Length:** 38″ over-all.
Stock: Walnut.
Sights: Blade front, step adj. rear.
Features: Shortened version of Allen & Thurber Special rifle especially suited for tree stand shooting. Made by Mowrey, available from Interarms.
Price: Complete gun **$251.00**

INTERARMS HAWK
Caliber: 45, 50 54 or 58.
Barrel: 32″.
Weight: 9½ lbs. **Length:** 49″ over-all.
Stock: Walnut, sporter-type with cheek-piece, walnut fore-end.
Sights: Open, fully adj. for w. and e.
Features: Hawkins-type buttplate and action housing of brass. Adj. trigger. Made by Mowrey, available from Interarms.
Price: Complete **$268.00**

INTERARMS ALLEN & THURBER SPECIAL
Caliber: 45, 50, 54 or 58.
Barrel: 32" octagonal.
Weight: 10 lbs. **Length:** 48" over-all.
Stock: Walnut with curved brass buttplate, walnut fore-end.
Sights: Open, fully adj.
Features: Same design as A&T Replica except has walnut fore-end. Polished brass furniture. Made by Mowrey, available from Interarms.
Price: Complete **$251.00**

"TEXAS CARBINE" Model 1 of 1000
Caliber: 58, takes .575" mini-ball or round ball.
Barrel: 24" octagon, 4-groove.
Weight: 8 lbs. **Length:** 39" over-all.
Stock: Walnut stock and fore-end, brass fore-end cap.
Sights: Adjustable front and rear.
Features: "1 of 100" inscribed on first 100, "1 of 1000" on remaining 1000. Saddle ring with leather thong and Texas seal imbedded in stock. Distributed by Trail Guns Armory.
Price: **$250.00**

FRAZIER MATCHMATE PERCUSSION RIFLES
Caliber: 32, 36, 40, 45, 50 or 54.
Barrel: 26" to 38". Douglas Premium M/L. Octagon. Choice of diam.—$^{13}/_{16}$", $^7/_8$", $^{15}/_{16}$", 1" or 1$^1/_8$".
Weight: 8 lbs. and up. Varies with size and wood. **Length:** 52½" over-all (32" bbl.).
Stock: Laminated of 5 layers of imported exotic high figure hardwoods. Thumbhole p.g., cheekpiece in line with bore. Satin finish. Adj. hooked buttplate.
Sights: Globe front on detachable base (insert set included), Redfield #75 micro peep rear.
Features: A unique rifle designed for competition shooting. Underhammer action with Anschutz-Mauser set triggers. Comes with set of 8 weights to control balance, Lyman mould, short starter and rod. Adj. coil mainspring; stainless steel flashguard around nipple. Action housed in breech but removes easily for cleaning. Write for full specifics. From Clark K. Frazier.
Price: Standard Offhand Rifle, from **$600.00**
Price: Custom Offhand Rifle, from **$700.00**
Price: "National Unlimited" bench rest rifle (illus.), from **$700.00**

TINGLE M1962 MUZZLE LOADING RIFLE
Caliber: 36, 44 or 50.
Barrel: 32" octagon, hook breech, 52" twist.
Weight: 10 lbs. **Length:** 48" over-all.
Stock: One-piece walnut with concave cheekpiece.
Sights: Blade front, step adj. V notch rear.
Features: Solid brass furniture, double-set trigger with adj. pull, percussion lock.
Price: **$159.95**

KODIAK DOUBLE RIFLE
Caliber: 58 (std.), 50 cal. and 50-cal./12 ga. optional.
Barrel: 28", 5 grooves, 1-in-48" twist.
Weight: 9½ lbs. **Length:** 43¼" over-all.
Stock: Czechoslovakian walnut, hand checkered.
Sights: Three leaf folding rear, adjustable gold bead front.
Features: Hooked breech allows interchangeability of barrels, matted raised rib. Comes with sling and swivels. Engraved lock plates, top tang and trigger guard. Locks and top tang polished, rest browned. From Trail Guns Armory, Inc.
Price: 58 cal. SxS **$385.00**
Price: 50 cal. SxS **$385.00**
Price: 50 cal. x 12 ga. **$360.00**
Price: Spare barrels, 58 cal. SxS, 50 cal. SxS **$200.00**
Price: Spare barrels, 50 cal. x 12 ga. **$175.00**

H & R HUNTSMAN PERCUSSION RIFLE
Caliber: 45, 58, 12 gauge, single shot.
Barrel: 28", 30", 32" (58 cal.).
Weight: 6¼ lbs. (12 ga.), 7¼ lbs. (58 cal.), 8 lbs. (45 cal.). **Length:** 43".
Stock: Walnut finished hardwood.
Sights: Open, rear adj. for w. and e., blade front.
Features: Action similar to Model 158 Topper. Enclosed nipple (#11 size). Supplied with rifle are brass ramrod with wood handle and nipple wrench. Blue-black finish with color case hardened frame. From Harrington & Richardson.
Price: 12 ga. **$79.50**
Price: 45 and 58 cals. **$88.50**
Price: 58 cal. 32" bbl. **$97.50**

CENTURY "KENTUCKY" TYPE SHOTGUN

Gauge: 24.
Barrel: 29" (Cyl.).
Weight: 4¼ lbs. **Length:** 44" over-all.
Stock: European walnut, checkered at wrist.
Sights: Bead front only.
Features: English style stock, inletted patch box; percussion or flintlock; steel ramrod. From Century Arms.
Price: Percussion, full stock $34.95
Price: Flintlock, full stock $37.95
Price: Percussion, sporter $32.95
Price: Flintlock, sporter $36.95

DOUBLE BARREL PERCUSSION SHOTGUN

Gauge: 12.
Barrel: 30" (I.C.& Mod.).
Weight: 6¼ lbs. **Length:** 45" over-all.
Stock: Hand checkered walnut, 14" pull.
Features: Double triggers, light hand engraving. Details vary with importer. Imported by Navy/Replica, The Armoury, Dixie, EMF.
Price: . . . . $125.00 to $175.00
Price: Model 100 Mag. (Navy) $225.00

CENTURY DOUBLE BARREL SHOTGUN

Gauge: 20.
Barrel: 28" (Cyl. & Cyl.).
Weight: 5¾ lbs. **Length:** 43½" over-all.
Stock: One piece, walnut finish hardwood; checkered at wrist.
Sights: Bead.
Features: Inletted brass patch box; back lock action; blued barrels, lock and trigger guard; wooden ramrod; matted raised rib. From Century Arms.
Price: $59.95

CENTURY SINGLE BARREL PERCUSSION SHOTGUN

Gauge: 28.
Barrel: 31" (Cyl.), part octagon.
Weight: 4¼ lbs. **Length:** 48½" over-all.
Stock: Walnut finish hardwood; checkered at small of butt.
Sights: Bead front only.
Features: Suitable for ball or shot; blue barrel; lock, buttplate, trigger guard, breech and patch box are case hardened; steel ramrod. From Century Arms.
Price: $44.95

DIXIE FLINT FOWLING PIECE

Gauge: 14 ga.
Barrel: 37".
Weight: 5½ lbs. **Length:** 52½" over-all.
Stock: Walnut stained birch.
Sights: Fixed.
Features: Uses basic Harpers Ferry Pistol flintlock lock. Sling swivels. Bright-finished metal. From Dixie Gun Works.
Price: $96.50

INTERARMS A. & T. 12 GAUGE SHOTGUN

Gauge: 12 ga. only.
Barrel: 32", octagon.
Weight: 7½ lbs. **Length:** 48" over-all.
Stock: Maple, oil finish, brass furniture.
Sights: Bead front.
Features: Available in percussion only. Uses standard 12 ga. wadding. Made by Mowrey.
Price: Complete $229.00

MORSE/NAVY SINGLE BARREL SHOTGUN

Gauge: 12 ga.
Barrel: 26".
Weight: 5 lbs. **Length:** 41½" over-all.
Stock: American walnut, full p.g.
Sights: Front bead.
Features: Brass receiver, black buttplate. From Navy/Replica.

SINGLE BARREL PERCUSSION SHOTGUN

Gauge: 12, 20, 28.
Barrel: 28".
Weight: 4½ lbs. **Length:** 43" over-all.
Stock: Walnut finish, choice of half or full stock.
Features: Finish and features vary with importer. Imported by The Armoury, Dixie.
Price: . . . . $32.95 to $59.95

SINGLE BARREL FLINTLOCK SHOTGUN

Gauge: 28.
Barrel: 28".
Weight: 4½ lbs. **Length:** 43" over-all.
Stock: Walnut finish, choice of half or full stock. Imported by The Armoury.
Price: $37.95

TINGLE PERCUSSION SINGLE BARREL SHOTGUN

Gauge: 12 only.
Barrel: 30" cylinder bore.
Weight: 5 lbs.
Stock: Lacquered walnut.
Features: Mule ear side hammer lock, iron trigger guard, rubber recoil pad.
Price: Blued $114.95

A BASIC GLOSSARY FOR BLACKPOWDER GUNNERS

If Some Of The Terms Sound Confusing, Here Are Some Helpful Definitions!

ACID ETCHING: *A process of marking gun barrels that was common to the early 1800s. The metal surface first was coated with wax; the initials or name then was scribed through the thin layer of wax, until the metal that would bear the markings was exposed. A minute amount of acid then was applied to the etched lines and this would discolor the exposed metal. The process was not permanent and was abandoned for the most part in the search for a better way to mark gun barrels.*

AMPCO NIPPLE: *A modern design percussion nipple made of Beryllium, an alloy that resembles brass but is much harder and more resistant to erosion of the flashhole. AMPCO nipples feature an extremely small flashhole at the bottom; this results in a hotter flame, as the fire concentrates to pass through the tiny opening. The hotter ignition flame, in turn, ignites the powder more readily in the breech, giving a more spontaneous shot than with ordinary nipple designs.*

APERTURE SIGHT: *Often referred to as a peep sight, because it requires the shooters to visually center the front sight in the center of a small round hole in the rear sight while aiming. This arrangement makes it one of the most accurate metallic sights.*

APPLEWOOD: *Occasionally used in the making of gunstocks. The fine grain of this wood resists warpage and a rifle so stocked maintains its zero. Applewood is one of the easiest to work with, rounding and shaping nicely; also, inlays are installed easily in a stock made of this wood.*

ARQUEBUS: *An early term for matchlock shoulder guns. The term originated from the German word of Hakenbuchse, meaning hook gun. The French equivalent to hook, or Haken, is arque. The German Buchse, or gun, became a suffix to be tacked onto the end of the French word and, by the turn of the 16th Century, all such guns were know as arquebuses.*

BACK ACTION LOCK: *A later type of percussion lock. A true side-lock, this type of lock features a mainspring that is to the rear of the tumbler and hammer.*

BALL: *Spherical lead projectile used most commonly in the majority of the muzzleloading rifles and nearly all black powder pistols and cap and ball revolvers. In many cases a certain size of buckshot works well in such guns of a caliber of the same size; the shot then becomes a ball, being loaded one at a time.*

BALL SCREW: *Resembling a wood screw, this attachment threads into the end of the ramrod and is used for removing the ball from an unfired loaded round. The threaded point of the ball screw digs into the soft lead of the ball and grips it firmly enough so that it can be pulled from its seating and through the length of the barrel.*

BALTIC LOCK: *Crude and early version of the flintlock. Guns fitted with this type of lock appeared around 1600. Design soon was replaced with advanced versions of the flintlock.*

BAYONET: *A metal knife-like blade — occasionally doubling as a knife — made to be attached to the muzzle of a shoulder arm and used in hand-to-hand combat.*

BAND SPRING: *The spring attached to barrel bands on a musket to hold them securely in place. To remove these bands, the band springs are depressed and the bands slip off.*

BAR ACTION: *The more common of the side locks; the mainspring of this lock is in front of the tumbler and hammer.*

BARREL: *The round, octagonal, et al., metal tube through and from which the ball, bullet or buckshot emerges upon being fired.*

BARREL KEY: *The wedge-shaped flat key that holds the barrel assembly to the forestock on many half-stock rifles and shotguns.*

BARREL PIN: *On most early full-stock rifles these were used to fasten the barrel to the long fore-stock.*

BELTED ROUND BALL: *A special design lead ball that was purposely cast with a raised belt of lead around its circumference. Belted round balls were mechanically started into the muzzles of deep two groove rifled bores found on many of the British rifles. The belted ring acted as a gas seal, at the same time being guided through the length of the barrel by the rifling groove on the bullet caused by the mechanical starter. The result was a bullet that was somewhat faster and more accurate than the standard patched ball.*

BENCH RIFLE: *A heavy muzzleloading target rifle especially designed and built for firing from a benchrest with the shooter seated.*

BLACK POWDER: *A mixture of potassium nitrate, charcoal and sulphur. Combined, these ingredients form the standard propellant for muzzleloading guns.*

BLUNDERBUSS: Arms of this type were used most commonly aboard ships to repel boarders during Naval conflicts. The blunderbuss featured a flared muzzle that probably was just as frightening to anyone unfortunate enough to view it from that angle as it was deadly. Although it is doubtful that such a flared muzzle did actually spread the shot any considerable amount over a gun with just a straight cylinder choke, it was nonetheless a deadly close range gun.

BOOT: A water resistant leather cover that fits over the flash pan of a flintlock rifle. The shield sheds rain and helps keep the priming powder in the pan dry during inclement weather.

BORE: The drilling or hole through which the bullet or load of shot travels the length of the barrel.

BORE BUILD-UP: Continuous firing of a black powder rifle, pistol or shotgun will result in a build-up of powder foulings in the barrel. For regular target practice, lining of sights or just plinking, this is cleaned out usually after a dozen or so shots with a few swipes with solvents and a jag threaded into the ramrod. Serious competitors, however, often wipe the barrels of their guns after every shot.

BOX LOCK: The hammer on this type of lock is fastened on the inside and projects above it.

BREECH: The rear end of a muzzleloader's barrel; the area immediately in front of the loaded round.

BREECH PLUG: The threaded plug that is screwed into the breech end of a muzzleloader's barrel. This forms a gas tight seal and is actually the rear or bottom of the chamber; the barrel tang usually is attached to the breech plug.

BREECH (CHAMBER) PRESSURE: As the loaded charge of powder is ignited and rapidly burns it results in trapped pressures as this pushes the projectile up the barrel. The pressure caused by these gases is known as the breech pressure and is measured in pounds per square inch — psi.

BROWN BESS: Smoothbore flintlock musket used by the British forces during the Revolutionary War. The long barrel and approximately .75 caliber made it fairly accurate and a hard-hitting military arm.

BROWNING: Predating bluing, browning is the result of an oxidation process. It is probably the result of some long ago gun owner unknowingly storing his gun in a damp or extremely humid spot and not remembering where it was until the bright metal had turned brownish red from rust. If treated properly, browning results in a beautiful barrel finish.

BUCKSHOT: Large spherical shot commonly used for big game hunting, combat and riot control. Shot ranging in sizes from .240 to .380 is occasionally used for loading muzzleloading rifles and pistols.

BUGGY RIFLE: Sometimes appearing in the form of a long barreled single shot pistol; many short barreled, lightweight rifles were commonly carried for protection, hunting small game and target shooting during the second half of the 1800s. These were known as buggy rifles and were usually of around .36 caliber, though there were many sawn off military rifled muskets of around .58 caliber used for this purpose also.

BULLET: It is a common practice to refer to an entire cartridge as the bullet. Actually the bullet is just the lead projectile that is fired from the assembled cartridge.

BULLET MOULD: Usually made from a soft iron, bullet moulds are nothing more than two pieces of metal that have hollow cavities into which molten lead is poured; when sufficiently cooled and the lead hardened, a bullet is formed.

BUTT PLATE: The plate that is fitted to the rear of the butt stock and fits into the shoulder as the gun is being fired. These can be made of metal, bone, horn, plastic or just about anything that suits the gun owner's fancy.

CALIBER: Diameter of the bore of a firearm, most commonly expressed in thousandths of an inch, although some are in millimeters.

CANNELURE: A shallow groove that encircles the circumference of a conical bullet. This serves as a grease groove and affords both the bore and the bullet some lubrication.

CAP BOX: Usually appearing as a hinged compartment on the butt stock of a rifle or shotgun, the cap box is exactly as the name suggests: a place to carry caps. It may, however, be located in places other than the butt stock and in some pistols is in the butt of the grip. The term also was used to describe a small leather belt pouch used during the Civil War for carrying musket caps.

CAPLOCK: A term often used to describe a percussion lock.

CARBINE: A shortened rifle; although usually not as accurate as rifles with longer barrels, the carbine is easier to manuever when hunting or shooting in brushy areas.

CAST-ON: Shaping of a gunstock that aligns the barrel of a gun to the left of what is considered normal alignment. This aids in sighting and shooting for the southpaw. When the alignment is in the other direction — to the right — for aiding a right handed shooter, it is termed, "cast-off."

CHAMBER: Although not commonly found in muzzleloaders in the true sense, a chamber is the unrifled portion of a barrel that holds the loaded round.

CHARGER: A term used to describe anything — flask, horn, dipper, et al. — that measures out one exact charge of powder.

CHERRY: A steel burr that has cutting edges running its vertical circumference or length, of an exact size. These are used to cut the cavities of bullet moulds. An old practice was to clamp a cherry between two pieces of soft iron or any other suitable metal in a vise. The elongated shank connected to the cherry was turned in the direction of the cutting edges until they had cut away enough metal for the cherry to turn freely. The vise then was tightened further and the process repeated until a cavity the exact proportion of the cherry had been formed.

CHOKE: The varying constrictions of shotgun barrels that determine the type of pattern the gun will throw. The tighter the constriction, usually the tighter the pattern. Some muzzleloading rifles also feature a slight choking at or near the muzzle that improves the gun's accuracy.

COACH PISTOL: An inaccurate pistol of the 1700s that was carried for protection while traveling. These were nearly always smoothbores — accounting for the lack of accuracy — and small enough to be concealed easily.

COCK: A term once used to describe the hammer of the early locks, today it is used to describe the action of drawing back the hammer.

COMB: The raised line of the butt stock that runs to the rear of the

wrist: the area of the stock that the cheek comes into contact with when a rifle or shotgun is being aimed and fired.

COMBUSTIBLE CARTRIDGE: Muzzleloading cartridge that contains the powder and projectile rolled in a paper casing. This paper is nitrated and the entire unit is loaded into the gun, the paper being completely combustible.

CONE: An early term for a percussion nipple.

CORNED POWDER: An early attempt to form black powder into grains, powder of this type was crude and grain sizes were inconsistent.

CORROSION: The worst enemy of muzzleloading guns; the deterioration of metal parts through chemical reaction or oxidation.

CULOT: An expanding wedge made of iron that was originally used in the hollow base of the Minie bullet. This wedge was abandoned by American shooters.

CURLY MAPLE: Early gunsmiths favored this wood for stocking Kentucky and Pennsylvania rifles. The best wood comes from trees that have grown to maturity in hard and rocky soil; this results in a fine grained dense wood. The popularity of this wood is still seen in today's black powder rifles.

C-SHAPED SERPENTINE: An early matchlock, as the term implies, a lock of this type was fitted with a C-shaped cock, which ignited the primed flash pan by being struck rearward mechanically.

CYLINDER: The revolving multi-chambers of a percussion revolver; these commonly had six chambers, but those with five are not uncommon.

CYLINDER BORE: The unrestricted bore of a shotgun, having no choking at all; improved cylinder barrels have been choked slightly to improve patterns.

DAMASCUS BARRELS: Early barrels formed by welding together strips of various steels. These were wrapped and hammer forged around a mandrel that was the same diameter as the intended finished bore — in the case of smoothbore or shotgun barrels — or on the smaller side if the finished barrels were to be rifled.

DAG: An early English term used to describe any massive, heavy and powerful pistol. Its origin is unknown.

DETENT: A fly added to the tumbler when a set trigger is installed. This cams the sear nose to some extent during firing by missing the half-cock notch.

DERRINGER: A short barreled pocket pistol of a general type and not particularly a gun made by Henry Deringer. The word, however, is now used to describe the type of small handgun; born through public recognition of a Deringer-built pistol used in the assassination of President Lincoln; the second 'r' was added to differentiate the two.

DISC PRIMER: During the transitional period appeared a Sharps rifle that self-primed itself for each shot. The rifle's hammer action caused a tiny magazine to place a disc-like primer over the nipple for each shot.

DOG LOCK: The manually operated hammer catch on many early snaphaunce and crude flintlocks.

DOGHEAD: The spring loaded arm found on wheellocks to hold the pyrite against the rotating wheel.

DOUBLE ACTION: The process of cocking the hammer, rotating the cylinder and firing the round with one single movement of the trigger to the rear; a double action revolver also can be cocked and fired manually single action.

DOUBLE-NECK HAMMER: Reinforced hammers found on many later flintlock rifles, especially on military rifles that were built for hard use.

DOUBLE RIFLE: A popular side-by-side rifle that was used mainly for big game hunting in Africa and India.

DRIVELL: An early term for a ramrod.

DUELLING PISTOL: Usually a single-shot percussion or flintlock pistol of superb quality — Manton, Purdey, etc. Aristocrats, being as they were, often found it necessary to defend one's honor by placing a well aimed bullet into their oponent. Unfortunately the procedure was outlawed!

ESCUTCHEON: The metal inlay through which the barrel key is inserted. This is reinforced for obvious reasons.

FALSE MUZZLE: Used to improve accuracy by preventing possible damage to the bullet, this device is placed on the muzzle of the finer target rifles as the bullet is started into the muzzle; this helps prevent possible damage to the crown of the muzzle also.

FENCE: Also known as the flash guard, this small projection located on the rear of a flintlock's flash pan diverts the flash of the igniting priming powder from the shooter's eyes; today's flintlock fancier would be wise to wear a pair of good shooting glasses in case the sparks and flame happen to by-pass the diversion.

FINIAL: The decorative ending lines of an inlayed patch box, trigger guard strap or most any other pieces of furniture; these ornate touches are usually what make truely one-of-a-kind guns.

FLASH: As the hammer on a flintlock strikes the hardened frizzen it results in a minute portion of molten metal falling into the priming powder located in the flash pan. This ignites the powder and the result is an audible and visible flash that can cause the shooter to flinch.

FLASH PAN: Rifles and pistols that rely on the sparking of flint against steel for ignition have a small pan located below the frizzen or striking arm. A fine granulation of black powder — FFFFg — is placed in the pan; this serves as a primer for the main charge that is located in the chamber which is ignited by the flame that shoots down the flashhole leading from the flash pan.

FLINTLOCK: The principal arm used during the late Seventeenth and Eighteenth Centuries; the first appeared in France around the end of the first quarter of the Seventeenth Century. It was the principal lock until the introduction of the percussion lock.

FORESIGHT: English term meaning front sight.

FORE-STOCK: Also known as the forearm and forend, the wooden area of a one piece stock or the wooden section of a two piece stock that lies under the barrel.

FORSYTH LOCK: The first successful percussion lock, designed and built by Reverend Alexander Forsyth, an amateur chemist from Scotland. Forsyth obtained a patent for his invention in April, 1807, and the following year went into the commercial production of this lock — this actual manufacturing being supervised by his assistant, James Purdey.

FOWLING PIECE: *This was an early term used to describe a gun that was intended for use with a load of shot instead of a single solid projectile. With the exception of the type of shot used, these were loaded practically the same as today's reproduction muzzleloading shotguns. Early shot had been small cubes chopped from a strip of lead, not the well formed spherical shape known today.*

FRENCH LOCK: *The earliest successful flintlock; this type of lock first appeared around Paris sometime about the end of the first quarter of the Seventeenth Century.*

FRIZZEN: *The hardened steel surface which the flint strikes to ignite the primed flashpan of a flintlock. Occasionally this may be referred to as the pan cover, steel, battery or by a similar term.*

FRIZZEN SPRING: *An external spring that controls the position of the frizzen, sometimes applying pressure on the frizzen to make better contact with the flint when the trigger is pulled.*

FULMINATE OF MERCURY: *An explosive priming charge used in the making of percussion caps. The discovery of fulminate of mercury — announced on March 13, 1800 — led to the invention of the percussion cap around 1820. Other detonating agents, such as fulminate of gold and silver, had been around since the 1600s, but had no practical use.*

FURNITURE: *The metal trim found on muzzleloaders, usually made of brass or German silver; this trim is usually decorative and adds to the overall appearance of the gun.*

FUSIL: *A late 1600 military flintlock; this gun resembled a kind of French woodcock gun and is the reason why the English cavaliers referred to them as fusils or fusees — a French term meaning any non-military sporting gun.*

GAIN TWIST: *Rifling of a bore that increases in the number of turns as it progresses toward the muzzle.*

GAUGE: *The size of a shotgun bore. This is determined by the number of spherical lead balls of the bore's diameter it takes to weigh exactly one pound. For example; a 20-gauge cylinder bore would weigh out twenty lead balls to the pound; the same with 16 gauge and 12 gauge, the number of lead balls to the pound equalling the bore size. This term also is used to describe various types of measuring devices.*

GERMAN RING TARGET: *A popular match ring target of the mid to late 1800s. This type of paper target was used extensively during the formal shooting matches of the Schuetzen era of the 1880s.*

GERMAN SILVER: *Another name used to describe nickel silver. An alloy of copper, zinc and nickel, its silver white appearance makes it ideal for furniture on muzzleloaders.*

GLOBE SIGHT: *A fine front sight blade with an extremely small bead. This delicate sight is almost always shaded in a cylindrical tube.*

GOOSE-NECK HAMMER: *The type of hammer found on many beautiful early flint and percussion sporting arms. Unlike the thick and heavy hammers found on military arms, these hammers were slender in proportion and graceful in design.*

GROOVES: *The spiral channels cut in the rifling of a bore, the raised portions are known as the lands or flats. The lands and grooves of a rifle's bore make the bullet rotate during flight and are instrumental in a gun's accuracy.*

GROUP: *The consistent placement of bullets into any distinguishable area on the target, not necessarily the point of aim. These are desirably in close proximity of one another and hopefully measure in diameter under that magic minute of angle mark. If the shots are placed tightly in one area, the sights can be adjusted to place them at the point of aim.*

GUNFLINT: *High quality flint shaped with a forward chisel edge, used for firing a flintlock.*

HAIR TRIGGER: *The extremely light trigger pull of the front trigger on a set trigger mechanism. These usually are adjustable and many can be adjusted to the point that they will release at the slightest amount of pressure.*

HALF-COCK: *A safety position of the hammer on rifles and pistols; the half-cock position of revolvers allow the cylinder to be freely rotated for easier loading.*

HALF-STOCK RIFLE: *A term occasionally used to depict the mountain and plains rifles used by early westward traveling settlers or adventurers. These were built to withstand rugged use and the graceful lines of the Pennsylvania and Kentucky long rifles weren't usually found on these guns; this was also the gun of the famed mountain man.*

HAMMER: *The arm that strikes the detonating device on percussion and cartridge guns or the arm that contains the flint on flintlock guns. This part was known as the cock on earlier wheellock guns.*

HAMMER SPUR: *The contoured protrusion found on the hammer of cartridge and percussion guns; on flintlocks, this appeared in the form of a part of the jaw that held the flint.*

HAND: *The part of a revolver's working mechanism that protrudes through the rear inside of the frame and turns the cylinder as the hammer is cocked or the trigger pulled on double action revolvers.*

HAND CANNON: *The earliest form of a small arm; first used during the mid-1400s, although its origin is unknown and the exact date it was first introduced remains a mystery to historians. Nearly every force in Europe was using one form or another of this type of armament by the turn of the Sixteenth Century. Resembling a metal tube, the cannoneer ignited the loaded round by placing a touch to the exposed flashhole, which was extremely hard on the finger tips!*

HANDGUN: *Originally this term was used to describe all guns that were held by hand, later to depict only pistols and revolvers.*

HANG-FIRE: *A dangerous situation, a hang-fire actually is what appears to be a misfire but discharges after a short delay. Perhaps more common with flintlocks than percussion locks, it's good practice to keep the muzzle pointed downrange should an apparent misfire occur. Never place your face near the muzzle in case of such a situation, the delayed ignition could cause serious injury to you or anyone else unlucky enough to be in front of the muzzle.*

HEEL: *The rear top corner of the buttstock, the portion of the stock that is in conjunction with the top of the butt plate.*

HORSE PISTOL: *An early pistol used by horsemen; the large and chiefly military pistol was most often carried in a pommel holster.*

IGNITION: *The method used to fire the main charge in the breech; a number of different means have been used or tried in the past, among which are the slow match, wheellock pyrites, flintlock, percussion cap.*

INCISE: *To cut the surface of a stock to a certain depth in preparation to relief carving, inlaying, et al.*

INLAYS: The decorative touches added to the stock of many rifles, these may either be of different woods, metal, ivory or just about anything the stock makers chooses to use. These are finished flush with the surface of the stock; such inlays are the little extras that make a gun one-of-a-kind.

INLETTING: The precise removal of wood from the stock in preparation for the fitting of a lock, barrel or other parts that come into contact with the wood's surface and demand some removal.

JAG: An accessory that fits into the end of the ramrod to aid in cleaning the barrel; this is usually in the form of a buttonlike device that has serrated edges to grip the cleaning patch.

KENTUCKY RIFLE: A term mistakenly used in reference to the numerous long rifles, many of which were manufactured in other armsmaking states, such as Pennsylvania or North Carolina. Such rifles are traditionally long flintlocks that saw much use in the settling of what is now the state of Kentucky, in which armsmaking never reached the level as that found in several other states.

KNAPPER: A professional craftsman who chips out gunflints. This work is nearly all done with the aid of handtools, with perhaps the only mechanized help occuring during the mining of the flint. Today the only remaining professional knappers operate in the village of Brandon, England.

LAP: The process of smoothing out rough areas of a bore. This is most commonly done with the use of a lead bit or mandrel and various abrasive materials, such as diamond paste.

LINEN: This cloth material, woven from flax fibers, is one of the best patching materials.

LOADING BLOCK: A wooden block that has been drilled with holes for carrying pre-patched balls. To use, the hole in the block is aligned with the muzzle and with the use of a short starter the ball is seated into the muzzle. When carried hunting, a loading block saves a lot of time when loading succeeding shots and makes packing the round balls less tedious when it comes time to dig one out for loading.

LOADING LEVER: The lever that is attached underneath the barrel on the majority of the cap and ball revolvers, used to seat the balls over the charge of powder in the chambers.

LOCK PLATE: The metal base for the mechanism of a conventional muzzleloader's lock; all screws, pins, etc., are usually mounted to this.

LOCK SCREW: The screw that runs laterally through the stock to hold the lock in place.

LONG RIFLE: Acutally the only true term that should be used to describe the type of rifle most common to this country during the period from the mid 1700s to the end of the second quarter of the Eighteenth Century. Many people erroneously refer to this type of rifle as a Kentucky Rifle, even though that same type could have been produced in Pennsylvania or North Carolina.

MAGAZINE CAPPER: A device used to dispense percussion caps directly onto the nipple. These are commonly spring-loaded and hold a quantity of percussion caps; the spring keeps the cap in line for jam free feeding. To use, the percussion cap that is extending or appearing in the exit hole of the capper is placed over the nipple and a slight tug frees it from the capper. Such devices are most commonly used for loading cap and ball revolvers, eliminates fumbling for caps in pockets or removing them from the tin.

MAINSPRING: A heavy spring that controls the fall of the hammer.

Early springs were commonly of the flat leaf type, later and improved springs appeared in the form of a V, some of today's modern black powder rifles utilize even superior coil springs.

MATCHCORD: Another term for the burning match of early matchlock guns.

MATCHLOCK: The earliest form of mechanical lock; first matchlocks required shooter to lever match into touchhole, later versions mechanically struck match into primed flash pan.

METALLIC SIGHTS: Any open, hooded or tube sight that does not rely on the magnification of the target through the use of precision-ground glass lenses.

MINIE BALL OR BULLET: Developed into its present state by Captain C. E. Minie of France in 1848, the Minie is an aerodynamically stable cylindrical ogive bullet with a hollow base. This bullet is easily seated in the dirtiest of bores, usually requiring very little effort. When fired, the expanding gases of the rapidly burning powder in turn expands the hollow base of the Minie into the rifling. Immortalized as the "minny ball" during the Civil War, the Minie-designed bullet made quick reloading in battle possible.

MISFIRE: A state when the round loaded in the chamber fails to fire as the primer — powder in flash pan or percussion cap on the nipple — ignites. It is also possible to have a misfire as a direct cause of the primer not igniting.

MRT: Mid Range Trajectory; the curved flight of a bullet as measured halfway between the muzzle and the target or game.

MIQUELET: Forerunner of the true flintlock, this type of lock followed the Dutch snaphaunce lock. The main improvement over the miquelet and the snaphaunce was that it featured a frizzen and pan cover that was combined into a single part; mainspring on this type of lock was located on the outside of the lock plate.

MULE EAR LOCK: Percussion lock that features a flat side hammer that pivots horizontally.

MUSKET: The long full stocked shoulder guns used by early military force. These were commonly smoothbore, those that featured rifled bores are referred to as rifled muskets. The soldier that carried one of these as his principle means of armament was known as a musketeer. A shortened carbine version of this type of arm is a musketoon.

MUZZLE: The end of the barrel opposite the breech; the point where the bullet, shot load, projectile leaves the barrel.

MUZZLE ENERGY: The amount of force exerted by the projectile as it leaves the muzzle; this is expressed in foot/pounds.

MUZZLELOADER: Gun loaded through the muzzle with an enclosed breech. To load, the powder is dropped in first, followed by the projectile, shot or ball, the lock is then primed and the gun is ready to fire. Commonly used to describe nearly all black powder guns that rely on percussion or flint ignition, although cap and ball revolvers aren't actually loaded through the muzzle.

MUZZLE VELOCITY: Speed of the projectile as it leaves the muzzle; usually measured in feet per second.

NIPPLE: On muzzleloading percussion guns, the small metal cone that the percussion cap is fitted to; flame from exploding cap is passed through hollow cavity of the nipple to the main charge of powder loaded in the chamber.

NIPPLE WRENCH: A tool used for replacing or removing nipple from percussion type guns. Nipples come in a variety of sizes and so do nipple wrenches.

OCTAGONAL BARREL: *An eight sided barrel commonly found on many of the early muzzleloading rifles and a number of pistols and revolvers; once just as common as the round barrel.*

OGIVE: *The radius of the curve of a bullet nose, commonly expressed in calibers.*

OPEN SIGHTS: *Metallic sights that usually appear in the form of adjustable or fixed V-notch rear and fixed blade front sight.*

PATCH BOX: *An inlaid lidded box that is found on some of the muzzleloading rifles, although an assortment of accessories now find their way into these, they were originally intended for carrying greased patches or tallow for lubricating patching material.*

PATCH CUTTER: *A circular cutter used for pre-cutting patches; this is placed with the cutting edge down on a piece of suitable material and rapped with a mallet, resulting in a perfectly circular patch. Often confused with a patch knife, which is a bladed instrument used to trim excess patch material from around the ball as it is being seated into the muzzle.*

PATCHING: *Cloth used to form a gas tight seal around the round ball loaded into a muzzleloading rifle or single-shot pistol; this also improves accuracy by engaging the rifling and causing the ball to rotate better as it leaves the muzzle and while in flight.*

PATINA: *As a gun ages the stock takes on a mellow yellowish tint, this is patina. Too often the nimrod gun enthusiast tries feverishly to remove this and give the gun that new look; as with fine furniture, this is a mistake.*

PATTERN: *The spread of the pellets from a shotgun's barrel. The choke of a gun is best established by the percentage of pellets placed inside a thirty inch circle from a distance of forty yards.*

PEPPERBOX: *A small repeating pistol of the mid 1800s, so named since its usual multi-barrel appearance resembles a pepper shaker, or pepperbox.*

PERCUSSION CAP: *Small metallic cup containing a minute charge of fulminate of mercury; when placed on a nipple, the striking of the hammer causes the fulminating charge to explode which in turn ignites the powder in the chamber or breech.*

PICKET BULLET: *An early conical bullet used in this country; the base of this bullet was the only area that was of bore size, tapering toward the nose, care had to be taken in loading to ensure that bullet was seated straight. Such loading problems are the reason that the bullet never became as popular as the Minie.*

PILL LOCK: *An early type of percussion lock; a small globule of fulminate was used in place of the percussion cap — which wasn't around when this lock first came out.*

PIN-FIRE: *An early cartridge; casing had small hole near the head of the brass, a percussion-type cap was inserted into this, followed by a small pin. The cartridge was loaded into the chamber, the pin and chamber walls holding the cap in place. The hammer struck the pin which ignited the percussion cap when fired.*

PISTOL: *A small, usually concealable and short-barreled handgun, generally not a term used to describe a revolver. Some sources claim that the term originated from the Italian gunmaking center of Pistoia, others claim the word was derived from a short Bohemian handgun known as the pist'ala; actually its origin remains unknown.*

POCKET PISTOL: *A general term used to depict nearly any small pistol or revolver that can be easily concealed. Certain short barreled pistols that are actually pocket pistols became known as derringers after the assassination of President Lincoln with a Henry Deringer-made pocket pistol.*

POWDER FLASK: *Carrying container for powder, commonly made of metal having characteristics of copper and brass, but occasionally made from stag horn or like materials. Powder flasks usually have some type of charger mounted on top.*

POWDER MEASURE: *A graduated measuring device that can be adjusted to measure out different grain loads, the weights of which are usually shown on scale form.*

POWDER TESTER: *Also known as an eprouvett. A device for measuring the comparative strength of powders. The ignition of the powder registers on some sort of needle or gauge — there were various types — and depending on the strength of powder being tested, the needle or whatever was used to measure the burning force would register. As a rule such devices weren't very reliable.*

PRICKER OR VENT PICK: *A piece of fine wire used to clear the vent of a nipple or flashhole, on a flintlock, of foulings or obstructions.*

PYRITES: *Commonly known as fool's gold, this material actually is iron pyrite; when struck against a hardened steel surface it results in sparks. Early wheellocks and later early versions of the flintlock relied upon this principle for ignition.*

QUEEN ANNE PISTOL: *A screw barrel breechloading style flintlock pistol commonly found in England during the early 1700s; pistols of this design lacked forends.*

RAMROD: *Usually made of wood, although brass and steel ones aren't uncommon. A rod that is used to seat the ball over the powder charge in muzzleloading rifles. Ramrods are commonly carried under the barrel, held by ramrod pipes or thimbles.*

REVOLVER: *A multi-shot handgun, using a revolving cylinder to align the chambers with the barrel.*

REVOLVING RIFLE: *The perfection of the cap and ball revolvers and the noticeable need for a repeating rifle resulted in a combination of the two, a revolving rifle. This gun sported nearly the same mechanism as the revolver, but had a longer barrel and rifle-like butt stock. Remington and Colt were the chief producers of these during the mid 1800s.*

RIFLED MUSKET: *Occasionally a thin barreled musket was produced that featured a rifled bore. Erroneously these sometimes are referred to as rifles when actually they are rifled muskets; rifles have much thicker barrel walls.*

SALTPETER: *Potassium nitrate, used in the production of black powder.*

SCHNABEL: *Often misspelled and commonly referred to as a nose cap; the metal cap found on the front of most muzzleloading rifle forearms, especially on guns featuring a full stock.*

SCREW BARREL PISTOL: *A breechloading black powder pistol that required the barrel to be unthreaded from its specially designed breech plug in order for it to be loaded. Pistols of this design were most common during the first half of the Eighteenth Century.*

SEAR: *The lock part — usually in the form of a notch — that is* engaged by the tumbler and hammer until it is released by exerting pressure on the trigger.

SELF-COCKING REVOLVER: *A forerunner to the first true double action revolvers; this type of revolver was developed by London gunmaker Robert Adams during the early 1850s. Unlike the true double action, it had no provision for manually cocking the hammer back, but instead relied upon trigger action to work the hammer and rotate the cylinder.*

SERPENTINE POWDER: *The crude first black powders, since corning powder into grains was discovered later, this first powder appeared in the form of meal.*

SET TRIGGER: *A double trigger mechanism in which the rear trigger is first pulled to set up the front trigger so that it can be released with a very slight amount of pressure. This type of trigger usually is found on target rifles and occasionally on the finer hunting rifles.*

SHOT: *Small spherical balls commonly used in a shotgun load; these range in size from .33 inch diameter — 00 buck — to .04 inch diameter — dust shot. Occasionally the larger shot may be used to load smaller bore rifles and pistols, but in general use shot is loaded in given quantities — the smaller the shot, the increase in the number of projectiles — in shotguns.*

SHOT POUCH: *A container, most often made of leather, used for carrying shot.*

SHORT STARTER: *A short, five to six-inch rod fitted with a round or flat palm fitting handle used for starting patched balls down the muzzle of rifles and some pistols.*

SKIN CARTRIDGE: *An advanced combustible cartridge; propellant is encased in nitrated animal intestine. This cartridge was introduced by Captain John Hayes in 1856.*

SLUG GUN: *Term used to denote an extremely heavy barreled match gun; slug gun shooters may spend as much as ten to fifteen minutes to load their guns, meticulously checking and rechecking every loading step.*

SNAPHAUNCE: *Early forerunner to the flintlock; frizzen and flash pan cover were two separate parts.*

SPANNER: *Key or wrench like device used to cock or span a wheel-lock.*

SPERM OIL: *The oil extracted from the flesh of the sperm whale. Among its many uses it once was a favorite gun lube.*

STEEL: *The hardened surface of the frizzen that causes spark when struck by the flint on a flintlock; on some early locks it was a strip of hardened metal that was attached to the pan cover to cause the spark for igniting the primed flash pan.*

STRAIGHT BARREL: *A barrel on which the outside diameter remains the same its entire length; barrels that gradually decreased in outside diameter to the muzzle are known as tapered barrels; barrels that taper toward the middle then return to the original diameter at the muzzle are known as tapered and flared barrels.*

SUPERIMPOSED ROUNDS: *Among the first repeating smallarms appeared ingeniously designed guns that featured two or more locks located at intervals along the rear area of the barrel. These then were loaded one round on top of another, the powder charge of each shot coinciding with the lock that was to fire that round, the lead ball*

sealing the flame of the first round from igniting the one directly behind it — hopefully. Care surely had to be taken not to fire the last round first! Such guns appeared as early as the Sixteenth Century.

SWAGING: *The precision sizing of a conical bullet to bring it to an exact size; done with the aid of precision tools.*

TANG: *Most often an extension from the breech plug, the tang is the retainer for the long screw that runs vertically through the stock, holding the breech portion of the barrel securely in place. The screw that holds this in place is known as the tang screw, which commonly fastens to the trigger assembly and helps hold it in place also.*

TANG SIGHT: *A rear sight aperture that attaches to the barrel tang; commonly a folding type that allows the usage of regular open sights.*

TAPE PRIMER: *A strip or roll of paper tape that has small charges of fulminating powders attached to it; designed for use with specially modified rifles during the Civil War.*

TENON: *The metal loop or flat piece of metal that extends from the bottom of the barrel which engages the barrel key or pin that holds the barrel to the stock.*

THIMBLE: *The metal ferrules located along the ramrod channel or under the barrel for storing and carrying the ramrod.*

TOE: *The rear bottom point of the butt stock; the area of the stock located at the bottom of the butt plate. Occasionally a rifle will have a metal plate running along the bottom of the butt stock. This is the toe plate; most commonly found on Kentucky type-rifles.*

TOMPION: *Plug used to prevent dust and moisture from getting into a muzzleloader's barrel during storage.*

TOP JAW: *The upper area of a flintlock's hammer that holds the flint; the screw that forms the vise that holds the flint is the top jaw screw.*

TOW: *Unspun flax, an early patching material for shotguns and often used as cleaning patches for rifles; coarse fibers made it undesirable for patching round balls in rifles or pistols.*

TOWER LOCK: *The type of flintlock found on the Brown Bess; locks are usually stamped with a crown and the initials GR on the area of the lock plate that is located in front of the hammer and the date of manufacture and the word Tower to the rear of it. Locks of this type were being installed first on Brown Bess muskets at the turn of the Eighteenth Century; occasionally a lock of this type is found on various muskets and fowling pieces.*

TOUCHHOLE: *The vent hole leading from the pan of a flintlock to the powder charge in the chamber; originally used to describe the vent hole on hand cannons which required the cannoneer to ignite the round by placing or touching a burning stick, hot coal, etc. to this vent.*

TUBE LOCK: *An early percussion type lock; to fire, a small copper tube five-eighths inch in length and a sixteenth inch in diameter — filled with percussion powder — was inserted into the vent hole. All but about an eighth of the tube went into the hole, the remainder rested on a small anvil shaped piece of metal. The hammer striking this would ignite the powder inside the tube, which in turn ignited the charge in the chamber.*

TUMBLER: *The central piece of a conventional lock that turns with the hammer; contains the half-cock and full-cock notches as well as the detent if the lock has one.*

UNDER HAMMER STRIKER: *A percussion type lock that features the hammer underneath; as on some of the modern made under hammer muzzleloaders, the trigger guard doubles as the spring to power the striking of the hammer.*

UNDER RIB: *The metal rib running beneath the barrel on a half stock rifle; supports the thimbles for the ramrod.*

VENT: *The small hole on muzzleloaders through which the priming flame reaches and ignites the main charge.*

VERNIER SIGHT: *A precision rear aperture commonly found on target rifles of the 1800s.*

V-SPRING: *Flat V-shaped spring used in locks; stronger and more durable than the flat single leaf spring.*

WAD CUTTER: *Nearly identical to a patch cutter, a small handtool featuring a circular cutting edge. By placing this edge onto wadding material and hitting the handle with a mallet, a perfect circular wad is punched out. This tool also can be used to cut patches for small rifles.*

WHEELLOCK: *The lock that made the first pistols practical; ignition relies upon the sparks created by the iron pyrites held in the cock coming into contact with the serrated edge of a rotating wheel. The first wheellocks were introduced during the first quarter of the Sixteenth Century.*

WINDAGE: *A term used to describe any lateral adjustment made to the rear sight.*

WIPING ROD: *A separate rod used to wipe the bore clean of powder fouling between shots.*

WORM: *A corkscrew type device used to remove a cleaning patch stuck in the bore of a muzzleloading rifle or removal of a shotgun wad; screws into the threaded tip of a cleaning rod.*

WRIST: *The small of the stock; the portion of the stock that forms the grip.*